WITHDRAWAL

Understanding Online Instructional Modeling:
Theories and Practices

Robert Z. Zheng
University of Utah, USA

Sharmila Pixy Ferris
William Paterson University, USA

INFORMATION SCIENCE REFERENCE

Hershey · New York

Acquisitions Editor:	Kristin Klinger
Development Editor:	Kristin Roth
Senior Managing Editor:	Jennifer Neidig
Managing Editor:	Sara Reed
Copy Editor:	Katie Smalley
Typesetter:	Jeff Ash
Cover Design:	Lisa Tosheff
Printed at:	Yurchak Printing Inc.

Published in the United States of America by
Information Science Reference (an imprint of IGI Global)
701 E. Chocolate Avenue, Suite 200
Hershey PA 17033
Tel: 717-533-8845
Fax: 717-533-8661
E-mail: cust@igi-global.com
Web site: http://www.igi-global.com/reference

and in the United Kingdom by
Information Science Reference (an imprint of IGI Global)
3 Henrietta Street
Covent Garden
London WC2E 8LU
Tel: 44 20 7240 0856
Fax: 44 20 7379 0609
Web site: http://www.eurospanonline.com

Library of Congress Cataloging-in-Publication Data

Understanding online instructional modeling : theories and practices / Robert Zheng & Sharmila Pixy Ferris, editors.

      p. cm.

  Summary: "Online learning has become an integral factor in higher education--both in distance learning and as an adjunct to the traditional classroom. This book focuses on both theoretical and practical aspects of online learning by introducing a variety of online instructional models and best practices that help educators and professional trainers to better understand the dynamics of online learning"--Provided by publisher.

  Includes bibliographical references and index.

  ISBN 978-1-59904-723-2 (hardcover) -- ISBN 978-1-59904-725-6 (ebook)

  1. Computer-assisted instruction. 2. Internet in higher education. 3. Education, Higher--Computer network resources. I. Zheng, Robert. II. Ferris, Sharmila Pixy.

  LB1028.5.U516 2008

  378.1'734--dc22

                    2007023501

British Cataloguing in Publication Data
A Cataloguing in Publication record for this book is available from the British Library.

All work contributed to this book set is new, previously-unpublished material. The views expressed in this book are those of the authors, but not necessarily of the publisher.

Table of Contents

Section I
Online Instructional Modeling: A Theoretical Perspective

Section II
Online Instructional Modeling: Teaching and Learning

Detailed Table of Contents

Section I
Online Instructional Modeling: A Theoretical Perspective

Chapter I

Online instruction will more likely be effective if it fits with, and is perceived by, students as being functionally relevant for their education, work, or other personal contexts. Existing practice may emphasize an ad hoc approach to online design by being pragmatic and somewhat unsystematic. It is proposed that using a functional relevance perspective, as described in this chapter, is more likely to have designers and online learners attain a greater advantage in using the capacity of the Internet to support teaching and learning. This chapter introduces the concept of functional relevance and identifies some of the underlying theories. Discussions are made on how the concept of functional relevance can be used as a conceptual framework to identify and to drive decision-making processes that occur during the design and development of instruction.

Chapter II

The purpose of this chapter is to discuss how instruction, technology, and models converge to create online model-facilitated learning environments. These instructional environments are designed in such a manner that the interaction with the model on the computer network is essential to the learning experience. The idea is to use these models to maximize the pedagogical power that helps students construct conceptual mental representations that lead to a greater degree of retention and overall recall of information. How students will act and learn in a particular environment depends on how the instructional designer creates the environment that maximizes their learning potential, considering the interrelationships between the learning experience, the technology, cognition, and other related issues of the learner.

Flexible learning is a term becoming increasingly prevalent in distance education. The concept of having a flexible learning environment is appealing to distance learners. Many learners choose a flexible environment over the traditional classroom so that learning can fit into their busy lifestyle. This chapter will define and discuss flexible learning theory, describing how it is used in the distance education setting and how it is a changing tide in education.

This chapter presents a unified theory of instructional design in the cognitive domain; this includes, of course, online instructional modeling. The theory differs from specific instructional design theories in that it describes how all instructional systems operate (regardless of their goals) in terms of resources and dialogues common to all instructional systems; it predicts certain instructional outcomes (related to groups of learners, not to individual learners) based on given initial conditions. The theory affords practical and theoretical advantages. Practically, it (1) simply and accurately describes the mechanisms at play in instructional systems, (2) presents readily quantifiable operational definitions, (3) suggests hypotheses that may be evaluated empirically, and (4) points the way toward optimizing instructional systems. Theoretically, it (1) subsumes all current theories of instructional design and (2) views campus-based, distance and online instructional systems as a single discipline.

Section II
Online Instructional Modeling: Teaching and Learning

Designing online trainings or courses for large numbers of participants can prove to be challenging for instructors and facilitators. Online learning environments need to be structured in a way that preserves actual or perceived levels of interaction, participant perceptions of value and utility, and achievement of the learning objectives. This chapter describes five large-scale interaction strategies that offer guidance for addressing some of these online instructional design issues. Evaluation data are presented in support of two of the strategies, and recommendations are provided about how future research in this area might be conducted.

The ubiquity of instructional technology necessitates a more critical look at the theories that drive adoption and the practical implications of its usage. Blended learning has been offered as one compromise to fully online learning or strict adherence to traditional lecture-based instruction that seems outdated. A particular approach to blended learning is examined in the present chapter through the use of an online learning system. Concept Keys was developed to assist instructors of social skills in breaking down these abstract concepts into manageable units of information appropriate for daily delivery via e-mail. This program is shown to be easily integrated into existing curriculum through two studies. A concluding section attempts to tie these studies together and suggests potential limitations and avenues for future research.

Establishing social presence in a text-based environment can be a challenge to teachers. This chapter discusses the main issues, controversies, and problems of social presence; provides conceptual frameworks of teacher's role and teaching presence on computer mediated communication (CMC); and presents a sound practical approach incorporating teaching presence and social presence in a graduate asynchronous online course.

This chapter focuses on how faculty can effectively determine their technological needs as they move from the traditional classroom to an online teaching environment through strategic planning. SIMPLE is a technology planning model, which can be used by faculty and administrators to stair-step themselves through this transition period. SIMPLE is an acronym representing six areas which should be addressed when developing and implementing technology strategies: (1) student/instructor assessment, (2) inventory, (3) measurement, (4) planning, (5) leadership, and (6) evaluation. These six components represent common threads throughout the literature on the subject of technology planning, which were utilized to develop the SIMPLE model, and can be easily utilized to guide faculty.

As e-learning keeps growing, an increasing amount of learning activities can be expected to take place through interactivity between the learner and e-learning materials. To better understand the processes and qualities of interactivity in e-learning, the chapter proposes a framework for analyzing and promoting interactivity from an information processing perspective. The framework consists of the dimensions of accessibility, information attributes of multimedia, learner control versus system control, hypermedia navigation, and cognitive engagement.

In the virtual environment created by asynchronous posting boards, e-mail lists, chat rooms, and other communication tools, it may not be easy for an instructor to detect communication problems among the participants. In this chapter, a research study where social network analysis (SNA) methods were applied to a sample of online classes to investigate interaction patterns and compare to instructors' perceptions is used to address social interactions in online environments. This study proves that SNA metrics and visualization of interactions are useful and potentially effective tools to analyze asynchronous online interaction patterns. The comparison of the results of a questionnaire administered to the instructors with the SNA results showed that the use of the SNA metrics and visualizations could reveal information the instructor is not aware of. Based on the findings from the study, recommendations for further research are provided. In the first part of this chapter, the importance of investigating interaction patterns in online environments is analyzed and basic SNA methodology is described. In the second part, the SNA methodology is utilized for analyzing online interactions.

This chapter explores the pros and cons of anonymity in cyber education and discusses possible ethical and social implications for online learning. It evaluates both sides of the anonymity issue and presents strategies that may help cyber educators and instructional designers safeguard academic integrity. The educational implications include concern for authenticity and academic integrity, and the dynamics found in social presence. This chapter discusses pertinent policy while analyzing anonymity's potential for limiting and monitoring academic freedom and the social benefits it brings. Strategies are suggested to enhance social presence by planning for interaction through the instructional design process. The far-reaching effects of anonymity within online educational settings and group dynamics have immediate and long term implications for instruction and learning.

Section III
Online Instructional Modeling: A Multi-Disciplinary Perspective

Instructional gaming has historically been used as a means of rehearsal and motivation. A majority of research in this area has attempted to identify the most effective method of rehearsal that maximizes student achievement and minimizes information loss over a specified time period. A few studies have suggested that instructional gaming environments have the ability to provide corrective feedback and reinforcement of previously taught information. The author investigates whether or not instructional online and computer gaming and the use of different forms of feedback produce a significant difference in improving delayed retention of different instructional objectives.

Chapter XIII

This chapter provides a perspective on the problems, challenges, and unique opportunities faced by instructors and designers of information technology in helping students who are differently-abled learn more effectively in online environments. The proposed solution is provided in the form of a cognitive-adaptive instructional system. This system provides menu-driven adaptive options or online assessments that evaluate a student's cognitive and sensory needs. These needs are translated into cognitive-sensory profiles, which are linked to compensatory and remedial actions. These actions render content automatically and dynamically in ways that provide adaptations that compensate for a student's special-needs while complementing their strengths.

Chapter XIV

Supervision is both a special case of instruction and a critical aspect of professional development. The ongoing development of Web-based infrastructures and communication tools provides opportunities for cybersupervision. Advantages of cybersupervision for counselor training include opportunities to provide location-independent, "live" supervision of counseling sessions in which: (a) evaluative feedback is communicated in "real time" using text or graphical modalities; (b) audio evaluative feedback is digitally recorded in "real time" for post-session playback; and, (c) weekly, hour-long, supervision sessions are conducted using either synchronous (e.g., multifeatured video conferencing, chat room) or asynchronous (video recording, email) Web-based communication tools. Challenges to quality online supervision include communicating critical supervisor characteristics, developing an effective supervisor/supervisee online relationship, insuring requisite personal dispositions and computer skills, implementing a theoretical model of supervision, and resolving legal and ethical problems. Authors examine these advantages, challenges, and solutions in the context of two online supervision/instructional models for training counselors (i.e., professional counselors, psychologists, clinical social workers, and psychiatrists) and discuss the generalizability of the cybersupervision model for professional training in a variety of fields that include medicine, law, and education.

Chapter XV

Recognizing the value, as expressed by the Association of College and Research Libraries Information Literacy Competency Standards for Higher Education, of incorporating information literacy instruction into a subject discipline, LSU Libraries partnered with the instructor of an environmental management course to develop online information literacy instruction with direct tie-ins to the subject matter of the course. This chapter discusses the results of that effort, including the advantages and problems encountered.

Preface

Education is constantly changing to reflect student needs as well as changing pedagogies. The most interesting and important innovation in education, in recent years, is the widespread introduction of computers. Of particular interest in the 21st century are the Internet and, more specifically, the World Wide Web. Just as in the turn of the century the pressures of change created by industrialization forced the educational system to respond by rethinking the structures of the institutions and the roles of the educators (see Strover & Bryant, 1987), so do the pressures generated by the Internet today mandate changes in education. A consideration of the pedagogical applications of computer and Internet technologies is of considerable importance to educators. That this is recognized by institutions of higher education is clear in that "instructional integration of information technology" was reported by CIOs in the United States as the "single most important IT issue confronting their institutions over the next two-three years (Campus Computing Project, 2004).

When considering issues of pedagogy and computer/Internet technologies, educators must look beyond the traditional classroom. The economic, social, and cultural changes in higher education have led to an irreversible shift from the traditional, space-and-time bound institution to one that offers increasingly cost-effective, technologically-enhanced programs. Online learning has thus become a force to reckon with, both in distance learning and as an adjunct to the traditional classroom. This trend is likely to increase rather than decrease. With access to the Internet now all but universal for faculty members in the United States (Office of Higher Education at NEA, 2002), faculty are increasingly using the Internet in their teaching. As well, more students than ever are studying online—over 1.9 million students in the United States alone, in the fall of 2003. Amazingly, the projected growth in online enrollment (of 20% a year) exceeds the overall expected growth for the entire higher education student population (Sloan Consortium, 2004).

Given these facts, it is alarming that the growth of online education has not been accompanied by a concomitant growth in pedagogical resources for educators. Yet, research shows that teaching methods have been slow to adapt to the technology (Twigg, 2001), and the need for pedagogical change is pressing. An equally urgent need is for such growth to be under-girded by sound learning theories and instructional modeling. Although there is a wealth of instructional *design* theories, designing online courses through the incorporation of appropriate theories can be challenging to educational practitioners and instructional designers who are often unfamiliar with theoretical materials. Studies show an inconsistency in online teaching and learning due to a discrepancy between theories and practice in online education (Irlbeck, Kays, Jones, & Sims, 2006). Clearly there is an imminent need to provide guidance in online teaching and learning so that educators and designers use technology more effectively in teaching practice and instructional design.

INSTRUCTIONAL MODELING AND ONLINE LEARNING

Instructional modeling, by definition, is the use of instructional models to systematically demonstrate how to incorporate an integrated set of strategy components in instruction, using Reigeluth's (1983) terminology, to achieve desired learning outcomes. While instructional models present a particular way that the content is sequenced, the instructional modeling is focused more on a strategic scheme that promotes effective teaching and learning and an action that demonstrates the strategic scheme. Differing from instructional models, instructional modeling reflects a theory-to-practice process in action where teaching and learning follow the steps of an instructional model and present perceivable effects of the model on a target population.

In traditional classrooms, instructional modeling is often subsumed under the broader, more recognizable term "best practices." However, this interchangeable use of the terms may cause some confusion, particularly when instructional modeling means a schematic approach to demonstrating effective teaching. As we understand it, best practices do not necessarily entail an integrated set of strategy components. They could be an instructional technique to teach students how to retell a story, or a particular method to solve a problem. Therefore, for our purposes in this book, we prefer to distinguish the term instructional modeling from "best practices" by defining the former as a process in action that demonstrates a strategic scheme for effective teaching and learning, and the latter as effective instructional techniques and methods in teaching and learning.

Online learning differs significantly from traditional classroom learning in terms of the instructional mode, ways of communication, pace of learning, and many other characteristics that have posed enormous challenges to educators and instructional designers. And, as we have previously noted, they suffer from a relative lack of pedagogical resources. One of the recent efforts attempted by practitioners who have experienced success in their online teaching is to disseminate best practices to offset this lack of pedagogical resources. However, the ability to generalize the best practices is often limited by such factors as social and economic status, geographic regions, and related demographic information (Wright, 2000). Besides, the use of isolated instructional techniques or methods (as identified by best practices) to address issues of an entire online course can be inefficient from the instructional design perspective. An organized and efficient approach to these issues is crucial. The goal of this book focuses on online instructional modeling as a systematic approach to effective online teaching and learning. However, readers may also benefit from the inclusion of some best practices as identified by the online community of educators, which can most effectively be used in conjunction with the instructional models to effectively design, develop, and manage online teaching and learning.

THE CONTRIBUTION OF THIS BOOK

This book addresses pressing needs in online education by (a) bridging theories with practice, (b) addressing emerging issues in online pedagogy and instructional modeling, and (c) identifying best practices in online teaching and learning. The book targets educators globally with an emphasis on diverse aspects in online design and modeling that include learner characteristics, media, communication, social-economic, and cultural differences. A major contribution of this book is to bring together online theories and practices with an emphasis on instructional modeling. Thus, the book is significant both theoretically and practically. At the theoretical level, it contributes to the knowledge base in online learning. It enhances our understanding of the underlying principles of online learning. At the practical level, the book provides an array of instructional models ranging from Wilmes, Huffman and Rickman's "SIMPLE" model, Giguere et al's asynchronous online discussion model, to Yang's "STEP" model which, among others, readers will find beneficial in online instructional practices.

This book also reflects the collective effort of online learning theorists and practitioners who challenge the traditional theoretical boundaries in instructional design, identify parameters critical to building online instructional models, and propose models applicable to online teaching across disciplines. Fortunately, we are able to bring together a group of excellent authors who represent perspectives on teaching and learning from a broad range of academic institutions—from private to public comprehensive, teaching to research, and from state and national to international. This book should thus appeal to readers from the United States to the international educational community. Practitioners in K-12 system should find this book of particular note, given that the nearly 49.5 million students enrolled in schools in 2003 (Enrollment Management Report, 2005) are members of the Net Generation who have grown up with exposure to, and familiarity with, the Internet. Beyond the educational community, anyone interested in e-learning, including corporations who will employ students from the Net Generation, will find this book a useful companion as they discover helpful information in online instructional modeling and practices that are under-girded by sound theories.

THE ORGANIZATION OF THIS BOOK

The three sections of this book are organized to maximize the value for the readers as they move from the theoretical to the practical and from a focus on models to specific issues of teaching and learning to multidisciplinary perspectives.

Section I presents a theoretical perspective on online instructional modeling, and includes four chapters which go beyond the boundaries of traditional instructional theories to propose a more holistic approach.

In Chapter I, the concept of functional relevance is introduced by Glenn E. Snelbecker of Temple University, Susan M. Miller, Kent State University, and Robert Z. Zheng, University of Utah. Functional relevance theory posits that educational technologies can succeed only to the extent their relevance to teaching and learning is clear. The authors focus on the importance of functional relevance to design in online and Web-based instruction, with emphasis on learners' needs and their perceptions of the relevance between learning and instruction.

Chapter II reflects a philosophical thinking on the relationship between instructional environments and model-facilitated learning. Glenda Hostetter Shoop, Patricia A. Nordstrom, and Roy B. Clariana, Pennsylvania State University, consider the ways in which models, as pedagogical tools, can come together with technology to facilitate successful learning. Although their focus is largely pedagogical, pedagogy is strongly supported by a theoretical framework.

The focus on theory continues in Chapter III, with Deb Gearhart's, Troy University, theory-to-practice perspective on online learning through the understanding and application of Flexible Learning Theory in a technologically-supported flexible learning environment. Gearhart's elaboration on the theory of flexible learning provides a theoretical framework for educators in teaching and design.

Finally, in Chapter IV, Paul Gorsky, Avner Caspi, and Eran Chajut of the Open University of Israel, offer a meta-level approach to instructional design in terms of resources and dialogues common to all instructional systems. In their focus on building an infrastructure for theory of instructional design, the authors work towards a much-needed unified theory, sorely lacking in online learning today.

Section II deals with issues of teaching and learning in online instruction. The models in this section cover a wide range of topics in online learning: from interactivity, learning systems and planning, to online assessment. The models focus on both theoretical and practical aspects of online learning by including case studies and empirical data that help illustrate the complexity of online learning.

In Chapter V, Paul Giguere, Tufts University, and Scott W. Formica, Wayne M. Harding, and Michele R. Cummins, SSRE at the Harvard Medical Hospital, consider interaction strategies appropriate for learning in large classes. They address a range of interaction strategies designed to facilitate effective learning in large (over 40 students) online courses, supporting their recommendations with empirical evaluations of two strategies in seven courses.

In Chapter VI, Graham Bodie, Purdue University, Margaret Fitch-Hauser, Auburn University, and William Powers, Texas Christian University, introduce an online learning system, Concept Keys, which allows a blended learning approach by integrating the use of two or more complementary approaches to teaching social skills and advancing pedagogical goals. The authors support their discussion with empirical data from two studies.

In Chapter VII, Harrison Hao Yang, State University of New York at Oswego, presents an approach to enhancing social presence in online learning through the use of the STEP approach. The STEP approach to teaching includes *S*caffolding before starting new learning topic, *T*ransaction during the learning process, *E*valuation during and after each learning topic and *P*resentation of outcomes. The author supports the use of this method with empirical data assessing students' perceptions in an online class.

In Chapter VIII, Barbara Wilmes, Stephanie Huffman, and Wendy Rickman, from the University of Central Arkansas, present another model—a technology planning model for online instruction. The SIMPLE model encompasses a consideration of *S*tudent/instructor assessment, *I*nventory, *M*easurement, *P*lanning, *L*eadership, and *E*valuation. The authors present clear guidance for educators on how to use this model for strategic technology planning.

In Chapter IX, Haomin Wang, Dakota State University, considers an important issue in online instruction: the means of promoting interactivity between learners and instructional sources (which are primarily online learning materials and activities). Wang's framework for promoting interactivity includes the following components: ensuring accessibility, enhancing legibility and readability, using multimedia, promoting cognitive engagement, supporting learner control, and maintaining system control. Both teachers and instructional designers can avail of this clearly articulated framework to improve their teaching-learning experience.

In Chapter X, Pedro Willging, University of La Pampa of Argentina, considers a different aspect of online interactions—human-to-human social interactions in online classes. Willging uses social network analysis (SNA) methods to investigate interaction patterns among students in comparison to their instructors' perceptions of these interactions. Educators can utilize the data from this study to analyze online interactions in their own classes and thus improve teaching and learning.

In the final chapter in Section II, Bobbe Baggio, of Advantage Learning Technologies, and Yoany Beldarrain, of Florida Virtual School, examine the issue of anonymity in online instruction. While anonymity is an important issue in teaching and learning, the authors frame this chapter in a larger context, considering both issues pertinent to learning, as well as broader social, cultural and educational implications.

Section III presents broad multi-disciplinary perspectives on online instructional modeling by including models and best practices that extend beyond the traditional concepts of teaching and learning.

The section opens with an investigation by Brian Cameron, of Pennsylvania State University, on the relationship between online gaming, cognitive style, and feedback type on academic achievement. Gaming has become an accepted aspect of life for the Net Generation and Cameron addresses this issue by investigating how teachers can utilize gaming to model effective teaching and learning in an online environment.

In Chapter XIII, Bruce J. Diamond, of William Paterson University, and Gregory M. Shreve, of Kent State University, consider another unique but pressing issue: ways to facilitate the learning of students with special needs. The authors offer an information technology adaptive model for helping students, especially those with learning disabilities or deficiencies in basic skills or academic achievement, to learn more effectively using an adaptive hypermedia system.

In Chapter XIV, Kenneth L. Miller, of Youngstown State University, and Susan M. Miller, of Kent State University, discuss another specialized issue: online supervision in clinical training. Although the focus in this chapter is on advantages and challenges of cyber-supervision in the clinical training of counseling professionals, the issues are largely generalized to cyber-training in a range of professional fields, academic and medical. The authors support their application of cyber-supervision across multiple disciplines with an examination of two models: the Cognitive-Behavioral model and Integrative-Developmental model.

Another inter-disciplinary application is developed by Michael F. Russo, Sigrid Kelsey, and Maud Walsh, at Louisiana State University, in Chapter XV. They posit a model integrating information literacy into a discipline-specific content area, partnering the university library partners with the instructor. E-struction has the multiple goals of introducing learners to electronic (library) resources and teaching them the basic concepts of information literacy in the context of any discipline-specific content area.

Robert Z. Zheng
Sharmila Pixy Ferris
August 2007

REFERENCES

Campus Computing Project. (2004). *The 2004 national survey of information technology in U.S. higher education*. Retrieved February 18, 2007, from http://www2.nea.org/he/techno.html

Enrollment Management Report. (2005). Use emerging technologies to recruit today's millennial students. *Enrollment Management Report, 9*(9).

Office of Higher Education. (2002). Higher education on the web. *NEA Research Center Update*, 7(1). Retrieved February 18, 2007, from http://www2.nea.org/he/heupdate/images/vol7no1.pdf

Irlbeck, S., Kays, E., Jones, D., & Sims, R. (2006). The phoenix rising: Emergent models of instructional design. *Distance Education, 27*(2), 171-185.

Reigeluth, C. (Ed.). (1983). *Instructional-design theories and models: An overview of their current status*. Hilldale, NJ: Lawrence Erlbaum.

Sloan Consortium. (2004). *Sizing the opportunity: the quality and extent of online education in the united states, 2002 and 2003*. Retrieved February 18, 2007, from http://www.sloan-c.org/resources/survey. asp

Strover, S., & Bryant, M. T. (1987). Higher education in the information society. In R. J. Schement & L. A. Lievrouw (Eds.), *Competing visions, complex realities: Social aspects of the information society* (pp. 69-89). Norwood, NJ: Ablex.

Twigg, C. A. (2001). *Innovations in online learning: Moving beyond no significant difference.*. Retrieved February 18, 2006, from the Center for Academic Transformation, Tensselaer Polytechnic Institute at http://www.center.rpi.edu/pewsym/mono4.htm

Wright, P. W. (2000). A best practices approach to the use of information technology in education. In *Proceedings of the Society for Information Technology and Teacher Education International Conference*, San Diego, CA. (ERIC Document Reproduction Service No. ED444575).

Acknowledgment

This book would not have been possible if it were not for the hard work of the many individuals who have written chapters for it. As a group, they voluntarily spent hundreds of hours putting together a series of chapters that provide readers with an excellent overview of the theoretical and practical perspectives of online instructional modeling, as well as trends and issues that are affecting the field. We would like to express our deepest thanks and sincere appreciation to all these authors for their outstanding efforts.

Our appreciation also goes to our reviewers who provided insightful input and suggestions. We thank all of our authors for their own expert assistance. We would also like to thank the following reviewers in particular for their hard work, generous donation of their time, and their attention to detail: David Arentsen, LIM College; Graham Bodie, Purdue University; Jill Flygare, University of Utah, Jason Huett, University of Web Georgia; Lawrence Hugenberg, Kent State University; Karen Mallia, University of South Carolina; Dewar MacLeod, William Paterson University; Matt McAlack, Philadelphia Biblical University; Kenneth Miller, Youngstown University; Maureen Minielli, Kingsborough Community College; Jacquee Williamson, University of Utah; and Milda Yildiz, William Paterson University. The first editor would like to especially thank his graduate assistant Stephanie Donnelly at the University of Utah who assisted with proof-reading the chapters.

We would like to thank our editors at IGI Global, Kristin Roth, Meg Stocking, and Jessica Thompson for their efficiency and generosity in working with us, and the publishing team at IGI Global for their competence and expertise.

And last, but far from least, we owe a continual debt of gratitude to our families for their encouragement, love and support, the warm reception they give our work, and for their allowances for our work schedules. We could not have done it without them!

Robert Z. Zheng
Sharmila Pixy Ferris

About the Editors

Robert Z. Zheng (EdD, Baylor University, 1998) is an assistant professor and program director in the Department of Educational Psychology, University of Utah, USA. His research agenda includes online learning and pedagogy, multimedia and cognition, and educational technology and assessment. He has authored and co-authored several book chapters and published papers in peer-reviewed journals on topics of cognitive load, multimedia, Web-based instruction, and problem solving in multimedia learning.

* * *

Sharmila Pixy Ferris (PhD, Pennsylvania State University, 1995) is a professor in the Department of Communication and Director for the Center for Teaching Excellence at William Paterson University, USA. Her research brings an interdisciplinary focus to the computer-mediated communication in which area she has published in a variety of print and electronic journals. She has coauthored a book in faculty development, *Beyond Survival in the Academy*, and edited books in the areas of virtual teams and virtual learning including *Virtual and Collaborative Teams: Theories, Process, and Practice* and *Teaching and Learning with Virtual and Collaborative Teams*. She is an experienced communication consultant who has worked with a range of corporate clients.

Section I
Online Instructional Modeling:
A Theoretical Perspective

Chapter I
Functional Relevance and Online Instructional Design

Glenn E. Snelbecker
Temple Universtiy, USA

Susan M. Miller
Kent State Universtiy, USA

Robert Z. Zheng
University of Utah, USA

ABSTRACT

Online instruction will more likely be effective if it fits with, and is perceived by, students as being functionally relevant for their education, work, or other personal contexts. Existing practice may emphasize an ad hoc approach to online design by being pragmatic and somewhat unsystematic. It is proposed that using a functional relevance perspective, as described in this chapter, is more likely to have designers and online learners attain a greater advantage in using the capacity of the Internet to support teaching and learning. This chapter introduces the concept of functional relevance and identifies some of the underlying theories. Discussions are made on how the concept of functional relevance can be used as a conceptual framework to identify and to drive decision-making processes that occur during the design and development of instruction.

CHAPTER OBJECTIVES

The reader will be able to:

1. Understand the meaning of—and conceptual foundation for—functional relevance
2. Apply functional relevance as a conceptual framework to clarify and drive decision-making processes during the design and development of online instruction
3. Recognize how general guidelines from this chapter may be applied to the design of online instruction
4. Understand how a functional relevance perspective can aid designers to:

   - Decide whether particular theories or research findings might improve some aspects of their instruction
   - Identify those situations where social presence might constitute an area that merits careful study and possible important modifications in the online instruction, and
   - Consider which learner attributes may be most relevant for the instruction being designed and to discern how those particular attributes may warrant additional instructions of modification of the online instruction

INTRODUCTION

The proliferation of Internet use in general and online learning in particular has dramatically changed the landscape in K-16 education (DuCharme-Hansen & Dupin-Bryant, 2005; Salpeter, 2003). Fernback (2003) pointed out that Web-based instructional delivery has allowed educators to experiment with flexible, innovative, and progressive learning techniques that "permit students to contribute the learning process in new and active way" (p. 28). Although

the idea of delivering instruction online has been heralded by teachers, administrators, parents, and students, doing so effectively takes more than a mere shift in modalities (DuCharme-Hansen & Dupin-Bryant, 2005). Recently, there has been a concerted effort among educators to create a successful online learning environment through *design* (Lim, Plucker, & Nowak, 2001). For example, DuCharme-Hansen and Dupin-Bryant's model of distance education planning and Jones, Harmon and Lowther's (2002) framework for online instructional implementation reflect the efforts in that direction.

Several important issues in online instructional design involve pedagogy and theoretical orientation. These issues include deciding whether: (a) an existing or a new pedagogical or instructional approach would be appropriate for learning; (b) someone's research findings are likely to "fit" with teaching and learning; and (c) using a new pedagogical approach or new research findings might cause a change in the design of teaching. Some instructors respond to these issues by using an ad hoc approach to online design. This is to say that often they take a pragmatic but unsystematic approach, which usually, in the end, fails to take advantage of the capacity of the Internet for teaching and learning. An alternative position is taken by some who propose that online practice should be grounded in theory through a systematic application of evidence-based strategies (Wilson, 1999). With this position, what is important is the congruence between practice and theory, rather than selection of a correct theory (Bednar, Cunningham, Duffy, & Perry, 1992; Wilson, 1999). An example of congruence is the inclusion of scaffolding strategies in constructivist-based instruction, or the use of prescriptive strategies associated with cognitive theory that aid encoding and retrieval of information (Wilson, 1999).

All this reflection still leaves the designer uninformed on how to proceed. Wilson (1999) suggested a problem or practitioner-centered approach in which theory plays a supporting but non-limiting role. Jonassen (1999) suggested that a designer possess the skills to include multiple perspectives, such as the inclusion of objectivist and constructivist views. Miller and Miller (2000) suggested five variables that need to be considered by a designer of online instruction: (a) theoretical orientation of the instructor and of the students; (b) learning goals, either explicit or implicit; (c) nature of the content, such as well or ill-structured subject matter; (d) learner characteristics including cognitive and motivational characteristics; and (e) technological capabilities including available infrastructure to support various types of online communication exchanges.

Snelbecker (1984, 1989, 1993) proposed that a designer should keep in mind the concept of *functional relevance* requirements regarding both the subject matter and delivery of that material to the learner. This idea suggests a perspective that addresses and integrates theoretical, technical, and practical context concerns. Functional relevance is congruent with the design considerations mentioned in the previous paragraph. In fact, functional relevance can be used as a conceptual framework to identify and to drive decision-making processes that occur during the design and development of instruction.

This chapter discusses (a) the concept of functional relevance from a design perspective, particularly how it can be applied to online instruction design and other Web-based learning, and (b) the relationship between functional relevance and design issues involved with pedagogical theory, social presence, and learner characteristics. The chapter focuses on these topics:

- Meaning of, and conceptual foundation for, functional relevance as a perspective that can yield fruitful implications for the success of online instruction
- Problems, learner needs, and online issues that are met by the inclusion of functional relevance

- Exploration of functional relevance as it relates to three aspects of online design: theoretical orientation, social presence, and learner characteristics.

CONCEPTS, PROBLEMS, AND SOLUTIONS

Functional Relevance

The concept of functional relevance can be depicted as the extent to which technology applications, including online learning environments, are actually supportive of learner activities and are perceived as such by learners as being relevant for how they function in a particular context (Snelbecker, 1989, 1991, 1993). The assumption is that it is only the degree to which technology is seen as potentially helpful that it will actually foster and support educational achievement and its use.

The importance of functional relevance for technology applications became apparent during the first author's (GES) work with various technology projects starting in the 1970s (e.g., Aiken & Snelbecker, 1991; Ball & Snelbecker 1982a, 1982b, 1983; Ball, Snelbecker, & Schechte, 1985; Roszkowski, Devlin, Snelbecker, Aiken, & Jacobsohn, 1988; Snelbecker, 1986; Snelbecker, Bhote-Edjulee, Aiken & Wilson, 1992; Snelbecker, Bhote, Wilson, & Aiken, 1995). Participants in these technology training projects initially consisted of nurses and physicians, but later mainly involved K-12 teachers. Many were computer novices who expressed some level of anxiety about using computers. Researchers involved in those projects also observed that teachers' *anxiety* was a barrier or restriction in their effective use of computers and related technology resources.

The solution of choice that emerged from those projects and related research was to focus on how computers can be relevant and useful for what teachers need to do in their work with students. Stated another way, once teachers were shown how computers could help them to function more effectively as teachers, indications of so-called computer anxiety and fear were no longer a major concern. Functional relevance involved providing concrete examples demonstrating how the participants could help their students gain technology mediated content. One method was the use of sample scripts—used first by teachers and then modified for their students. Teachers who previously had only limited computer and Internet experiences were hesitant about using computers. However, once they recognized how they could get useful ideas and activities for their students, they were much more willing to take cognitive risks and explore technology resources and the Internet by themselves. Quite commonly with the different groups it was found that, even early in the training sessions, teachers and other trainees began to have more confidence, rejecting offers of help even though they initially had regularly sought help.

The initial experiences of these teachers reflect the experiences of many end-users. When computers and other technology resources became more readily available, available instructions and manuals almost exclusively focused on how computers functioned. In contrast, end-users need instructions and examples clearly describing how they could benefit from using computers in their respective learning or work contexts. Unfortunately, the trend to focus on how technology works rather than on its functional relevance continues today. All too often, many user manuals emphasize key-strokes (i.e., push X key followed by Y key) rather than guidelines about how the hardware or software can enhance how people function relevant to their respective learning or work contexts. One key idea derived from functional relevance is that fear of computers is less likely to occur when users recognize clearly how the computer resources can support and enhance their functioning.

During the previously mentioned school-related technology projects, the first author (GES) used his background and experiences as a clinical psychologist and as an educational psychologist to create and develop the concept of functional relevance. A number of theorists' ideas were helpful in developing facets and use of this concept. Carl Rogers (1969) is widely known for his concept of personally relevant learning, that is, students may be apathetic about teachers' comments but will become engaged in learning when students perceive learning to be personally relevant for themselves. This idea stimulated Snelbecker to explore ways that teaching-learning activities might have greater impact if and when students perceive those activities can be relevant for how they function in personal, work, or other contexts. Concurrently, Heider's pioneering work regarding common sense psychology and interpersonal relationships (Fredenborg, 1995; Harvey, 1989; Heider, 1958; Snelbecker, 1988) provided insights and research methods to discern how people develop beliefs as to what can be functionally relevant for them.

Other theorists' ideas were helpful in developing procedures for selecting and improving interventions related to functional relevance. Many people are familiar with Selye's (1956, 1980) concept of distress, which is stress from highly undesirable or even potentially painful experiences. But, comparatively, few seem aware of Selye's concept of eustress, which is stress in conjunction with highly desirable but challenging experiences, such as getting a job or promotion, getting married, or having other challenging responsibilities. This raised questions about how to cope with challenging experiences during online and other learning activities.

Certain researchers' ideas were helpful in addressing cognitive operations that are regularly used by experts and that could be valuable for novices to learn. Herbert A. Simon and Alan Newell's key work on administrators' and other professionals' approaches to problem solving showed that, quite often, those experts were not aware of the many steps or sequences of actions they use in formulating or solving problems (Simon, 1981; Simon & Newell, 1971). Lev Landa (Landa, 1987; Landa & Kopstein, 1974, 1976; Main, 1987) created procedures (a) to uncover actual procedures used by experts—including logical steps that experts have described and also other cognitive operations that they could not describe, and (b) for teaching novices, effectively and efficiently, how to emulate experts in complex real world problem solving contexts. Those procedures and other ideas from Landa, Newell, and Simon proved to be helpful in designing functional relevance guidelines for teachers and students. Other aspects of functional relevance were influenced by the work of educational technology leaders and various psychology learning theorists, including the views of scholars about the creation, modification, and use of theories and research findings (Azar, 1999; Oswald, 2002; Snelbecker, 1974, 1985). Thus, functional relevance draws from and is based on a synthesis of observations and ideas from formal theories and research findings, as well as common sense psychology and other so-called real world learning, ideas, and perspectives.

When Design Lacks Functional Relevance

Our premise is that potentially helpful technology applications will foster or support meaningful educational achievement successfully only in the degree to which they are clearly relevant for how students and teachers function. This requires having such helpful resources perceived, respectively, by students and teachers, as being functionally relevant for them in their particular context. Functional relevance overcomes frustration and anxiety, two human emotions that frequently accompany use of technology. We now need to recognize briefly some inherent, potentially problematic, attributes of technology

before addressing ways to maximize learning benefits from technology.

It is a mistake to assume that the frustrations encountered by users in the aforementioned technology projects are a thing of the past. There are unending streams of examples about the frustrations people endure when trying to use technology resources. A June 16, 2004 *PC Magazine* article, entitled *Help Us Define PC Ease of Use,* depicted a PC as behaving like a stubborn child, including being obstinate and hard to figure out, much too often taking even simple tasks consume too much time. Also criticized were too frequent occurrences of poor design, inherent incompatibilities, and having things not working the way they should. Advertisements and articles in major IT industry publications (e.g., the June 28, 2004 issue of *ComputerWorld*) contain requests such as, "Can't there be a machine that adapts to my business, not the other way around?" More recently some IT industry publications have been proposing that an "IT attitude" (or, "IT" emphasis) should be discarded in favor of focusing on ways in which IT resources can enhance business, professional, or personal productivity. Each of these comments reflects a condition in which technology is *not* functioning in a manner that is recognized by users as being relevant for them. All too often, it seems intended end-users tend to judge that technology resources or ideas offered are so markedly different from their perspective that any benefit from such ideas would be too costly in time, frustration, or effort that they are judged as being simply *not* worth the effort needed to learn and use them.

Unfortunately, one source of frustration stems partly from inherent attributes of modern-day technologies, which constitutes strengths as well as frustration-laden weaknesses. These inherent aspects of technology resources include, but may not be limited to, the following: (a) complex software that can deal with complicated processes, and (b) general purpose software that can be modified for a variety of purposes. These attributes make it difficult for developers to know how and when software may malfunction. For example, once we know that a board can support 210 pounds we also know that the board can support objects weighing less than 210 pounds. Unfortunately, the same *may not* be true for many technology resources. Even if we know that software can handle complicated tasks, we cannot safely say that this software can separately handle all simpler tasks. That gap could exist even when those same simple tasks are being addressed successfully in the process of handling more complicated tasks. An example would be to create a universal design compatible website. It is believed that by adding technical features such as ALT tags for web graphics and enclosed captions for streaming videos, we are able to create a website that would address the needs for all people. Such an assumption may not be warranted. Even though the website is designed based on the principles of universal design, it still lacks the capability to address the specific needs for all people who use the website.

A second source of frustration is the apparent tendency of designers to forget or ignore the fact that the main goal of online instruction is to facilitate learning that will be beneficial for learners. Instead, too often, designers apparently see a project from their own perspective, perhaps focusing on the technological "bells and whistles" and not through the eyes of the users who want to achieve or complete successfully a particular task. Some designers seem to think that their real goal is to convince others that only the best technology and technical details have been incorporated in their online instruction. It is very easy for online designers to get excited about some new gadget, device, or technology with many new features. Designers and developers of online instruction must be extremely cautious and sensitive about the selection and deployment of appropriate online instruction resources and become aware of the design related issues in online learning. Studies have shown that educators and designers tend to focus more on the technical aspects than the

relevant functions in online learning (Baer, 2000; Carr, 2000; Tu & McIsaac, 2002). For example, many online instructional designers are fascinated by the nonlinear, associative nature of the Web and assume that learning will occur when such features are built into instructional Websites. However, physical connection between concepts in online courses does not necessarily guarantee the types of cognitive connections that occur during learning. According to Perkins (1990), "… 'Connections' is an effort to try to confront the need for conceptual understanding of subject matter on one hand and the need for general thinking skills on the other" (p. 53). Oftentimes, designers are overly concerned with the physical aspects of a connection, that is, how many links are needed and where to insert them, and so forth, leaving little room for examining the cognitive connections that are needed to support learning.

Some technology designers, developers, and vendors seem to misunderstand why technology resources are not readily usable. That reaction is evident each time designers assert that the solution to end-user problems is to make the software simpler (less capable) or watered down (i.e., providing less information rather than providing the valuable information more clearly). Instead, the designers should be trying to find out how their technology resources, whether intended for experts or novices, can be relevant to the ways that their target group functions. This means that the added value of the online learning for the user's productivity or other aspects of work is effectively and explicitly provided. Adding value or getting a return on one's investment (ROI)—time as well as monetary, personal, or business investment—is routinely expected by end-users, (but not necessarily recognized by designers) much of the time in business and professional contexts. Recognizing the perspectives of targeted end-users—during needs assessment and identification of purposes for the instruction and throughout the development process and follow-up evaluations—rather than depending so much on how designers perceive things is very important. Involvement of potential end-users can benefit the ultimate end—and also can help improve the productivity and positive impact of applications designers and developers in online learning.

What is needed is to have designers of online learning focus more on the learning benefits that can be derived from online learning, rather than only or mainly on the subject matter and technical aspects of the technology resources. Of course, all three of these plus practical and other matters must be considered. Online resources should be designed so that they provide students with learning experiences of relevance to the ways that they function in their educational program, personal lives, and/or work.

In the next sections we will offer some examples of how a functional relevance perspective can be useful in addressing online learning instruction issues and problems. We'll offer some suggestions from a functional relevance standpoint regarding three online learning matters: theoretical orientation, social presence, and learner characteristics.

Functional Relevance and Design

Functional relevance is proposed here as an approach that can help improve and enhance the quality of online instruction. Although functional relevance can *not* be expected to solve all online instructional design problems, it can help the designer make decisions about students' likely reactions to online instruction and thus possibly avoid some problems. Here are some general guidelines to consider:

1. Before starting any design or development activities, get as much information as is feasible about the nature and attributes of learning that is desired and likely to be successful.
2. In addition to discerning what instructors, subject matter experts, and administrators consider to be important attributes and learning outcomes of the online instruction, also get the views and expectations of people who are presumed to be potential students. Where feasible, also be attentive to ideas from students who completed previous relevant instruction.
3. Online instruction quite commonly involves potential students who are not in the same geographical area. However, to the fullest extent that is feasible, seek information from those potential students. Identify similarities as well as differences among those students and note patterns that may have design implications. Use technology resources to communicate with geographically remote potential students.
4. Do *not* wait until you have set the final design of the instruction before getting potential students' views. Instead, as much as possible, have representatives of potential students somehow involved in providing relevant ideas prior to, during, and after the actual design and development of the online instruction. Be especially attentive to their views and expectations, concerns they may have, and any special accommodations or other issues that might impact on their access to and active participation in the online instruction.
5. As you should do regarding your reactions to ideas from theories, professionals, and other resources, consider the ideas you gain from potential students in the context of all other ideas you're using to design and develop the online instruction.

Theoretical Orientation

One rather common question occurs when designing online instruction: Should a particular theory guide design and implementation? Many different views have been expressed, ranging from those who think that theories are quite useful to those who think that theories are not helpful because they do not take into account practical realities of online learning contexts. Based on our functional relevance standpoint, we offer ideas for you to consider, but we will not pretend that there is one correct position about the use of theories. In brief, we will propose that it could be appropriate to use theories in some contexts more than other contexts or with some facets of instruction without relying on theories for other facets. Theories, research findings, practical information, and so-called wisdom of the profession (e.g., knowing previous customary ways of doing things) all can be very helpful in organizing online instructional design plans. For example, theories can stimulate or facilitate insights and variations in ways to think about online learning.

At the core of instructional theories are their respective epistemologies (or, philosophies about the nature of knowledge). Various frameworks have been used to describe how respective theories compare regarding epistemology, with some people suggesting that they might be both complementary and competitive while others contend that there exists a continuum from objectivist to constructivist views. The objectivist perspective is that knowledge is observable and measurable. Instructional theories based on this assumption tend to be prescriptive, that is, the theory specifies particular strategies to help the instructor transmit knowledge to the novice learner and strategies that aid the learner in acquiring this knowledge. The assumption of constructivism is that knowledge is the making of meaning about a phenomenon and this meaning-making involves either personal or social agreement. The constructivist approach to instruction uses strategies such as collaboration, authentic context, and diverse perspectives to aid the learner's understanding (Bednar, et al., 1992; Cronin, 1997; Jonassen, 1999; Wilson, Jonassen, & Cole, 1993).

In a sense, we need to consider both the potential value that we might derive from theories and research findings and any costs (time, frustration,

incompatibility) involved—particularly any costs that may be imposed on our student end-users. We should not do so simply to proclaim that our design is based on good theory. Using good theory can obviously be a good idea when it is reasonably clear that theories we have selected enhance learning. But, theories collectively cannot address all aspects and attributes that exist in practical situations. Functional relevance can serve as a framework within which to decide whether particular theories or research findings support the design and development of training for the types of skills desired for a particular situation.

One can make the case that applying learning theories to online design after judicious consideration of costs and benefits constitutes a value-added decision. For example, by identifying constructivism with online design, we recognize that constructivist approach in teaching fits with the unique characteristics of online learning environments which promote positive and active student learning. Head, Lockee, and Oliver (2002) described the facilitating functions of the nonlinear, associative structure of the Web in promoting learners' knowledge association. According to Miller and Miller (1999, 2000), the nonlinear, associative structure can be used to provide more accurate representations of experts' knowledge structures or to permit learners to build their own representations of knowledge (Ayersman, 1995; Wilson & Jonassen, 1989; Yang, 1996).

Discussions about the relative merits of different theories, and sharply different views about whether instruction should or should not be driven by theories, have occupied the attention and interest of researchers and practitioners. Thus, this chapter can not address all issues involved in such matters. However, from the standpoint of functional relevance, we propose that one or more theories should be applied to online instruction depending on the extent to which such theories offer some added value for the online instruction of interest. It may be possible, and even desirable in some situations, to apply so-called competitive approaches in our online instruction.

Previously, in this chapter, it was acknowledged that some designers consider objectivist and constructivist approaches to be incompatible with each other, often asserting that you have to choose one approach or the other. But, with careful attention to overall design requirements, it is plausible that certain aspects of our online instruction could benefit from applying objectivist procedures and other aspects could benefit from constructivist procedures. This can be accomplished successfully by observing that different components of online instruction can be identified and that those components may have contrasting design requirements. Moreover, it seems unlikely that any one theory will address all aspects of our instruction. A functional relevance perspective could be helpful for designers in identifying and making decisions about such responsibilities as the following: (a) make reasonably certain that procedures within each component make sense to students, (b) provide students with transition instructions and support so that they can move successfully from one component to another, and (c) help instructors and students to recognize how the various online instruction components "fit together" and collectively have been designed to enable students to attain the respective purposes, goals, and benefits to be derived from that online instruction.

Social Presence

Social presence is an important concept for online instruction, but too often its significance and impact seem to be ignored or minimized. *Social presence* refers to the extent to which one feels that certain other persons are either both physically and psychologically present or feels the sensation of their being "socially present," even though said persons are not with us physically. Connectedness is one term that sometimes is used in discussions about social presence. Think for a moment when you were in the same room with another person but the other person seemed to be oblivious to the fact that you were in that same room. That is the kind of situation where you most likely felt that you were not at all connected with this person, and you may even have wondered whether there was any social presence between you and this person. If this person is an instructor of a face-to-face classroom course you are taking, your feelings probably would depend on the size of the class or on other factors. As one member of a class with several hundred students you might have mixed feelings, but as one of only five students, you probably would not feel very happy.

How we perceive other people, and how they perceive us, has been of interest in psychology and other disciplines for at least half a century. Earlier terms for this area include personal perception, interpersonal perception, social perception, and other terms related to communications theory. Some of the earlier work focused on implications when people do not have accurate perceptions of each other. However, for several decades it has been recognized that how one perceives another person may be more important than whether or not such a perception is accurate. For example, Sundland (1960) found that patients' outcomes were correlated with their person-perceptions of their psychotherapists along relevant dimensions; however, the extent to which those person-perceptions were accurate was not correlated with their outcome. Snelbecker (1967) found that college students' perceptions of psychotherapists in a laboratory analog were correlated with their perceptions of two therapists. Both of those studies used Barrett-Leonard's (1959) idea of Relationship, which was based on Carl Rogers' theory concerning person-perceptions of patients.

Online instruction designers might want to examine contemporary instruments and research findings both to inform their practice. At least with instructional design of some online courses, it may be important for designers to examine the extent to which students' views regarding social presence could help identify what students expect with regard to social presence. It is important to note that the studies previously mentioned were conducted in psychotherapy relationships decades ago. However, lessons from studies of those relationships do raise some possibilities today. First, how students perceive social presence matters in online instruction may be important, no matter how accurate they are. Second, it seems plausible that online students' personal attributes might influence their perceptions and feelings regarding social presence and also influence designers' plans for creating instruction that is functionally relevant.

Although the term social presence is not always used, there is growing concern that increasing use of automated resources generally in society might be having an adverse impact, partly because of reduced interactions with an actual person. This concern has been expressed about various instances in society today where people are using technology resources as a replacement of person-to-person interactions. For example, James (2006) suggested that the automated systems that make banking activities readily available as needed may actually be creating emotionally detached customers. One recent major study (Katz, 2006) suggests that, despite their proficiency with technology, today's college students do not necessarily prefer to have more than moderate levels of technology in their college courses. More directly related to online instruction, Reio and Crim (2006) expressed their concern about the lack of personal connection among learners while engaging in asynchronous online learning. They pointed out that the online educators were overly enthusiastic about the features of asynchronous learning and overlooked the factor of social presence, which may result in overall learner dissatisfaction with online learning.

These contemporary observations, along with earlier views, suggest that there may be insufficient attention given to social presence (Baer, 2000; Hill, Raven, & Han, 2002). Hill et al., pointed out that "explanation for high dropout rates and dissatisfaction with distance delivered courses may relate to a lack of a perception of community in courses" (p. 384). Tu and McIsaac (2002) emphasized that it is essential to explore the social presence in online classes, the relationship between media and the social-cultural construction of knowledge. Many commercial Web systems like Web CT and Blackboard include built-in tools to accommodate and facilitate education-related communication—such as synchronous and asynchronous online chat rooms. However, many online courses continue to create "cyber cubicles," where learners are separated from each other and where the level of communication is limited to "logon" without meaningful social communication among learners. Good quality effective online instruction involves more than introducing cutting edge technology. It involves building functionally relevant components such as those that address social presence issues, meaningful communication, and so forth, to create a positive and socially supportive environment for learning. A recent effort in this direction is Yang's (2007) STEP model, which includes scaffolding, transaction, evaluation, and presentation. The STEP model underscores the importance of establishing social presence in online learning. It reflects the effort of designers and practitioners to build functionally relevant components in online learning by enhancing learner self-awareness in online learning environment, facilitating social comfort of expressing and sensing affect, and providing effective social navigation.

Learner Characteristics

Students who engage in online instruction often come with different motivational demands. Carr (2000) pointed out that some students attended the online courses because of external motivation such as job promotion, while others attended the online courses for internal motivational reasons such as self-improvement. Thus, online instructional design should attend to both external and internal motivation demands. Some students enrolled in online courses became very frustrated because the courses were poorly designed and failed to address students' internal and external motivational demands associated with the online courses (Carr, 2000; Hill et al., 2002). A design issue in online learning is how to address the differing motivational demands that each learner brings to a learning experience.

In most real life situations, people may share a common interest in some event (e.g., an observation or activity) while concurrently having considerable differences in the perspective they bring to that event. Despite such common interest, it does not necessarily mean that all of these people will have similar perspectives about that particular event. This same co-occurrence of shared common interest along with diverse perspectives can involve (a) preparing good online instruction, (b) writing a good book chapter, (c) designing good research studies, (d) practical application of some theory, or (e) even attending a sporting event. Thus it is not unreasonable to expect diversity and common interests among students who are intended recipients of the online instruction.

Similarly, students enrolled in online courses or some role in making decisions about online learning can be expected to share some common interest but also have co-occurring perspectives with very different views about what constitutes quality of online learning. In addition to the intended beneficiaries of this online instruction, other people with some interest in and views about the topics addressed in the online instruction could include: the authors and designers of the topics, instructors or employers of potential recipients, and various theorists or researchers who focus on online learning.

We suggest that, of all these potential perspectives, too often the intended beneficiaries' perspectives about the online instruction are not adequately considered. More often, it seems that the designers' and other professionals' perspectives predominate. This is not surprising because

designers and developers are so busy dealing with their online instruction responsibilities and pressures—typically also while wondering about potential critics' views about the technical standards that are supposed to be met in good quality online instruction.

Why is it important to place the emphasis on clients' or learners' perspectives (instead of mainly designers' perspectives)? Simply stated, if the needs and expectations of those intended beneficiaries are not met in a reasonable manner, it is quite likely that this online instruction will be judged to be either deficient or even a failure. Functional relevance suggests that we need to maintain our focus on the intended beneficiaries of the online instruction from inception of the idea, iterative tests and revisions of the online instruction. That includes not only design and development processes but also follow-up evaluations and implications for making any changes in this present offering or in future online instruction.

In recent years, certain commercial design firms regularly involve intended learner groups or other targeted end-users throughout the design and development process. Although such firms recognize that additional costs are involved, this practice is accepted because it can help ensure that online learning will have higher prospects for success. A key question is: By what cost-effective ways can we obtain reasonably valid information about potential students' characteristics? As a start, let us acknowledge that designers should not be expected to recognize all possible motivations and expectations of students. Available funds, timeframes, and administrative requirements need to be considered when making design plans. Although a first inclination might be to survey potential students, it is usually best to start with pertinent existing information. Such available information could be valuable in designing, conducting, and analyzing surveys of potential students.

In established institutions with ongoing classroom courses and online courses, some useful information may be readily available. Reviews of literature about distance learning for the particular subject matter area may yield some other helpful insights about matters that should be considered for our online course. In the case of a new course, at many institutions this information about students would be required and carefully reviewed before the new course proposal was approved. Thus, it would be very important to obtain all pertinent documents about the new online course. When an online course is replacing or extending an established classroom course, helpful ideas could be obtained from current students or accessible students who previously completed this or similar courses.

Along with these ways for seeking information about learner characteristics, at some point it may be advisable to use a combination of procedures for collecting new information. One approach is to alternate between using interviews or focus groups and surveys. For example, one possibility would be this: (a) after having reviewed available information, formulate a series of questions and interview or hold group discussions with potential students. A goal here would be to ensure that we're asking reasonably appropriate questions. These interviews and focus group discussions could help guide identification and formatting of appropriate questions; (b) conduct surveys (in class, mailed surveys, or online surveys) of potential students; (c) conduct interviews or focus groups to help clarify and interpret survey results as well as to get answers to questions that only emerged during or after the surveys were conducted.

This information about potential students can be compared and integrated with ideas expressed by the experts. This should result in making decisions so that our resulting online instruction can be more relevant to how our intended online students function.

CONCLUSION

The chapter calls attention to an important aspect in the design of online instruction: that online instructional process will more likely be effective if and when they fit with and are perceived by students as being functionally relevant for their education, work, or other personal contexts. Designers typically must cope with many different—and sometimes competing—responsibilities. They must address subject matter requirements and expected outcomes, provide effective and efficient means for attaining designated educational standards, make professional decisions about cost-effective means for using technology resources, and comply with numerous other conceptual, administrative and practical matters. However, it is a key thesis of this chapter that those efforts may not be so successful if intended students ultimately do not recognize that the resultant online instruction is consistent with their needs and expectations.

It is suggested that unnecessary deficits may exist in online instruction causing students to have unanticipated problems that may cause serious downtime in learning. For example, problems may occur when technology resource instructions are confusing or not clear, when incompatibilities exist between technology resource requirements and students' available equipment or software, with subject matter content that is different from what students had expected, or when students are not familiar with some particular pedagogical procedures.

The concept of functional relevance focuses on learners' perspectives and perceptions as to whether instruction might be relevant for and fit with the way(s) that students function in their work, studies, personal lives, and so forth. It is proposed that teachers, trainers, and other educators become aware of the functional relevance aspect of their designs and programs. Doing so could help improve and enhance the design and development of successful online instruction. In particular, such efforts can lead to online learning outcomes that intended learners will view as being more relevant to their prior knowledge and as being compatible with they function in their studies, work and personal lives. Those efforts may facilitate students' application and extension of their online learning.

FUTURE RESEARCH DIRECTIONS

Two general directions can enhance our ability to design and provide better online learning: (1) study and classify the nature of respective approaches to designing online learning, (2) create ways to incorporate learners' perspectives throughout the design-development-dissemination process.

1. For good reasons, novices initially are encouraged to focus on only one or a few approaches because trying to learn too many different approaches could be counterproductive. But, with greater knowledge and experience, they will learn about "new" approaches and wonder if some might be preferable in certain situations. Snelbecker (1999) suggested that facilitating such advanced proficiency in design might benefit from psychotherapists' experiences with their Society for the Exploration of Psychotherapy Integration (SEPI). SEPI helps psychotherapists learn psychotherapy approaches' strengths, weaknesses, and situations where each can be especially helpful. A SEPI-type group could help instructional designers study and discuss merits of design approaches.

2. To create functionally relevant online learning, it is important that intended learners' perspectives be considered throughout the design-development process — from initial ideas through design-development-evalua-tion-revision, and during follow-up studies in various settings.

Of course, some of this work already is included in most (if not all) instructional design-development approaches, such as doing needs assessments of intended students, and getting reactions of students at various stages. Research could help clarify cost-effective ways (a) for identifying the nature of potential constituent groups, (b) detecting the range of views within each group, (c) discerning similarities and differences in perspectives of constituent groups, and (d) most importantly, research especially is needed to identify cost-effective means whereby we can integrate these groups' perspectives *throughout* the instructional design-development process.

Snelbecker, Miller, and Zheng (2004 & 2006) have reported ways that two commercial design groups began incorporating intended end-users' perspectives throughout the design process from conception of products and continuing throughout development and release of the new products. For example, end-users participate along with graphic designers, information scientists, and other professionals who traditionally designed and developed such products and services. Instead of waiting until products are ready for "Beta testing" the trend now for some design companies is to have end-users' views made a part of the entire design-development process.

There is need for studies on: identifying the kinds of people who might benefit from proposed online learning, obtaining and understanding the perspectives of constituent groups, clarifying similarities/differences among constituent groups, and indicating ways potential students' perspectives can be *synthesized* with information more conventionally used during design-development of online instruction.

There is long-term and continuing need for this research. Snelbecker (1974) described the need to synthesize information from various resources to design effective instruction, and proposed the importance of focusing on practical matters along with theory. Milsum (1966) explained: "When the biologist, social scientist, and indeed natural scientist collaborate with the engineer on these large new system's problems, their classical roles as analyzers of existing systems in contrast to the engineer's role as the synthesizer of previously non-existing 'hardware' systems needs reappraisal" (Milsum, 1966, p. vii).

REFERENCES

Aiken, R. M., & Snelbecker, G. E. (1991). Hindsight: Reflections on retaining secondary school teachers to teach computer science. *Journal of Research on Computing in Education, 23*(3), 444-451.

Ayersman, D. J. (1995). Introduction to hypermedia as a knowledge representation system. *Computers in Human Behavior, 11*(3-4), 529-531.

Azar, B. (1999). Crowder mixes theories with humility. *APA Monitor, 30*(10), 18.

Baer, W. S. (2000). Competition and collaboration in online distance learning. *Information, Communication & Society, 3*(4), 457-473.

Ball, M. J., & Snelbecker, G. E. (1982a). Overcoming resistances to telecommunication innovations in medicine and continuing medical education. *Computers in Hospitals, 3*(4), 40-45.

Ball, M. J., & Snelbecker, G. E. (1982b). Physicians' perceptions of present and future computer usage. *Hospital Information Management, 2*(3), 12-16.

Ball, M. J., & Snelbecker, G. E. (1983). How physicians in the U.S. perceive computers in their practice. In *MedInfo 1983: Proceedings of the Forth World Conference on Medical Informatics, Part 2* (pp. 1169-1172).

Ball, M. J., Snelbecker, G. E., & Schechte, S. L. (1985). Nurses' perceptions concerning computer uses before and after computer literacy lecture. *Computers in Nursing, 3*(1), 23-31.

Bednar, A. K., Cunningham, D., Duffy, T. M., & Perry, J. D. (1992). Theory into practice: How do we link? In T. M. Duffy & D. H. Jonassen (Eds.), *Constructivism and the technology of instruction* (pp. 17-34). Hillsdale, NJ: Lawrence Erlbaum.

Barrett-Leonard, G.T. (1959). *Dimensions of perceived therapist response related to therapeutic change.* Unpublished doctoral dissertation, University of Chicago.

Carr, S. (2000). As distance education comes of age, the challenge is keeping the students. *Chronicle of Higher Education, 46*(23), A39-41.

Cronin, P. (1997). *Learning and assessment of instruction.* Retrieved from http://www.cogsci.ed.ac.uk/~paulus/Work/Vranded/litconsa.htm

DuCharme-Hansen, B. A., & Dupin-Bryant, P. A. (2005). Distance education plans: Course planning for online adult learners. *TechTrends, 49*(2), 31-39.

Fernback, J. (2003). The nature of knowledge in web-based learning environments. *Academic Exchange Quarterly, 7*(4), 28-32.

Fredenborg, J. (1995). *Fritz Heider's "The sychology of interpersonal relations": A detailed citation analysis.* Oslo, Norway: University of Oslo Library, Faculty of Social Sciences Library.

Harvey, J. H. (1989). Fritz Heider, (1896-1988) (Obituary). *American Psychologist, 44*, 570-571.

Head, J. T., Lockee, B. B., & Oliver, K. M. (2002). Method, media, and mode: Clarifying the discussion of distance education effectiveness. *Quarterly Review of Distance Education, 3*(3), 261-68.

Heider, F. (1958). *The psychology of interpersonal relations.* New York: John Wiley & Sons, Inc.

Help Us Define PC Ease of Use. (2004, June 16). *PC Magazine.* Retrieved October 24, 2006, from http://www.pcmag.com/print_article2/0,1217,a=129735,00.asp

Hill, J. R., Raven, A., & Han, S. (2002). Connections in web-based learning environments: A research-based model for community building. *Quarterly Review of Distance Education, 3*(4), 383-393.

James, V. L. (2006). *The creation of emotionally detached customers.* Retrieved December 22, 2006, from www.crmmarketplace.com/content/news/article.asp?docid=%7B8C7798E0-E36E-433C-BEBE-00085E5E6167%7D

Jonassen, D. (1999). Designing constructivist learning environments. In C. M. Reigeluth (Ed.), *Instructional-design theories and models: A new paradigm of instructional theory, Vol. II* (pp. 215-239). Mahwah, NJ: Lawrence Erlbaum.

Jones, M. G., Harmon, S. W., & Lowther, D. (2002). Integrating web-based learning in an educational system: A framework for implementation. In R. A. Reiser & J. V. Dempsey (Eds.), *Trends and issues in instructional design and technology* (pp. 295-306). Upper Saddle River, NJ: Merrill/Prentice Hall.

Katz, R. N. (2006). *The ECAR study of undergraduate students and information technology, 2006: Key findings.* Retrieved December 22, 2006, from http://www.educause.edu/ers0607/

Landa, L. N. (1987). The creation of expert performers without years of conventional experience: The Landamatic method. *Journal of Management Development, 6*(4), 40-52.

Landa, L. N., & Kopstein, F. F. (Scientific Editor), & Bennett, V., Translator. (1974). *Algorithmicization in learning and instruction.* Englewood Cliffs, NJ: Educational Technology Publications.

Landa, L. N., & Kopstein, F. F. (Scientific Editor), & Desch, S., Translator. (1976). *Instructional regutlation and control: Cybernetics, algorithmicization, and heuristics in education.* Englewood Cliffs, NJ: Educational Technology Publications.

Lim, B., Plucker, J., & Nowak, J. (2001). We are what we weave? Guidelines for learning by web design. *Educational Technology, 41*(6), 23-27.

Main, J. (1987). The Russian who makes pros out of amateurs. *Fortune, 76.*

Miller, S. M., & Miller, K. L., (1999). Using instructional theory to facilitate communication in web-based courses. *Educational Technology and Society, 2*(3). Retrieved from http://ifets.gmd.de/periodical/vol_3_99/miller.html

Miller, S. M., & Miller, K. L. (2000). Theoretical and practical considerations in the design of web-based instruction. In B. Abbey (Ed.), *Instructional and cognitive impacts of web-based education.* Hershey, PA: Idea Group Publishing.

Milsum, J. H. (1966). *Biological control systems analysis.* NY: McGraw-Hill.

Oswald, D. F. (2002). A conversation with Glenn E. Snelbecker. *Educational Technology*, September-October, 59-62.

Perkins, D. (1990). On knowledge and cognitive skills: A conversation with David Perkins. *Educational Leadership, 147*(5), 50-53.

Reio, T. G., & Crim, S. J. (2006). *The emergence of social presence as an overlooked factor in asynchronous online learning.* Paper presented at the Academy of Human Resource Development International Conference (AHRD). Columbus, OH.

Rogers, C. (1969). *Freedom to learn.* Columbus, OH: Merrill.

Roszkowski, M. J., Devlin, S. J., Snelbecker, G. E., Aiken, R. M., & Jacobsohn, H. G. (1988).

Validity and temporal stability issues regarding two measures of computer aptitude and attitudes. *Educational and Psychological Measurement, 48,* 1029-1035.

Salpeter, J. (2003). Web literacy and critical thinking: A teacher's tool kit. *Technology and Learning, 23*(8), 22-34.

Selye, H. (1956). *The stress of life.* New York: McGraw-Hill.

Selye, H. (Ed.) (1980). *Selye's guide to stress research.* New York: Reinhold.

Simon, H. A. (1981). Herbert Simon: A software psychologist who isn't. *Psychological Association Monitor,* 15.

Simon, H. A., & Newell, A. (1971). Human problem solving: The state of the theory in 1970. *American Psychologist, 26,* 145-159.

Snelbecker, G. E. (1967). Influence of therapeutic techniques on college students' perceptions of therapists. *Journal of Consulting Psychology, 31,* 614-618.

Snelbecker, G. E. (1974). *Learning theory, instructional theory, and psychoeducational design.* New York: McGraw-Hill.

Snelbecker, G. E. (1984). *"Functional Relevance": Key to successful computer applications.* Unpublished manuscript. Wyndmoor, PA: Snelbecker, G.E.

Snelbecker, G. E. (1985). *Learning theory, instructional theory, and psychoeducational design.* Latham, MD: University Press of America. (Reprint of book originally published by McGraw-Hill in 1974).

Snelbecker, G. E. (1986). *Will computers survive in education? Some practical suggestions.* Luncheon Address at the Fifth Annual Microcomputer Conference, Sagninaw, Michigan.

Snelbecker, G. E. (1988). Heider's comprehensive contributions. *Contemporary Psychology, 33,* 925.

Snelbecker, G. E. (1989). *Instructional design, teachers, and functional relevance.* Paper presented in the symposium "Instructional Design and the Public Schools: A Conversation with the Authors of the Journal of Instructional Development. Special Issue." Presented at the Annual Meeting of the Association for Educational Communications and Technology, Dallas, TX.

Snelbecker, G. E. (1991). *Global concepts: An instructional perspective—differentiated instructional systems design.* Presented in Symposium at the National Conference of the American Society for Training and Development, San Francisco, CA.

Snelbecker, G. E. (1993). Practical ways for using theories and innovations to improve training. In G. M. Piskurich (Ed.), *The ASTD handbook of instructional technology* (pp. 19.3-19.26). New York: McGraw-Hill.

Snelbecker, G.E. (1999). Some thoughts about theories, perfection, and instruction. In C.M. Reigeluth (Ed.), *Instructional-design theories and models: A new paradigm of instructional theory, bolume II,* (pp. 31-50). Mahwah, NJ: Erlbaum.

Snelbecker, G. E., Bhote-Edjulee, N. P., Aiken, R. M., & Wilson, J. D. (1992). *Demographic variables, experience, aptitudes and attitudes as predictors of teachers' learning about computers.* Paper presented at the Annual Meeting of the American Educational Research Association, San Francisco, CA. (ERIC Document Reproduction Service No. 344 877, SP 033 785).

Snelbecker, G. E., Bhote, N. P., Wilson, J. D., & Aiken, R. M. (1995). Elementary versus secondary school teachers retaining to teach computer science. *Journal of Research on Computing in Education, 27*(3), 336-347.

Snelbecker, G. E., Miller, S. M., & Zheng, R. (2004). Thriving, not merely surviving, with technology in education: Implications for teachers, administrators, policy makers, and other educators. *Journal of Christian Education and Information Technology, 6*, 13-53.

Snelbecker, G. E., Miller, S. M., & Zheng, R. (2006). Learning sciences and instructional design: Observations, reflections, and suggestions for further exploration. *Educational Technology, 46*(4), 22-27.

Sundland, S. M. (1960). *Psychotherapists' self-perceptions, and patients' perceptions of their therapists.* Unpublished doctoral dissertation, The Ohio State University.

Tu, C., & McIsaac, M. (2002). The relationship of social presence and interaction in online classes. *The American Journal of Distance Education, 16*(3), 131-150.

Wilson, B. (1999). *The dangers of theory-based design.* Retrieved from http://www.cudenver.edu/~brent_wilson/dangers.html

Wilson, B. G, & Jonassen, D. H. (1989). Hypertext and instructional design: Some preliminary guidelines. *Performance Improvement Quarterly, 2*(3), 34-39.

Wilson, B. G., Jonassen, D. H., & Cole, P. (1993). Cognitive approaches to instructional design. In G. M. Piskurich (Ed.), *The ASTD handbook of instructional technology* (pp. 21.1-21.22). New York: McGraw-Hill. Retrieved from http://www.cudenver.edu/~brent_wilson/training.html

Yang, H. (2007). Establishing social presence for online collaborative learning: STEP and practices. In R. Zheng & P. S. Ferris (Eds.), *Understanding online instructional modeling: Theories and practices.* Hershey, PA: Idea Group Publishing.

Yang, S. C. (1996). Designing instructional applications using constructive hypermedia. *Educational Technology*, November-December, 45-50.

Chapter II
Model–Facilitated Learning Environments:
The Pedagogy of the Design

Glenda Hostetter Shoop
Pennsylvania State University, USA

Patricia A. Nordstrom
Pennsylvania State University, USA

Roy B. Clariana
Pennsylvania State University, USA

ABSTRACT

The purpose of this chapter is to discuss how instruction, technology, and models converge to create online model-facilitated learning environments. These instructional environments are designed in such a manner that the interaction with the model on the computer network is essential to the learning experience. The idea is to use these models to maximize the pedagogical power that helps students construct conceptual mental representations that lead to a greater degree of retention and overall recall of information. How students will act and learn in a particular environment depends on how the instructional designer creates the environment that maximizes their learning potential, considering the interrelationships between the learning experience, the technology, cognition, and other related issues of the learner.

CHAPTER OBJECTIVES

The reader will be able to:

- Discuss models
- Describe online model-facilitated learning
- Find evidence that supports decisions to design online model-facilitated learning experiences
- Define complex systems and their association with online model-facilitated learning
- Understand the role of collaboration in the design of online model-facilitated learning
- Consider specific issues and challenges in designing online model-facilitated learning experiences

INTRODUCTION

You are, once again, preparing your lesson plans for a fall semester online science class. For the past two years, your students have expressed problems learning certain scientific principles, and their opinions have been substantiated in their overall test scores. You are trying to decide how to revise your instruction to teach some of the more complex scientific concepts. To your credit, you are aware of the challenge and are willing to consider alternative instructional methods. You become curious about *model-facilitated learning* after reading Hestenes (1987, 2006) describe a decade of successes using modeling in physics, chemistry, and physical science classrooms. In addition, today's powerful computers allow you to go beyond traditional methods of instruction by breaking down the limitations and constraints of conventional methods of teaching and assessment. They give you the capability to use electronic applications and processes to deliver the content, and situate learners in a domain of information and a set of circumstances that maximize the cognitive potential of learners. By creating these online learning environments, you can give the students the opportunity to use computer-based models and simulations to explore, and better comprehend and communicate complex ideas (Maier & Größler, 2000). In an extensive review of the literature to examine computer-mediated communication in educational applications, Luppicini (2006) reported that learners in online courses did just as well as face-to-face courses, therefore, it seemed a favorable alternative.

Online model-facilitated learning has its roots in the learning sciences, an interdisciplinary field of study that focuses on building innovative learning environments that incorporate multimedia and computer-based technology. Therefore, we define online model-facilitated learning as an instructional experience whereby the instructional materials and resources are managed and run on a computer system. The system is connected by a network of devices that are used and manipulated by the students to support and enhance their participation in the learning experience. Students are placed in experiences that allow them to learn with and from other students in a system that uses a model. The model is the artifact structurally designed and created to represent or to demonstrate a theoretical construct of a system or some chosen phenomenon. The instruction is designed in such a manner that the interaction with the model on the computer network is essential to the learning experience. The instructors and students may or may not be geographically separated.

The intent of this chapter is to discuss how instruction, technology, and models converge to create online model-facilitated learning environments, and discuss the pedagogical structures within which they operate. More specific objectives for the chapter are:

a. Define models and their function in online model-facilitated learning
b. Develop a theoretical platform and related principles as these apply to online model-facilitated learning

c. Apply pedagogical principles to teaching and assessment in online model-facilitated learning

MODELS

Models are instructional tools that teachers can use to enhance the human cognitive power (Kozma, 1987) and enhance higher order thinking as they "function as intellectual partners with the learner" (Jonassen, 1996, p. 9). They are used to provide a learning situation that is more contextually bound than most conventional instructional approaches because they situate the students in an experience that gives them the chance to experience and "play with" selected aspects in the domain of knowledge. As a *representation*, a model is the tangible depiction or portrayal of some original object or phenomenon. For example, a globe is a representative model of Earth that the learners can interact with to find different locations around the world; the interaction between the learners and their interaction with the model are most important. As a *demonstration*, a model becomes the means to demonstrate or show the learner how to do something without having to actually build a model. For example, a scale model of the solar system demonstrates the size of the planets in relation to each other. Regardless if it is a representation or a demonstration, a model is primarily a tangible communication device for conversing with self and others immediately and through time (Pea, 1994).

How Are Models Used In Instruction?

Instructors can employ models in different ways. They can create a model that the student can use or they can instruct the students to build their own model. Bliss (1994) refers to this as explorative modeling and expressive modeling respectively.

Using Models

Students can be instructed to use instructor-created dynamic models (computer simulations and games) or static models (illustrations and concept maps) to learn about a domain of content. These models are usually designed and created by instructors for learners to use within a specific sphere of interrelated knowledge. Löhner, van Joolingen, Savelsbergh, and van Hout-Wolters (2005) say, "Learners explore a given model representing someone else's ideas by trying it out and perhaps modifying it" (p. 442).

The primary learning objective of using models is to acquire domain content at the application level. For example, intuiting the effects of supply on demand or grasping the possible affects of global warming on hurricane strength are case in point.

Building Models

Students can be instructed to build models in order to construct their own new understanding of a domain content area or of the dynamics of a system. Students learning about the human cardiovascular system can build a concept map (e.g., a static model) of the content and then use their concept map to write an expository essay of the content. Or they can build a dynamic model of the same system using *Stella*®[1] (a software modeling program for creating *dynamic systems)* and examine the structure and function of the heart. With both strategies, students build their own understanding of the content. If decision making is your instructional aim, there are software packages that students can use to build a model of a system that needs to be managed (e.g., SIMPROCESS® is a product that can be used to build models that support decision making[2].).

Model building typically seeks to answer questions of inquiry (Kolb, 1984). The knowledge gained allows the student to understand causal relationships and make predictions. The overarching learning objective is aimed at the students' ability to gather information; to communicate knowledge; to transfer the knowledge; and to apply complex cognitive skills to other novel real-life encounters (van Merrienboer, Clark, & de Croock, 2002). Thus building models directs attention to higher-order, transferable cognitive skills and develops a domain-specific base of content knowledge.

Tasks Accomplished with Models

We propose that the tasks learners are asked to accomplish with models in online settings fall under one of two categories: *peremptory* and *dialectic*.

Peremptory Online Task

A peremptory online task invites either acceptance or rejection, it is "a-dialectic" and it brings along an underlying worldview. Working alone on a computer-based simulation or game is a peremptory task. A learner who has become proficient in *Simcity* has acquired important concepts and principles regarding city planning that reflect the theory that undergirds this simulation, including a positive bias (but perhaps misplaced trust) towards public transportation. Said differently, the learner 'wins' when their intuitive planning actions and interactions with the simulation most agree with the hidden theory and the learner *appropriates the theory usually without reflection* (rather like brain washing). This assumption is derived from the research on implicit learning.

Reber (1967) refers to implicit learning as a process by which knowledge is acquired independently of conscious and deliberate attempts to do so. What is implicitly (unconsciously) learned about the domain through simulations and games can probably be evaluated only within the simulation or game. This is an important issue that is overlooked. Further, learners will internalize the "grammar" of the technology tool that they are

using; for example, thinking in terms of stocks and flows when using *Stella*, or in terms of variable control when programming. At a minimum, given enough model-facilitated exposure, students will begin to think about everything as a system, and this represents a substantial mental shift that may not be measured by traditional tests.

Dialectic Online Task

In contrast to the peremptory online task, a dialectic online task invites argument or participation. The learner must 'fill-in-the-blanks.' If the instructor posts a detailed concept map of a topic and requires students to study it for a test, this approach is highly peremptory. However, if the students are given the same concept map and are told to work individually to find the errors and correct it, then it becomes less peremptory. If the students complete this same concept map task in a collaborative group with appropriate ground rules, then this becomes a dialectic experience.

In summary, the model is a contextual representation whose primary function is to provide the basis of an experience where the students can experience and investigate the fundamental attributes and properties of what is to be learned. If the instructional intent in online model-facilitated learning is to promote a conceptual change, according to Windschitl (1996), allowing students to interact with the dynamics of a modeling system can create unique ways to help students conceptualize the information. Common to both uses of models is simulating a situation, specifically designed to situate learners in experiences that serve to stimulate their process of inquiry and understanding (Kolb, 1984).

A THEORETICAL PERSPECTIVE

Learning, as we know it, is an active cognitive process whereby knowledge is built on existing knowledge as the learner seeks to understand the information and experience as it is presented (Duffy & Cunningham, 1996; Winn & Snyder, 1996). In online model-facilitated learning environments, regardless whether the learner builds or uses the model, he/she takes the information from the model and adopts mental representations of the system to help organize the information in a *personally* coherent and meaningful way. The degree of learning rests in how well the learner can connect the existing facts, concepts and principles with the new information that is given or discovered in the modeling experience.

How this information is stored in memory and how it is linked in this complex, abstract and interconnected network of memory structures is the schema (Bruning, Schraw, & Ronning, 1999; Driscoll, 2000; Rumelhart, 1980; Schunk, 2000; Winn & Snyder, 1996). If you think of the brain as a neural file cabinet, these schemas are neural memory files that hold information about specific concepts. Over time, we make associations between and among them, and this intricate network of neural files become highly elaborate, interconnected, and cross-referenced. Online model-facilitated learning environments provide a powerful way for learners to develop these conceptual arrangements and manage the interrelationships and integration of these complex systems. In online model-facilitated learning, Papert (1993) argues that constructing and manipulating "quasi-concrete" representations of knowledge on computers leads to more robust internal knowledge structures.

Online model-facilitated learning is a generative learning approach that uses strategies to encourage learners to actively create and consider the relationships among various elements of information, between lesson information, and personal knowledge, and find personal meaning (Jonassen, 1988; Jonassen & Wang, 1993; Wittrock, 1992). Following the theory of generative learning, it is the process of generating relationships between and among the information and integrating that with memory, whereby "meaningful understanding and comprehension are predicted outcomes" (Grabowski, 1996, p. 898). Generative strategies, such as asking the learner to formulate new questions, form direct inferences, and demonstrate and represent how the concepts connect, typically require learners to consider *multiple information elements at the same time*, thus encouraging the development of the organizational and structural relationships between the information elements (Grabowski, 1996; Ritchie & Volkl, 2000). The focus is to generate new conceptual understandings, not just transform what is already known (Grabowski, 1996).

The view that students actively participate to construct their own knowledge through direct participation in the modeling experience (whether using or building the model) is from the philosophical point of view called constructivism—a doctrine of beliefs that knowledge is constructed by the learner through experiences and direct participation with the environment (Duffy & Cunningham, 1996). Based on what we know of online model-facilitated learning environments, Cobb's (1994) interpretation of the complementary nature of the two perspectives of constructivism and socioculturism apply. According to Cobb (1994), the cognitive constructivist perspective explains the unique configuration of knowledge constructed by the learner and the quality of the individual interpretation of the experience in constructing that knowledge, while the sociocultural constructivist perspective emphasizes the construction of knowledge when individuals engage in discussion and activity about shared problems and experiences in a community of learning. Accordingly, *social interaction is necessary for the construction of knowledge*, and meaning will differ among the learners because meaningfulness is an individual interpretation based on past experiences. These interactions are uniquely understood by the learner through personal reflection and dialogue with others as they gain a shared understanding of the complexity of the concept being explored (Gasparini, 2004).

In the online model-facilitated learning environment, the student is situated in the learning experience in a manner that directly confronts the intellectual, practical, personal and social aspects the model brings to the experience. According to Collins's (1988) definition of situated learning, knowledge, and skills are learned in contexts that reflect the way they will be used in real life (p. 2), and he goes on to cite benefits of situated learning that we feel are applicable to the design of online model-facilitated learning instruction:

- Students are placed in the conditions for applying knowledge
- Students are situated in conditions to apply information and problem solve
- Students learn the implications of knowledge as they work through the problem
- Students are supported in structuring knowledge in ways appropriate to later use by gaining and working with that knowledge in context

Brown, Collins and Duguid (1989) suggest that embedding information in the situation provides essential parts for its structure and meaning. The knowledge gained in the learning experience becomes coded in such a way that it is connected to that situation; therefore, context and authenticity become important considerations. In online model-facilitated instruction, the idea is to create models that simulate authentic practice.

We have continued to talk about the role of the experience in online model-facilitated instruction. We believe it is the hallmark and the distinguishing characteristic in your design. How you create the online modeling experience and then situate the learner in that experience will greatly influence the success of achieving the learning outcomes. Carl Rogers (1969) paved the way for student-centered, experiential education, and any instructional method that gives the student the opportunity to actively participate in the encounter with a goal of acquiring knowledge

is considered experiential learning. The students directly experience the subject matter, either by using or building models.

PEDAGOGICAL CONSIDERATIONS AND ISSUES IN THE ONLINE MODEL-FACILITATED LEARNING EXPERIENCE

Among the pressing issues for instructors in designing online model-facilitated learning experiences lie in understanding of the complex systems taught with models, and appreciating the role of collaboration. Placing a student in the experience, knowing how information is cognitively processed, and understanding the role of the social and collaborative aspects of learning about complex systems are important considerations in building a theoretical framework to support the pedagogical decision to use online models. These aspects are mutually connected and interrelated.

Complex Systems

Wilensky and Resnick (1999) describe complex systems as having multiple levels of simultaneous hierarchical interactions; the system under study may in fact be a sub-system of a larger system. An example of this would be the human body. When you consider the body as a functioning "whole" the interrelated, interdependent, and simultaneous interactions among the sub-systems, for example, oxygen transport system, the renal system, the cardiovascular system, the nervous system, and so forth, are essential for life. These complex systems are becoming increasingly important to understand in the 21st century as the relationships among the systems becomes more integrated (Lesh, 2006). But, learning about these systems is difficult because of the amount and complexity of subject matter within and across domains and disciplines (Hmelo-Silver & Azevedo, 2006).

These systems tend to be defined by the dynamic interactions and interrelationships among and between the multiple constituent parts and frequently cannot be explained by a set of linear, functional rules (Lesh, 2006). As stated by van Merrienboer et al. (2002), "In complex learning, the whole is clearly more than the sum of its parts because it also includes the ability to coordinate and integrate those parts" (p. 40). Therefore, approaching it from a traditional, behaviorist learning point of view will not suffice. The theories in behaviorism focus on forming associations between a stimulus and a response, and they do not account for the complicated and involved nature of systemic thinking in these complex online model-facilitated learning environments. The memorization of facts limits knowledge to the constituent parts rather than fully comprehending how these parts fit together into one cohesive whole (Feltovich, Coulson, & Spiro, 2001). The instructor must break down the prevailing "silo" mentality so that the students can more easily find meaningful associations and see the patterns of relationships, and the control and influences among the parts. These relationships are not necessarily linear and the pattern of differentiation makes them complex. Specifically, Milrad, Spector, and Davidson (2002) suggest learners usually experience difficulty in the following:

- Comprehending nonlinear relationships
- Understanding and viewing the problem within the context of the system
- Considering the full range of connections, influences, and controls within a system
- Transferring what is learned in one context to find the solution to a problem in another

Kukla (1992) claimed that using models designed to represent various situations and complex systems will help develop cognitive systems that enable the learner to process information, solve problems by reasoning, infer consequences, form hypotheses about the world that's external to the "microworld," and make predictions about the future with reasonable accuracy.

The Association with Complex Systems

When learners are plunged into a system, they become more aware of the system's dynamics in terms of the processes, relationships, and consequences of decisions. To illustrate this, we turn to work done by Colella (2000), who designed a microworld using miniature computers called *thinking tags* to explore viral transmission. Each learner in this "participatory simulation" wore a *thinking tag* [3]. To begin the session, only one *thinking tag* contained the virus. As the experience unfolded the virus jumped from tag to tag infecting the other learners. Colella created this model of the dynamic system of viral transmission so the students could experience the transmission of a virus, understand the problem, develop hypotheses, explore the underlying rules (cause and effect) of the system, and learn the consequences if the rules were broken. Colella could have taught the students about viral transmission without giving them the chance to experience it; however, the power of using a model to explore this helped the students discover the knowledge of how a virus is transmitted, understand the social relationships in this community of learners, and feel the accompanying emotion when infected with the disease. According to Hmelo-Silver and Azevedo (2006), learning about these systems confronts our cognitive, meta-cognitive, and social resources.

Regardless if the students are instructed to use a model or build a model, the microworld becomes the place for the group to learn. The instructor creates these microworlds and models to simulate the real world so the topic of instruction can be taught in the safety of an instructional environment yet learned in a real-world context. Context and authenticity are important considerations in the design and creation of models because the model represents domain-specific situations and systems constrained within "microworlds" that are meant to activate the cognitive system in ways that traditional teaching by lectures often cannot accomplish (Colella, 2000; Kukla, 1992). According to Colella (2000, p. 474-475), "the flexibility of microworld environments opens up the range of possible experiences that can be created." Thus a critical design issue in online model-facilitated instruction is determining the "level" of the microworld and the "size" of the model.

Role of Collaboration

Collaborative online projects are some of the most exciting ways to motivate students. Getting students involved with posting projects on the web, emailing other students or experts, discussing issues on a threaded discussion, or chatting online is a great way to motivate students. Stahl (2004, p. 64) defines collaborative learning in terms of building "the gradual construction and accumulation of increasingly refined and complex cognitive and linguistic artifacts." The students commit to a shared goal and work together in a mutual and joint effort to construct meaning, share learning tasks to build a knowledge base, clarify issues, explore a topic, and solve a problem (Hron & Friedrich, 2003; Nevgi, Virtanen & Niemi, 2006). In online model-facilitated learning environments, students gathered together in virtual groups not only learn from their own individual experiences as they solve a problem, but they learn from each other. The nature of the task, the context of the experience, the learner characteristics, and the group relations all affect the collaboration (Dillenbourg & Self, 1995).

Clark and Mayer (2003) make a distinction between two alternative collaborations: product-oriented and process-oriented. The product-oriented collaboration results in some tangible output. These types of assignments need sufficient instructional guidance and resources that guide the experience, yet allow enough openness

for the student to explore, be creative and feel challenged. The process-oriented collaboration focuses on learning that is gained from structured group exchange rather than the production of a tangible finished product. The learning is stimulated by how the instructor designs interactions around the model. In either case, structuring the online model-facilitated learning environment to promote collaboration and maximize the power of the interactions is important and is critical for a successful outcome as suggested by Clark and Mayer (2003). During collaboration, all members *should* contribute equally to the model and begin to develop a sense of co-ownership of the model. In cooperative association, each member individually completes a discrete portion of the task in detail, and then brings that portion or piece back to the group. A properly designed collaborative task engenders dialectic interactions as the group works together reaching consensus or compromise on every part of the project. Although the online model-facilitated learning itself may vary among different authors (Kanuka, Rourke, & Laflamme, 2006; Roberts, Andersen, Deal, Grant & Shaffer, 1983; van Merrienboer, 1997; van Merrienboer et al., 2002; Wolstenholme, 1990), the process generally moves through the following phases as described below:

1. **Problem orientation:** The problem is presented and the learner is oriented to the modeling task, which includes goal setting and engagement. These problems or scenarios are not only authentic and relevant but also have the correct level of complexity for the learners.

2. **Conceptualization:** The learner puts the problem into some context. Important components and causal relationships are recognized.

3. **Formulation:** The learner develops hypotheses and a method of collecting the data he/she needs to move forward with the problem.

4. **Rules and Principles:** The learner explores the cause and effect relationships.
5. **Testing:** The learner verifies in that their evolving mental model does not contradict data from the real-world system.
6. **Application:** The learner transfers the knowledge and applies the cognitive skills to authentic situations to solve problems (Perkins & Unger, 1999).

Collaboration in online learning, by its very nature, requires attention to the social interactions and communication strategies because this is very different than face-to-face collaborative learning experiences many students are familiar with.

PEDAGOGICAL CONSIDERATIONS

Instruction must be designed to teach students how to apply skills in a coordinated and integrated fashion (van Merrienboer et al., 2002). The instructor-created experience must be thoughtfully designed because it is paramount for learning. Rogers (1969) has provided us with essential guidelines to create an environment for learning. Although these guidelines were developed for face-to-face instruction, we believe they are so fundamental to learning that they are noteworthy considerations in creating online model-facilitated learning environments:

1. Setting the initial mood or climate of the group or class experience
2. Elicit and clarify the purpose of the individuals in the class as well as the more general purposes of the group
3. Make easily available the widest possible range of resources for learning
4. Take the initiative in sharing feelings with the group in ways which do not demand nor impose but represent a personal sharing

Just as important is the course design. Goldman, Williams, Sherwood, Hasselbring and the Cognition and Technology Group at Vanderbilt (1999) have provided us with these four principles for course design:

1. Organize it around the solution of meaningful problems
2. Provide scaffolds for achieving meaningful learning
3. Provide opportunities for practice with feedback, revision, and reflection
4. Promote collaboration, sharing of expertise and independent learning

Milrad (2002) concludes that the design of these environments should include multiple perspectives of the problem, support for learning and cognitive development, opportunity to develop meaningful collaborative interactions among the learners, and concrete feedback to facilitate the learners' understanding. However, there are specific issues and challenges in designing these collaborative learning environments due to the unique characteristics of online instruction and online learning groups, most specifically in the areas of social context, the nature of the communication, cognitive load, and the emotional state of the learner (Hron & Friedrich, 2003). Suitable instructional supports must be considered in each area.

The social context of online model-facilitated learning experiences cannot be ignored because it differs from face-to-face experiences. There are no facial expressions, body gestures, voice inflections, or head nods to help the instructor or the students make judgments on interest, response, or participation. In addition, the "whose next" question can become an issue in deciding when and who takes the next turn to participate. How the instructor communicates the idea and how he/she draws all the participants into the model will determine the collaboration among the participants. The instructor must take the lead to establish clear ground rules and set the convention of etiquette for the communication at the onset of the experience so the students know what to expect and how to manage their role. It is the challenge of the instructors to ensure that the student interactions and discussions are engaging, productive, and meaningful in developing knowledge and understanding (Littleton & Whitelock, 2005). In a study conducted by Navarro and Shoemaker (2000), students enrolled in an online economics course were generally satisfied with the online student-to-instructor interactions, however, students were generally unsatisfied with their student-to-student interactions. Instructors, by providing appropriate supporting materials and resources, activities that support the learning, and feedback will enhance the quality of interaction between students and instructors.

Communication in online collaboration is an important consideration in terms of the technology and the quality of the message. Tolmie and Boyes (2000) have found that asynchronous communication not just facilitates discussions between students but "any disagreements which occur will promote growth and understanding (p. 121). The technology greatly expands the potential of the instruction, but it does not come without problems. Navarro and Shoemaker (2000) found that technical problems are pervasive in online learning environments. The system can go down, the students may have problems accessing some instructional materials, the software may not be compatible, the video and audio system might malfunction; indeed, a whole host of problems could occur. Technical support to students and instructors must be available, and instructors must match the course design to the technology that is available to the students. How the information is delivered to the students is very important because messages are more enduring and permanent in online collaboration (Hron & Friedrich, 2003). They can be accessed or sent at any time, and the sheer volume and the task of following them can seem unmanageable. Instructors must be concerned with the effect in how the message is interpreted, the value of the messages produced, and the manner in which the messages motivate the learners. In addition, it is the instructor's responsibility to ensure that the students are not learning the "wrong" concepts that are transmitted in the messages. This is particularly important when the students are working and learning from each other. The instructor should intervene to bring the students back on track if this occurs.

Cognitive load can overwhelm the student (Hron & Friedrich, 2003). The complicated computer network, the complex subject matter, the sheer volume of information, and the different pattern of communication all contribute to this. It is important for the instructor to provide help for students to cope with the complexity. Technological support systems should be included in the design of the instruction so that problems can be dealt with in a reasonable manner and without disruption to the learning. In designing online model-facilitated learning environments when multimedia is used, instructors must create experiences that maximize the opportunities for the learner to mentally organize the information in meaningful and coherent cognitive structures for meaningful learning to occur, while at the same time paying attention to the cognitive load associated with multimedia learning (Mayer & Moreno, 2003). This becomes particularly important when the model uses and presents visual and verbal representations of information. Mayer and Moreno (2003) highlight the potential for cognitive overload in multimedia learning environments due to the substantial cognitive processing that is necessary for meaningful learning to occur. They report that in their research on multimedia learning, they are "repeatedly faced with the challenge of cognitive load" (p. 43). In response, they explored nine ways to reduce cognitive load in processing information aimed at redistributing the demands of cognitive processing (Mayer & Moreno, 2003): off-load processing demands on the visual and verbal channels, segmenting, pre-training, eliminate extraneous information, provide signaling cues, minimize incidental cognitive load, eliminate redundancy, synchronize the presentation of material, build in ways for it to be individualized to the learner's characteristics. In addition, other strategies to help manage this cognitive load might include breaking a larger problem into sub-problems, the inclusion of the heuristic aids, or the integration of metacognitive self assessment tools (Malopinsky, Kirkley, Stein, & Duffy, 2000). Instructional supports in online model-facilitated learning experiences would include a plan to monitor the messages, coach the students, build in scaffolding strategies, and provide reflection and feedback mechanisms.

The emotional state of the learner cannot be ignored in online model-facilitated learning experiences. Interest and motivation are important learner attributes to the success of these experiences whether you use or build models. This is a concern, because low participation in discussions in online learning environments has been reported across the board (Tolmie & Boyle, 2000). Instructors must find ways to stimulate and motivate the learners to participate. They should include mechanisms to involve all students and not let a few dominate the discussions. Techniques used by experienced instructors include personal electronic workbooks as well as records of their contributions to the group projects; participating in instructor supported computer conferences; and having the students use critical reflection on both the content and the process. In a discussion on issues related to designing inquiry on the Web, Lim (2004) suggests using questions, student planning, careful sequencing of activities, and reflection to engage the students.

ASSESSMENT CONSIDERATIONS

Online model-facilitated instruction is aimed at teaching complex, higher-order thinking skills; therefore, online model-facilitated learning is defeated if the focus of the assessment is on declarative knowledge only, and using the traditional methods, such as paper and pencil tests. These methods are unlikely to measure the full range of knowledge, skills, and attitudes accumulated by the learner.

When developing an assessment plan in an online model-facilitated learning environment, the question is, "what should be assessed—the process (contribution and interaction), the product (the model), or both?" The assessment of process and product are equally important; yet, assume different types of assessment strategies and methods. In online model-facilitated instruction, the model represents the group's understanding of a large amount of information from multiple disciplines due to the complexity of the modeling experience, and so assessing the model (the product) makes sense. The evaluators(s) must assess the breadth and depth of information represented in the model as well as the students' thinking and reasoning strategies. A process assessment would be used to measure the students' contribution to the group structure, and participation in the discussion and information gathering.

Educational assessment plans should include two functional categories: formative or summative. *Formative assessment* supports the progression of learning by providing immediate, contextualized feedback and encourages self-reflection. Formative assessments should focus less on how closely student responses match a pre-determined model and more on the competency of the performance as a whole (Pellegrino, Chudowsky, & Glaser, 2001). In online model-facilitated learning, students work collaboratively to construct their own knowledge within the structure of the course objectives. Instructors must be diligent to guide the students "back on track" through either coaching or scaffolding or other pedagogical techniques if the students stray too far from the learning objectives. *Summative assessment* is done at the conclusion of a course or some larger instructional period to determine individual student success or to what extend the program/ project/course has met its learning objectives. Because of the complex nature of online model-facilitated learning, we suggest that summative assessment must be designed to measure higher order thinking skills to learn how they reason through situations, how they transfer knowledge, how they make decisions, and how they critically think through problems. Reeves (2000) suggests three alternative assessment methods to use in an online environment:

- Cognitive assessment is the assessment of a wide range of abilities, including attention, memory, problem-solving, language skills and intellectual functioning. It is the process of determining a student's cognitive strengths and weaknesses through observed behavior
- Performance assessment requires that a student carry out an extended, complex process or produce a product, such as a model
- Portfolio assessment can be either formative or summative. An example of a formative assessment portfolio is a "growth and learning portfolio," which contains the student's work that demonstrates their program toward a goal. A summative assessment portfolio is a "best works portfolio" which is representative of the student's work that provides evidence that they have a specific learning target (Nitko, 2004).

Assessment must not be an afterthought to be effective, but strategically integrated into the instructional design plan from the very beginning, so it has the ability to assess the transfer and integration the conceptually-complex ideas, which are best measured through complex, authentic assessment methods (Erickson, 2001; Nitko, 2001).

CONCLUSION

This chapter provides a framework for online model-facilitated learning environments that offers pedagogical considerations not seen in traditional instruction. These models embedded in carefully constructed "microworlds" are artifacts within a specific sphere or domain of information that instructors create for learners to interact with and experience. The idea is to use these models to maximize the pedagogical power that helps students construct conceptual mental representations that lead to a greater degree of retention and overall recall of information.

Based on what we learned in this chapter, learning and most importantly, the comprehension of complex systems, are enhanced in online model-facilitated learning instructional environments because students can interact with the content and each other to apply it to real-world scenarios. The overarching goal is to teach students a body of knowledge that may draw from the integration of many disciplines, and get this stored in long-term memory so it can be recalled and transferred to solve problems in different situations.

Perhaps the greatest value of online model-facilitated learning environments is in developing a student's "thinking skills." Reasoning and making judgments is a multi-layered, complex process of constructing evidence that is based on a social interaction with others and gathering evidence to support the claim. Learners must have the ability to organize large amounts of information through complex cognitive processes and mental associations to critically analyze many facets of a problem, reach an informed conclusion, develop a plan to solve the problem, and systematically justify their response by making a reflective judgment of their decision (Bruning et al., 1999; Winn & Snyder, 1996).

How students act and learn in a particular environment depends on how the instructional designer creates the environment that maximizes their learning potential, considering the interrelationships between the learning experience, the use of the technology, the cognitive conditions and other related issues of the learner. Pedagogical decisions depend on the interrelationships between the instructional goal, the instructor, the theory, and all the resources. The importance of considering these factors in the design of an online model-facilitated learning environment cannot be overstated. Surging ahead without this understanding will result in a situation that does not maximize the learning potential in online model-facilitated experiences.

FUTURE TRENDS AND RESEARCH

This area of online model-facilitated learning environments is relatively new and educators are at the fringe of gathering empirically valid and reliable data to support the pedagogical decisions. As suggested by Hmelo-Silver and Pfeffer (2004) in talking about the complexity of the systems we are trying to teach, we are still at an early stage of understanding how this all fits together. For this reason, much more needs to be learned. The decision to choose model-facilitated instruction should not be solely driven by the available advances in technology, but by the principles grounded in empirical research findings. The major elements of model-facilitated instruction, learning and assessment, and the inherent relationships among them, provide important areas for investigation.

A pressing issue in online model-facilitated instruction lies in the complexity of the system being taught, and how the instructor integrates the breadth and depth of a vast amount of knowledge related to that system. These modeling systems cross disciplines and cross themes within a unit of study as they relate complex concepts and generalizations, yet are all linked to the common topic of interest (Erickson, 2001). Therefore, designing these learning environments takes a highly coordinated approach, sometimes involv-

ing experts from several disciplines because the instructional designer must be concerned with the integration of content (what essential topics to cover and which experts need to be involved in those decisions) and the integration of process (strategies to maximize learning and promote thinking). What we want from the design of online model-facilitated instruction is to integrate all the concepts associated with these complex systems in careful associations to the students to "integrate their thinking at a conceptual level (Erickson, 2001, p. 64), and commit this to long-term memory.

Complex dynamic systems surround us and it is critical that students are provided with the tools to understand these systems. We as instructional designers and educators have the tools and the knowledge to provide students with the learning environments to develop these skills. However, Stahl (2004, p. 9) argues that in spite of the wide recognition of artifacts as "an embodiment of shared understanding," only a few education scientists have focused on how new users learn to use them. To fully implement online model-facilitated instruction, we must learn how to use models to expand the capacity and capability to help students process the information, and construct conceptual models that lead to greater retention, and recall and application of knowledge to new and complex situations. Mayer, Dow, and Mayer (2003) focused on the pedagogic features of agent-based microworlds to begin to address how to promote deep learning in the next generation of highly interactive computer-based environments. How best we can facilitate learning in these complex environments and how our cognition changes to do this is an area to be explored.

REFERENCES

Bliss, J. (1994). From mental models to modeling. In H. Mellar, J. Bliss, R. Boohan, J. Ogborn, & C. Tompsett (Eds.), *Learning with artificial worlds:*

Computer based modeling in the curriculum. London: The Falmer Press.

Brown, J. S., Collins, A., & Duguid, P. (1989). Situated cognition and the culture of learning. *Educational Researcher, 18*(1), 32-42.

Bruning, R. H., Schraw, G. J., & Ronning, R. R. (1999). *Cognitive psychology and instruction.* Upper Saddle River, NJ: Prentice Hall, Inc.

Clark, R. C., & Mayer, R. E. (2003). *E-Learning and the science of instruction.* San Francisco, CA: Jossey-Bass/Pfeiffer.

Cobb, P. (1994) Where is the mind? Constructivist and sociocultural perspectives on mathematical development. *Educational Researcher, 23*(7), 13-20.

Colella, V. (2000). Participatory simulations: Building collaborative understanding through immersive dynamic modeling. *The Journal of the Learning Sciences, 9*(4), 471-500.

Collins, A. (1988). *Cognitive apprenticeship and instructional technology.* (Technical Report No. 6899). BBN Labs Inc., Cambridge, MA.

Dillenbourg, P., & Self, J. A. (1995). Designing human-computer collaborative learning. In C. O'Malley(Ed.), *Computer supported collaborative learning.* Berlin: Springer.

Driscoll, M. P. (2000). *Psychology of learning for instruction, 2nd Ed.* Needham Heights, MA: Pearson Education.

Duffy, T. M., & Cunningham, D. J. (1996). Constructivism: Implications for the design and delivery of instruction. In D. Johassen (Ed.), *Handbook of research for educational communications and technology* (pp. 170-198). New York: Simon and Schuster Macmillan.

Erickson, H. L. (2001). *Stirring the head, heart, and soul: Redefining curriculum and instruction, 2nd Ed.* Thousand Oaks, CA: Corwin Press Inc.

Feltovich, P. F., Coulson, R. L., & Spiro, R. F. (2001). Learners' (mis)understanding of important and difficult concepts. In K. D. Forbus & P. J. Feltovich (Eds.), *Smart machines in education: The coming revolution of educational technology* (pp. 349-375). Menlo Park, CA: AAAI/MIT Press.

Gasparini, S. (2004). Implicit versus explicit learning: Some implications for L2 teaching. *European Journal of Psychology of Education, 19*(2), 203-219.

Grabowski, B. L. (1996). Generative learning: Past, present, future. In Jonassen, D. H. (Ed.), *Handbook for educational communications and technology* (pp. 897-907). New York: Simon and Schuster Macmillan.

Goldman, S. R., Williams, S. M., Sherwood, R. D., Hasselbring, T. S., & Cognition and Technology Group at Vanderbilt. (1999). *Technology for teaching and learning with understanding: A primer.* Nashville, TN: Vanderbilt University.

Hestenes, D. (1987). Toward a modeling theory of physics instruction. *American Journal of Physics, 55*(5), 440-454.

Hestenes, D. (2006). *Modeling instruction in high school physics, chemistry, and physical science.* Retrieved July 25, 2006, from http://modeling. asu.edu/modeling-HS.html

Hmelo-Silver, C. E., & Azevedo, R. (2006). Understanding complex systems: Some core challenges. *The Journal of the Learning Sciences, 15*(1), 53-61.

Hmelo-Silver, C. E., & Pfeffer, M. G. (2004). Comparing expert and novice understanding of a complex system from the perspective of structures, behaviors, and functions. *Cognitive Science, 28*, 127-138.

Hron, A., & Friedrich, H. F. (2003). A review of web-based collaborative learning: Factors beyond technology. *Journal of Computer Assisted Learning, 19*, 70-79.

Jonassen, D. H. (1988). *Instructional designs for microcomputer courseware.* Hillsdale, NJ: Lawrence Erlbaum Associates

Jonassen, D. H. (1996). *Computers in the classroom: Mindtools for critical thinking.* Englewood Cliffs, NJ: Prentice-Hall.

Jonassen, D. H., & Wang, S. (1993). Acquiring structural knowledge from semantically structured hypertext. *Journal of Computer-Based Instruction, 20*(1), 1-8.

Kanuka, H., Rourke, L., & Laflamme, E. (2006). The influence of instructional methods on the quality of online discussion. *British Journal of Educational Technology.* Retrieved from http://www.blackwell-synergy.com/doi/pdf/10.1111/j.1467-8535.2006.00620.x

Kolb, D. A. (1984). *Experiential learning: Experience as the source of learning and development.* Englewood Cliffs, NJ: Prentice-Hall, Inc.

Kozma, R. B. (1987). The implications of cognitive psychology for computer-based learning tools. *Educational Technology, 27*(11), 20-25.

Kukla, R. (1992). Cognitive models and representation. *The British Journal for the Philosophy of Science, 43*(2), 219-232.

Lesh, R. (2006). Modeling students modeling abilities: The teaching and learning of complex systems in education. *The Journal of the Learning Sciences, 15*(1), 45-52.

Lim, B-R. (2004). Challenges and issues in designing inquiry on the web. *British Journal of Educational Technology, 35*(5), 627-643.

Littleton, K., & Whitelock, D. (2005). The negotiation and co-construction of meaning and understanding within a postgraduate online learning community. *Learning Media and Technology. 30*(2), 147-164.

Löhner, S., Van Joolingen, W. R., Savelsbergh, E. R., & Van Hout-Wolters, B. (2005). Students'

reasoning during modeling in an inquiry learning environment. *Computers in Human Behavior, 21,* 441-461.

Luppicini, R. (2006). Review of computer mediated communication research for education. *Instructional Science.* Retrieved from http://www.springerlink.com.ezaccess.libraries.psu.edu/content/v023l4727u816016/fulltext.pdf

Maier, F., & Größler, A. (2000). What are we talking about? A taxonomy of computer simulations to support learning. *Systems Dynamics Review, 16*(2), 135-148.

Malopinsky, L., Kirkley, J., Stein, R., & Duffy, T. (2000, October 26,). *An instructional design model for online problem based learning (PBL) environments: The learning to teach with technology studio.* Paper presented at the Association for Educational Communications and Technology Conference (AECT), Denver, Colorado.

Mayer, R. E., Dow, G. T., & Mayer, S. (2003). Multimedial learning in an interactive self-explaining environment: What works in the design of agent-based microworlds? *Journal of Educational Psychology, 95*(4), 806-813.

Mayer, R. E., & Moreno, R. (2003). Nine ways to reduce cognitive load in multimedia learning. *Educational Psychologist, 38*(1), 43-52.

Milrad, M. (2002). Using construction kits, modeling tools and system dynamics simulations to support collaborative discovery learning. *Educational Technology & Society, 5*(4), 2002. Retrieved August 16, 2006, from http://ifets.ieee.org/periodical/vol_4_2002/milrad.html

Milrad, M., Spector, J. M., & Davidson, P. (2002). Model facilitated learning. In S. Naidu (Ed.), *eLearning: Technology and the development of learning and teaching.* London: Kogan Page Publishers.

Navarro, P., & Shoemaker, J. (2000). Policy issues in the teaching of economics in cyberspace: Research design, course design, and research results. *Contemporary Economic Policy, 18*(3), 359-366.

Nevgi, A., Virtanen, P., & Niemi, H. (2006). Supporting students to develop collaborative learning skills in technology-based environments. *British Journal of Educational Technology, 37*(6), 937-947.

Nitko, A. J. (2001). *Educational assessment of students, 3rd Ed.* Upper Saddle River, NJ: Merrill Prentice-Hall.

Nitko, A. J. (2004) *Educational assessment of students, 4nd Ed.* Upper Saddle River, NJ: Pearson/Merrill Prentice-Hall.

Papert, S. (1993). *The children's machine: Rethinking school in the age of the computer.* New York: Basic Books.

Pea, R. D. (1994). Seeing what we build together: Distributed multimedia learning environments for transformative communications. *Journal of the Learning Sciences, 3*(3), 285-299.

Pellegrino, J., Chudowsky, N., & Glaser, R. (Eds.). (2001). *Knowing what students know: The science and design of educational assessment.* Washington, DC: National Academy Press.

Perkins, D. N., & Unger, C. (1999). Teaching and learning for understanding. In C.M. Reigeluth (Ed.), *Instructional-design theories and models* (Vol. 2, pp. 91-114). Mahwah, NJ: Lawrence Erlbaum Associates.

Reber, A. S. (1967). Implicit learning of artificial grammars. *Journal of Verbal Learning and Verbal Behaviour, 5,* 855-863

Reeves, T. C. (2000). Alternative assessment approaches for online learning environments in higher education. *Journal of Educational Computing Research, 23*(1), 101-111.

Reisetter, M., & Boris, G. (2004). What works: Student perception of effective elements in online learning. *Quarterly Review of Distance Education, 5*(4), 277-291.

Ritchie, D., & Volkl, C. (2000). Effectiveness of two generative learning strategies in the science classroom. *School Science and Mathematics, 100*(2), 83-89.

Roberts, N. G., Andersen, D. F., Deal, R. M., Grant, M. S., & Shaffer, W. A. (1983). *Introduction to computer simulation: The system dynamics modeling approach.* Reading, MA: Addison-Wesley.

Rogers, C. R. (1969). *Freedom to learn.* Columbus, OH: Merrill.

Rumelhart, D. E. (1980). Schemata: The building blocks of cognition. In R. J. Shapiro, B. C. Bruce, & W. F. Brewer (Eds.). *Theoretical issues in reading comprehension.* Hillsdale, NJ: Erlbaum.

Schunk, D. H. (2000). *Learning theories: An educational perspective.* New Jersey: Prentice-Hall.

Stahl, G. (2004). Building collaborative knowing. Elements of a social theory of CSCL. In J. W. Strijbos, P. A. Kirschner, & R. L. Martens (Eds.), *What we know about CSCL: And implementing it in higher education* (pp. 53-86). Amsterdam, Kluwer.

Tolmie A., & Boyle, J. (2000). Factors influencing the success of computer mediated communication (CMC) environments in university teaching: A review and case study. *Computers and Education, 34,* 119-140.

Van Merrienboer, J.J.G. (1997). *Training complex cognitive skills: A four-component instructional design model for technical training.* Englewood Cliffs, NJ: Educational Technology Publ.

Van Merrienboer, J.J.G., Clark, R. E., & de Croock, M. B. (2002). Blueprints for complex learning: The 4C/ID-model. *Educational Technology Research and Development Journal, 50*(2), 39-64.

Wilensky, U., & Resnick, M. (1999). Thinking in levels: A dynamic systems approach to making sense of the world. *Journal of Science Education and Technology, 8*(1), 3-19.

Windschitl, M. (1996). Student epistemological beliefs and conceptual change activities: How do pair members affect each other? *Journal of Science Education and Technology, 6*, 24-38.

Winn, W., & Snyder, D. (1996). Cognitive perspectives in psychology. In D. Johassen (Ed.). *Handbook of research for educational communications and technology* (pp. 112-142). New York: Simon and Schuster Macmillan.

Wittrock, M. C. (1992). Generative learning processes of the brain. *Educational Psychologist, 27*(4), 531-41.

Wolstenholme, E. (1990). *System enquiry: A system dynamic approach.* New York: Wiley & Sons.

ENDNOTES

[1] STELLA® is a registered trademark of the isee systems and can be accessed at http://www.iseesystems.com/softwares/Education/StellaSoftware.aspx

[2] SIMPROCESS® is a registered trademark of the CACI International Inc. and can be accessed at http://www.caci.com/asl/solutions_simprocess_demo_model.shtml

[3] Thinking Tag technology was developed at the MIT Media Lab, 20 Ames Street, Cambridge, MA.

Chapter III
Understanding Flexible Learning Theory and How it is Used in Online Learning

Deb Gearhart
Troy University, USA

ABSTRACT

Flexible learning is a term becoming increasingly prevalent in distance education. The concept of having a flexible learning environment is appealing to distance learners. Many learners choose a flexible environment over the traditional classroom so that learning can fit into their busy lifestyle. This chapter will define and discuss flexible learning theory, describing how it is used in the distance education setting and how it is a changing tide in education.

CHAPTER OBJECTIVES

The reader will be able to:

- Define flexible learning theory and distinguish its difference from providing a flexible learning environment
- Explain the advantages and issues related to using a flexible learning environment
- Design an online course based on flexible learning theory

INTRODUCTION

The term anytime, any place is common when discussing online learning. The phrase should be changed to anytime, anyplace, for everyone to include the concept of flexible learning. The term flexible learning is a term with a dual meaning. It is both a term used by many programs instead of distance education, especially internationally, and it is also a learning theory. Forms of delivery that were appropriate for education in the industrial age of mass production are now viewed as inappropriate in the emerging information age (George & Luke, 1995). Flexibility and access are important to the success of education in the information age. In order to provide flexible learning, an instructor must consider the issues facing online education such as pedagogy, learner needs and characteristics, interaction and communication between and among instructor, learner and content, outcomes, and assessment.

Flexible learning, seen as a shift in basic educational paradigm, brings together three dimensions: learner learning styles, forms of delivery, and content (George & Luke, 1995). Flexible learning encompasses the belief that learners should be viewed as active participants in the learning process. Thusly, flexible learning is learner-centered and the instructor makes a pedagogical shift to a facilitating role in learning, with technology being the enabler. Although this seems to be common in theory related to online learning, flexible learning theory is much more aggressive in modeling learner-centered instruction.

Defining the term flexible learning and explaining how it is not, just another term for distance education or distance learning is the prerequisite to understanding the theory of flexible learning. Indeed, flexible learning is the term used interchangeably with distance learning by many international programs, however not all distance learning is flexible. For the purposes of this paper, flexible learning will be defined as providing educational opportunities that are focused on meeting the needs and circumstances of individual learners (Bryant, Campbell & Kerr, 2003; George & Luke, 1995,). Flexible learning is an approach to providing educational opportunities that are focused on the varying learning needs and circumstances of individual learners.

BACKGROUND

Definitions

Defining flexible learning theory includes placing learner educational needs and choices as the center of educational decision-making. It signifies a shift from locating formal, whole classes, didactic teaching at the center of the learning process towards individuals or group management of learning, through the provision of structured resource materials (Drennan, Kennedy, & Pisarski, 2005). Flexibility is generally understood to mean offering choices in the learning environment so that a course of study better meets the individual needs of learners (Bryant et al., 2003). In the broadest sense, flexible learning is about a learner-centered, rather than an instructor-centered, approach to learning. In this view technology is an enabler; flexible learning and flexible delivery are used interchangeably (Radcliffe, 2002). Flexible delivery is a term which signifies the desirable social goals of increasing access to education and democratizing and learning processes by giving greater control over learning to learners—also means an educational environment in which unfettered individuals and choice are the values which ultimately determine the shape of education through the competitive marketing of educational products and processes (Nunan, 1996).

Whom Can Flexible Learning Serve?

All types of learners can be served by flexible learning. Research has found that at-risk learners, not normally considered to be suitable online learners, are doing well in flexible learning environments (Bryant et al., 2003). Learners of all abilities are becoming comfortable with using hypermedia, leveling the playing field. Using flexible learning and focusing on gains in performance, instructors can individualize learning in online courses to reach low-ability and high-ability learners. Bryant et al. conducted a research project based on an information systems course to try and support the concept that a Web-based flexible learning mode will have a positive impact on learning. In this study the traditional classroom was compared to the flexible classroom, with assessments carrying the same weight. The results demonstrated that Web-based flexible learning can be as an effective learning environment as the traditional classroom, with the flexible learning learners doing better than average on exams and lower than the traditional learners in group work. When truly using an individual flexible learning environment, group work can be a struggle, especially with the learners at different times and places.

Instructional Strategies

As described in the previous study, using technology, in particular multimedia, in flexible learning is crucial. How does one go about setting up such an educational environment? Newman (1990) proposed a framework which needs to be in place before developing a flexible learning environment:

1. The identification of strategies that create effective teaching and learning environment
2. Analysis of how technology can support the strategies
3. Exploring new technologies to improve teaching and learning environments
4. Proposing new areas of research

The objective of any learning environment should be to ensure there are prospects for learners to develop competencies in the material taught. Strategies for creating an efficient and effective learning environment must be established to identify how technology can best support learning before the technological infrastructure required to support them can be devised. Once the infrastructure is in place then faculty can move to making the classroom, including virtual one, to a flexible environment.

Egbert (1993) identified strategies that applied to almost any classroom situation will create an effective flexible learning environment.

1. Providing occasions for learners to interact
2. Providing an authentic audience and opportunities to negotiate meaning
3. Creating and using real tasks
4. Promoting exposure to and production of rich language
5. Providing learners opportunities to formulate ideas and thoughts
6. Promoting intentional cognition
7. Creating an atmosphere with optimal stress and anxiety
8. Creating a learner-centered classroom

Keeping in mind the definition of flexible learning theory, for an instructor to successfully take these strategies and develop courses in a flexible learning environment the strategies must take into consideration the needs of individual learners. It has been argued that flexible delivery is not just a new option, but a shift in the basic paradigm of course design and delivery.

Issues and Barriers to Flexible Learning

The primary issue on flexible learning revolves around the question of whether or not flexible learning approaches provide a pedagogically sound foundation on which to provide educational programs. That is do flexible learning approaches, particularly those employing the use of Internet technologies, result in learning outcomes equivalent to that of traditional education? Further, do Web-based flexible learning environments provide adequate reward for the extra development effort required to create a course in a flexible environment? (Bryant et al., 2003,). According to Bryant et al. flexibility is generally understood to mean offering choices in the learning environment so that a course of study better meets the individual needs of learners. This would include class times, course content, instructional approach, learning resources, location, technology use, entry/completion dates, relevance of assignments to the workplace, and communication medium. In offering flexibility, educators must recognize and understand who their learners are and where their experiences and interests lie. Flexible learning is an educational approach that uses a variety of learner-centered teaching and learning methods and resources to reach a diverse learner population; and one where learners are personally and socially motivated to achieve and learn. Further, the introduction of flexibility encourages greater self-reliance and the development of lifelong learning skills. Although the use of technology is not a requirement for flexible learning (print based courses are viewed as being very flexible), it is generally seen as an important element in supporting learner-centered learning and improving the quality of education. Educational technology is used to enhance learner independence and control over access to course content and other resources.

Another issue common to flexible learning is the short time frame for development and delivery of content (Witherby, 1997). Learners interested in anytime, anyplace learning are often looking for courses and programs to be ready immediately. It is a challenge for institutions and programs developed for delivery in the timeframe the learners are looking for. Quality of content can be at issue in distance education, particularly for flexible learning, when course design and development is compressed into short time frames.

Askham (1997) presented barriers to learning that learners often face and discussed how to overcome some of the barriers through flexible learning. Barriers for learners include: support, clarity of information about courses and of learn-

ing outcomes of the courses, motivation, time pressures, morale, relevance, and confidence. Some of these barriers are faced by learners universally, motivation, time pressures, morale, and confidence. Adjusting for these barriers in a flexible learning environment is helpful. The Askham study did address some of the barriers with the following suggestions:

- Provide a clearer definition of the course/ program's aims and objectives
- Learning outcomes should be written in relevant terms to the learners
- Provide greater flexibility in learning outcomes and assessments which provide choice and negotiation by the learner
- Develop a workable support system, with input from the learners
- Develop course administration processes which involve the learners
- Use streamlined and flexible assessment strategies
- Refocus ownership of learning on the learner and away from the institution and employer

To assist in understanding the issues and barriers faced by learners, a series of case studies are described in following paragraphs. These four case studies review different issues and perspectives related to flexible learning and lead into suggestions for online course design for a flexible learning environment.

CASE STUDIES IN FLEXIBLE LEARNING

Case Study 1: Aligning Education with the Workplace

The Radcliffe article presented a case study where flexible course design uses real work tasks as assignments. The case study was based on an engineering program at the University of Queensland. The challenge was to see if it was possible to develop a program which provided industry experience in the program without extending the length of the program. The concept of a work program was pedagogically and operationally different than done in the past. Students who entered the work program covered the same syllabus as those on campus and assessments were conducted on site. The program included 12 weeks on site and the final four weeks on campus. Flexible learning theory came into play in that the curriculum was redesigned to be more learner-centered, work being done under an industry mentor and learning through reading and private study, using a combination of technologies for communication and research. The blended learning environment enhanced the culmination of the engineering program and a similar model has been adopted in the US. From this project it was established that the alignment of course objectives with assessments based on real work tasks provides a learning environment flexible for adults to use their educational experiences directly in the workplace. Figure 1 provides course development cycle for this case study.

Case Study 2: Flexibility from Learners' Perspective

In Dunning's (1997) study, the learners' perception of flexibility in the course and the perceived quality of the learning experiment were assessed. Flexibility was paradigm in the choices learners had with regard to how and when they studied and this group found the module format of course design most flexible. The flexible learning environment enabled learners to synthesize personal experience with at least some of conceptual framework set up in each course module. The study did point out that some learners coped better with the change to a flexible learning environment better than others, reinforcing the need to design courses based around learners' learning styles to help with the transition to flexible learning.

Case Study 3: Student Performance and Satisfaction

In the case study conducted by Smith (1997), the flexible course discussed was designed and delivered entirely by e-mail in a modular format. Although, not all learners were successful in the

Figure 1. Aligning course assignments with real work tasks in a flexible learning environment (Adapted from Radcliffe, 2002)

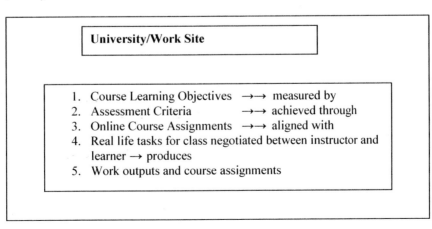

course by virtue of the final grade, the learner performance on and satisfaction with the modules were both high. The learners felt that the e-mail modules provided an unusual degree of flexibility and support, which contributed to their success. Learners felt they were successful with this medium, even though grades did not necessarily show that. This supports the concept discussed in the issues section of the chapter, that flexible learning is not necessarily a good alternative for some learners, even when the learner is satisfied with the flexibility provided in the course.

Case Study 4: Engaging Learners in Flexible Learning

McArdle and McGowan (1997) recognized that it is critical to engage learners from the onset in flexible learning so that learners can use their prior and current experiences in combination with their learning to develop new constructs of knowledge. This case study used reflective inquiry as the process for combining experience with learning as demonstrated in Figure 2. The course was designed with features to allow the learners to find their own appropriate route to course outcomes, with the use of personal portfolios and the construction of personal support structures.

This author's experiences, with similar flexible course structures, allowed learners input on the projects to meet course learning outcomes and the results were met with mixed reviews. Many learners liked the ability to create a course project, which allowed them to use the project in the workplace; however, many learners were uncomfortable with the vagueness of the assignments and often sought more guidance.

From these case studies, it becomes apparent that the key elements of flexible learning are for the learners to take control of their learning, determining time and place for learning, and being able then to apply learning to the workplace. These demands can be formalized into the course environment by engaging the learners. For most faculties, this is challenging the teaching methods they have long been accustomed to. The next section of this chapter looks at solutions and recommendations for course design course in a flexible learning environment.

Figure 2. Integration of process, content and context (Adapted from McArdle & McGowan, 1997)

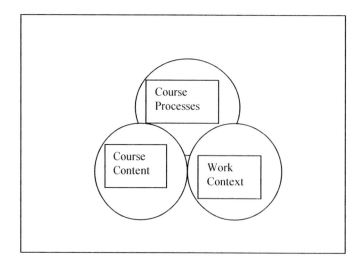

SOLUTIONS AND RECOMMENDATIONS FOR DESIGNING ONLINE COURSES IN A FLEXIBLE LEARNING ENVIRONMENT

Flexible Delivery

Developing courses with flexible delivery is critical to in today's learning environment because, as described in flexible learning theory, it is the learner that is driving how and when education should be delivered. Flexible delivery of courses will result in a blurring of classroom boundaries with increased choices available to learners and will be multidimensional. However, flexible delivery will need to be economically feasible and pedagogically sound.

According to George and Luke (1995), flexible delivery brings together three dimensions:

1. *Learner learning,* including place, time, and pace of delivery; considerations of entry and exit points; and assessment methods
2. *Forms of delivery,* including place, time and pace of delivery; collaborative ventures between teaching institutions and community organizations; and the variety of media and technologies employed
3. *Content,* including partnerships with industry, consideration of previous learning experiences through recognition of prior learning policies, credit transfer and articulation arrangements

To make flexible delivery work institutions will need to maximize the use of resources and change the paradigm, seeking to reconstruct the educational practices of universities to become learner-centered. Faculties are no longer the primary resource, but one of the many resources, which includes the use of information and technology. This will have implications for information literacy and makes technology a central aspect of this paradigm shift. Learners and faculty alike need to become knowledgeable users of technology mediated information and be able to evaluate the identified sources of information in respect to their validity, quality and usefulness for a given purpose.

To emphasize how critical information literacy is in the educational environment George and Luke (1995) have provided the following list of skills learners should possess as they move on to the work world:

- The possession of a body of knowledge of sufficient depth to begin professional practice or to facilitate the acquisition of new knowledge through postgraduate studies
- An ability to communicate effectively within their profession and the community;
- An ability to solve problems using a systematic approach and applying logical, critical and creative thinking
- A capacity to work both independently and cooperatively within a team;
- An understanding of and commitment to ethical practice together with a concern for social justice
- A commitment to lifelong learning through ongoing personal and professional development

There is an implication that learners need skills beyond just the understanding of course content, and that learner numbers and diversity require that effective teaching be inclusive of a wide range of orientations, styles, contexts, abilities, and life experiences. Many learners, using flexible learning, are already be working in their profession and want to bring work related experiences to the educational process. This is another aspect of the learner-centered or learner-controlled environment critical in flexible learning environments.

Race (1996) noted that learners interested in flexible learning are different; their expectations are more varied and they often feel stressed out and overwhelmed in all aspects of their lives. However, they are interested in obtaining their educational goals and look for flexibility. Besides the needs of the learners, within society there are new agendas: quality control is more important, the workplace is using more flexible learning. Learning how to learn is more important in today's information society than any other aspect of education. It is becoming a change agent in education and educators need to make a paradigm shift to provide flexible learning. The following table provides tips for designing courses based on flexible learning theory.

Developing Models for Flexible Learning

Drennan et al. (2005) developed and tested a model of learner satisfaction with flexible learning in a management course. Their research noted two key learner attributes for effective flexible learning: (a) positive perceptions of technology and (b) an autonomous and innovative learning style. Figure 3 demonstrates the model developed in their study.

Table 1. Tips for developing flexible learning courses (Adapted from Race, 1996)

Decide what is to be covered in the course
    Start with introductory or "remedial" content
    Provide study skill information

Keep in mind to design the course so learners can primarily work at their own pace, remaining flexible

Write clear objectives meant to meet the learning outcomes

Create course materials that are manageable chucks of the content or units with headings, sub-headings and white space making them easy to read

Design materials around activities that learners participate in, not just read

Provide multiple feedback formats for all areas of the course and feedback needs to provide guidance

Keep in mind learners view course materials from a variety of learning styles and provide activities and formats that meet multiple learning styles

Make sure the instructions on all assignments and assessments are clear and concise

Get to know the learners and ask them to comment on what they want from feedback on assignments and assessments

Make sure the assignments and assessments develop learner's abilities to master the course objectives and demonstrate their achievement of the intended learning outcomes

Figure 3. Model of flexible learning (Adapted from Drennan et al., 2005)

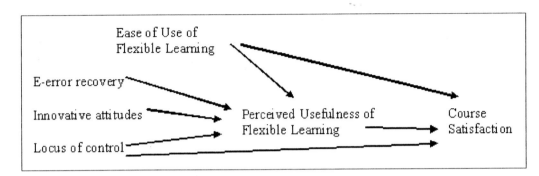

Drennan, et al. commented their results suggest that positive perceptions toward technology and an autonomous learning mode influence learner satisfaction with courses presented in a flexible learning mode. Specifically, course satisfaction was influenced directly by the perceived usefulness of flexible learning and by the learner's locus of control. The study also found that the ease of using flexible learning was directly related to course satisfaction at the beginning of the course.

Designing courses to meet the principles of flexible learning theory is a challenge. A study by Samarawickrema (2005) discovered that learning groups were often instructor-reliant. It is a major transition for learners to move from instructor-led learning to learner-centered learning. Course design needs to assist learners with that transition. In Samarawickrema's study from the perspective of the learner, flexible learning and flexible delivery attempt to increase learner opportunities for access and control. It has given universities the capacity to appeal to and serve specific learner groups or extend their service to wider and dispersed learner groups through specially designed learning resources and often through the use of communication technologies.

A study by Rennie (2003) described a modular structure for course design in a flexible learning environment. The modular format allows the developer of curriculum resources to experiment within a relatively small, self-contained area of study, which can be used to roll out good practice to other curriculum areas on an incremental basis. The Rennie study also discussed the concept of blended learning in a flexible environment providing the following benefits:

1. Support is not dependent on a single medium
2. The format gives time and distance flexibility
3. A consistency of learning resources
4. The mixed format is subject and learner sensitive
5. This enables the tutorial resources to be used in an appropriate context
6. The mixed format develops extra skills in learners
7. More power is invested in the learners

Radcliffe (2002) introduced dimensions of flexibility. According to Radcliffe (2002), any distance course design can adopt a profile of flexibility across combinations of these dimensions. Course effectiveness does not require maximum flexibility in all dimensions. It is a matter of matching a degree of flexibility on each dimension to achieve the objective. It is worth noting, for example, that the most flexible media is print. This counters the expectations many faculty have when the

Table 2. Dimensions of flexibility in flexible learning (Adapted from Brown in Radcliffe 2002)

Dimensions	Less Flexible → More Flexible
Access	Time/place bound → Anytime/any place
Structure	Fixed, instructor developed → Blended/choices
Content	Determined by instructor → Learner negotiated
Media	Face-to-face → Online → Print
Methods	Lecture → Self-directed
Interaction	Passive → Highly interactive
Assessment	Instructor determined → Negotiated

topic of flexible learning, as compared to flexible delivery, is discussed. In this chapter there has been an emphasis on technology in flexible learning environments. However, in the field of distance education print based instruction has been around for over 100 years. With increased use of technology many print based courses are developing into hybrid courses, where e-mail submission is possible and online resources are available to accompany the print based course. This hybrid print-based course is very appealing in a flexible environment.

CONCLUSION

This book is dedicated to the understanding of instructional modeling for online courses. Flexible learning theory, among the models selected for this text, is becoming a popular theory with the expansion of "on-demand" learning. This instructional model, an excellent model for both online and hybrid course design, works primarily with a modular structure to provide flexible delivery and learner-centered design, something the distance learner expects. Flexible learning theory is becoming a key theory for online courses and programs where the workplace and work related tasks are emphasized. In looking at future directions, flexible learning strategies for online course design are cornerstones to deep learning, enhancing the quality of education.

FUTURE TRENDS AND RESEARCH

According to Nunan (1996), to be competitive educational institutions need to restructure their practices and relationships with their learners, a key characteristic of flexibility. Flexibility is a characteristic, which satisfies many stakeholders in education. It can serve the interests of managers and politicians who focus on effectiveness and efficiency and cost savings solutions to the delivery of a service. For learners and instructors, it can suggest a learner-centered approach to learning and the democratization of processes of learning and teaching. For curriculum developers it can mean the availability of a range of approaches to suit learner diversity. For those marketing educational services it can mean the production of commodities which can be used competitively in a global educational market. And for those learners who cannot, or choose not to, attend an educational institution it can spell the end of campus bound teaching, with education being delivered to home and workplace in ways and times to suit their circumstances.

Flexible learning is viewed by many educators as a direct consequence of the ways that information technologies are changing education. Basically, the argument is that flexible learning is the form of learning delivered through a variety of technologies and that learners' expectations, about teaching and learning and their approach to learning, are increasingly a factor of their experience of using information technologies. Recruitment and retention are terms common in higher education today. According to Nunan (1996), flexibility of operation and flexible learning are seen strategically as both a defense and offense for educational institutions in their competition for learners with institutions striving for recruitment and retention of learners.

The argument for the educational value of flexible learning is based around the assertion that flexible delivery encourages approaches to learning which support deep learning. Deep learning is defined by Weigel (2002) as learning that promotes the development of conditionalized knowledge and meta-cognition through communities of inquiry. A constructivist framework for learning, deep learning is seen to be compatible with the processes and techniques of flexible delivery. There is a belief that teaching and learning environments which arise from flexible delivery strategies are likely to encourage an approach to learning which is highly valued—namely, a "deep approach." This approach is not just to boost course enrollments or to economize resources for an institution but to enhance the quality of education. Institutions that move to embrace the theory of flexible learning will be setting the standard of education in this information age and for the future.

REFERENCES

Askham, P. (1997). Workplace learning: Removing the barriers. In R. Hudson, S. Maslin-Prothero, & L. Oates, (Eds.), *Flexible learning in action case studies for higher education.* (pp. 67-72). London: Kogan Page.

Bryant, K., Campbell, J., & Kerr, D. (2003). Impact of web based flexible learning on academic performance in information systems. *Journal of Information Systems, 14*(1) 41-50.

Drennan, J., Kennedy, J., & Pisarski, A. (2005). Factors affecting learner attitudes toward flexible online learning in management education. *The Journal of Educational Research, 98*(6) 331-338.

Dunning, L. (1997). Don't lecture me about flexible learning! Being flexible in the delivery of an undergraduate education studies module. In R. Hudson, S. Maslin-Prothero, & L. Oates (Eds.), *Flexible learning in action case studies for higher education* (pp. 17-21). London: Kogan Page.

Egbert, J. (1993). Group support systems for computer assisted language learning. In L. M. Jessup & J. S. Valacich (Eds.), *Group support systems: New perspectives* (pp. 294-310). New York: Macmillan.

George, R., & Luke, R. (1995, November). *The critical place of information literacy in the trends towards flexible delivery in higher education contexts.* Paper delivered at the Learning for Life Conference. Retrieved March 15, 2006, from http://www.city.londonmet.ac.uk/deliberations/flex.learning/rigmor_content.html

McArdle, K., & McGowan, I. (1997). Professional development through reflective inquiry. In R. Hudson, S. Maslin-Prothero, & L. Oates, (Eds.), *Flexible learning in action case studies for higher education* (pp. 61-66). London: Kogan Page.

Newman, D. (1990). Opportunities for research on the organizational impact of school computers. *Educational Researcher, 19*(3), 8-13.

Nunan, T. (1996, July). *Flexible Delivery—What is it and why is it a part of current educational debate?* Paper presented at the Higher Education Research and Development Society of Australasia annual Conference "Different Approaches:

Theory and Practice in Higher Education. Perth, Western Australia. Retrieved March 15, 2006 from http://www.city.londonmet.ac.uk/deliberations/flex.learning/nunan_content.html

Race, P. (1996). *Practical pointers to flexible learning.* Retrieved March 15, 2006, from http://www.city.londonmet.ac.uk/deliberations/flex.learning/race_content.html

Radcliffe, D. F. (2002). Technological and pedagogical convergence between work-based and campus-based Learning. *Educational Technology & Society, 5*(2). Retrieved March 15, 2006, from http://ifets.ieee.org/periodical/vol_2_2002/radcliffe.html

Rennie, F. (2003). The use of flexible learning resources for geographically distributed rural learners. *Distance Education, 4*(1), 25-39.

Samarawickrema, R. G. (2005). Determinants of learner readiness for flexible learning: Some preliminary findings. *Distance Education, 26*(1), 49-66.

Smith, C. (1997). Teaching by e-mail. In R. Hudson, S. Maslin-Prothero, & L. Oates (Eds.), *Flexible learning in action case studies for higher education.* (pp. 34-38). London: Kogan Page.

Weigel, V. B. (2002). *Deep learning for a digital age.* San Francisco: Jossey Bass, a Wiley Company.

Witherby, A. (1997). Peer mentoring through peer-assisted study sessions. In R. Hudson, S. Maslin-Prothero, & L. Oates (Eds.), *Flexible learning in action case studies for higher education* (pp. 28-33). London: Kogan Page.

Chapter IV
The Theory of Instructional Dialogue:
Toward a Unified Theory of Instructional Design

Paul Gorsky
Open University of Israel, Israel

Avner Caspi
Open University of Israel, Israel

Eran Chajut
Open University of Israel, Israel

ABSTRACT

This chapter presents a unified theory of instructional design in the cognitive domain; this includes, of course, online instructional modeling. The theory differs from specific instructional design theories in that it describes how all instructional systems operate (regardless of their goals) in terms of resources and dialogues common to all instructional systems; it predicts certain instructional outcomes (related to groups of learners, not to individual learners) based on given initial conditions. The theory affords practical and theoretical advantages. Practically, it (1) simply and accurately describes the mechanisms at play in instructional systems, (2) presents readily quantifiable operational definitions, (3) suggests hypotheses that may be evaluated empirically, and (4) points the way toward optimizing instructional systems. Theoretically, it (1) subsumes all current theories of instructional design and (2) views campus-based, distance and online instructional systems as a single discipline.

CHAPTER OBJECTIVES

The reader will be able to:

* Understand the unified theory of instructional design as a paradigm change
* Identify variables and processes common to *all* instructional systems
* Design instructional systems in accord with the theory's rules of thumb
* Do research within the framework afforded by the theory

INTRODUCTION

This chapter presents a unified theory of instruction in the cognitive domain. The theory was originally proposed as a general theory of distance education (Gorsky & Caspi, 2005a) to replace the "Theory of Transactional Distance" (Moore, 1993), which may be construed as tautology (Gorsky & Caspi, 2005b). It is our belief that this theory can provide a most useful working model for analyzing, designing and evaluating any instructional system, be it "online" or "on-ground."

The importance of theory to a discipline can hardly be overemphasized. The discipline of instruction, however, is characterized by a proliferation of theories (see Kearsley, 2004 and Reigeluth, 1998) that include a wide array of corresponding instructional approaches. Such approaches are routinely characterized as "anchored instruction" (Bransford, Sherwood, Hasselbring, Kinzer & Williams, 1990), "advance organizers" (Ausubel, 1963), "experiential learning" (Rogers, 1969), and "mastery learning" (Bloom, 1981; Carroll, 1963; Gagne, 1985), to name only a limited few. These theories and approaches, however, use different terminologies, use unique sets of variables and emphasize particular aspects of instruction, some of which are mutually exclusive. One outstanding example is the seemingly irreconcilable divide between behaviorist and constructivist theories. For example, in "experiential learning," student control of curriculum and evaluation is emphasized while in "mastery learning," instructor control of both is emphasized. In discussing the proliferation of instructional design theory and practice, Tennyson and Schott (1997) wrote that "it can lead to fruitless separations in our discipline so that specialists tend to forget the forest when looking to their trees of interest" (p. 13). Hannafin (1997) wrote:

New perspectives and approaches have, alternately, been the target of widespread skepticism, the focus of unbridled advocacy, and the object of scorn as advocates and critics position themselves to support or refute the legitimacy of a particular approach. (p.101)

We cite two practical alternatives for dealing with this current state of affairs. The first accepts theoretical diversity and suggests a methodology for dealing with it. Hannafin (1997) contended that instructional design decisions should be grounded in *any* defensible theoretical framework and defined criteria for doing so. He wrote:

Grounded design, therefore, argues not for the inherent superiority of one theoretical position or methodology over another, but for articulation of and alignment among the underlying principles that define them. It does not marginalize differences among perspectives, where such differences exist, but advocates approaches that reflect them. (p. 3)

The second alternative is to seek what Duchastel (1998) calls a "Physics-like grand theory of instructional design that would unify the current elements of disparity that we witness" (p.1). Although he does not suggest a solution, he cites four attributes required for any such theory or theoretical framework: comprehensiveness, abstractness, utility, and validity. Such a theory would enable research to progress from isolated case studies couched in idiosyncratic terminology to a common set of constructs and variables shared by researchers around the world.

The key element of the proposed theory is dialogue which, since Socrates, has been viewed from both philosophical and pedagogical approaches. On the one hand, philosophical approaches to interpersonal instructional dialogue tend to emphasize either its epistemological advantages in the pursuit of knowledge and understanding (Socrates and Plato) or, more recently, its moral and political foundations based on egalitarianism and mutual respect (Bruner, 1966; Buber, 1965; Dewey, 1916; Freire, 1972; Rogers, 1969; Vygotsky, 1978). For example, regarding the moral aspects of educational dialogue, Martin Buber (1965) wrote "...the basic movement of genuine dialogue, and thus of education itself, is a truly reciprocal conversation in which teacher and students are full partners" (p.184). According to Buber, the relationship between teacher and students is based on honesty, equality, openness, and mutual respect. Genuine dialogue is not located *within* any one of the participants, but rather is found in their "betweeness," in what Buber called the reality of the "interhuman." Jerome Bruner and Carl Rogers also emphasized the importance and necessity of dialogue between teacher and student. Bruner (1966) wrote that instructor and student should engage in an active dialogue (i.e., Socratic learning); Rogers (1969) discussed the centrality of the interpersonal relationship in the facilitation of learning alongside the need to provide freedom in educational environments.

The problem with such philosophical approaches to dialogue, however, is that they are highly idealized and prescriptive. They tell us how people *should* relate to each other and what outcomes *should* result from dialogue. They tell us little about what real dialogues look like and how they work, or fail to work, in real situated learning environments, concrete or virtual. Such philosophical approaches are biased *a-priori* toward an anti-empirical approach to the study of dialogue.

On a more practical level, pedagogical viewpoints of interpersonal dialogue, such as proposed in this unified theory, tend to emphasize actual, situated dialogic behavior. Some dialogues converge toward predetermined answers and conclusions (instructivism) while others are divergent and open-ended (constructivism); some are friendly (conversation), some antagonistic (debate). They may be investigated empirically and correlated with learning outcomes.

In the next section, we describe what the unified theory is and what it is not. Here, we hope to create reasonable expectations for the reader and to suspend, at least momentarily, the widespread skepticism and disbelief generally associated with "grand-unified" theories in the social and behavioral sciences.

WHAT THE PROPOSED UNIFIED THEORY IS, AND ISN'T

The proposed theory may be seen as a *meta-theory* of instructional design, *not* as a specific design theory. We begin by clarifying the latter concept.

Simon (1969) contends that certain man-made phenomena or processes (e.g., medicine, business and architecture) are "artificial" in that they are contingent on the goals or purposes set by their designer. In other words, the processes would have been different had the goals been different (as opposed to natural phenomena and processes which necessarily evolve from given natural laws). Such artificial processes are characterized by "design theories," which are goal-oriented; that is, they identify means for achieving goals and they are maximally useful to practitioners. The professional responsibility of doctors, managers, or architects, is not to decipher the laws of the universe but to act responsibly in order to transform existing situations into more preferable ones.

Within this frame of reference, instruction may also be seen as an "artificial" process characterized by diverse theories of design. Indeed, it is the diversity of instructional goals that generates the multitude of instructional design theories.

As opposed to design theories, the proposed unified theory identifies phenomena and processes common to *all* instructional systems, regardless of their goals. It enables us to map activities and strategies engaged in by teachers and students as observable and quantifiable behavior. We may predict certain instructional outcomes (related to groups of learners, not to individual learners) based on given initial conditions. The theory does not attempt to explain how individuals learn in terms of internal mental processes.

The ultimate goal of the theory is to determine "rules of thumb" for the design of instructional systems. A rule of thumb is defined by Wikipedia (2007) as "a principle with broad application that is not intended to be strictly accurate or reliable for every situation. It is an easily learned and easily applied procedure for … making some determination." The theory's rules of thumb (e.g., group size, instructor accessibility, etc.) will enable designers to make top-down strategic decisions about any instructional system with confidence. In this sense, we are looking at a meta-theory of instructional design. Rules of thumb will be determined through logical inference grounded in empirical research; they will be probabilistic, not deterministic; they will be bounded by confidence factors. Rules will be determined by: (1) identifying the critical resources in instructional systems that account for most of the variance vis-a-vis the type, amount and duration of dialogue that occurs both in-class and out, and (2) by finding correlations between specific, situated dialogues and learning outcomes.

At this point, we wish to emphasize three important issues that place the proposed theory in a proper and modest perspective. First, the theory is skeletal; it needs fleshing out. To date,

basic constructs and variables have been named (Gorsky & Caspi, 2005a); dialogic behavior in different kinds of instructional systems has been observed and analyzed, and tentative rules of thumb for predicting dialogic behavior as a function of structural and human resources have been formulated (Caspi & Gorsky, 2006; Gorsky, Caspi, & Smidt, 2007; Gorsky, Caspi, & Tuvi-Arad, 2004; Gorsky, Caspi, & Trumper, 2004, 2006). Rules of thumb for predicting learning outcomes as a function of dialogic behavior have not yet been investigated.

Second, no valid instructional design theory is discarded. Third, no startling, heretofore unknown discoveries have emerged. Each rule of thumb is familiar, unsurprising, and even reassuring. What we believe important and innovative, however, is that these heretofore anecdotal and unrelated truisms are now grounded and linked in a unified theory of instructional design.

TOWARD A UNIFIED THEORY OF INSTRUCTIONAL DESIGN

The one, all-encompassing, underlying assumption of the theory is that instruction is dialogue. Three propositions are derived from this assumption:

1. Every element in an instructional system is *either* a dialogue (intrapersonal or interpersonal) *or* a resource which supports dialogue.
2. Certain structural and human resources, common to all instructional systems, correlate with the type, amount and duration of interpersonal dialogue that occurs, or may occur, both in-class and out.
3. Specific, situated dialogues correlate with learning outcomes.

Proposition 1

This proposition states that every element in an instructional system is *either* a dialogue (intra-personal or interpersonal) *or* a resource which supports dialogue.

Intrapersonal Dialogue

Intrapersonal dialogue is defined formally as the interaction between student and subject-matter that occurs when, *and only when*, it is mediated by a given instructional resource. A structural resource for intrapersonal dialogue is defined as any instructional material of any kind specifically and intentionally made available to students. For example, when students read books or text from computer screens, listen to lectures or to dialogues engaged in by others, use computer simulations or watch educational television with the intent to learn, they are said to be engaging in intrapersonal dialogue. The construct intrapersonal dialogue is operationalized along three dimensions: the human resource, the structural resource and the resulting interaction.

The human resource, the student, utilizes structural resources as he or she sees fit in accord with his or her: *age, prior knowledge, motivation, learning styles, perceived course difficulty, and other possible variables that define the student's predisposition toward learning.* These variables differ for each learner and they determine the extent of intrapersonal dialogue that occurs and its quality. Groups of students, too, may be characterized by these same variables which should be taken into account by instructional designers.

Variables associated with structural resources and the resulting intrapersonal dialogue, include, for example:

- **Media choice:** The specific resources utilized
- **Utilization rates:** The number of times each resource was used

- **Time on task:** Duration of each dialogue
- **Instructional outcomes:** Degrees of success achieved
- **Efficiencies:** Ratios of time on task versus outcomes
- **Resource mobility:** When and where dialogues occurred

Students, of course, may interact with subject-matter *without* the presence of any given resource. In fact, this may be a desirable instructional outcome indicating "reflection" (Dewey, 1916) or "deep-level" learning (Biggs, 1987; Marton & Saljo, 1976) or "critical thinking" (Garrison, 1992). These processes, however, are *not* defined as intrapersonal dialogue which, within the domain of the instructional theory, deals only with quantifiable learner-resource interactions. The internal mental processes that presumably occur during intrapersonal dialogue lie within the domain of learning theory.

Interpersonal Dialogue

Interpersonal dialogue is defined formally as a verbal interaction between instructor and student or between student and student. Interpersonal dialogue *facilitates* learning (Buber, 1965; Bruner, 1966; Dewey, 1916; Rogers, 1965, 1969; Vygotsky, 1978). Specifically, Rogers (1965) wrote: "We cannot teach another person directly; we can only facilitate his learning (p.389)." Interpersonal dialogue may be face-to-face or mediated by communications media; if mediated, synchronous or asynchronous. Operational definitions are structural and typological. In structural terms:

- Interpersonal dialogue is a message loop; it may be Instructor-Student-Instructor *or* Student-Instructor-Student *or* Student A-Student B-Student A.
- Messages are mutually coherent.

Relevant variables for these coherent message loops are the number of occurrences, their duration and the number of "threads" (defined as an initial message, all replies to it and all subsequent responses to the replies) that exist in an ongoing dialogue.

In typological terms, there are two distinct classes of output: subject-matter oriented and non-subject-matter oriented. One or both types may characterize an interaction. Subject-matter oriented dialogue is characterized by hypothesizing, questioning, interpreting, explaining, evaluating, or rethinking issues or problems at hand. Such a dialogue has occurred if at least one of these activities is evident in an interaction. Judgments may be reached by analyzing qualitative data derived from observations, interviews, and questionnaires (see Silverman, 2001). Such dialogues have been named "cognitive presence" (Garrison & Anderson, 2003).

Subject-matter oriented dialogues may be further classified as inquiry, conversation, instruction or debate (Burbules, 1993). Formal qualitative definitions of each dialogue type are:

- *Inquiry* addresses a specific problem to be solved or answered; it investigates a question, resolves a disagreement or formulates a compromise.
- *Conversation* is an open-ended discussion. Its aim is to achieve understanding, rather than finding the answer to any specific question or problem.
- *Instruction* is an intentional process in which a teacher "leads" a student to formulate certain answers or understandings.
- *Debate* is an antagonistic engagement for and against opposing positions. Alternative points of view can each be clarified through such an engagement.

A subject-matter oriented dialogue may include one or more of these dialogue types. Burbules (1993) pointed out that, at times, dialogues may serve educational purposes; at other times, they may have deleterious and anti-educational effects. One further point is noteworthy—intent. Subject-matter oriented dialogue may be directed intentionally toward achieving instructional goals such as increasing learner understanding *or* a dialogue may have no specific instructional intent; that is, although subject-matter oriented, neither participant presumes to "instruct" the other.

Non-subject-matter oriented interpersonal dialogue is a discursive relationship devoid of subject-matter concerns. Such dialogues have been categorized as "social presence" and "teaching presence." Garrison, Anderson and Archer (2000) defined "social presence" as "the ability of participants in the community of inquiry to project their personal characteristics into the community, thereby presenting themselves to the other as "real people" (p.89). Henri (1992) defined "social message" as a "statement or part of a statement not related to formal content of subject matter" (p.126). An example of such socio-emotional content may be the expression of emotions, use of humor, self disclosure, or expressing feelings of group cohesiveness.

Anderson, Rourke, Garrison, and Archer (2001) defined "*teaching presence*" as "the design, facilitation, and direction of cognitive and social processes for the purpose of realizing personally meaningful and educationally worthwhile learning outcomes" (p.5). Instructors, but sometimes also students, may achieve this by setting time parameters for a study, encouraging students, creating a climate that facilitates learning, and so on.

Structural Resources for Interpersonal Dialogue

It has been found that three structural resources determine to a large degree the extent of interpersonal dialogue that may occur in an instructional system. The first two resources relate to in-class interpersonal dialogue while the third relates to out-of-class dialogue.

- Instructional strategy (Clark, 1983; Garrison & Cleveland-Innes, 2005; Gorsky, Caspi, & Trumper, 2006; Kearsley & Shneiderman, 1998)
- Group size (Caspi, Gorsky, & Chajut, 2003; Chen & Willits, 1998)
- Student/instructor accessibility (Chen, 2001a,b; Gorsky, Caspi, & Tuvi-Arad, 2004; Gorsky, Caspi, & Trumper, 2006)

The variable "instructional strategy" is defined formally as the approach a teacher takes to achieve learning objectives. This includes creating learning environments and specifying the nature of the activities in which the teacher and learner will be involved during the lesson. Five general strategies, cited from Saskatchewan Education (1991), provide a framework for categorizing instructional strategies:

1. **Direct instruction:** This strategy is highly teacher-directed and is among the most commonly used. It is effective for providing information or developing step-by-step skills.

2. **Indirect instruction:** This strategy is mainly student-centered. It seeks high level student involvement in observing, investigating, drawing inferences from data, or forming hypotheses from an environment created by the teacher. Here, the role of the teacher shifts from lecturer/director to that of facilitator, supporter, and resource person.

3. **Experiential learning:** Experiential learning is inductive, learner centered, and activity oriented. Often, activities are suggested by the students. The emphasis in experiential learning is on the process of learning and not on the product.

4. **Independent study:** Independent study refers to the range of instructional methods which foster the development of individual student initiative and self-reliance. Independent study is usually carried out under the guidance or supervision of a classroom teacher.

5. **Interactive instruction:** This strategy relies heavily on discussion and sharing among participants. Students can learn from peers and teachers; they may also learn from computer programs.

This formal definition is complemented by an operational one appropriate for any instructional strategy namely, the type and number of in-class interpersonal dialogues that occurred, their duration and the number of "threads" that exist in ongoing dialogues. This variable, instructional strategy, appears to have the most profound impact on the extent of interpersonal dialogue that occurs within a classroom, real or virtual. The instructor, in accord with his beliefs or the beliefs held by the organization that employs him, implements an instructional strategy that, within the constraints imposed by "group size," determines who talks to whom, why, where, when, in what manner, and for how long.

The variable "group size" is defined operationally as a "fuzzy variable" quantified through the use of "fuzzy logic" (Zadeh, 1976, 1989). This analytic procedure enables us to assign a numeric range instead of a discrete integer value to such an imprecise concept. Group size has only an indirect impact on the extent of interpersonal dialogue that may occur. It is, in fact, a mediating variable that influences the kinds of instructional strategies that teachers may reasonably adopt. Two extreme examples follow. First, assume a group size of one student. It is highly unlikely, even absurd, that a teacher would lecture to this lone student. Second, assume a group size of 500 students linked in a video conference. In the same vein, it is highly unlikely that a teacher would adopt a conversation based instructional strategy.

As a mediating variable for implementing a given instructional strategy, "group size" is not only the actual number of students present, but a variable that also takes into account group attributes that include students' age, goals for the course, prior knowledge, motivation, intelligence, learning styles and anxiety. A group of 50 mature and highly motivated students may be amenable to interpersonal in-class dialogue while a group of 10 immature and unmotivated students may not.

The resource, out-of-class instructor/student accessibility, includes two variables. First, "out-of-class instructor accessibility" is defined operationally as follows:

1. The time allotted to personal conversation, be it through face-to-face meetings, telephone consultations or participation in synchronous forums. This time allocation is usually published prior to the start of courses.
2. Instructor "lag time" (the time interval between a message sent to the instructor and the instructor's response) for email and asynchronous forums. Instructor accessibility decreases as lag time increases.

Second, "out-of-class student accessibility" is defined operationally as the availability or non-availability of (1) students' online and "on-ground" addresses and telephone numbers (2) technological means for communication, and (3) provisions for aiding and abetting study groups.

Human Resources for Interpersonal Dialogue

Instructors and students are the human resources associated with interpersonal dialogue. Instructors, characterized by "facilitation skills" (e.g., Bruner, 1966; Rogers, 1969), play a critical role in creating and maintaining dialogue in the classroom, be it traditional or virtual. Students, characterized by personality traits, especially "autonomy" (Caspi & Gorsky, 2006; Moore, 1993), and by the need to overcome conceptual difficulty or to solve an insoluble problem (Gorsky, Caspi,

& Trumper, 2004, 2006; Gorsky, Caspi, & Tuvi-Arad, 2004) engage in interpersonal dialogue to greater or lesser degrees.

Reliable procedures for ranking "facilitation skills" and degrees of "autonomy" appear in the literature cited previoulsy; for the sake of brevity, they are not presented here.

Learning Outcomes

The theory includes four outcomes that relate to instructional systems (e.g., a program, a course, a lesson). The first three are students' achievements (knowledge and skills), attitudes and satisfaction; the fourth outcome is efficiency.

Practical Applications of Proposition 1: Describing Instructional Systems

Practical applications of the theory include generating simple, accurate, and useful descriptions of the mechanisms at play in all instructional settings (educational, military or industrial) and systems (online or on-ground). The following examples use the theory's variables to describe instructional events and processes.

1. An instructor lectures; there is no discussion. The lecture is a structural resource for intrapersonal dialogue.
2. A student reads a book. The book is a structural resource for intrapersonal dialogue.
3. Student A phones Student B to discuss the concept of angular momentum that he doesn't understand. The availability of students' telephone numbers is a structural resource for interpersonal dialogue. Students are human resources for interpersonal dialogue. A subject-matter oriented dialogue between them occurs.
4. Student J wants the answer to an assigned exercise and posts a message in an asynchronous discussion group. Student K answers. The discussion group is a structural

resource that enables interpersonal dialogue. A subject-matter oriented dialogue occurs between Students J and K; both students are human resources for interpersonal dialogue.

5. A face-to-face tutorial session is led by an instructor who encouraged discussion. The tutorial is a structural resource for *both* intrapersonal and interpersonal dialogue. Instructor and students are human resources for dialogue.

   - Student X attended and listened attentively, but did not actively participate. This student utilized the resource for intrapersonal dialogue only; he chose not to utilize the human resources, instructor and fellow students, for direct interpersonal dialogue.
   - Student Y attended the same tutorial and, in addition to listening attentively, also asked the instructor several questions that were answered to her satisfaction. This student utilized the resource for *both* intrapersonal and interpersonal dialogue.

6. An instructor distributes exercises to her students. A student solves the assigned exercises and submits them to the instructor who corrects, grades, and returns them to the student. The student reads the corrected exercises and understands the source of his mistakes.

   - The assigned exercise is a structural resource for *both* intrapersonal and interpersonal dialogue. The dialogue is intrapersonal as the student solves the exercises. It becomes interpersonal when the student submits the completed exercise to the instructor thereby closing the loop—instructor to student, student to instructor. An additional interpersonal link (or thread)

occurs when the instructor returns the corrected exercise to the student. A further *intra*personal dialogue occurs when the student reads the corrected exercises with the intent to learn from them.

Proposition 2

This proposition states that certain structural and human resources correlate with the type, amount and duration of interpersonal dialogue that occurs, or may occur, both in-class and out. The following rules of thumb (or simply "Thumb-Rules") are the basis of Proposition 2. They are derived from the empirical research cited throughout this paper and described below. Thumb-Rules 1-4 relate to structural resources; 5-7, to human resources.

- **Thumb-Rule 1:** *Group size and attributes* determine to a very high degree the kinds of instructional strategies that an instructor may reasonably implement.
- **Thumb-Rule 2:** *Instructional strategy* determines to a very high degree the type, the amount and duration of both in-class and out-of-class interpersonal dialogue that occurs.
- **Thumb-Rule 3:** *Out-of-class instructor accessibility* determines to a very high degree the type, amount and duration of out-of-class instructor-student dialogue that occurs.
- **Thumb-Rule 4:** The availability of *communications media and support systems* (e.g., students' telephone numbers, e-mail addresses, etc.) determine to some degree the type, amount and duration of out-of-class student-student dialogue that occurs.
- **Thumb-Rule 5:** An instructor's *facilitation skills* determine to some degree the type, amount and duration of in-class interpersonal dialogue that occurs.
- **Thumb-Rule 6:** A student's *autonomy* determines to some degree the type, amount

and duration of interpersonal dialogue that he or she engages in.

- **Thumb-Rule 7:** *Perceived course difficulty* (from a student's perspective) determines to some degree the type, amount and duration of interpersonal dialogue that a student engages in.

These Thumb-Rules are familiar and unsurprising, at least in retrospect. What we believe of special significance though, is that they are now linked in a unified theory of instructional design. A rich research agenda, may be derived from each rule. We believe that additional Thumb-Rules will be found. We reiterate that the quest for additional rules is for those that account for a significant and meaningful level of variance.

Structural Resources and Interpersonal Dialogue: Potential Dialogue

The cumulative effect of the first four structural resources/Thumb-Rules cited previously was defined by Gorsky and Caspi (2005a) as the variable "*potential dialogue*." Currently, the potential dialogue associated with given structural resources may be estimated prior to the start of a course; eventually, through empirical research, it may be quantified to higher degrees of precision. Although other structural resources may influence potential dialogue (i.e., seating arrangements, the physical environment of the classroom, time of day, etc.), so far as known, their impact, if any, is minimal or yet to be studied.

Table 1. Impact of structural resources on the potential for interpersonal dialogue

INSTRUCTOR-STUDENT POTENTIAL DIALOGUE		
Structural Resource	Low Potential	High Potential
Instructional design	Recorded lecture	"Live" discussion and Q&A
Group size	500 students	1 student
Out-of-class accessibility	1 hour per month	24 hours/day; 7 days/week
STUDENT-STUDENT POTENTIAL DIALOGUE		
Structural Resource	Low Potential	High Potential
Instructional design	Individual assignments	Collaborative problem-based learning (PBL)
Out-of-class accessibility	students' e-mail addresses and telephone numbers not available; no web-based media	students' e-mail addresses and telephone numbers are given; web-based forums (synchronous and asynchronous) exist

Two values of potential dialogue, one for each interpersonal dialogue type (instructor-student, student-student), may be estimated or measured for any given instructional system. To illustrate the impact of these variables on potential dialogue, Table 1 presents some extreme examples.

The construct "potential dialogue" is especially useful for optimizing the efficiency of instructional systems. Two examples follow:

- In courses perceived by students as "very easy" or "easy," group size per instructor may be increased since less interpersonal dialogue is needed. Appropriate research can help to optimize instructor/group size ratios.
- Students' dialogic behavior may be correlated with a changing rate of instructor accessibility. Instructional outcomes may be correlated with the extent of subsequent out-of-class dialogic behavior. Such findings could be helpful in optimizing instructor accessibility.

Proposition 3

This proposition states that specific, situated dialogues correlate with learning outcomes. Thumb-Rules that predict learning outcomes as a function of dialogic behavior have not yet been investigated within the framework of the unified theory. However, there is an extraordinary volume of empirical findings about the relations between instructional environments, instructional processes, and learning processes triggered by instruction, on the one hand, and learning outcomes, on the other hand. We contend that the unified theory is able to integrate these findings into a coherent whole thereby increasing our understanding of how instructional systems achieve their goals. Two examples of very large-scale research programs ("problem-based learning" and "class size reduction") that support this proposition follow. Together, these two research programs have generated thousands of studies.

Problem-Based Learning and Student Achievement

A great deal of research has been directed toward studying the instructional strategy known as problem-based learning or PBL. For example, Dochy, Segers, Van de Bossche and Gijbels (2003) conducted a meta-analysis that investigated the effects of problem-based learning on two categories of outcomes, skills and knowledge. According to Barrows (1996), PBL environments are characterized by student centered learning in small groups that deals with authentic problems and instructors who serve as facilitators. He found statistically significant and meaningful correlations between the PBL environments and the learning outcomes. In other words, these findings from the realm of problem-based learning clearly support the theory's proposition that predicts a correlation between a structural resource ("instructional strategy") and the ensuing dialogue types and amounts. The ensuing dialogue, in turn, correlates with learning outcomes.

Class Size Reduction and Student Achievement

A second example involves one of the most widely researched topics in education, namely the correlation between class size and student achievement. Several large-scale studies (Connor & Day, 1988; Glass & Smith, 1978, 1979; National Education Association, 1986; Word, Johnston, Bain, Fulton, Boyd-Zaharias, Lintz, Achilles, Folger, & Breda, 1990) all found that reduced class size enhanced the achievement of elementary school aged children in statistically significant and meaningful ways. These studies also investigated particular variables that lead to the improved performance found in small classes. For example, Word et al. (1990) found that the following outcomes resulted from the instructional strategies enabled by small class size; namely, students had:

- More individual attention
- Increased time on task
- Increased opportunities to participate
- Improved self-image
- Greater interest and improved attitude towards learning
- Improved attendance

In terms of the theory and in its clear support, these outcomes are correlated with the structural variables "class size" and "instructional strategy" which determine the extent of "dialogue" that may occur.

To summarize, the findings from research on PBL and "group size" offer clear support for the propositions of the unified theory. All these findings, so obvious in retrospect, are now grounded in a unified theory of instructional design. Figure 1 presents an overview of the theory.

Figure 1. An overview of the unified theory of instructional design

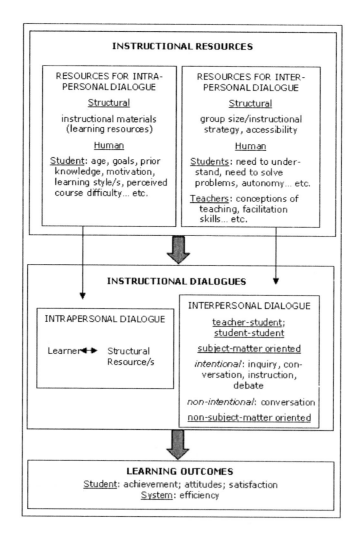

PRACTICAL AND THEORETICAL IMPLICATIONS

Findings from Preliminary Empirical Studies Using the Theory

We adopted a grounded theory approach (Glaser & Strauss, 1967; Strauss & Corbin, 1998) that begins with small naturalistic studies carried out in order to generate models and hypotheses that can then be tested on larger populations using traditional statistical techniques. To date, five studies have been carried out using the theory's variables to map students' dialogic behavior.

Two small-scale naturalistic studies investigated the dialogic behavior of distance education students while learning chemistry and physics at the Open University of Israel. In the first (Gorsky, Caspi, & Tuvi-Arad, 2004), 10 out of a total of 128 students who completed the introductory level course "Pathways in Chemistry" participated in the study. In the second (Gorsky, Caspi, & Trumper, 2004), eight students, out of 41 who had completed the introductory level course "Foundations of Physics II" participated. In both studies, participating students met the following two criteria: the successful completion of at least two science courses in previous semesters and a willingness to explore their own learning processes. The former criterion ensures that students had amassed enough experience in distance learning so that dialogue preference would be the result of conscious decision making and not the result of random trial and error. That is, they have acquired a sense of knowing how to learn based on direct personal experience. In addition, a total of three faculty members who led tutorials also participated in the study.

Data from all participants were gathered from semi-structured interviews. A constant comparative method (Silverman, 2001) was used in which provisional hypotheses were generated and then tested in subsequent interviews with different students until no more new knowledge was gathered.

Hypothesis validation involves seeking patterns in the thoughts and actions of the participants (Hill & Hannafin, 1997).

Several findings were reported. First, it was possible to categorize *all* activities engaged in by students in terms of dialogue type and resource utilization. The studies showed how students went about the tasks of studying/learning introductory level undergraduate chemistry and physics courses. Second, a general approach to the use of dialogue was discerned. For all students participating in the two studies, intrapersonal dialogue was the primary and preferred study mode. The primacy of intrapersonal dialogue (also referred to in the literature as learner-content interaction) is supported by several other research studies (Rourke & Anderson, 2002; Rourke, Anderson, Garrison, & Archer, 1999). At the start of a course, self-instruction texts and tutorials were the primary structural resources utilized by learners. Only when assigned problems could not be solved did students opt for interpersonal dialogue, especially with peers. Instructor-student dialogues were generally used as a last resort. The preferred communication modes in such meetings were synchronous: telephone conversations were most popular followed by face-to-face meetings. This general course of action, individual study through self-instruction materials, is indeed the paradigm of distance education at the Open University of Israel. Students studied and solved problems alone until they were unable to do so successfully.

In a third small-scale study, Gorsky, Caspi, and Trumper (2006) investigated the dialogic behavior of campus-based college and university students learning physics and chemistry in large and small classes. A total of 14 students participated in the study: four physics majors and four chemistry majors from a large university alongside six physics majors from a small college. As in the previous two studies, it was possible to categorize *all* activities engaged in by students in terms of dialogue type and resource type. Three main findings emerged from this study:

1. For university students participating in large introductory level lecture-based courses (about 175 students), interpersonal dialogue was not a significant dialogue mode engaged in while learning physics and chemistry in the classroom. At any given lecture, more than 90% of the students did not engage in interpersonal instructor-student dialogue. Even though tutorials were more interactive than lectures, they constituted only 20% of total instruction time.

2. For college students participating in small introductory level courses (about 12 students), interpersonal dialogue was a significant dialogue mode for learning in the classroom.

3. For both college and university students, interpersonal student-student dialogue was the primary dialogue mode engaged in for the purpose of solving problems. In other words, students predominately turned to one another for help in problem solving, not to instructors.

The first two findings illustrate clearly the impact of group size and instructional strategy on dialogue. The small group size at the college (a structural resource) afforded the *potential* for discussion-based class sessions while faculty (human resources) *chose* to implement this instructional strategy. Furthermore, the first finding illustrates clearly the tension between instructional theories on the one hand and actual practices engaged in by campus-based students participating in large lecture oriented courses, on the other. Instructional theories, such as those advanced by Bruner (1966) and Rogers (1969), often assign to interpersonal dialogue, especially between instructor and student, an importance that may not be realized in practice (Beyth-Marom, Saporta & Caspi, 2005). Indeed, instructor-student dialogue in large lecture courses was very limited in scope. The third finding illustrates the importance of peer dialogue in the learning process.

Based on findings from the naturalistic studies, we developed a "Tactical Approaches to Study" questionnaire, (see Appendix A) appropriate for large-scale studies. In our fourth study (Caspi & Gorsky, 2006), this questionnaire was distributed via e-mail to 3,512 students at the Open University of Israel. 521 questionnaires were returned. Findings replicated those from the smaller-scale ones. Here, participating students represented all faculties and disciplines, not just natural science. Faculty distribution for the reported courses: 73.1% Social sciences, 9.1% Natural sciences, 8.2% Computer sciences, 7.6% Mathematics, and 2.0 % Humanities. Mean age was 27.8 (range: 15-62). Men accounted for 48.8% of the participants.

In the fifth study (Gorsky, Caspi, & Smidt, 2007), the dialogic behavior of 121 Open University, UK students was investigated as a function of perceived course difficulty. Here, all 355 students studying an advanced level quantum mechanics course were sent written questionnaires posted to their home addresses. 123 students returned the questionnaires; 121 perceived the course as difficult or very difficult. We found that a very large majority of students turned to instructors for help, not to their peers. This finding differed from the previous ones wherein students turned overwhelmingly to peers, not to instructors. Several scenarios, vis-a-vis adult students in undergraduate science courses, have emerged:

1. In courses perceived as difficult, (UK) students turned to instructors for help when confronted with difficulty.

2. In courses perceived as moderately difficult, (Israeli) students turned primarily to peers for help when confronted with difficulty.

3. In courses perceived as easy, (Israeli) students generally studied alone; levels of interpersonal dialogue were low.

These may be universal phenomena or culturally biased ones. Further research will provide answers. In practical terms, such answers will help us optimize instructional systems in terms of perceived course difficulty/class size. On the one hand, if instructor-student dialogues are limited in "easy" or "moderately difficult" courses, then a large class size is feasible and justifiable, both from economic and pedagogical points of view. On the other hand, if levels of instructor-student dialogue are high in "difficult" courses (as these findings indicate), then a small class size is feasible and justifiable, both from economic and pedagogical points of view (a higher rate of student success along with a reduction in drop-out rates may be attained given a higher level of instructor presence).

All these findings are obvious and not surprising, *at least in retrospect*. Again, what we believe important, however, is that these anecdotal and unrelated truisms are now grounded and linked in a unified theory of instruction. Furthermore, and quite possibly of utmost importance, is the standardization of variables for the purpose of research. We suggest that the widespread use of the theory's variables will end the "Tower of Babel Syndrome" (Guri-Rosenblit, 2001) thereby enabling researchers to work from a common frame of reference with a common set of variables toward a common goal.

Theoretical Implications

Three theoretical implications are discussed: the unity of distance and campus-based instructional systems, the place of learning theories in the hierarchy of curriculum and instruction, and implications for online instructional design.

The Unity of Distance and Campus-Based Instructional Systems

Findings from the studies described above indicate that modern distance and campus-based instructional systems may be viewed as one. Dialogue types in both systems are identical as

are the human and structural resources. It seems that modern communication technologies, which enable efficient synchronous and asynchronous interpersonal dialogue (instructor-student and student-student), readily compensate for the physical separation. Furthermore, students' dialogic behavior in both systems is similar. Undergraduate campus-based students in the large lecture based science courses, like their distance education counterparts, engaged initially in intrapersonal dialogue. The only difference found between the two student populations was in the particular structural resource that enabled intrapersonal dialogue: campus-based students generally *listen* to lectures and make notes while distance students generally *read* texts or computer screens and highlight relevant segments. Furthermore, both distance and campus-based students used interpersonal student-student dialogue almost exclusively for seeking help to solve problems.

The analytic framework afforded by the theory may help clarify research that compares students' achievements in campus and virtual systems, whether in search of a "no significant difference" phenomenon (Russell, 1999) or for significant differences in academic performances (Shachar & Neumann, 2003).

The Place of Learning Theories in the Hierarchy of Curriculum and Instruction

We contend that broad curriculum issues (what to teach and how much time should be devoted to each topic) have priority over learning theory and instructional design. These issues, resolved by those responsible for running the organizations that wish to instruct, severely limit the instructional options available to designers. Duchastel (1998) compares instructional design to architecture:

Instructional design ... builds to the client's specifications, but does not determine those specifications. Architects (and instructional designers) might assist a client ... to determine the goals, but the choices are not fundamentally theirs.

In other words, an instructional designer should implement a client's goals. For example, on the one hand, constructivist approaches, based on making students aware of their prior knowledge and then building on that often idiosyncratic knowledge, are generally very time consuming. Instructivist approaches, on the other hand, are often less time consuming, but may perpetuate misconceptions. The decision to use a given approach might necessarily be based on organizational constraints as opposed to the ultimate veracity of this theory or that. In other words, decisions about the use of an instructional strategy must first match the constraints of the proposed instructional system as defined by those responsible. Only afterwards, decisions about instructional design and strategy may be grounded in an appropriate and defensible learning theory as Hannafin (1997) suggested.

The Unified Theory: Implications for Online Instructional Design

Before attempting to link the unified theory to online instructional design practices, we sought a clear and generally agreed upon definition for the latter concept (often referred to as e-learning). An extensive literature review revealed an array of definitions that indicate a general lack of clarity and agreement vis-a-vis defining online instructional design. Some researchers (Firdiyiyek, 1999; Govindasamy, 2002) claimed that online instruction is essentially another way of teaching and learning. Govindasamy (2002) defined e-learning most generally as "instruction delivered via all electronic media including the Internet, intranets, satellite broadcasts, audio/video tape, interactive TV, and CD-ROM" (p.288). In other words, online instruction is simply technology-enabled learning. Rosenberg (2001) limited this very broad definition to learning that is based on networked Internet technology. Tavangarian,

Leypold, Nolting, Roser, and Voigt (2004) contended that "a proper definition should demand that the electronic media give specific support to the learning process itself, which probably could not be achieved by other media" (p.274). However, they limited their definition to a constructivist learning model, thereby excluding any behaviorist approaches to online instruction. We find this restraint arbitrary and overly restricting.

Anderson (2004) noted the similarities between "online" and "on-ground" instruction in terms of curricular goals, content, orchestration of learning activities, assessment of learners' needs, etc. He also noted the disparities: (1) the release from "time and place" constraints, (2) the ability to support diverse content formats (e.g., multimedia, video), (3) the access to vast amounts of information, and (4) a communications-rich learning context for both human-machine interaction as well as asynchronous and synchronous interpersonal forums.

We accept Anderson's description of online instruction as a most useful working model. We now discuss how the unified theory relates to online instructional design. Put simply: In precisely the same manner that it relates to any and all instructional systems. This is the essence of a unified theory. The critical structural resources for intra- and interpersonal dialogue (instructional materials, group size, instructional strategy, and instructor/peer accessibility) are the same. The only difference lies in the amount and type of resources, not in the instructional dialogues that occur or not. In addition, the same human resources for interpersonal dialogue (instructors' facilitation skills; students' autonomy and their need to overcome conceptual difficulty or to solve an insoluble problem) are also the same. Furthermore, we contend that the existence of additional online resources and their utilization has no significant effect on the learning process itself, although it may change students' satisfaction or attitudes toward learning.

The disparities that Anderson pointed out are reflected in instructional strategy, be it for online or on-ground systems. For example, in terms of achievement, an on-ground lecture and an on-line recorded copy of the lecture have essentially the same impact on learners (Beyth-Marom et al., 2005). The fact that all instructional resources are available for on-line and on-ground learners implies that there is nothing unique about on-line instruction *per se* and the subsequent learning that occurs or not. In other words, the same design principles that comprise the unified theory are appropriate for all instructional systems.

SUMMARY AND FINAL REMARKS

We have presented the infrastructure for a unified theory of instructional design in the cognitive domain based on dialogues and their supporting resources. We hope to create a top-down "instructional design checklist" for all kinds of instructional systems. The end product will be two finite and complete sets of Thumb-Rules linking: (1) initial conditions of instructional systems to dialogic behavior, and (2) dialogic behavior to learning outcomes. Regarding the first set of rules, the research described above is part of a detailed, large-scale research program. Some typical additional research questions follow:

- In courses perceived by students as "very easy" or "easy," group size per instructor may be increased since less interpersonal dialogue is needed. What are the optimal limits of group size per instructor, given particular age ranges?
- Students' dialogic behavior may be correlated with a changing rate of instructor accessibility. What are the optimal limits for instructor accessibility, especially for courses perceived as difficult by students?
- To what extent, if any, should expensive communications media be made available?

Regarding the second set of rules, the relationship between dialogic behavior and learning outcomes, three typical research questions follow:

- What kinds of interpersonal dialogue types (inquiry, conversation, instruction and debate) facilitate or retard students' abilities to make conceptual changes?
- What kinds of intrapersonal structural resources (hypertext, simulations, etc.) best support constructivist pedagogy and under what circumstances?
- Assuming a relation between "communities of inquiry" and learning outcomes, what is an effective ratio between non-subject-matter (social) and subject-matter oriented dialogues?

Once again, the research questions are not new. Innovation lies in their inter-relatedness in a single unified theory that begins with a new paradigm, that instruction is dialogue. To conclude, we're talking about building working models for *all* instructional systems in the cognitive domain based on a relatively small number of rules. We believe that such an endeavor, based on valid qualitative and quantitative research, will advance our field to new levels.

ACKNOWLEDGMENT

The authors gratefully acknowledge the valuable insights and comments contributed by Ms. Rakefet Nitzani-Hendel, CEO at Science and Reasoning 2000, Israel, and by Terry Anderson, Professor and Canada Research Chair in Distance Education at Athabasca University. The former for her ongoing efforts and the latter for fine-tuning the final version.

REFERENCES

Anderson, T. (2004). *Teaching in an online learning context.* New York: Oxford University Press.

Anderson, T., Rourke, L., Garrison, D., & Archer, W. (2001). Assessing teaching presence in a computer conferencing context. *Journal of Asynchronous Learning Networks, 5*(2), 1-17.

Ausubel, D. (1963). *The psychology of meaningful verbal learning.* New York: Grune and Stratton.

Barrows, H. (1996). Problem-based learning in medicine and beyond: A brief overview. In L. Wilkerson, & W. Gijselaers (Eds.), *New directions for teaching and learning.* San Francisco: Jossey-Bass Publishers.

Beyth-Marom, R., Saporta, K., & Caspi, A. (2005). Synchronous vs. asynchronous tutorials: Factors affecting students' preferences and choices. *Journal of Research on Technology in Education, 37*(3), 245-262.

Biggs, J. (1987). *Student approaches to learning and studying.* Melbourne: Australian Council for Educational Research.

Bloom, B. (1981). *All our children learning.* New York: McGraw-Hill.

Bransford, J., Sherwood, R., Hasselbring, T., Kinzer, C., & Williams, S. (1990). Anchored instruction: Why we need it and how technology can help. In D. Nix, & R. Spiro (Eds.), *Cognition, education and multimedia.* Hillsdale, NJ: Erlbaum Associates.

Bruner, J. (1966). *Toward a theory of instruction.* Cambridge, MA: Harvard University Press.

Buber, M. (1965). *Between man and man.* New York: Macmillan.

Burbules, N. (1993). *Dialogue in teaching: Theory and practice.* New York: Teachers College Press.

Carroll, J. (1963). A model of school learning. *Teachers College Record, 64,* 723-733.

Caspi, A., Gorsky, P., & Chajut, E. (2003). The influence of group size on non-mandatory asynchronous instructional discussion groups. *The Internet and Higher Education, 6*(3), 227-240.

Caspi, A., & Gorsky, P. (2006). The dialogic behavior of Open University students. *Studies in Higher Education, 31*(6), 735-752.

Chen, Y. (2001a). Transactional distance in world wide web learning environments. *Innovations in Education and Teaching International, 38*(4), 327-338.

Chen, Y. (2001b). Dimensions of transactional distance in World Wide Web learning environment: A factor analysis. *British Journal of Educational Technology, 32*(4), 459-470.

Chen, Y., & Willits, F. (1998). A path analysis of the concepts in Moore's theory of transactional distance in a videoconferencing learning environment. *The American Journal of Distance Education, 13*(2), 51-65.

Clark, R. (1983). Reconsidering research on learning from media. *Review of Educational Research, 53,* 445-460.

Connor, K., & Day, R. (1988). *Class size: When less can be more.* Sacramento, California: Senate Office of Research, State of California.

Dewey, J. (1916). *Democracy and education.* Toronto: The Macmillan Co.

Dochy, F., Segers, M., Van de Bossche, P., & Gijbels, D. (2003). Effects of problem-based learning: A meta-analysis. *Learning and Instruction, 13*(5), 533-568.

Duchastel, P. (1998). Prolegomena to a theory of instructional design. *Online ITFORUM presentation and archived discussion.* Retrieved January 15, 2007, from http://itech1.coe.uga.edu/itforum/paper27/paper27.html.

Firdiyiyek, Y. (1999). Web-based courseware tools: Where is the pedagogy? *Educational Technology, 39*(1), 29-34.

Freire, P. (1972). *Pedagogy of the oppressed.* Harmondsworth: Penguin.

Gagne, R. (1985). *The conditions of learning* (4th ed.). New York: Holt, Rinehart, and Winston.

Garrison, D.R. (1992). Critical thinking and self-directed learning in adult education: an analysis of responsibility and control issues. *Adult Education Quarterly, 42*(3), 136-148.

Garrison, D.R., & Anderson, T. (2003). *E-Learning in the 21st century: A framework for research and practice.* London: Routledge.

Garrison, D.R., Anderson, T., & Archer, W. (2000). Critical inquiry in a text-based environment: Computer conferencing in higher education. *The Internet and Higher Education, 2*(2-3), 87-105.

Garrison, D.R., & Cleveland-Innes, M. (2005). Facilitating cognitive presence in online learning: Interaction is not enough. *American Journal of Distance Education, 19*(3), 133-148.

Glass, G., & Smith, M. (1978). *Meta-Analysis of research on the relationship of class-size and achievement.* San Francisco, California: Far West Laboratory for Educational Research and Development.

Glass, G., & Smith, M. (1979). *Relationship of class size to classroom processes, teacher satisfaction and pupil affect: A meta-analysis.* San Francisco, California: Far West Laboratory for Educational Research and Development.

Glaser, B., & Strauss, A. (1967) *The discovery of grounded theory: Strategies for qualitative research.* New York: Aldine de Gruyter.

Gorsky, P., & Caspi, A. (2005a). Dialogue: A theoretical framework for distance education instructional systems. *British Journal of Educational Technology, 36*(2), 137-144.

Gorsky, P., & Caspi, A. (2005b). A critical analysis of transactional distance theory. *Quarterly Review of Distance Education, 6*(1), 1-11.

Gorsky, P., Caspi, A., & Smidt, S. (2007). Use of instructional dialogue by university students in a difficult distance education physics course. *Journal of Distance Education, 22*(1), 1-22.

Gorsky, P., Caspi, A., & Tuvi-Arad, I. (2004). Use of instructional dialogue by university students in a distance education chemistry course. *Journal of Distance Education, 19*(1), 1-19.

Gorsky, P., Caspi, A., & Trumper, R. (2004). University students' use of dialogue in a distance education physics course. *Open Learning, 19*(3), 265-277.

Gorsky, P., Caspi, A., & Trumper, R. (2006). Campus-based university students' use of dialogue. *Studies in Higher Education. 31*(1), 71-87.

Govindasamy, T. (2002). Successful implementation of e-Learning Pedagogical considerations. *Internet and Higher Education, 4,* 287-299.

Guri-Rosenblit, S. (2001). The tower of babel syndrome in the discourse on information technologies in higher education. *Global E-Journal of Open and Flexible Learning, 1*(1), 28-38.

Hannafin, M. (1997). The case for grounded learning systems design: What the literature suggests about effective teaching, learning, and technology. *Educational Technology Research and Development, 45*(3), 101-117.

Henri, F. (1992). Computer conferencing and content analysis. In A.R. Kaye (Ed.), *Collaborative learning through computer conferencing: The Najaden papers* (pp. 115-136). New York: Springer.

Hill, J., & Hannafin, M. (1997). Cognitive strategies and learning from the world wide web, *Educational Technology Research and Development, 45,* 37-64.

Kearsley, G. (2004). *Explorations in learning and instruction: The theory into practice database.* Retrieved January 15, 2007, from http://tip.psychology.org/

Kearsley, G., & Shneiderman, B. (1998). Engagement Theory: A Framework for technology-based teaching and learning. *Educational Technology, 38*(5), 20-23.

Marton, F., & Saljo, R. (1976). On qualitative differences in learning: 1. Outcome and process, *British Journal of Educational Psychology, 46,* 4-11.

Moore, M. (1993). Theory of transactional distance. In D. Keegan (Ed.), *Theoretical principles of distance education* (pp. 23-38). New York: Routledge.

National Education Association. (1986). *What research says about class size.* Washington DC: Professional and Organizational Development/ Research Division.

Reigeluth, C. (1998). *Instructional design theories and models: A new paradigm of instructional theory. Volume II.* Mahwah, NJ: Erlbaum.

Rogers, C. (1965). *Client-centered therapy.* London: Constable.

Rogers, C. (1969). *Freedom to learn.* Columbus: Merrill Publishing Co.

Rosenberg, M. (2001). *E-learning. Strategies for delivering knowledge in the digital age.* New York: Merrill Lynch.

Rourke, L., Anderson, T., Garrison, D., & Archer, W. (1999). Assessing social presence in asynchronous text-based computer conferencing. *Journal of Distance Education, 14*(2), 50-71.

Rourke, L., & Anderson, T. (2002). Exploring social presence in computer conferencing. *Journal of Interactive Learning Research, 13(3), 259-275.*

Russell, T. (1999). *The no significant difference phenomenon.* Montgomery, AL: International Distance Learning Certification Center.

Saskatchewan Education. (1991). *Instructional approaches: A framework for professional practice.* Regina: Saskatchewan Education.

Shachar, M., & Neumann, Y. (2003). Differences between traditional and distance education academic performances: A meta-analytic approach. *International Review of Research in Open and Distance Learning, 4*(2), Retrieved January 15, 2007, from http://www.irrodl.org/content/v4.2/

Silverman, D. (2001). *Interpreting qualitative data: Method for analysing talk, text, and interaction.* London: Sage.

Simon, H. (1969). *The sciences of the artificial,* Cambridge, MA: MIT Press.

Strauss, A., & Corbin, J. (1998) *Basics of qualitative research: Techniques and procedures for developing grounded theory.* Thousand Oaks, CA: Sage Publications.

Tavangarian, D., Leypold, M., Nolting, K., Roser, M., & Voigt, D. (2004). Is e-learning the solution for individual learning? *Electronic Journal of e-Learning, 2*(2), 273-280.

Tennyson, R., & Schott, F. (1997). Instructional design theory, research, and models. In R. Tennyson, F. Schott, N. Seel, & S. Dijkstra (Eds.), *Instructional design: International perspectives. Vol. 1.* Mahwah, NJ: Erlbaum.

Vygotsky, L. (1978). *Mind in society.* Cambridge, MA: Harvard University Press.

Wikipedia: The Free Encyclopedia. (2007). Retrieved January 15, 2007 from http://en.wikipedia.org/wiki/Rule_of_thumb

Word, E., Johnston, J., Bain, H., Fulton, D., Boyd-Zaharias, J., Lintz, M., et al.(1990). *Student/ Teacher Achievement Ratio (STAR): Tennessee's K-3 class-size study.* Nashville: Tennessee State Dept. of Education.

Zadeh, L. (1976). A fuzzy-algorithmic approach to the definition of complex or imprecise concepts. *International Journal Man-Machine Studies, 8,* 249-291.

Zadeh, L. (1989). Knowledge representation in fuzzy logic. *IEEE Transactions on Knowledge and Data Engineering, 1,* 89-100.

APPENDIX A

Tactical Approaches to Study Questionnaire (for distance education students)

1. Age: _____
2. Gender: M / F
3. How do you rate your motivation to achieve a high grade? very high, high, moderate, low or very low
4. How difficult do you consider the course to be? very difficult, difficult, moderate, easy or very easy
5. How do you prefer to learn? independently or with others
6. Did you know at least one other student in the course before you started? Y / N
7. How did you typically address conceptual difficulties that occurred while reading the course materials? Mark *all* actions undertaken:
   a. Reread the text(s) Y / N
   b. Found alternative texts or instructional materials Y / N
   c. Without participating, browsed the (asynchronous) course forum Y / N
   d. Contacted another student from the course   Y / N
   • If yes, then typically how (circle the appropriate response):
     1. Face-to-face meeting
     2. Telephone
     3. E-mail
     4. Asynchronous course forum
     5. Other _____
   e. Contacted your tutor Y / N
   • If yes, then typically how (circle the appropriate response):
     1. Face-to-face meeting
     2. Telephone
     3. E-mail
     4. Course forum
     5. Other _____
   f. Contacted someone from outside the course (parent, friend, employer, etc.) Y / N
   g. Asked a question at the next tutorial Y / N
   h. Gave up Y / N
   i. Enter any other additional actions taken: _____

8.   List the order in which your <u>first four actions</u> were carried out (enter the appropriate letter) and estimate the relative contribution made by each (Total 100%).

1st action: ___ ;   relative contribution: ___%
2nd action: ___ ;   relative contribution: ___%
3rd action: ___ ;   relative contribution: ___%
4th action: ___ ;   relative contribution: ___%

Questions 9 and 10 are identical to questions 7 and 8 except that they refer to solving difficult problems or exercises.

Section II
Online Instructional Modeling:
Teaching and Learning

Chapter V
Large–Scale Interaction Strategies for Asynchronous Online Discussion

Paul Giguere
Tufts University, USA

Scott W. Formica
Social Science Research and Evaluation, Inc., USA

Wayne M. Harding
Social Science Research and Evaluation, Inc., USA

Michele R. Cummins
Social Science Research and Evaluation, Inc., USA

ABSTRACT

Designing online trainings or courses for large numbers of participants can be challenging for instructors and facilitators. Online learning environments need to be structured in a way that preserves actual or perceived levels of interaction, participant perceptions of value and utility, and achievement of the learning objectives. This chapter describes five large-scale interaction strategies that offer guidance for addressing some of these online instructional design issues. Evaluation data are presented in support of two of the strategies, and recommendations are provided about how future research in this area might be conducted.

CHAPTER OBJECTIVES

The reader will:

- Explore the relationship between levels of interaction and the number of participants in an online learning environment
- Learn about five strategies for organizing discussion areas in online learning environments
- Examine evaluation findings from the real-world application of two of the five large-scale interaction strategies presented
- Understand areas for future research on the strategies and issues presented.

INTRODUCTION

This chapter describes five large-scale interaction strategies that, if used properly, can help minimize the potentially detrimental effects of increasing the number of participants in a Web-based training course beyond what research and the wisdom of practice suggest is the maximum threshold. Evaluation findings from seven Web-based professional development trainings for adult learners provide preliminary evidence in support of two of these strategies. The outcome variables under study were participants' satisfaction with the training, willingness to recommend the training to their peers, satisfaction with the facilitator, and perceived utility of the training. The central hypothesis was that the use of these strategies in Web-based trainings that served large numbers of participants would preserve participant outcomes that the literature suggests are only associated with a small number of participants. The chapter closes with recommendations about how future research on large-scale interaction strategies might be conducted.

There is a large body of research on the role and importance of interaction between instructors and learners in both academic and non-academic settings. In a recent study examining the effects of participant-instructor interaction in a higher education setting, Kuh and Hu (2001) found that participants place a high value on interaction with the instructor. Another study by King and Doerfert (1996) found that interaction is a key factor in participants' learning satisfaction, and it assists in deterring attrition or dropout. It is logical to assume that any threats to the nature and level of interaction in an online educational setting will result in lower levels of participant satisfaction, lower levels of participant performance, and/or lower levels of participant retention. But, what constitutes the optimal number of participants to ensure a high level of interaction, and how can instructors and educators maintain a high level of interaction when the number of participants exceeds this threshold? The large-scale interaction strategies presented in this chapter offer one solution for structuring online educational opportunities in a manner that either preserves the small-group atmosphere and/or allows participants to engage the instructor/educator at a level that meets their individual needs.

Our current understanding of what constitutes the optimal number of participants or students in a Web-based training course is based largely on anecdotal evidence and non-rigorous studies. As noted by Simonson (2004), there is still a paucity of research on the relationship between the number of participants in Web-based trainings courses and the associated outcomes. The focus of most outcome studies to date have been on demonstrating the extent to which Web-based trainings and courses can produce outcomes that are commensurate with face-to-face training and educational approaches. In contrast, little has been done to test empirically how outcomes might vary with characteristics of the training course, such as the number of participants and the pedagogical approach or strategy utilized. Even rarer are studies examining participant perceptions of the value and utility of the courses as opposed to outcome-based models focusing on increases in knowledge, behaviors, and academic gains.

Much of what *is* known about the optimal number of participants in a Web-based training has come from early adopters of online educational approaches within institutions of higher education, and is based on the wisdom of practice rather than on experimental study. For example, Palloff and Pratt (1999), citing lessons learned from Harasim, Hiltz, Teles and Turoff (1997), indicate that given the large amount of time needed for facilitators and students to engage in substantive interaction, limiting the number of participants seems to be a logical and necessary strategy to maximize the quality of interaction that occurs in an online learning environment. This view is consistent with Ko and Rossen (2001), who advise in their guide for online teaching that it is not possible to have a high level of interaction when more than 40 people participate in a Web-based course.

Evidence from the application of Web-based courses in college settings indicates that the majority of faculty teaching courses that utilize distance learning approaches tend to limit these courses to fewer than 40 students. Results from interviews conducted by the National Education Association with 402 higher education faculty members who taught at least one distance learning course between 1995 and 2000 found that two-thirds of faculty members taught a course with 40 or fewer students (National Education Association, 2000). The reason for adopting this cut-off is not entirely clear, but is likely the result of several factors including: word of mouth from other faculty using distance learning approaches; familiarity with anecdotal best practice guides and articles such as those mentioned above; lack of student demand for larger courses; and/or a desire of faculty to limit enrollment either to increase interaction, to limit the amount of time needed to facilitate and monitor discussion boards, or as a test of the modality before moving it to scale.

While more research is clearly needed to determine what constitutes the optimal number of participants or students in a Web-based training, conventional wisdom and real-world application seem to indicate that instructors and facilitators are limiting audiences to 40 participants or fewer. Although this approach may make sense from a purely pedagogical point of view, it does not provide solutions for: (1) bringing distance learning approaches to scale as their popularity increases, (2) obtaining enough return on investment to make the adoption of distance learning approaches more cost-effective, or (3) structuring trainings or courses that are less dependent on personal interaction. Limiting the size of Web-based training courses to 40 participants or fewer abides by the more traditional physical limitations of a face-to-face training without taking full advantage of the potential offered by technologies with more malleable boundaries.

Limiting the size of Web-based training courses would seem to work when demand for such distance learning offerings is low, but this is only a temporary solution as an increasing number of trainers, faculty members, and students become more familiar and comfortable with different online instructional methods and the demand for and use of these approaches increase. In this situation, it would seem that limiting the training to fewer than 40 participants would necessitate hiring additional instructors and/or reducing course offerings as the demand on instructors' time begins to exceed their availability. For example, a trainer or instructor who delivered a training or introductory course that could accommodate 200 participants in a face-to-face setting would need to offer five different trainings or classes online in order to maintain a 1:40 ratio. This would not be very cost-effective as compared to the face-to-face implementation. Furthermore, it is questionable whether or not this would even be feasible given Colwell and Jenks' (2004) estimates of the amount of time it takes to actually moderate and facilitate online discussion areas.

The return on investment needed to make online instruction cost-effective would also be difficult to meet while limiting a training or course to fewer than 40 participants. Administrators and organization heads often desire to increase the number of participants enrolled in Web-based training because of the high development costs associated with creating new online offerings or translating existing curricula to the Web (Boettcher, 1999). Increasing the number of participants reduces the per-participant development and maintenance costs of delivering a training or course online. Again, increasing the number of participants would require either sacrificing what the literature suggests is the optimal number of participants, increasing the number of times the training or course was offered, and/or hiring additional instructors or trainers.

A final consideration is whether or not it makes sense to limit online courses to 40 participants when the objectives have less to do with personal interaction, such as building a community of learners, and more to do with providing a means of reinforcing elements from the content of a face-to-face course or training. Examples include blended models where participants engage in both face-to-face and online instruction, and non-credit-based professional development training targeting practitioners in the field. The latter example is perhaps most salient for social service providers who already have advanced degrees, but who need access to training opportunities about current best practices in rapidly changing fields such as substance abuse prevention, youth mental health services, and childhood special education (Ludlow, 2002). Here, the high level of interaction that seems to be necessary for higher education credit-based courses might not be necessary, or, in the case of blended credit-based courses, the high level of interaction *online* might not be necessary.

The issue, then, is the nature of the interaction strategy used and how to minimize the potentially detrimental effects of increasing the number of participants in a Web-based training or course beyond what research and the wisdom of practice suggest is the maximum threshold. One potential solution is the use of large-scale interaction strategies that allow a large group of learners (more than 40) to engage in asynchronous discussion in an online environment. (The term asynchronous refers to discussions that unfold in an electronic bulletin board format as opposed to being held in real-time.) Large-scale interaction strategies constitute a formalization of some of the various ways in which large numbers of participants can be managed in online trainings and courses. The goal of these strategies is to increase the number of participants served without sacrificing participants' perceptions of the value and utility of the trainings or courses. This is accomplished by either sheltering participants from the entire group and/or allowing them to participate at a level appropriate to their needs.

The primary focus of this chapter is on professional development training that is used as a means of reinforcing elements from the content of a previous face-to-face training, but generalizations are also made about how these strategies might be utilized in institutions of higher learning in traditional credit-based academic courses. To set the stage for a discussion of the five large-scale interaction strategies and the evaluation studies that follow, we use real-life examples drawn from the experience of middle school coordinators, a group of adult professionals working in the substance abuse prevention field who were exposed to Web-based training courses.

The United States Department of Education (USED) provides funds for virtually every school district in America to support drug and violence prevention programs. To help schools identify and adopt effective drug and violence prevention programs, the 1999 appropriation included funds for a new middle school coordinator (MSC) initiative available to communities through a competitive grant process. This initiative supported the hiring and training of 925 full-time MSCs between 1999 and 2001. The USED appropriation also included funds for the creation of a training and technical assistance center charged with providing MSCs with training and professional development opportunities. MSCs were required to attend a five-day, face-to-face training that provided an introduction to the topics that would be relevant to their work in schools. MSCs were also eligible to participate in up to seven continuing education Web-based training events designed to supplement and provide a more in-depth presentation of a topic that was introduced at the face-to-face training.

LARGE-SCALE INTERACTION STRATEGIES

For the purposes of this discussion, the five strategies will be based on the presence of 100 MSCs participating in a single Web-based training that utilizes an asynchronous bulletin board-style Web-based discussion area. In each scenario, all MSCs have unrestricted access to the content of the training (materials, activities, etc.). The five strategies do not represent all possible interaction strategies that can be used in combination with computer-mediated communication tools. They

do, however, represent the principle models for large-scale interactions. Advantages and disadvantages of the strategies are summarized in Table 1 at the end of this section.

Strategy 1: Multi-Group Interaction

Using the multi-group interaction strategy, the 100 participants are divided into four groups of 25 (see Figure 1). Participants can self-select into one of the four groups, be assigned randomly, or assigned according to criteria such as their skill level. Each group has a facilitator and is given its own closed discussion area in which only group members can see what is posted and respond to a posting or start a new thread of discussion. Group members are not able to view or participate in other groups' discussions during the online training. Regardless of the group to which a participant is assigned, s/he will engage in the same activities and address similar issues in the discussion areas with regard to the topic. If we choose to group participants according to skill level each group may address the topic with varying levels

Figure 1. Multi-group interaction

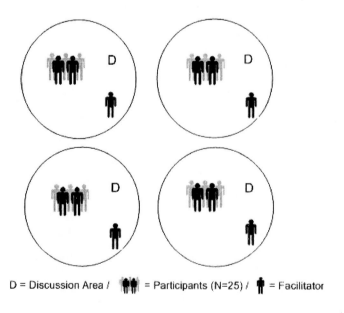

D = Discussion Area /   = Participants (N=25) /   = Facilitator

of intensity and depth. In the MSC example, we might chose to vary group membership according to previous experience conducting a school-based needs assessment or the number of years they have been working in prevention.

The multi-group interaction strategy serves 100 participants by essentially maintaining a single Website for training materials and activities while providing four separate discussion areas for each of the groups to engage with their facilitator. High levels of interaction are achieved by limiting discussion area membership to 40 or fewer participants, while simultaneously saving resources by having only one space for the actual content of the training. This strategy might be best used in an online training where otherwise multiple sections or event offerings would be needed in order to accommodate the numbers of enrolled trainees.

One benefit of using the multi-group interaction strategy is that by adding additional discussion areas, as needed, a large number of participants can be accommodated. Another benefit is that, because each discussion area has a facilitator, this strategy provides for more in-depth discussion and analysis of the training topic than a single facilitator attempting to train 100 participants without additional assistance could handle.

A disadvantage of the multi-group strategy is that each discussion area is isolated so participants cannot eavesdrop on other groups' discussions that may be of interest. Another disadvantage is that organizational or institutional capacity to host four or more discussion areas at once may not be present. The availability of qualified facilitators to facilitate the discussions in each group may also be limited. Even when available, the use of multiple facilitators may require the added burden of hiring a supervisor to ensure high levels of fidelity across discussion areas.

To extend the multi-group strategy to a higher education setting, an instructor may have teaching assistants serve as facilitators, while limiting their own role to reviewing and monitoring the

discussions and only weighing-in either as needed or requested by one of the facilitators. Depending on the length of the course and the number of discussion areas, the instructor might also rotate among the different sections spending a week or several days at a time with each section by either taking over facilitation for that week or co-facilitating.

Strategy 2: Forum Interaction

Structurally, the forum interaction strategy is identical to the multi-group strategy. As shown in Figure 2, the 100 participants are divided into four groups of 25 either through self-selection, random assignment, or by skill level or some other characteristic. As with the multi-group strategy, each of the four groups has its own facilitator. The difference between the multi-group and forum interaction strategies is that all groups using the forum interaction strategy are able to view other groups' discussions during the training. Participants are only able to post or contribute to their own discussion area, but they are able to view or eavesdrop on the other groups. Participants are no longer "blind" to discussions that are occurring in groups other than their own.

This strategy makes it possible to have individual groups address different objectives, activities, and topics in-depth, and then make the results of these interactions available to all groups either in summary form, through group presentations, or through other methods. Using the MSC example, each of the four discussion groups might be tasked with reviewing the pros and cons of different substance abuse prevention programs. Participants would then be able to review the discussions in the other groups without the burden of having to participate in multiple simultaneous discussions.

As with the multi-group interaction strategy, high levels of interaction are achieved using the Forum Interaction strategy by limiting discussion area membership to 40 participants or fewer, while

Figure 2. Forum interaction

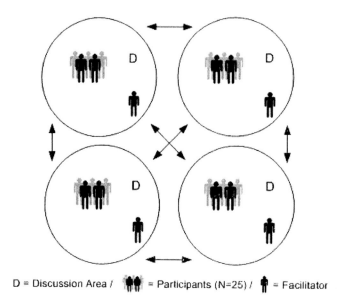

D = Discussion Area / = Participants (N=25) / = Facilitator

simultaneously saving resources by having only one space for the actual content of the training. The benefits of the forum interaction strategy are that adding additional discussion areas, as needed, can accommodate large numbers of participants, and each discussion area has a facilitator. This allows for more in-depth discussion and analysis of the training topic. An added advantage of the forum interaction strategy is that more information is made available to participants because they can read postings made to discussion areas in which they are not members.

A disadvantage of the forum interaction strategy is that participants may experience "information overload" trying to follow too many discussions at one time. Another potential disadvantage is that participants may become frustrated if they find an interesting discussion in another group in which they cannot participate. In this situation, they might either request to switch groups or attempt to initiate a similar discussion in their own group. The other potential disadvantages of the Forum Interaction strategy are the same as for the multi-group strategy: lack of institutional

capacity to host multiple discussion areas, lack of qualified facilitators, and the need to monitor fidelity across discussion areas.

Generalizing to a higher education setting, an instructor using the forum interaction strategy would still have the opportunity to rotate among the different sections spending a week or several days at a time with each section. As with the multi-group strategy, the instructor could choose to either take over facilitation for the week or co-facilitate. The potential advantage to students of the forum interaction strategy is that they could view the instructor's contributions to other groups while simultaneously engaging in parallel discussions with the facilitator in their own discussion group.

Strategy 3: Sub-Group Interaction

The sub-group interaction strategy constitutes the first major structural change in the strategies presented to this point. In the sub-group strategy, not every participant has the ability to interact with the facilitator or to post comments to a discussion area. As shown in Figure 3, the sub-group strategy provides 25 participants with a discussion area and a facilitator while the remaining 75 participants have "read-only" access to the discussion area. As with the previous strategies, selection of the interactive group of 25 can be accomplished through self-selection, random selection, or selection based on participant characteristics. A potential advantage of random selection is that the discussion will likely better represent the strengths, weaknesses, interests, and other aspects of the group of 100 participants as a whole.

While the sub-group strategy might seem counterintuitive if the goal is to achieve a high level of interaction, it offers participants the ability to participate at a level that is suitable to their needs and interests. As discussed later in this chapter, given the opportunity to self-select into the active participant or auditor groups depicted in Figure 3, it is possible to obtain equal levels of participant satisfaction and learning outcomes even among the less active group. Another potential benefit of the sub-group strategy is that participants are able to view all of the discussion that is occurring while possibly avoiding the "information overload" phenomenon that might occur if using the forum interaction strategy.

An obvious disadvantage of the sub-group strategy is that no feedback loop exists for participants who are not part of the active group of 25, nor can these participants contribute to the discussion. The implication is that non-active participants may derive less benefit from the experience since they are not able to directly engage the instructor or other participants. In reality, this is not much different than a training or academic course in which a small number of participants or students actively participate with a large portion simply listening to the discussion that unfolds. The sub-group strategy was one that was used in the MSC studies that follow, so it is discussed in more detail later in the chapter.

The application of the sub-group strategy may be less ideal for use with credit-based courses in institutions of higher learning since it would be difficult to ensure participation among the non-active group. On the other hand, the sub-group strategy might provide students with the opportunity to audit courses with preferred or highly esteemed faculty members whose class they might not otherwise be able to register for due to space limitations or scheduling conflicts. The institution would, of course, needs to decide whether or how students would receive credit for this kind of participation.

Figure 3. Sub-group interaction

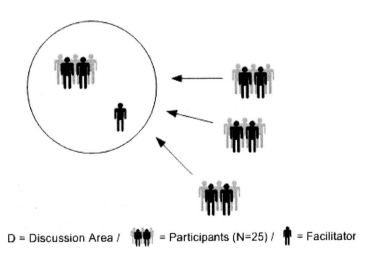

D = Discussion Area / = Participants (N=25) / = Facilitator

Strategy 4: Large-Group Interaction

The large-group interaction strategy is the only one presented where all 100 participants have access to the same discussion area. As shown in Figure 4, the large-group strategy entails the use of a single discussion area with one facilitator for all 100 participants. As the training progresses and the amount of participation in the discussion area increases, additional facilitators can join in the discussion, as needed, to accommodate the volume of postings. High levels of interaction are achieved through the introduction of additional facilitators, as needed, and through participants' ability to participate at a level suitable to their needs and interests.

A potential disadvantage of the large-group strategy is that too many threads of discussion can occur, making it difficult for participants to keep track of individual threads in which they are most interested. A possible solution might be the use of discussion rules or protocols to keep discussions manageable. Another potential disadvantage is that adding facilitators may confuse participants since the additional facilitators are not part of the training from the beginning. The large-group strategy was the second strategy that

was used in the MSC studies that follow, so it too will be discussed in more detail later.

There are several possibilities for applying the large-group strategy to a higher education setting. For example, the instructor might post overall comments while delegating responsibility for managing the discussion threads to teaching assistants if the volume of student postings became unmanageable. The advantage here, as opposed to several of the strategies previously described, is that students would have more opportunity to interact with the instructor on a one-to-one basis than if they were auditing a discussion or if the instructor was rotating among different discussion groups.

Strategy 5: Meta-Interaction

The meta-interaction strategy, shown in Figure 5, functions like a radio talk show. The 100 participants are not provided with a discussion area, but are able to submit questions or comments to a facilitator through e-mail or a Web-based form. The questions or comments are synthesized and then posted by the facilitator for deliberation and discussion by a panel of experts and/or selected participants in an asynchronous discussion area.

Figure 4. Large group interaction

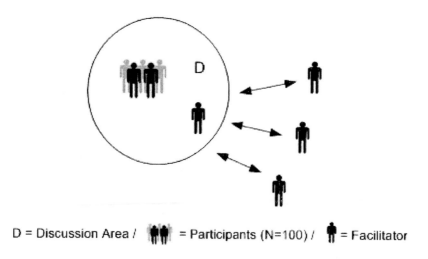

D = Discussion Area / ![participants] = Participants (N=100) / ![facilitator] = Facilitator

Figure 5. Meta interaction

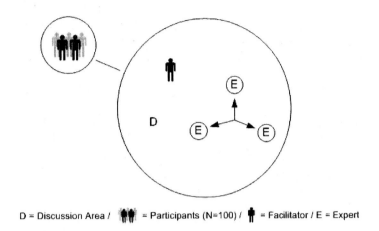

D = Discussion Area / = Participants (N=100) / = Facilitator / E = Expert

Table 1. Advantages and disadvantages of large-scale interaction strategies

Strategy	Advantages	Disadvantages
Multi-Group Interaction	• Large number of participants can be accommodated • Each discussion area has facilitator	• Discussion areas are isolated from each other • Technological ability to host multiple discussion areas may be limited • Availability of facilitators may be limited • Using multiple facilitators may reduce fidelity
Forum Interaction	• Large number of participants can be accommodated • Each discussion area has facilitator • Participants across discussion areas can view postings in other discussion areas • Discussion areas can be organized according to thematic topics and results shared	• Technological ability to host multiple discussion areas may be limited • Availability of facilitators may be limited • Participants can get information overload following too many discussions • Participants can only post in their own discussion area • Using multiple facilitators may reduce fidelity
Sub-Group Interaction	• Allows participants to participate at a level suitable to them • All participants can view discussions • Large number of participants can be accommodated	• Not all participants can contribute to discussions • No feedback loop exists for participants not actively part of the discussion area
Large-Group Interaction	• All participants can participate in discussions • Large number of participants can be accommodated • Facilitators can be added as needed to accommodate increased discussion activity	• Availability of facilitators may be limited • Facilitators who join the training late may not have a solid overview of discussion themes • Frequency of postings to discussion areas may exceed participants' ability to follow discussion threads • Discussion rules/protocols may need to be used to keep discussions manageable
Meta-Interaction	• All participants can contribute to discussions • Panel of experts can add to the discussion • Experts can be added as needed and appropriate • Large number of participants can be accommodated	• Postings must filter through a facilitator, which can slow down the training • Postings and/or questions are not immediately available for all to see • Comments or questions may lose their meaning when synthesized • No direct student-to-student interaction

The facilitator then engages the panel participants in a discussion that is viewed as "read-only" by participants in the training. Participants can then continue asking questions or making comments through e-mail or the Web-based form to the facilitator, who again synthesizes these messages and posts them for panel discussion.

High levels of interaction are achieved because all participants can contribute to the discussion by submitting questions to the facilitator. This allows for one-on-one interaction, as needed, regardless of the number of participants in the training. The use of experts also carries with it the advantage of adding more information and perspective to the discussion than reliance on participants and facilitators alone. A disadvantage of this strategy is that all participant postings and questions must filter through a facilitator, which can slow down the training. Participant comments or questions may also lose their meaning or their context when synthesized with other similar comments. Also, no direct student-to-student interaction is possible using this strategy.

If this strategy had been used with MSCs, the experts might have been MSCs that had been in their roles longer and, therefore, could offer practical start-up advice to newcomers. In a higher education setting, this strategy could be used in several ways. For example, the instructor could serve as the sole expert or several faculty members with expertise in the content area might teach the course jointly.

EVALUATION STUDY

Large-Scale Interaction Strategies Utilized

Delivery of the seven online trainings for MSCs mentioned earlier constituted a natural experiment for studying whether Web-based trainings serving large numbers of participants would preserve participant outcomes that the literature

and conventional wisdom suggest are only associated with a small number of participants. The first three online trainings utilized the sub-group interaction strategy (3). Participants were self-selected from the population of all MSCs and were able to choose whether or not they wanted to be an interactive participant or non-interactive participant on a first-come-first-served basis. Once 25 participants indicated their preference to be in the interactive group, all additional registrants were assigned to the non-interactive group. The sub-group strategy was chosen because it served to maximize the number of participants in the overall training while limiting the discussion area to 40 participants or fewer. It was hypothesized that the experience of the 25 active participants would not be detrimentally affected by the presence of the unseen participants.

The other four trainings were conducted using the large-group interaction strategy (4), in which a single discussion area with one facilitator was provided for all participants. The large-group strategy was adopted when evaluation results from the first three training events using the sub-group strategy revealed that differences between interactive and non-interactive participants were both small and statistically not significant (Formica & Harding, 2001).

Web-Based Training Structure

The purpose of the seven Web-based trainings for MSCs, which each lasted five days, was to deepen skills the MSCs acquired during a five day face-to-face training, and foster the exchange of information and ideas that help transfer knowledge into practice. Each of the trainings covered a different job-specific topic that was introduced briefly at the face-to-face training. Although the content of the events differed, they shared many structural characteristics. Each training consisted of: (1) an introduction and overview of the topic to be covered, (2) a narrative component presenting information using examples from real-life situations, (3) a facilitated discussion area, (4) a set of daily activities, (5) links to additional resources, and (6) an annotated bibliography of materials used to generate the training content.

Each of the online trainings was designed in accordance with best practices in the field of adult learning, such as the use of facilitated discussions, case studies, and links to additional resources (Galbraith, 1998; Knowles, Holton, & Swanson, 1998). Subject matter experts usually acted as the lead facilitator in the online discussion area. In addition to being skilled face-to-face trainers and workshop facilitators, these experts were provided with resources describing effective strategies for moderating online discussions (e.g., Collison, Elbaum, Haavind, & Tinker, 2000).

Evaluation Design and Methods

MSCs were given the opportunity to register for each of the seven online trainings. Participation in these trainings was encouraged, but not required. Participants, therefore, were self-selected and likely represented MSCs who felt that they needed further skills in the areas targeted by the trainings. Due to the necessity of offering all MSCs the opportunity to participate in these trainings and the uniqueness of the MSC initiative, it was not possible to construct a control or comparison group.

Common items that appeared on post-training online questionnaires were used to assess participants' perceptions of the trainings. Specifically, the post-training questionnaires included items designed to assess participants' overall satisfaction with the training, whether or not they would recommend the training to other MSCs, satisfaction with the role of the facilitator, and usefulness of the information presented. All MSCs who registered for training were sent e-mail invitations immediately after the training to take part in an online posttest. A hyperlink to the posttest was included in the last day of the training, a reminder message was posted in the training discussion area, and an e-mail was sent to all non-respondents one week after the end of the training in an attempt to increase the response rate. The response rate across all seven trainings was 59% (range 44% to 84%).

Evaluation Findings

The purpose of this section of the chapter is to provide descriptive information about participants' perceptions of the value and utility of these large-scale interaction strategies taken as a whole. The impact of the seven trainings on participants' knowledge, attitudes, and behaviors in both the short-term and long-term have been described elsewhere (Formica & Harding, 2001; Formica & Harding, 2002; Harding, Formica, & Scattergood, 2001)

To assess participants' perceptions of the trainings, both percentages and mean scores were calculated for each of the four variables. As shown in Table 2, participants gave consistently high ratings to each of these aspects across all of the seven trainings: 92% of participants indicated that they were *somewhat* or *very satisfied* with the overall training, 93% that they would *probably* or *definitely recommend* the training to other practitioners, 75% that they were *somewhat* or *very satisfied* with the facilitator, and 97% that the information presented would be either *somewhat* or *very useful*.

Group Differences

As reported in a previous study (Giguere, Formica, & Harding, 2004), two sample independent *t*-tests were used to compare aggregate group means for the trainings using the sub-group strategy and those using the large-group strategy in order to determine whether or not participants' perceptions differed based on the strategy used. Overall, participants who took part in the trainings that used the large-group strategy had higher mean scores on all four variables. Although these differences

Table 2. Participant ratings on perception items

Web-Based Trainings	Percent of Respondents Providing the Two Highest Ratings[a] and (Mean Score)			
	Overall Satisfaction [b]	Would Recommend Training [c]	Satisfaction With Facilitator [b]	Usefulness of Information [d]
Sub-Group Interaction Events				
1: Using Existing Data to Inform Prevention Program Selection (N=37)	83% (4.11)	92% (4.39)	81% (4.19)	94% (3.32)
2: Identifying Priorities and Strategies for Your Prevention Initiative (N=86)	79% (4.05)	88% (4.33)	63% (3.91)	99% (3.54)
3: Promoting Prevention through School-Community Partnerships (N=60)	89% (4.30)	89% (4.35)	71% (4.11)	96% (3.37)
Large-Group Interaction Events				
4: Selecting Research-Based Programs for Your School (N=93)	92% (4.51)	95% (4.53)	73% (4.17)	96% (3.59)
5: Implementing Research-Based Prevention Programs in Schools (N=58)	90% (4.45)	91% (4.40)	80% (4.36)	97% (3.47)
6: Sustaining Your Prevention Initiative (N=73)	96% (4.59)	99% (4.52)	76% (4.17)	100% (3.65)
7: Linking Violence & Substance Abuse Prevention to Academic Success (N=97)	96% (4.58)	95% (4.57)	86% (4.46)	98% (3.65)
OVERALL	**92% (4.40)**	**93% (4.46)**	**75% (4.20)**	**97% (3.55)**

[a] *For example, participants who selected "somewhat" or "very satisfied" on a 5-point satisfaction scale.*

[b] *Based on a 5-point scale from very dissatisfied (1) to very satisfied (5).*

[c] *Based on a 5-point scale from strongly recommend they NOT participate (1) to strongly recommend they participate (5).*

[d] *Based on a 4-point scale from not at all useful (1) to very useful (4).*

were statistically significant, the effect sizes were generally small for each of these variables with the exception of training satisfaction, which approached a medium effect size as defined by Cohen (1977). In other words, although significant, the magnitude of differences between the two groups was relatively small with the exception of overall satisfaction, which more heavily favored trainings that utilized the large-group interaction strategy.

Comparison to Other Trainings

The MSC project used a "modified blended" approach to their training events. MSCs were required to participate in a five-day, face-to-face training, which included lectures and small group work, before they were eligible to participate in one of the online trainings. Unfortunately, there was no way within the current study to test the extent to which the substantive face-to-face training was a necessary or contributing factor to the success of the online trainings.

Although not a perfect comparison, the evaluators for the MSC initiative also evaluate another technical assistance center, the Center for Substance Abuse Prevention's Northeast Center for the Application of Prevention Technologies (CAPT). Between June and November, 2003, the Northeast CAPT conducted three online training events with self-selected participants using the large-group interaction strategy. As opposed to the

MSC trainings, participants in the CAPT trainings did not have the shared experience of a five-day, face-to-face training prior to participation. These three trainings using the large-group interaction strategy with a similar target population (self-selected, substance-abuse preventionists) and similar content, also yielded positive participant ratings for participants' overall satisfaction with the training and whether or not they would recommend the training to other people who do the type of work that they do. As shown in Table 3, 95% of participants across the three trainings indicated that they were either *somewhat* or *very satisfied* with the overall training, and 95% indicated that they would either *probably* or *definitely recommend* the training to other prevention practitioners. Data on satisfaction with the training facilitator and usefulness of the information presented were not collected from these participants.

DISCUSSION AND CONCLUSION

Designing online trainings courses can prove to be challenging for instructors and facilitators, particularly when they do not have either sound theory or empirical evidence to guide them. In the absence of reliable information about best practices, early adopters of online instructional approaches were left in the position of having to forge new approaches not grounded in theory, or they had to adapt theories and pedagogical approaches from traditional face-to-face educational settings. A serious limitation of modeling online learning on traditional face-to-face instruction is that it treats online learning environments as simply extensions of the classroom, and fails to take into account the potential offered by these new technologies. As discussed in this chapter, designing online learning environments that are structured in a way that preserves actual or perceived levels of interaction while simultaneously allowing for the accommodation of large numbers of participants is one area in which educators need more guidance.

The five large-scale interaction strategies presented in this chapter offer several options for structuring Web-based trainings, and potentially academic courses, for large numbers of participants. Preliminary evidence from evaluations of

Table 3. Participant ratings on perception items for CAPT online trainings

Web-Based Trainings	Percent of Participants Providing the Two Highest Ratings[a] and (Mean Score)	
	Overall Satisfaction[b]	Would Recommend Training[c]
1: Locating, Hiring, and Managing an Evaluator (N=32)	100% (3.73)	100% (3.74)
2: What Now? Effective and Useful Data Presentation (N=33)	87% (3.52)	87% (3.41)
3: Linking Substance Abuse and Violence Prevention to Academic Success (N=39)	100% (3.56)	100% (3.65)
OVERALL	**95% (3.59)**	**95% (3.59)**

[a] *For example, participants who selected "somewhat" or "very satisfied" on a 4-point satisfaction scale.*

[b] *Based on a 4-pont scale from very dissatisfied (1) to very satisfied (4).*

[c] *Based on a 4-point scale from definitely would NOT recommend it (1) to definitely WOULD recommend it (4).*

two of the five strategies suggest that adopting these strategies may help instructors ward off the undesirable effects of increasing the number of participants without making provisions for maintaining a suitable level of interaction. One of the overarching benefits of the strategies presented is that they allow for participants to either interact in a small setting and/or to interact at a level that suits their individual needs.

The main results from evaluation study suggest that participant perceptions of the value and utility of the Web-based training were not negatively impacted when using either the sub-group interaction strategy or the large-group interaction strategy. Based on the structural similarities between the five strategies, it is probable that similar results would have been obtained if the other three strategies had been utilized. The three strategies that were not utilized, along with other characteristics of the trainings, still warrant additional study.

Although participants in the four trainings that used the large group interaction strategy rated these trainings significantly higher than participants in the trainings that used the sub-group interaction strategy, the magnitude of these differences was generally small as assessed by effect size. We hypothesized that the differences in ratings between these two strategies were attributable to lower ratings by the non-interactive participants in the Sub-Group Interaction strategy trainings. Analyses within the sub-group participants showed no differences in ratings between non-interactive participants and the participants who had access to the on-line discussion (Giguere et al., 2004). While these data do not support the initial hypothesis, they do lend support to the idea that "perceived interaction" might be as important as actual interaction. In other words, as long as participants are initially offered the opportunity to be part of an interactive discussion area and are allowed to choose their level of interaction to fit their personality/needs, this might be sufficient to buffer against any negative affect from the participants.

We were also able to test the possibility that the intensive five-day, face-to-face training with the MSCs was a necessary factor in achieving high ratings in their Web-based trainings by examining results from three trainings delivered by the Northeast CAPT to a group of preventionists who did not participate beforehand in a face-to-face training. These trainings, which used the large group interaction strategy with a similar target population and similar content, also yielded very positive participant ratings.

In the absence of a comparison group we cannot be certain how the MSC or CAPT ratings compare to ratings for Small-Scale Interaction strategies. It may be that the content or some other characteristic of these trainings account for the positive ratings obtained. Nevertheless, the consistency of the results for both the MSC and the CAPT trainings does support the conclusion that these large-scale interaction strategies can produce very positive participant ratings for overall satisfaction and similar outcome measures. It should also be noted that these strategies may still not provide the cost-efficiency that administrators may desire due to the fact that some strategies require additional trainers, facilitators, and/or assistants in order to implement the strategy effectively (Colwell & Jenks, 2004).

FUTURE RESEARCH DIRECTIONS

The limitations of these studies help identify some of the questions and the methodological challenges that future research should address. Perhaps the single most important task will be to construct studies with appropriate comparison groups, ideally control groups employing random assignment to condition, to specify the degree to which large-scale *as compared to* small-scale interaction strategies produce positive outcomes. Assuming that small-scale interaction strategies produce some added amount of participant satisfaction, or some other positive outcome, knowing the amount of this difference would allow the calculation of how much, if anything, the incremental gain costs per-participant. This kind of cost-effectiveness information is certainly among the most critical to improving decisions about which Web-based training strategy to use.

The need for more rigorous experimental studies extends to comparisons among and between all the large-scale interaction strategies we have identified, and small-scale interaction strategies designed to be more dependent on close participant-to-facilitator or participant-to-participant interaction. It also extends to other populations and settings. An issue of great importance is whether the findings drawn from studies of Web-based professional trainings, such as ours, will hold for non-professional students in universities and other academic settings. While we have offered suggestions about how these strategies might be generalized to higher education settings, their adoption in these settings has not yet been studied.

Other issues that should be addressed in future research concern the outcome measures used and the timing of measurement. Our work measured some, but not all potentially important outcomes. Examples of outcomes to be assessed in future studies comparing Web-based training strategies include the extent to which: (1) participants fail to complete the course or training (attrition), (2) participants in one course or training enroll in subsequent trainings—an indicator of their satisfaction, (3) the course or training succeeds in creating a community of learners who continue post-training interaction yielding continued benefits, (4) the course or training produces positive changes in knowledge and skills, and (5) course or training participants apply the gains made to their work and obtain positive results from doing so (Formica et al., 2002; Porter, 2004). The last issue is perhaps the single most important outcome to be considered. If the training increases knowledge, skills, and is perceived as enjoyable, but is not applied and does not contribute to improved "real world" performance, its value is, at

least, questionable. In our experience evaluating a wide rage of training and technical assistance services, this is also the outcome addressed least often. This is probably in part because of the widespread, almost unconscious acceptance of the dominant assessment model used in schools, where the focus is on determining whether a course builds a student's capacity and not on whether or how successfully students use that capacity. The issue of when to measure is implied in the above previous discussion on what should be measured. Future evaluation studies should employ pretest-posttest designs, with follow-up testing to determine whether gains in knowledge and other short-term changes persist over time and to assess long-term outcomes concerning the application of gains made during the training (Formica & Harding, 2002; Formica et al., 2002).

Lastly, future research should examine moderating variables that seem likely to impact outcomes. These include individual differences among participants, such as the MSCs' prior experience in prevention, their motivation for participating, their previous experience and comfort with Web-based trainings, and the usual background characteristics of gender, age, and so forth (Formica et al., 2002; Sener, 2004). These analyses will speak to the question of whether outcomes found for different strategies apply broadly or vary significantly by the type of participant.

REFERENCES

Boettcher, J. V. (1999). Cyber course size: Pedagogy and politics. *Syllabus, 12*(8), 42-43.

Cohen, J. (1977). *Statistical power analysis for the behavioral sciences* (Rev. Ed.). New York: Academic Press.

Collison, G., Elbaum, B., Haavind, S., & Tinker, R. (2000). *Facilitating online learning: Effective strategies for moderators*. Madison, WI: Atwood.

Colwell, J., & Jenks, C. (2004). *The upper limit: The issues for faculty in setting class size in online courses.* Paper presented at the Teaching Online in Higher Education 2004 Conference, Online.

Formica, S. W., & Harding, W. M. (2001). *Evaluation results for middle school drug prevention and school safety coordinators online continuing education events: Summary report.* Report prepared for Education Development Center, Inc., and the United States Department of Education.

Formica, S. W., & Harding, W. M. (2002). *Evaluation results for middle school drug prevention and school safety coordinators online continuing education events: Six-month follow-up report.* Report prepared for Education Development Center, Inc., and the United States Department of Education.

Formica, S. W., Harding, W. M., & Giguere, P. J. (2002, November). *Evaluation results from distance learning courses for U.S. Department of Education Middle School Coordinators.* Paper presented at the annual conference of the Association for Educational Communications and Technology, Dallas, Texas.

Galbraith, M. W. (Ed.). (1998). *Adult learning methods* (2nd ed). Malabar, FL: Krieger.

Giguere, P. J., Formica, S. W., & Harding, W. M. (2004). Large-scale interaction strategies for Web-based professional development. *American Journal of Distance Education, 18*(4), 207-223.

Harasim, L., Hiltz, S. R., Teles, L., & Turoff, M. (1997). *Learning networks: A field guide to teaching and learning online.* Cambridge, Massachusetts: MIT Press.

Harding, W. M., Formica, S.W., & Scattergood, P. (2001, October). *Evaluation of trainings in substance abuse and violence prevention for middle school coordinators.* Paper presented at the 129th annual meeting of the American Public Health Association, Atlanta, GA.

Ludlow, B. L. (2002). Web-based staff development for early intervention personnel. *Infants and Young Children, 14*(3), 54-64.

King, J. C., & Doerfert, D. L. (1996). *Interaction in the distance education setting.* Retrieved January, 1996, from http://www.ssu.missouri.edu/ssu/AgEd/NAERM/s-e-4.htm

Knowles, M. S., Holton, E. F., & Swanson, R. A. (1998). *The adult learner: The definitive classic in adult education and human resource development.* Houston: GULF.

Ko, S., & Rossen, S. (2001). *Teaching online: A practical guide.* New York: Houghton Mifflin Co.

Kuh, G.D., & Hu, S. (2001). Effects of student-faculty interaction in the 1990s. *Review of Higher Education, 24*(2), 309-332.

National Education Association (2000). *A survey of traditional and distance learning higher education.* Washington, DC: Author

Palloff, R. M., & Pratt, K. (1999). *Building learning communities in cyberspace: Effective strategies for the online classroom.* San Francisco: Jossey-Bass.

Porter, C. E. (2004). A typology of virtual communities: A multi-disciplinary foundation for future research. *Journal of Computer-Mediated Communication, 10*(1). Retrieved December 2, 2004, from http:/www.ascusc.org/jcmc/vol10/issue1/porter.html

Sener, J. (2004). Escaping the comparison trap: Evaluating online learning on its own terms. *Innovate, 1*(2). Retrieved December 7, 2004, from http://innovateonline.info/print.php?id=11

Simonson, M. (2004). Class size: Where is the research? *Distance Learning, 1*(4), 56.

Chapter VI
Teaching Social Skills:
Integrating an Online Learning System into Traditional Curriculum

Graham Bodie
Purdue University, USA

Margaret Fitch-Hauser
Auburn University, USA

William Powers
Texas Christian University, USA

ABSTRACT

The ubiquity of instructional technology necessitates a more critical look at the theories that drive adoption and the practical implications of its usage. Blended learning has been offered as one compromise to fully online learning or strict adherence to traditional lecture-based instruction that seems outdated. A particular approach to blended learning is examined in the present chapter through the use of an online learning system. Concept Keys was developed to assist instructors of social skills in breaking down these abstract concepts into manageable units of information appropriate for daily delivery via e-mail. This program is shown to be easily integrated into existing curriculum through two studies. A concluding section attempts to tie these studies together and suggests potential limitations and avenues for future research.

CHAPTER OBJECTIVES

The reader will be able to:

- Understand the pedagogical goals driving the development of Concept Keys (CK)
- Understand the key elements of the CK system
- Identify two specific ways in which CK can aid in the teaching of specific social skills
- Determine the usefulness of the CK approach to his or her pedagogical needs

INTRODUCTION

Institutions of higher education continue to face challenges posed by online education and the ubiquitous nature of technology in the classroom. The concept of blended learning—the use of two or more complementary approaches when teaching the same material—has seen heightened attention in literature in the past decade and offers a unique approach to merging the availability of technology with traditional and tested pedagogical approaches. Examples of blended learning include using textbook supplements, peer-to-peer learning, and/or online modules while maintaining aspects of a more traditional, lecture-style format. The purpose of the present chapter is to outline the development, implementation, and effectiveness of one online learning system, Concept Keys (CK), that takes a blended learning approach to teaching social skills (see also Bodie, Powers, & Fitch-Hauser, 2006; Powers, Bodie, & Fitch-Hauser, 2005). In service of these aims, a brief background is offered that situates CK into the larger category of e-learning and examines its core components. Then, two studies are used to illustrate how the system is easily integrated into an existing curriculum and can be custom fit to address specific pedagogical goals. Finally, a concluding section ties these two studies together and offers insights for future research and exploration using the CK system.

BACKGROUND: E-LEARNING, SOCIAL SKILLS, AND CONCEPT KEYS

E-learning can refer to a wide range of online learning protocol. Systems can be created that allow individuals to self-manage their learning or that blend online and face-to-face instruction to greater or lesser degrees. Datamonitor (2004, July 14) predicts the global e-learning market for higher education to grow at a rate of 12% between 2004 and 2008. This growth has necessitated a more critical look at the theories that drive technology adoption and the practical implications of instructional technology usage. Intuitively, technology should not be utilized for its own sake; instead usage should be grounded in specific goals and objectives (see Moore, 2005). This translates to practical considerations of which types, how, and how often specific technologies will be used and in what combinations. Backing such claims, research suggests that, when grounded in pedagogical goals and objectives, technology has the potential to enhance learning outcomes (e.g., Dean, Stahl, Sylwester, & Pear, 2001; DeLacey & Leonard, 2002; Rainbow & Sadler-Smith, 2003). Conversely, using technology can impede the learning process if used poorly (Derntl & Motschnig-Pitrik, 2005; Sellnow, Child, & Ahlfeldt, 2005). Still other studies have found that students have certain expectations of instructor use of technology prior to the first day of class; violating these expectations can have deleterious effects on student learning (e.g., Witt & Schrodt, 2006).

Thus, it follows that instructors who teach social skills—communication-related skills such as listening and critical thinking (Leigh, Lee, & Lindquist, 1999)—are likely to benefit from the use of online learning systems; however, the adoption of a given system should be guided by specific curricular goals. Concept Keys (CK) is an online, empty engine approach that allows instructors who teach what are generally categorized as social skills the opportunity to offer students a blended learning approach to obtaining these skills. In other words, CK enables the educator an opportunity to define social skills as broadly or narrowly as needed for a particular application (e.g., how to communication effectively or how to give meaningful presentations). The system can accommodate educators interested in, for instance, enhancing sales-related communication skills as well as educators interested in teaching engineers how to present complex material or medical students how to be more patient-centered. Most importantly, the sytem is customizable based on pedagogical goals and objectives.

The Concept Keys Approach to Blended Learning

The CK system is a focused approach to classroom interaction grounded in educational theory (i.e., chunking, priming, and active learning) that blends Web-based education with face-to-face instructor direction and support. Concept Keys provides students with small bits of information over a long period of time culminating in an integrated store of knowledge about a set of skills and how to perform these skills in specified contexts. Along with daily commentary, or fundamental keys, this method has students rate these keys according to personal relevance. Additional classroom activities are also available, which add to the student-teacher interaction and increase the chances of information retention and skill acquisition (see Table 1 for a brief overview of program elements). Defining some key terminology within the system will aid in describing its basic components. Once key terms are explained, the CK process will be outlined.

Table 1. Concept keys online learning system components: Traditional integration options

Each Student in a Concept Keys Certification Achievement Program receives:
• 1 Personal CK website account
• 2 Certification Examination attempts at program conclusion
• 50 Daily "Gentle Reminder" emails
• 50 Daily Keys
• 50 Daily Micro-lessons; each micro-lesson has four paragraphs
• 50 Daily Food For Thought Segments (four questions and responses)
• 10 Weekly quizzes over previous 5 Keys
• 10 Weekly self-selections of the Most Important Key
• 10 Weekly self-determinations of what to do about the Most Important Key
• 70+ Days of availability to download all personal program material
• 70+ Days of Engagement Index Metric (degree of participation in the program)
• 700+ Cognitive engagements in learning and improvement activities
Each Teacher (or designate) in a Certification Achievement Program will receive the following:
• A free copy of the *Student Learning Instructor's Manual*
• Daily access to all student's program activity
• Daily opportunity to obtain detailed metrics for documentation, assessment, and accountability
• Daily option to download metric data for group comparative purposes
• Daily opportunity to provide immediate feedback to students regarding their progress

Keys

Keys are very brief statements reflecting small bits of information that make up some larger concept (hence, Concept Keys). This system is based on the notion that the best way to teach complex material is to break it into small, manageable units or bits of information that are systematically delivered over an extended timeframe. This organizational framework mirrors textbook and lecture organization in which students are taught steps, guidelines, and strategies that aid in the successful implementation of a competency (e.g., how to deliver bad news). As noted by Bodie et al. (2006), "information is more easily remembered (Cowan, Chen, & Rouder, 2004; Miller, 1956) and strategic choices more easily made (Gobet & Simon, 1996, 1998) if small bits of information are built into larger stores or chunks of information that can be recalled in necessary situations" (p. 121).

For example, if you were trying to teach a group of students how to deliver an effective presentation you might start with the necessity of audience analysis followed by appropriate topic selection, writing general and specific purposes and thesis statements, and so forth. These smaller components, if segmented even more, might result in the generation of hundreds or thousands of keys to successful presentational speaking (the concept). One such key might be "Walk a Mile in the Audience's Shoes." This key should elicit thoughts concerning the importance of audience characteristics and/or experiences that might differ from one's own.

Micro-Lessons

A micro-lesson is an extension of the key whereby specific elements of the short statement (e.g., Walk a Mile in the Audience's Shoes) are elaborated upon. Specifically, each micro-lesson contains 3 elements: the key, three to four bullet points expanding upon the core components of the key,

and food-for-thought (FFT) questions (see Figure 1). The paragraphs that follow the key are a combination of explanation and motivation.

Explanation refers to bullet points with the main purpose of explaining what the key means in ordinary language. In the example presented in Figure 1, the first three bullet points explain that "Walking a Mile in the Audience's Shoes" refers to taking the audience's perspective into consideration during the speech preparation and presentation process. They also provide specific examples of how to do this (e.g., use words and concepts the audience knows and is concerned about) in order to give students practical examples of recommended behavior. Motivation refers to the bullet points designed to include both the appropriate behaviors and an example of at least one situation in which the set of behaviors should be used. As seen in Figure 1, each bullet point attempts to provide motivation to utilize the key by suggesting positive outcomes of key use (e.g., increased audience interest) and ramifications for non-use (e.g., not achieving goals, audience not attentive).

In sum, this explanation-motivation sequence provides examples of what can happen when the key is used successfully and the possible negative consequences when the key is misused or not used. These examples are written to resonate with students insofar as they are likely to recall at least one instance in which miscommunication occurred in this particular context; the assumption is that students will connect the mishap with misuse of communication processes thus motivating behavior change. Such suggestions are also likely found in textbook treatments of public speaking; by presenting material in multiple ways and through multiple channels, likelihood of retention is increased (see Bodie et al., 2006).

Each micro-lesson also contains four FFT questions that act to encourage the learner to make a decision about how to increase his or her use of that day's key. Those questions are also presented in Figure 1. Questions build upon

Figure 1. An example of a CK micro-lesson

<u>*Concept Keys*</u> *-- Unlocking Knowledge, One Key at a Time*
Effective Presentational Speaking
Key #1: Walk a Mile in the Audience's Shoes.

- *Your audience will be better able to comprehend and understand your topic if they are able to relate it to their unique lives and experiences. So to have the attention of your audience, approach your topic from the audience's perspective, not your own. This will assist you in bridging the gap between you and your audience, making your presentation more effective.*
- *The audience will trust you more if you show that you can relate to them. This includes using words and concepts the audience knows and is concerned about. This breeds interest and an interested audience will allow for a better presentation.*
- *Make sure to incorporate ways in which your audience can benefit from the topic of your presentation. Explain to them how they would benefit if the problem you're addressing in your presentation could benefit them in some way. The audience will have a better understanding of your presentation if it involves something they are concerned about.*
- *A presentation that an audience views as not related to them will not succeed in winning attention or achieving its goals. Use words and concepts that your audience will perceive as effective yet understandable and you'll have no choice but to succeed.*

Food For Thought!
Now you want to make a decision about how to increase your use of this Key. Answering the following questions should point you in the right direction. Be sure to click on the Finish button below once you have answered all the questions.

1) How would you evaluate your use of this Key in your current work environment?
    A) Not Effective
    B) Slightly Effective
    C) Moderately Effective
    D) Very Effective
    E) Extremely Effective
2) To what extent would increasing your effective use of this Key help you achieve your short-term or your long-term goals?
    A) Not Helpful
    B) Slightly Helpful
    C) Moderately Helpful
    D) Strongly Helpful
    E) Extremely Helpful

3) To what extent do you plan to develop your ability to effectively use this Key?
    A) Not a Priority
    B) Slight Priority
    C) Moderate Priority
    D) Strong Priority
    E) Extremely High Priority

4) What are you actually going to do to improve your effective use of this Key? (Maximum: 360 characters)

© *Copyright All rights reserved.*

each other allowing the student to reflect on the present use of the key and how this aspect of the social phenomenon might be improved. The final question, especially, places the responsibility for learning on the student.

The Process

Once a student is signed up for a CK program, he or she goes to the CK Website, creates a unique username and password, and submits a working e-mail address.[2] This e-mail address is used to send the student daily reminders that a particular key is ready to be viewed (see Figure 2). Once the student clicks on the Web address located in the e-mail, he or she is sent to the login page. Once logged in, the student will be able to access the daily micro-lesson and answer daily FFT questions; past micro-lessons, quizzes, and so forth, not yet completed are also made available.

Summary

CK allows abstract and complex social skills that are otherwise ambiguous, vague, and/or vast in scope to be presented in manageable and meaningful units of information that can be tailored to course goals and individual learners. This information is presented to the learner though daily micro-lessons over a predetermined period of time. Each micro-lesson consists of (a) the daily key, (b) the cognitive and behavioral components of that key, and (c) "food for thought" questions.

CK achieves the objective of breaking down a complex concept like presentational speaking into manageable units of information for increased retention as well as increases the amount of time the student is likely to remain engaged with course material (small bits of information are delivered daily). This is enabled by the empty engine capabilities of the system—individual lessons can be customized as broadly or narrowly as desired. Components of this system, such as FFT questions and motivation-based behavioral examples, aid in student engagement and a sequentially-based learning approach that has been shown to be effective in several classrooms. The next section explores two such applications of the system.

CURRICULUM INTEGRATION

Concept Keys has been successfully implemented in several classrooms at three different universi-

Figure 2. An example of a daily reminder e-mail

Greetings, John!

This is your daily reminder that a key is ready for you to read! Today's key is:

Key #1: Take personal responsibility for quality communication!
http://www.conceptkeys.com/program.php?keyId=1&progId=99

If the above URL is 'clickable', simply click it to go to the key. You might need to log into your account as well. If you do need to log in, you will be directed to your participant page immediately upon successful log in where you will find the above key in your 'To Do List'.

If the URL is *not* clickable, simply copy and paste it into your web browser.

In addition, the following item has not yet been completed:

Key #1: Food for Thought Questions
http://www.conceptkeys.com/program.php?progId=99&keyId=1&fft=1

If you have any questions, comments, or suggestions, please feel free to reply to this message and one of our customer support agents will respond to you shortly.

Sincerely,
Dr. Will Powers
CEO Concept Keys, Inc.
wpowers@conceptkeys.com

ties. Initially, the system was built to provide instructors with 10-week programs that cover a wide variety of areas relevant to social skills. This has been the most widely used component of the system. Study One addresses this traditional integration. In this model teachers serve as *learning system coordinator* to students who are assigned, as one component of a larger class, one of eight e-books each with 50 micro-lessons. Typically, the teacher assigns CK as a supplemental text in a class that is largely focused on some large area of social interaction (e.g., business communication, listening). There are many options available to the teacher, some more appropriate in one level of learning than another (e.g., College students relate to some learning activities differently than would Junior High School students). A complete Instructor Manual detailing multiple options is available on the CK Website (see Table 2 for a sample of activities).

Thus, in study one we discuss the ways in which online material was blended into the classroom experience through particular assignments in one classroom; however, it should be noted that this is merely an example of traditional integration (for additional case studies see Bodie et al., 2006; Cook & Powers, in press; Powers et al., 2005). Although the class was small, the results from the study are useful in illustrating points about CK as well as elements of the system that seem to work as they were theoretically grounded.

Table 2. Two example activities for use with CK modules

Personal Improvement Plan Development

Once students identify a particular Key as having some level of special value for themselves as they look at their relationships and career aspirations, the first learning element has to be to get that Key into long-term memory. Thus, the emphasis in so many activities upon repetition leading to enhanced memory. But, memory without use is of value only at some future time—and then, the actual skill may not be as practiced or smooth as one would desire.

So, at the same time that memory is being developed, we may wish to ask the students to develop a plan that each student believes will lead to their personal improvement with specific Keys.

You could review the plan and have the student implement the final improvement plan and report their progress after a specified time period.

You could have Buddies or Teammates select a Key, develop a two-week personal improvement plan for each other, negotiate the plan to each person's satisfaction (you would want to review all plans to assure appropriateness), implement the plan, and have each partner report the progress of the other person.

The number of times you use this activity is optional. You could have students develop such a plan for the Most Important Key each week, thus producing 10 personal improvement plans. Or, you could use this activity on the basis of the Most Important Key each 25 Keys leading to two personal improvement plans.

Communication Cartoon of the Week

Newspapers, magazines and books are filled with cartoons that often have direct relationship to communication or to specific Tips. Students can clip these out and post them on bulletin boards or include them in the newsletter, along with how they relate to Concept Keys content. Or, Teams can present them in class along with their rationale. The best (or most relevant cartoon) can be identified by a vote, and the person/team contributing the cartoon can be recognized. These cartoons can be collected and saved in a photo album with the related Key itself and used later as a resource.

A unique twist to this idea could be having a cartoon posted in a central place and having other students figure out which Key(s) it applies to and why. The group or student with the most relevant Keys and explanations can be rewarded.

Also, a cartoon can be displayed without the caption, allowing students to write their own caption. Using cartoons allows a humorous look at how things can sometimes occur and also foster some learning.

More recently, the system has been modified to allow students or instructors to author e-books of varying lengths, thus taking full advantage of the empty engine application. Study two describes a student authorship approach that was recently incorporated into an introductory interpersonal communication course. This class was largely focused on theories and approaches to the study of interpersonal communication; therefore, the CK program was used as a supplement to provide a focus on basic communication skills that students often do not receive when taking such a class. The particular course represented in study two is required or offered as an elective for a wide range of student majors. Since this class is taught in multiple sections each semester, it is necessary to streamline material and textbooks as much as possible. CK offered a non-intrusive supplement that allowed one section to receive CK materials and still be exposed to the same concepts and theories as the other sections of the course. In other words, this context allows for exploring and illustrating a second specific case of integration made possible by the CK learning system.[3]

Study One: Traditional Integration

The first study looks at the traditional use of a CK e-book and subsequent exercises that are integrated into the requirements of a semester-long course on listening. Eleven students enrolled in a five-week mini-mester at a large southeastern university during the summer of 2006 subscribed to the *Listening Effectively* e-book which consists of 50 micro-lessons and ten retention quizzes—each quiz tests the retention of five keys. Time constraints of a five-week course altered normal key distribution. Instead of receiving one key per day for 10 weeks, students received three keys each day for three-and-a-half weeks. On day 17, students received the final two keys. Students received retention quizzes at the end of every five keys. These quizzes motivate students to remember each key and to think about the key

they find to be most meaningful out of each set by having each student establish his or her most important key (this culminates in each student having ten most important keys with a rationale of why this key is the most important to his or her unique situation). To further motivate students to remember the keys, students were encouraged to take a certification exam at the end of the term that tested overall retention and understanding. Students who correctly answer the questions at a 90% or better accuracy rate are certified at the highest level; those who score in the 80% range receive regular certification. Each student had two opportunities to take the certification test. All 11 students received certification. Two additional assignments designed to integrate the keys into the fabric of the class were used as pedagogical tools.

CK-Related Assignments

The first assignment was used to increase student engagement in classroom discussion by enhancing active leaning. This group project had students get into pairs (there was one triad) and write a skit that illustrated two keys which both students agreed were important for social interaction. In addition to writing the skit, the groups had to perform it in front of the class. To increase the number of keys covered, groups were told no keys could be repeated in the class; 10 of the 50 keys to effective listening were represented by this activity.[4] This activity provides a fun, but challenging opportunity for the students to translate the key into an active skill. For example, one skit illustrated the key "stop talking" by featuring an individual missing important instructions for a task because she continued to talk over her supervisor. The skit clearly demonstrated what the key means in a life-like situation and illustrated the importance of the skill. The clarity and creativity of the skits provided useful measures of how students interpreted and integrated the keys into their way of thinking about potential listening situations.

The second assignment required students to turn in, on a weekly basis, a two-page essay focused on how they had incorporated their two favorite keys (out of the previous nine) in their daily lives. The exercise was designed to keep students engaged in the program and provided one more means of getting them to think about the importance of the particular skill or suggestion. By getting them to focus specifically on how they were using a particular key, the students found they either already used a skill or explored how a new approach (as suggested by the key) could help them manage a situation more effectively.

At the end of the semester, the instructor asked volunteers to return copies of their individual CK reports for use in writing the present manuscript. A total of 15 out of a possible 55 reports were returned representing nine out of the 11 enrolled students. Most students returned their last one or two reports. A theme analysis was conducted

Table 3. Study one: Essay excerpts

Relating Keys to Personal Experience.	
Key(s)	Excerpt
"Take the Time to Respond"	Instead of hollering at one another, [my parents] took their time and came up with a good calm response. This is probably why they have been married so long. So I am going to try to emulate them in my listening behavior and always take my time to respond. From doing so, I can avoid situations where I say something I regret.
"Control Your Feelings About the Task" "Listen with Optimism"	...when it comes to doing certain things [at work], I tend to have a pessimistic attitude. Sometimes, I haven't heard the complete details of the task but I tend to block out the rest of the information being delivered to me. I catch myself doing this at work … when someone has an idea that I don't particularly like, I tend to focus on how it will not work as opposed to making the idea more effective…I think it's important to listen with optimism because if you don't, you may miss details that could lead to mistakes that will be hard to fix. …. I realize that this pessimism will not get me far, especially when I get a real job and will probably have to work with a group of people for a common goal. I have found that listening with optimism is also a great way to improve relationships among coworkers. . .

Relating Keys to relevant prior course work.	
Key(s)	Excerpt
"Be Aware of Nonverbal Messages while Listening"	Concept Key 48 is something I studied during the last mini-semester in nonverbal communication, Oculesics, or eye behavior, is one of the most important nonverbal behaviors to observe. Deception can be very easily detected by eye behavior. If the speaker avoids eye contact or has trouble maintaining eye contact it could be a sign that the truth is not being told. Kinesics or body language is very important for the listener as well as the speaker.

Applying the Keys	
Key(s)	Excerpt
"Reduce Distractions when Listening,"	I attend a devotional each week … After the devotional is over, we use the time together to catch up with friends and meet new people. The problem is we are still gathered in a large room with several people. There are a lot of conversations going on…. This is where I have been trying to practice this skill. I have found communication more successful when I try to block out all the noise and everything going on around me.

on the returned essays to determine whether or not they truly integrated the keys into everyday thinking. To show integration, the report should not only discuss the meaningfulness of the key itself, but it should also clearly relate the key to some area of the student's life. Common themes across essays included relating keys to personal experience, relating keys to relevant prior coursework, and applying the keys. Table 3 provides relevant excerpts for each theme.

Several essays were representative of students focusing on the impact certain keys have on their unique lives and personal experiences when engaged in interaction with others or when observing good and poor examples of listening behaviors. By personalizing the keys, students took the abstract skill of listening and its component parts, as presented by relevant micro-lessons, and added concrete and applicable dimensions to it. That is, rather than simply drawing general conclusions and applications, which may be equally accomplished by reading a chapter in a textbook, students focused on the actual use or observation of the key and the resulting impact. By ending with a listening lesson, they showed their ability to generalize from their own experience and integrate the concept into their daily behaviors.

Another focus in some reports was to write about how the keys fit with concepts learned in previous communication classes. This provides support for the notion that chunking helps increase one's knowledge base by allowing individuals to layer relevant information into proper mental category or schema. A core assumption of the CK system is that micro-lessons operate most effectively when students are not only able to relate to presented material but are also able to build mental stores of core concepts that can be recalled when certain aspects of the environment prime relevant information from long-term memory (see Bodie et al., 2006). The more students are able to do this, the more effective learning from such a system should be. This blending and combining of small bits of information is also facilitated by

the way in which current e-books are constructed and how authors are encouraged to write new material.

First, programs have been designed to include micro-lessons that are repetitive and cross over potential applications. For instance, the keys "Control Your Feelings about the Task" and "Listen with Optimism" share common aspects (this is also evident in the bullet points following the keys). Thus, the student who wrote about both keys in the same report also illustrated how students are relating previously learned information within the program to build larger stores (chunking) about the core concept (i.e., effective listening). Second, the micro-lessons are designed to reflect an explanation-motivation sequence which should resonate with students. This resonation should call forth life experiences from long-term memory (as illustrated by students who related keys to personal experiences) and further the chunking process.

A final way student's showed how thoughtful they were about the keys was experimenting with and practicing their application. The segment of one report presented in Table 3 clearly shows the student has used the key and has noticed an appreciable difference in his ability to listen. This application of course material is often what is sought as we teach social skills. The fact that student essays were illustrative of this goal is encouraging.

Discussion

While these results are only anecdotal, they do suggest that CK can be integrated into a traditional course with positive results. By providing students with the opportunity to link basic concepts and elements of a skill to their own lives in small, regular increments, educators can help students incorporate important skills into daily practice. As discussed previously, students related keys to their personal experiences and prior coursework, and experimented with keys to improve their listening ability.

These themes are also useful to illustrate the pedagogical goals to which a "traditional integration" is suited. One of the most important goals of the original CK system is to assist education in teaching basic social skills. Unfortunately, students not only place barriers to learning these skills, but by the time students get to college many of their inappropriate communication behaviors are ingrained. To "unlearn bad habits" and to simplify the presentation of large amounts of information, CK presents students with small bits of information on a daily basis that takes approximately five minutes to complete. Even this short amount of time can produce considerable reflection, sparked by FFT questions and application. This positive finding suggests that more extensive and statistically reliable research needs to be done in the future on the impact of this type of instructional tool.

Likewise, a five-week mini-mester places constraints on the ability for the system to be implemented as intended. However, it should be noted that results from the present case study do not deviate from those presented elsewhere (Bodie et al., 2006; Powers, Bodie, & Fitch-Hauser, 2006). It would also have been useful to obtain pre- and post-test measures from students related to listening habits and biases to assess change over time. Two reasons are offered for why these data were not collected. First, the small number of students limits statistical power needed to detect even large effects. Second, the length of the course places into question the amount of absolute change that is likely. The results of study two offer some appeasement to such concerns. It is to that integration method we now turn.

Study Two: Student Authorship Project

In the spring semester of 2006, 20 students enrolled in an upper-level interpersonal communication course at a large mid-western university took part in a group project that involved researching and authoring a skills training program, as well as acting as participants for a similar program authored by classmates. Specifically, students self-selected five-person groups then chose a general skill set on which to focus: intercultural communication competence, effective public speaking, effective parent-child communication, and effective employment interviewing. Students were responsible for two main tasks. First, groups developed a three-week CK program to enhance the skills of their chosen competency. Second, students were randomly assigned to take one of the four three-week programs near the end of the semester; the program ended one week before the final day of class and was scheduled to run Wednesday through Sunday with Monday and Tuesday as "off days."[5]

A series of smaller steps was employed to better facilitate the project. After students formed groups, they were required to turn in an initial bibliography consisting of journal articles, book chapters, books, and other sources. After this bibliography was approved by the instructor, the students developed a list of 50 keys to their chosen competency. These 50 keys were refined and reduced to 15 and approved by the instructor. It was at this point that the groups began work on their series of micro-lessons. Five different micro-lessons were due at three different points in the semester. After all micro-lessons received final approval by the course instructor, the instructor put them into the CK template and randomly assigned individuals to take a program that they did not create. Students were graded on the quality of their authored programs as well as their participation in the three-week program as participants. In all, this project counted for 40% of the total course grade.

Several different measurement instruments were employed to test the effectiveness of the different project stages. A series of self-report scales were employed after the completion of this class project to assess different learning-related outcomes. In addition, a pre-post design (week three and week 16) was used to test knowledge relevant to the four competencies represented in the CK programs.

Self-Report Learning and Knowledge Outcomes

Concept Keys Assessment Instrument

To assess student perceptions of the utility of the CK program a 21-item scale was implemented (see Table 4 for all items). The scale is a modified version of the ART-Q (MacGeorge et al., in press) and asks students to report on their experience using the CK system without regard to any other element of the course, the group to which they were assigned, or other elements of the classroom. The scale was originally intended to measure seven areas relevant to the CK experience: time, interest (in the course), motivation, self-perceived learning, ease of use, fun, and liking. When submitted to a principle components factor analysis with Varimax rotation, a two factor solution that explained 57.6% of the item variance was found.

Table 4. Factor analysis for concept keys assessment scale

Scale Items	Component				
	1	2	3	4	5
CK boost my enthusiasm for studying the material we covered in this course.	**.887**	.272	.153	-.116	.088
CK helped me learn course material better.	.583	.186	.323	.168	.605
I did not like using CK. (R)	**.847**	.061	.182	.253	.078
I enjoyed using the CK system.	**.629**	.359	-.177	.463	-.119
I felt more engaged with the class because we used CK.	**.812**	.285	.339	-.154	.146
I had a good experience with CK.	**.848**	-.019	- 023	.174	.017
I had no problems using the CK system.	.191	.158	-.410	-.351	.521
I understood more in this class because we used CK.	.244	**.838**	.023	.092	.182
If we didn't use CK, I would have been less interested in the topics we covered in this course.	-.054	**.834**	.021	-.011	.206
Investing time in the CK program was a worthwhile use of class time.	.518	.461	.417	.476	.026
It was exciting to get daily e-mails from the CK system.	.540	.078	.721	-.061	.228
My knowledge of course material was improved by using CK.	.200	**.832**	.159	-.247	-.079
The CK project was good use of class time.	.356	.349	.554	.239	-.059
Using CK did NOT get me any more involved in the class. (R)	.101	-.026	.058	.882	.005
Using CK heightened my interest in other aspects of the class.	**.750**	.386	.350	-.258	-.107
Using CK made me more motivated to learn in this course.	.203	**.873**	.154	.149	-.025
Using the CK system was a waste of class time. (R)	.510	.516	.220	.250	-.433
Using the CK system was boring. (R)	**.835**	.071	.199	.150	.397
Using the CK system was easy.	-.032	.012	-.939	-.058	.107
Using the CK system was fun.	.678	.285	.031	.152	.569
Using the CK system was pretty hard. (R)	-.154	-.199	-.889	.020	-.043

Notes: Extraction method: Principal component analysis; rotation method: Varimax with kaiser normalization.

These two factors were interpreted as CK enjoyment ($\alpha = .922$), how much the students enjoyed using the system, and CK knowledge ($\alpha = .871$), how much the students reported learning as a result of using the system (see Table 4 for items corresponding to these components).

Self-Reported Improvement

To assess student perceptions of learning several items were written that asked respondents to "refer to how much you think you learned as a result of the Concept Keys system." A principle components factor analysis with Varimax rotation indicated a three factor solution that explained 77.8% of the item variance. However, after inspecting the rotated factor structure and the corresponding reliability analyses, the following items seemed to comprise the only interpretable and reliable scale: "How well do you think you have comprehended the content of the CK system?"; "How much improvement have you noticed in your ability to communicate since you started the CK program?"; and "How much has your level of anxiety about communication decreased due to the CK program?" Thus the variable perceived communication improvement was calculated from the means of these three items ($\alpha = .757$).

Affective Learning

Affective learning is defined as "an increasing internalization of positive attitudes toward the content or subject matter" and "is viewed typically as an important motivator of students' willingness to learn, use, and generalize information and skills beyond the traditional classroom" (Rubin, Plamgreen, & Sypher, 1994, p. 81). To assess student affect toward learning with respect to the CK project, students completed a slightly modified version of Affective Learning Scale (Kearney, Plax, & Wendt-Wasco, 1985); they were instructed to "respond about how you perceived your learning as related to the CK system and

not to other elements of the course." Responses were recorded on a series of semantic differential scales (1 to 5) with respect to three areas of the CK program: behaviors recommended by the CK program (good/bad, worthless/valuable, fair/unfair, and positive/negative), content/subject matter of the CK program (bad/good, valuable/worthless, unfair/fair, negative/positive), and in "real life" situations, your likelihood of actually attempting to engage in behaviors recommended in the program (likely/unlikely, impossible/possible, probable/improbable, would not/would). Affective learning with respect to the CK project was calculated by taking the mean of all items. Internal consistency for this scale as measured by Cronbach's alpha was .921.

Pre-Post Design Measures

Intercultural Communication

Three measures were used to assess pre- and post-intervention knowledge of intercultural communication: the generalized ethnocentrism scale, the personal report of intercultural communication apprehension, and the uncertainty when communication with strangers scale. The generalized ethnocentrism scale (Neuliep, 2002; Neuliep & McCroskey, 1997a) consists of 22 items, only 15 of which are used, that assess the general tendency to see the world from ones own cultural perspective. The 15-item scale achieved excellent reliability both pre- ($\alpha = .908$) and post-test ($\alpha = .939$).

The Personal Report of Intercultural Communication Apprehension (PRICA) (Neuliep & McCroskey, 1997b) assesses anxiety within intercultural communication exchanges. This 14-item measure ($\alpha_{pre} = .881$; $\alpha_{pst} = .959$) produces scores between 14 and 70, with scores below 32 indicating low intercultural communication apprehension (ICA), scores above 52 indicating high ICA, and scores ranging between 32 and 52 indicating a moderate level of ICA.

Items from the Uncertainty When Communicating with Strangers Scale (Gudykunst, 1998) were modified slightly to measure confidence/uncertainly when engaged in cross-cultural communication. For example, the item "I am not confident when I communicate with strangers" was reworded to read "I am not confident when I communicate with members of other cultures." Alpha reliability for this scale was .830 pre-test and .520 post-test.[6]

Public Speaking

One measure was used to assess levels of competence with public speaking. The Personal Report of Public Speaking Anxiety (PRPSA) (McCroskey, 1970) consists of 34 items that are added to form a composite score between 34 and 170. Given excellent reliability estimates ($\alpha_{pre} = .962$; $\alpha_{pst} = .965$), scores could be interpreted as consistent with prior research: highly apprehensive (scores above 131), moderately apprehensive (scores between 98 and 131), and low apprehensive (scores below 98).

Parent-Child Communication

Self-reported competence when communicating with one's parents was assessed in two primary ways. First, eight questions were written and embedded in the interpersonal competence questionnaire (Buhrmester, Furman, Wittenberg, & Reis, 1988), a 40-item scale that assesses five social competencies. Four items concerned how comfortably respondents handled situations with their father (e.g., talking to your father about personal problems or issues.) and the same four items concerned how comfortably respondents handled situations with their mother (e.g., handling a conflict with your mother.). Responses were recorded using a 5-point scale: 1 = I'm poor at this; I'd be so uncomfortable and unable to handle this situation that I'd avoid it if possible; 2 = I'm only fair at this; I'd feel very uncomfortable and would have lots

of difficulty handling this situation; 3 = I'm okay at this; I'd feel somewhat uncomfortable and have some difficulty handling this situation; 4 = I'm good at this; I'd feel quite comfortable and able to handle this situation. 5 = I'm EXTREMELY good at this; I'd feel very comfortable and could handle this situation very well. Internal consistency was as follows: father and mother combined ($\alpha_{pre} = .858$; $\alpha_{pst} = .773$), father ($\alpha_{pre} = .920$; $\alpha_{pst} = .895$), mother ($\alpha_{pre} = .735$; $\alpha_{pst} = .855$).

Second, a family communication questionnaire was written to assess how likely a respondent is to talk with his or her father/mother about several situations. Those situations were as follows: (a) "If you are having problems with your homework," (b) "If you are trying to find a good book to read or a movie to watch," (c) "If you are thinking about your plans for the future," (d) "If you have had a quarrel with your best friend," (e) "If you want to know something about alcohol or other drugs," (f) "If you are really angry or upset about something," and (g) "If you feel bad or guilty about something you have done." Respondents recorded responses on a 5-point scale from Almost Never (1) to Almost Always (5) with the midpoint indicating Sometimes (3). The scale achieved excellent reliability for father-oriented responses ($\alpha_{pre} = .929$; $\alpha_{pst} = .895$). After removing one item (If you are thinking about your plans for the future), the mother-oriented scale also achieved excellent reliability ($\alpha_{pre} = .907$; $\alpha_{pst} = .906$). The combined scale achieved adequate reliability ($\alpha_{pre} = .823$; $\alpha_{pst} = .833$) after the removal of the same item.

Interviewing

Self-reported interviewing competence was assessed in two distinct ways. First, four interview competence questions were written and embedded in the Interpersonal Competence Questionnaire (Buhrmester et al., 1988). Those items were: (a) "During an interview, telling a potential employer my strengths," (b) "During an interview, telling a potential employer my weaknesses," (c) "Asking relevant questions at the end of an employment interview," and (d) "In a job interview, responding quickly and comfortably to questions." Response choices were the same as indicated in the previous section. Since alpha reliabilities did not indicate an internally consistent scale at either pre- (α = .381) or post-test (α = .591) this measure was not included in further analyses.

Second, a more objective measure of job interview knowledge was created which included

Table 5. Part one: Group size, means, standard deviations, and standard errors of cross cultural and public speaking measures

	Cross Cultural Communication				
	Program	N	Mean	SD	SE
Ethnocentrism Pre Test	Author	5	25.40	6.02	2.69
	Taker	5	32.60	8.62	3.85
	Neither	10	34.30	6.63	2.10
	Total	20	31.65	7.64	1.71
Ethnocentrism Post Test	Author	5	25.20	5.45	2.44
	Taker	5	32.60	7.80	3.49
	Neither	8	36.00	13.67	4.83
	Total	18	32.06	10.93	2.58
Intercultural Communication Apprehension Pre Test	Author	4	30.75	7.54	3.77
	Taker	4	32.00	1.63	0.82
	Neither	10	34.90	8.88	2.81
	Total	18	33.33	7.46	1.76
Intercultural Communication Apprehension Post Test	Author	5	28.40	12.52	5.60
	Taker	5	30.80	4.76	2.13
	Neither	8	34.13	11.56	4.09
	Total	18	31.61	10.17	2.40
	Public Speaking				
Personal Report of Public Speaking Anxiety Pre Test	Author	6	107.83	26.71	10.90
	Taker	5	107.60	20.89	9.34
	Neither	9	95.78	21.55	7.18
	Total	20	102.35	22.63	5.06
Personal Report of Public Speaking Anxiety Post Test	Author	5	99.40	35.66	15.95
	Taker	4	108.00	26.92	13.46
	Neither	9	115.11	20.07	6.69
	Total	18	109.17	25.76	6.07

both general (e.g., what is the purpose of the job interview?) and more applied questions (e.g., what is the best way to respond to the request, "Tell me about yourself?"). Respondents were given three answers in a multiple choice format. Questions had one correct and two incorrect answers, thus scores could range between 0 and 10.

Results

Self-Report Learning and Knowledge

To assess student self-perceived learning, a series of single sample t-tests were conducted with a value of 3 (the mean of all three variable scales)

Table 5. Part two: Group size, means, standard deviations, and standard errors of parent-child and interviewing measures

	Program	N	Mean	SD	SE
Parent-Child Communication					
Family Communication Competence Pre Test	Author	4	4.06	0.63	0.31
	Taker	5	3.63	0.99	0.44
	Neither	11	3.46	0.66	0.20
	Total	20	3.62	0.74	0.17
Family Communication Competence Post Test	Author	4	3.78	0.28	0.14
	Taker	4	3.25	0.92	0.46
	Neither	10	3.45	0.65	0.21
	Total	18	3.48	0.65	0.15
Family Communication Questionnaire Pre Test	Author	4	3.85	0.57	0.29
	Taker	5	3.05	1.46	0.65
	Neither	11	2.73	0.62	0.19
	Total	20	3.03	0.95	0.21
Family Communication Questionnaire Post	Author	4	3.35	0.28	0.14
	Taker	4	3.02	1.24	0.62
	Neither	10	2.85	0.86	0.27
	Total	18	3.00	0.84	0.20
Interviewing					
Job Interview Knowledge Pre Test	Author	5	5.20	2.59	1.16
	Taker	5	6.20	1.30	0.58
	Neither	10	5.10	0.57	0.18
	Total	20	5.40	1.47	0.33
Job Interview Knowledge Post Test	Author	4	5.25	1.71	0.85
	Taker	5	6.40	1.52	0.68
	Neither	9	6.00	1.00	0.33
	Total	18	5.94	1.30	0.31

as the test value. Results showed statistically significant differences (90% CI) for CK knowledge, $t(17) = -2.05$, $p = .057$, $M = 2.63$, $SD = .778$, affective learning, $t(16) = 2.57$, $p = .021$, $M = 3.56$, $SD = .894$, and perceived communication improvement, $t(17) = 2.68$, $p = .016$, $M = 3.51$, $SD = .805$; there was a non-significant difference for CK enjoyment, $t(17) = .091$, $p = .929$, $M = 2.98$, $SD = .740$. An additional analysis was run to assess the utility of the CK project beyond simple classroom purposes. As previously mentioned, one subscale within the affective learning scale refers to the "likelihood of actually attempting to engage in behaviors recommended in the program" in "real life situations." This composite subscale achieved excellent reliability at .90. A one-sample t-test with 3 as the test value produced a marginally significant and positive result, $t(16) = 1.99$, $p = .063$, $M = 3.59$, $SD = 1.22$.

Thus, students seemed to enjoy the CK program an average amount but perceived the program to aid in their comprehension and improvement of key communicative behaviors. Moreover, their affect toward learning material related to the programs as well as their likelihood of engaging in relevant behaviors was also above the mean. The negative result with respect to CK Knowledge can be explained with respect to the specific items. As compared to the Perceived Communication Improvement and Affective Learning items, the CK Knowledge items seem to measure the CK program as assisting in learning course material. The course material was more theoretical than applied and exams were focused on this theoretical material. The CK program was highly applied and not tested explicitly on examinations. Thus, although the students did not feel as if the CK project heightened their understanding of course material per se, they still felt as if the project aided in their understanding of a core social skill and in the improvement of this skill.

Pre-Post Design Measures

After the four programs were finalized, students were randomly assigned to take a program they had not authored. Thus, all students fell into one of three groups for all programs: program author, program taker, or control group.[7] To control for possible differences in pre-test scores a series of one-way ANCOVAs were run to test the expectations that, within each context, the author group would achieve the greatest improvement from pre- to post-test, the taker group would achieve the second greatest improvement from pre- to post-test, and the control group would achieve the least improvement from pre- to post-test.[8] The rationale behind this hypothesized pattern of results is the

Table 6. Results of the ANCOVA analyses

	F	df	p	Partial η^2	Post-Test M in Predicted Direction?
Cross Cultural Communication —Ethnocentrism	.824	2,18	.459	.105	Yes
Cross Cultural Communication — PRICA	.104	2,16	.902	.017	Yes
Public Speaking — PRPSA	2.69	2,18	.103	.278	See contrast results
Parent-Child Communication — Family Communication Competence	.451	2,18	.646	.061	No
Parent-Child Communication — Family Communication Questionnaire	.072	2,18	.931	.010	Yes
Interviewing — Job Interview Knowledge	.136	2,18	.874	.019	No

time spent with the material. Individuals who engaged in the authoring process spent eight weeks engaged in researching and thinking about the concept under question. Meetings between group members and the instructor indicated the depth in which students were exploring the material and the exponential growth in their understanding as they attempted to translate scholarly research into real-life suggestions (in the form of micro-lessons) that took no more than five minutes for an individual to comprehend.

The dependent variable was always the post-test score, the fixed factor was group membership (author, taker, control), and the covariate was always the pre-test score. Given the small sample size, power analyses indicated that even a 90% level of statistical significance would be difficult to achieve: large effect (power = .40), medium effect (power = .20), small effect (power = .10) (Cohen, Cohen, West, & Aiken, 2003). Means, standard deviations, standard errors, and group sample sizes for all variables of interest are presented in Table 5. Table 6 presents the results of a series of ANCOVA analyses. As indicated in the table, the only significant result found was for public speaking anxiety. A series of simple contrasts showed that, as predicted, those students who authored the program had a lower level of public speaking anxiety post-test than did controls, Contrast Estimate = -27.2, SE = 11.9; however, authors did not differ significantly from takers, Contrast Estimate = -12.8, SE = 13.7, and takers did not differ significantly from controls, Contrast Estimate = -14.5, SE = 12.4. Given the power to detect significant effects and the exploratory nature of the present study, the discussion section presents explanations for all findings in light of inherent limitations.

Discussion

Adding to the descriptions of how students incorporate CK material into their personal and professional lives obtained in study one, the present investigation allows for a slightly more rigorous test of the assumptions that the CK system provides students with a meaningful learning experience. Although the sample size in this study warrants caution be taken when extrapolating the results to a larger population, this study does provide evidence that students in the present study felt as if the system aids in their understanding of a particular social skill (at least within the confines of a typical semester project). Moreover, they report that engaging in behaviors recommended by the system is likely. Insofar as the behaviors recommended are appropriate for the skill in question, the system shows promise in allowing instructors to engage in a blended learning approach to teaching skills that may otherwise be overlooked, ignored, or given peripheral treatment in a more theoretically-driven classroom. As mentioned previously, the course in study two is largely theoretical with little emphasis on skills training. Incorporating CK in this manner increased student engagement with both scholarly literature and application potential of this material.

In terms of the pre- and post-test knowledge assessment, power to detect significant differences between groups was dismally low. Nevertheless, several results are worth extended discussion. First, the public speaking program produced the only statistically significant result with program authors achieving lower public speaking anxiety scores post-test than controls; no differences were found between program takers and program controls. In addition, as indicated in Table 5, program authors seemed to decrease and controls seemed to increase their anxiety while program takers seemed to stay relatively stable. The fact that a significant result was found with respect with the public speaking program may reflect the fact that all students in the present class had been exposed to similar instruction prior to the class in the form of the basic speaking course (a course that is required for most students at this particular university). Thus, additional reinforcement may have triggered cognitive stores of information (i.e., chunks) and strengthened the links between this information (see Bodie et al., 2006).

One aspect of the class that may have influenced this result is the fact that all students were required to present an abstracted version of a scholarly article as a course requirement. Presentations were 15 to 20 minutes in length and basic public speaking criteria were used as a part of the grading rubric. This was done throughout the semester with approximately one student presenting per class period. It is possible that program authors, with an extended and in-depth exploration of this subject, felt better about this particular experience as a result of their research and program writing while the program takers did not have the opportunity in a three-week program to obtain all the positive benefits of such instruction. Those that neither authored nor took the public speaking program were not only exposed to an anxiety producing speaking event, but they had no further instruction as to how to manage their anxiety or how to improve their skills; they also lacked the potential additional feedback that such instruction may have afforded the other two groups. In other words, this recent public speaking event may have served as a reference point to all students as they answered the post-test questionnaire.

A second set of results that supports the utility of the CK system are those non-significant results that met expectations in terms of patterns of group means. Within the cross cultural communication program, program controls had the highest and authors had the lowest post-test ethnocentrism scores with the mean for program takers falling between. It is also notable that only the program controls exhibited a change of over .20 between pre- and post-test scores going from an average of 34 to an average of 36 on ethnocentrism over the course of the semester. Similarly, program controls had the highest and program authors had the lowest anxiety levels related to cross cultural communication with program takers falling in

between. As with the ethnocentrism variable, pre- to post-test change for each group was also in line with expectations; control participants showed the smallest decrease in cross cultural communication anxiety (.77) and program authors showed the greatest decrease in this variable (2.35), with program takers falling between these two (1.2). Given that cross-cultural communication is likely a new topic, especially in relation to the other programs, it is possible that none of the students had much prior exposure. Thus, there may be little information stored in long-term memory to which students can incorporate new bits of information to form larger chunks. With increased exposure, we would expect this mechanism to begin operating and for the observed mean pattern to remain. This also points to a potential limitation of the CK system, namely, some material may need to be presented in longer or shorter sessions with more or less repetition and cross application depending on the nature of the material and the individual learner.

Finally, the results related to parent-child communication showed some awkward patterns (and they were not statistically significant). This, along with the job interview results, may suggest that certain topics are not as productively taught in the present format. In the case of parent-child communication, it may be that some individuals were raised and continue to communicate in single- or split-parent households; even those whose parents are still married may experience more or less productive talk in this context. In the case of some students it might be irrelevant to discuss strategies in terms of parents or of specific recommendations related to one or the other parent. Likewise, when responding to questionnaire items individuals from "non-traditional" family structures may interpret items differently. For instance, for those with step parents to whom should the student refer when answering about conflict?

For the job interview results, it might be that students, most of whom were in their junior year, were not particularly motivated to engage with material so seemingly distant. Moreover, as with the intercultural communication material, students taking the job interview program may have had little prior knowledge from which to build large schema needed to fully become competent in this area. Alternatively, the material presented in the job interview program may have been at odds with previously learned tidbits about the job interview process. Investigation of, and comparison with, other material may be warranted with this and similar skills. It is possible that the CK system could also be used to integrate relevant opposing opinions and suggestions; however, the format of such a protocol would differ in substantial ways to that presented.

Overall, the student-authorship integration addressed goals similar to traditional integration (e.g., break down complex topics into small, manageable bits of information), but also dealt with the confines of a common service course. Theory and practice are inherently intertwined but semester time constraints often restrict serious focus on both. Incorporating CK as the skills-based component and using the online system as a group project allowed for the integration of theory, scholarly research pertinent to four areas of social skill, and direct hands-on application. The project was not without flaws, however. Limiting programs meant teaching social skills that have accumulated vast amounts of research to 15 keys. This poses problems of comprehensiveness and accuracy. It also limits repetition which can enhance code building and cross application which can help to build needed stores in long-term memory. Similarly, the programs contained material only as good as its authors. The potential downfalls of teaching either inappropriate or controversial information in a format meant to build mental stores that rest in a relatively stable long-term memory structure should not be overlooked and is one area in need of added attention if this integration is used in the future. Finally, multiple measures of similar constructs

were used thus necessitating alpha correction for t-tests and multivariate statistics for the pre-post design. Thus, appropriate statistical tests were not run in many instances and assumptions related to other tests were certainly violated. Thus, results should be replicated with larger samples in future research. Nevertheless, a second application was presented and seems to aid in achieving particular pedagogical goals.

CONCLUSION

Given the prevalence of technology for use in higher education, it is important for instructors to be informed of the ways in which different technology options can aid in or detract from achieving specific pedagogical goals and objectives. Concept Keys offers one way to break down complex topics into smaller, more manageable bits of information. This system is based on how students learn (see Bodie et al., 2006) and is easily integrated into existing curriculum. Two ways in which integration is possible were explored and data was presented that shows how students perceive the system and how learning may be affected. Although future research is needed, CK should be considered a viable alternative to traditional, lecture-based formats. This system provides instructors with an easy way to supplement textbook treatments of material or to offer an additional skills-based component to a more theoretically oriented class. Other integration strategies are also possible. For instance, basic communication course textbooks often do not treat listening in a thorough manner (Janusik & Wolvin, 2002). The CK program on effective listening might be used as a supplement for this lack of focus in such a course as opposed to a supplemental text in a course on listening. The sections below explore some reflections on why CK is likely to produce results seen thus far in our research.

Active Learning and Reflexive Thinking

Oftentimes lecture-based instruction does not allow for students to interact and wrestle with course material. Thus, good teachers structure the classroom in a way that promotes active learning. Active learning is seen most directly in the skit activity from study one and the overall implementation of a student authored e-book in study two. Each of these learning centered approaches allowed students to become involved in the learning experience. The second integration strategy furthermore allowed students to have a voice in the production of course material. In groups, students selected material that they wanted to engage with and present in a skills training program. This may be an even more productive form of active learning than producing skits about mandated material.

An additional way to foster such an environment is by allowing students to self-manage their learning by increasing the responsibility of the learner to think critically about course material (Thomas & Busby, 2003). When teaching listening, Cost, Bishop, and Anderson (1992) "encouraged [students] to explore and understand what words, phrases, or topics get them emotionally involved; what their listening strengths and weaknesses are; and how to recognize what motivates other people to speak and behave as they do" (p. 42). In this way, the student is actively engaged with course material, reflexively thinking about that material, more likely to relate the material to his or her circumstances, and able to incorporate what it means to be socially competent within in his or her unique frame of reference.

CK encourages reflexive thinking on a daily basis through the use of the FFT questions; reflexive thinking was also explored through weekly essay assignments used in study one. Similarly, each week, after all five keys were presented, instructors can have students prompted by the question, "Of the five (5) most recent Keys you have received, which one is most important to your (career, personal, social) success?"[9] After choosing this most important key students are asked, "How will you apply this most important Key in your everyday interaction?" In addition to these built-in personal relevance motivators (i.e., integrating, self-selection and self-determination) the expected success of the CK system is also contingent upon the instructor taking on the role of program leader and providing motivational leadership in the form of high student involvement in program decision-making and assisting in making the learning process enjoyable and individualized (see Powers et al., 2005). This was accomplished in the first study by a written essay assignment and a group skit activity. In the student-authored integration students were actively involved in both creating a unique e-book and taking an online course that was created by classmates. On course evaluations, students in study two wrote most extensively about CK and how "cool" it was to be a published author as an undergraduate. Although not conclusive, this at least suggests students took learning into "their own hands."

Our Continuing Challenge

It is not uncommon to hear students complain about taking courses on presentational speaking, listening, interpersonal communication, and other related topics because "I already know how to speak" or "I listen all the time." However, as one of the authors explains to his students: simply because an individual possesses a car and drives daily does not mean he or she is a skilled driver. Social skills, like driving, can be performed more or less successfully. Social skills, like driving, also have many manifestations—communicating interpersonally is qualitatively different from public speaking which is different from effective group interaction or handling conflict.

The challenge then becomes not only how to engage the students with learning social skills, but also how to change thoroughly ingrained (and oftentimes bad) habits. In other words, the educator's challenge is how to re-teach practices that are ingrained in the student's way of thinking and way of interacting in a social environment. CK approaches this by engaging the student in his or her learning environment via daily e-mails that incorporate elements of explanation and motivation. Given the likelihood of learning incorrect behavioral sequences related to social skills, CK attempts to aid the learning of correct behavioral and cognitive records to be recalled in the correct context in three distinct ways.

First, programs have been designed and future authors are encouraged to include micro-lessons that are repetitive and cross over potential applications. Not only will students attach different meanings to keys but the contexts in which the keys can be applied are inherently different. Thus, "repetition allows the student to build larger chunks of information based on similarities between Keys and allows for extended priming opportunities across contexts" (Bodie et al, 2006, p. 125). This motivation is furthered by the use of FFT questions which virtually force students to attach keys to personal experience. As mentioned above, the lack of such repetition in the form of repetitive keys was a main limitation of the student-authored study. Similarly, in study one learning was somewhat restricted to a three-and-a-half week delivery of material as opposed to the traditional 10 week structure. Even so, incorporating keys into personal experience was one of the three main themes found in study one.

Within the first study, the traditional 50 key sequence utilized the above components (explanation-motivation, repetition, etc.) in a way that was set previously by book authors. However, this same model was utilized when students authored their own e-books. Students were instructed that keys must be brief and clearly communicate the overall purpose for a particular day. It was also explained that the paragraphs constituting the remainder of the micro-lesson should both explain

and motivate proper key usage. This model can be used or other protocol developed to more easily fit instructor goals. For instance, instructors who want to author unique e-books for specific classes can begin to blend current materials with the CK system in order to produce a third type of integration similar to but not isomorphic with the authorship study. The point is that CK offers the hardware and online support some suggest (Bonk, 2001) as the primary obstacle for secondary educators instituting Web-based blended learning.

In sum, the CK system was built to teach social skills that are broad, ubiquitous, and often difficult to teach due to lack of student engagement and prior habits that are brought into the learning environment. Although the above studies do not cover the entire gamut of possibilities, we feel that what has been presented offers those who teach social skills the tools necessary to institute a fun and effective way to blend traditional instructional practices with Web-based learning. CK can be tailored to fit specific pedagogical objectives which is a mark of a useful instructional technology. Moreover, students appear to learn from the program in theoretically driven ways. The need for future research should not halt the extended use of this blended learning approach to social skill development.

FUTURE RESEARCH DIRECTIONS

The rapid rate at which technology is available to instructors presents a number of questions for future research. Questions specifically raised by this study include issues of online learning protocol in general and the CK system in particular. First, more research is needed that helps specify the boundary conditions for e-learning technology. For example, are some learning objectives, although possible to achieve online, better achieved in more traditional or blended classroom environments? If so, why? Is it because the classroom can foster active and peer learning, whereas online systems often stifle such learning potential? Are efforts to enable active learning and peer learning online effective and seen as productive? The answers to questions such as these should be based on sound theory. As previously discussed, the limitations of our research prevent us from making broad generalizations. Our findings do, however, provide a foundation for testing existing and yet-to-be-developed learning systems that are similarly based on theories of learning, memory, and information processing.

The research that has been conducted with the CK system has been small-scale and mainly presented in the form of case studies. Experimental studies that randomly assign participants to engage or not engage with the CK program would be an ideal next step for research to progress. If truly experimental studies are not possible due to the design of the system (designed for use in a classroom setting), research needs to examine the effects of variables that exist on multiple levels within the same study. Building and testing multilevel models that enable the simultaneous inclusion of aggregate, group-level, and individual variables are needed to test such effects. Likewise, research should address the longitudinal effects of empty engines such as CK. Specifically, issues such as the extent to which CK enables students to build large chunks of information that can be recalled from long-term memory with appropriate priming stimuli and the identification of those primes should be addressed. Future researchers will also need to refine measurement devices needed to test such propositions.

A second set of questions addresses whether students learn differently when material is presented online versus offline. Future research in this area should examine the impact of presenting online information in its entirety as opposed to presenting it gradually and sequentially. In addition, given some of the results from study two, we should address whether the CK approach of breaking down complex ideas into small, manageable units of information is a better approach

for all learners and for all subject matter. In other words, will online systems such as CK be able to provide more advanced learners with a meaningful learning experience? What about students who do not possess characteristics of self-motivated and self-managed learners? If not, how will it need to be modified to be the most effective?

Finally, future research should be conducted on potential additions and alterations to the CK learning system that are either currently unavailable or have the potential to evolve as technology itself evolves. For example, as video-conferencing capabilities develop for use in truly distance education contexts wherein teacher and student interactions will approximate the personal atmosphere found in the face-to-face traditional classroom and office environment, will increased or different learning outcomes be enhanced or comparable to the in-classroom or office face-to-face tradition?

Ultimately, the possibilities of research that are generated by the introduction of the CK and similar learning systems are limitless. Not only do we need to modify existing theories within education and learning, but we also need to build sound, novel theories that help explain the phenomena germane to online learning specifically. CK was developed from sound theories of education, and research is needed to support many of the assumptions underlying this approach. Further research and theory from the areas of technology acquisition, teacher immediacy, student-teacher interaction, learning and memory, and information processing, just to name a few, are also likely to prove fruitful for incorporation into and expansion of CK and similar learning systems.

REFERENCES

Bodie, G. D., Powers, W. G., & Fitch-Hauser, M. (2006). Chunking, priming, and active learning: Toward an innovative and blended approach to teaching communication related skills. *Interactive Learning Environments, 14*, 119-136.

Buhrmester, D., Furman, W., Wittenberg, M. T., & Reis, H. T. (1988). Five domains of interpersonal competence in peer relationships. *Journal of Personality and Social Psychology, 55*, 991-1008.

Cohen, J., Cohen, P., West, S. G., & Aiken, L. S. (2003). *Applied multiple regression/correlation analysis for the behavioral sciences* (3rd ed.). Mahwah, NJ: Erlbaum.

Cook, J., & Powers, W. G. (in press). A case study on strengthening workforce training outcomes. *Training and Management Development Methods.*

Cost, D. L., Bishop, M. H., & Anderson, E. S. (1992). Effective listening: Teaching students a critical marketing skill. *Journal of Marketing Education, 14*, 41-45.

Cowan, N., Chen, Z., & Rouder, J. N. (2004). Constant capacity in an immediate serial-recall task: A logical sequel to Miller (1956). *Psychological Science, 15*, 634-640.

Datamonitor. (2004, July 14). *E-learning in education.* Retrieved July 1, 2006, from http://www.datamonitor.com

Dean, P., Stahl, M., Sylwester, D., & Pear, J. (2001). Effectiveness of combined delivery modalities for distance learning and resident learning. *Quarterly Review of Distance Education, 2*, 247-254.

DeLacey, B. J., & Leonard, D. A. (2002). Case study on technology and distance in education at Harvard Business School. *Educational Technology & Society, 5*, 13-28.

Derntl, M., & Motschnig-Pitrik, R. (2005). The role of structure, patterns, and people in blended learning. *Internet and Higher Education, 8*, 111-130.

Gobet, F., & Simon, H. A. (1996). Templates in chess memory: A mechanism for recalling several boards. *Cognitive Psychology, 31*, 1-40.

Gobet, F., & Simon, H. A. (1998). Pattern recognition makes search possible: Comments on Holding (1992). *Psychological Research, 61*, 204-208.

Gudykunst, W. B. (1998). *Bridging differences: Effective intergroup communication* (3rd ed.). Thousand Oaks, CA: Sage.

Janusik, L. A., & Wolvin, A. D. (2002). Listening treatment in the basic communication course text. In D. Sellnow, (Ed.), *Basic Communication Course Annual* (Vol. 14, pp. 164-210). Boston: American Press.

Kearney, P., Plax, T. G., & Wendt-Wasco, N. J. (1985). Teacher immediacy for affective learning in divergent college courses. *Communication Quarterly, 33*, 61-74.

Leigh, W. A., Lee, D. H., & Lindquist, M. A. (1999). *Soft skills training: An annotated guide to selected programs.* Washington, DC: Joint Center for Political and Economic Studies.

MacGeorge, E. L., Homan, S. R., Dunning, J. B., Elmore, D., Bodie, G. D., Evans, E., et al. (in press). Student evaluation of audience response technology: Influences of aptitude, learning, and learning conceptualizations. *Journal of Computing in Higher Education.*

McCroskey, J. C. (1970). Measures of communication-bound anxiety. *Speech Monographs, 37*, 269-277.

Miller, G. A. (1956). The magical number seven, plus or minus two: Some limits on our capacity for processing information. *The Psychological Review, 63*(2), 81-97.

Moore, M. G. (2005). Editorial: Blended learning. *The American Journal of Distance Education, 19*, 129-132.

Neuliep, J. W. (2002). Assessing the reliability and validity of the generalized ethnocentrism scale. *Journal of Intercultural Communication Research, 31,* 201-215.

Neuliep, J. W., & McCroskey, J. C. (1997a). The development of a U.S. and generalized ethnocentrism scale. *Communication Research Reports, 14,* 385-398.

Neuliep, J. W., & McCroskey, J. C. (1997b). The development of intercultural and interethnic communication apprehension scales. *Communication Research Reports, 14,* 385-398.

Powers, W. G., Bodie, G. D., & Fitch-Hauser, M. (2005). Improving training outcomes: An innovative approach. *International Journal of Applied Training and Development, 1.* Retrieved April 1 from http://www.managementjournals.com/journals/training/index.php

Powers, W. G., Bodie, G. D., & Fitch-Hauser, M. (2006, April). *Initial testing of an online learning system in an extracurricular context.* Paper presented at the annual convention of the Southern States Communication Association, Dallas/Fort-Worth, TX.

Rainbow, S. W., & Sadler-Smith, E. (2003). Attitudes to computer-assisted learning amongst business and management students. *British Journal of Educational Technology, 34,* 615-624.

Rubin, R. B., Plamgreen, P., & Sypher, H. (1994). *Communication research measures.* New York: Guilford.

Sellnow, D. D., Child, J. T., & Ahlfeldt, S. L. (2005). Textbook technology supplements: What are they good for? *Communication Education, 54,* 243-253.

Thomas, S., & Busby, S. (2003). Do industry collaborative projects enhance students' learning? *Education & Training, 45,* 226-235.

Witt, P. L., & Schrodt, P. (2006). The influence of instructional technology use and teacher immediacy on student affect for teacher and course. *Communication Reports, 19,* 1-15.

ENDNOTES

[1] The authors would like to thank Dr. Steven Wilson and Dr. John Greene for their insights and help with various stages of the project reported in study two of this chapter. All correspondence regarding this chapter should be directed to the first author. Address: Department of Communication, Purdue University, 100 N. University Ave., Beering Hall 2114, West Lafayette, IN 47907-2098; Phone: 765-494-3429 E-mail: gbodie@purdue.edu.

[2] A space is created for this student that stores information relevant to programs in which he or she is enrolled, the number of keys completed and the number yet to be completed; answers to FFT questions, and the amount of time spent on each key. Other options available on the system include weekly retention quizzes and a final certification exam; all of this information is likewise stored in the student's individual database. Teachers or others in supervisory roles also have access to this information through the use of an administrative login. Readers are encouraged to visit www.conceptkeys.com, explore the options, and sign up for a trial program.

[3] Syllabi and other instructional material for either application will be made available upon request.

[4] This is a common practice when using the traditional CK system but is only one of several options included in the Student Learning Instructor's Manual (see also Table 2).

5   Technical difficulties (the beta version of the CK template software) and time constraints imposed by the semester format made Monday through Friday delivery impossible to implement. Participation indices obtained by the CK system indicated that this alternative delivery was not a problem for the majority of students. At most, students skipped one day, usually on the weekend, and completed two keys in one day in order to catch up.

6   Given the low reliability post-test, the measure of cross cultural uncertainty was excluded from further analyses.

7   Since all data are not independent, a main assumption of ANOVA has been violated. In addition, equal sample sizes were not achieved. Similarly, in most cases multiple dependent variables were used to measure pre-post differences. Thus, MANOVA and MANCOVA are arguably the more appropriate techniques (small sample sizes precluded a full multivariate form to be utilized). Thus, all results should be tempered by these limitations. However, given the primary goal of the project was for students to become "communication trainers" within an interpersonal communication course, this limitation was disregarded and considered less important than the pedagogical objective. Thus, the analyses presented show preliminary evidence of the success of this project based on previously validated measures of the constructs in which students attempted to train their classmates.

8   Although only one of the DVs showed a significant difference between pre-test scores based on group membership in a series of oneway ANOVAs (data not presented but available from first author upon request), the lack of power to detect even large effect sizes seemed to warrant controlling for these pre-intervention assessments. Nevertheless, a series of 3 X 2 mixed model ANOVAs were also run with repeated measures on the last factor (pre-test, post-test scores). The between-subjects factor was always group membership (author, taker, control). The results from these analyses produced results comparable to the oneway analyses and are not reported but are available from the first author upon request.

Chapter VII
Establishing Social Presence for Online Collaborative Learning:
STEP and Practices

Harrison Hao Yang
State University of New York at Oswego, USA

ABSTRACT

Establishing social presence in a text-based environment can be a challenge to teachers. This chapter discusses the main issues, controversies, and problems of social presence; provides conceptual frameworks of teacher's role, and teaching presence on computer mediated communication (CMC); and presents a sound practical approach incorporating teaching presence and social presence in a graduate asynchronous online course.

CHAPTER OBJECTIVES

The readers will be able to:

- Understand what is meant by social presence and distinguish it from related perspectives (such as "filtered-cues" and "be cultured" arguments)
- Identify and describe teacher's role and teaching presence in computer mediated communication

- Enhance social presence in a text-based asynchronous course based on categories and indicators of teaching presence

INTRODUCTION

Asynchronous text-based learning has been recognized more commonly than the synchronous face-to-face learning (Jonassen, 2000), which consists of two noteworthy advantages: first, it offers "anytime, anywhere" accessibility which makes it more convenient and flexible; second, "it allows students to reflect upon the materials and their responses before responding, unlike traditional classrooms" (Richardson & Swan, 2003, p. 69). While asynchronous distance learning programs are expanding, and participants are mounting, the question of how best to foster community among learners, as well as instructors who are physically and timely separated from each other has been raised (Palloff & Pratt, 1999; Rovai, 2002). Such separation may increase social insecurities, communication anxieties, and feelings of disconnectedness (Jonassen, 2000; Kerka, 1996); as a result, "the student becomes autonomous and isolated, procrastinates, and eventually drops out" (Sherry, 1996).

Previous studies suggested that establishing social presence, which related to open communication, emotional expression, and group cohesion, was essential for an asynchronous text-based communication (Anderson, Rourke, Garrison, & Archer, 2001; Garrison, Anderson, & Archer, 2000; Rourke, Garrison, & Archer, 2000; Rourke, Anderson, Garrison, & Archer, 2001; Rovai, 2002). As Garrison and Anderson (2003) noted, "it is inconceivable to think that one could create a community without some degree of social presence" (p. 49). This chapter reviews issues, controversies, and problems of social presence as gleaned from the literature. It then introduces the teacher's role and teaching presence for the involvement of online asynchronous learning in supporting social presence. It also provides a practical approach which systematically integrates categories and indicators of teaching presence into the text-based asynchronous course development with the preliminary results of effectiveness on social presence.

ISSUES, CONTROVERSIES, PROBLEMS OF SOCIAL PRESENCE

The genealogy of the construct social presence was rooted from the Mehrabian's (1969) concept of *immediacy*, which he defined as "those communication behaviors that enhance closeness to and nonverbal interaction with another" (p. 203). He claimed that nonverbal cues such as facial expressions, body movements, and eye contact would lead to more intense, affective, and immediate interactions (Rourke, Anderson, Garrison, & Archer, 2001).

For some time, communication theorists have attempted to apply Mehrabian's (1969) work in the field of communication technology. The term *social presence* was first introduced by Short, Williams, and Christie (1976), which had been defined as the "degree of salience of the other in a mediated communication and the consequent salience of their interpersonal interactions" (p. 65). They argued that social presence varied between different media; it affected the nature of the interaction, and it interacted with the purpose of the interaction to influence the medium chosen by a user who intends to communicate. The inability of these media to transmit nonverbal cues would have a negative effect on interpersonal communication. Similarly, other studies indicated that the critical difference between face-to-face and mediated communications was that many forms of media lacked social context cues, and the absence of such cues led to uninhibited communication such as "flaming" (i.e., hostile and intense language); greater self-absorption versus other-orientation; and the resistance to defer speaking turns to higher-status participants (Kiesler, Siegel, & McGuire, 1984; Sproull & Kiesler, 1986). Furthermore, based on the bandwidth or the number of cue systems available within various media, researchers have focused on "media richness." Face-to-face interaction is considered as the "richest" form of communication, for its capacity and availability of immediate feedback, the number of cues and channels utilized, nonverbal (facial and oral) cues, personalization, and language variety. Online learning interaction, which features mainly asynchronous text-based computer mediated communication (CMC), on the other hand, is considered to be a very "lean" form of communication and judged "low" on social presence, because nonverbal cues are not present (Daft & Lengel, 1984, 1986; Daft, Lengel, & Trevino, 1987; Lindlif & Shatzer, 1998; Rovai, 2002; Swinth & Blascovich, 2002; Trevino, Daft, & Lengel, 1990; Trevino, Lengel, & Daft, 1987;).

However, recent studies of social presence challenge the above "cues-filtered-out" or "filtered-cues" arguments, which view social presence largely as an attribute of the communication media. Some studies have not found that technology-mediated communications are less personal or socioemotional than face-to-face interactions (Tammelin, 1998; Walther, 1992, 1997), while other studies have even found that online users perceive CMC as a high social presence medium (Gunawardena, 1995; Gunawardena & Zittle, 1997; Perse et al., 1992;). Gunawardena and Zittle (1997) argued that it was important to examine whether the actual characteristics of the media were the causal determinants of communication differences or whether users' perceptions of media altered their behavior. Garrison and Anderson (2003) defined social presence as "the ability of participants in a community of inquiry to project themselves socially and emotionally, as real people (i.e., their full personality), through the medium of communication being used" (pp. 28-29). Related studies have suggested that social presence could "be cultured" among teleconference users (Gunawardena, 1995; Gunawardena & Zittle, 1997; Johansen, Vallee, & Spangler, 1988; Walther, 1992). User's perception of social presence in a mediated situation can depend on the effort made by the instructors/moderators. Therefore, "regardless of the mediated nature of the communication, it is the teacher's responsibility to precipitate and facilitate learning that has purpose and is focused on essential concepts and worthwhile goals" (Anderson, Rourke, Garrison, & Archer, 2001, p. 3).

TEACHER'S ROLE AND TEACHING PRESENCE ON ONLINE LEARNING

Although creating a warm, open, and trusting learning community can promote students' levels of social presence and allow them an opportunity for greater participation, it is extraordinarily difficult for educators to fulfill this responsibility in a mainly text-based and largely asynchronous online environment. When students are set free in a nonverbal communication environment within a 24-hour availability, students need to have the experience and knowledge base to sift the discussion for misinformation, and teachers need to have the skills and strategies to facilitate students for certain learning objectives. In his report, Karmers (1993) well described this new challenge as following:

...expecting that my students would follow me in discussion, I found instead that they much preferred to converse with each other, forcing me to the sidelines. I could not imagine that happening in my conventional classroom. No student had ever tried to take over the discussion in all my 20 years of teaching, even during my progressive period, when I arranged the desks in a circle. I had always set the direction, and the students had always done more or less what I wanted. (p. 113)

There is a growing number of research studies on the roles and responsibilities of online teachers in course-related computer conferences (Berge, 1995; Collins & Berge, 1997; Davie, 1989; Eastmond, 1992; Feenberg, 1989; Kerr, 1986; Paulsen, 1995, Salmon, 2000). Most of these studies suggest that in order to develop a socially responsive discourse that models a combination of social encouragement with pedagogical discussion, the teacher should play the role as more of a facilitator or moderator than the main source of information (Gunawardena & Zittle, 1997; Stacey, 2002). In addition, Mason (1991) and Paulsen (1995) divided the teacher's role as a moderator and facilitator into three major responsibilities: organizational, social, and intellectual. Berge (1995) also identified four major functions of the online facilitator/moderator as indicated in Table 1.

Garrison et al. (2000) developed the Community of Inquiry model and used it to illustrate the multifaceted components of teaching and learning in a text-based environment. This model proposes that learning occurs through the interaction of three core elements: cognitive presence, social presence, and teaching presence. They defined cognitive presence as "the extent to which the participants in any particular configuration of a community of inquiry are able to construct meaning through sustained communication" (p. 89). Social presence element was defined as the ability of participants to project themselves socially and emotionally in a community of inquiry. Teaching presence is the binding element in creating a community of inquiry for educational purposes. Garrison et al. claimed that "appropriate cognitive and

Table 1. The functions of the online instructor/facilitator (Source: Berge, 1995)

Pedagogical
- ✓ Have clear objectives
- ✓ Maintain as much flexibility as you can
- ✓ Encourage participation
- ✓ Be objective
- ✓ Don't expect too much
- ✓ Don't rely on offline materials
- ✓ Promote private conversations as well as in the computer conferencing (CC)
- ✓ Find unifying threads
- ✓ Use simple assignments
- ✓ Make the materials relevant
- ✓ Required contributions
- ✓ Present conflicting opinions
- ✓ Invite visiting experts
- ✓ Don't lecture
- ✓ Request responses

Managerial
- ✓ Informality
- ✓ Distribute a list of participants
- ✓ Be responsive
- ✓ Providing for administrative responsibilities
- ✓ Be patient
- ✓ Request comments on meta communications
- ✓ Synchronize and resynchronize
- ✓ Be mindful of the proportion of instructor contribution to the conference
- ✓ Procedural leadership
- ✓ Use private email for prompting as is appropriate for discussion
- ✓ Be clear
- ✓ Don't overload
- ✓ Change misplaced subject headings
- ✓ Handle tangents appropriately
- ✓ Very participants' amount of contribution
- ✓ Student leaders
- ✓ Preparation time
- ✓ End the sessions
- ✓ Have experienced instructors

Social
- ✓ Be accepting of lurkers
- ✓ Guard against fear in your conference
- ✓ Watch the use of humor or sarcasm
- ✓ Use introductions
- ✓ Facilitate interactivity
- ✓ Praise and model the discussant behavior you seek
- ✓ Don't ignore bad discussant behavior
- ✓ Expect that flames may occur

Technical
- ✓ Use technical support
- ✓ Provide feedback
- ✓ Develop a study guide
- ✓ Provide time to learn
- ✓ New methods of indicating feedback
- ✓ Promote peer learning
- ✓ Avoid lecturing
- ✓ Giving direction

Table 2. Categories and indicators of teaching presence (Source: Anderson et al., 2001)

Category	Indicator	Example
Design and organization	Setting curriculum	"This week we will be discussing…"
	Designing methods	"I am going to divide you into groups, and you will debate…"
	Establishing time parameters	"Please post a message by Friday…"
	Utilizing medium effectively	"Try to address issues that others have raised when you post"
	Establishing netiquette	"Keep your messages short"
Facilitating Discourse	Identifying areas of agreement/ disagreement	"Joe, Mary has provided a compelling counter-example to your hypothesis. Would you care to respond?"
	Seeking to reach consensus/understanding	"I think Joe and Mary are saying essentially the same thing"
	Encouraging, acknowledging, or reinforcing student contributions	"Thank you for your insightful comments"
	Setting climate for learning	"Don't feel self-conscious about 'thinking out loud' on the forum. This is a place to try out ideas after all"
	Drawing in participants, prompting discussion	"Any thoughts on this issue?" "Anyone care to comment?"
	Assess the efficacy of the process	"I think we're getting a little off track here"
Direct instruction	Present content/questions	"Bates says…what do you think"
	Focuses the discussion on specific issues	"I think that's a dead end. I would ask you to consider…"
	Summarize the discussion	"The original question was …Joe said… Mary said…we concluded that…We still haven't addressed…"
	Confirm understanding through assessment and explanatory feedback	"You're close, but you didn't account for…this is important because…"
	Diagnose misconceptions	"Remember, Bates is speaking from an administrative perspective, so be careful when you say…"
	Inject knowledge from diverse sources, e.g., textbook, articles, internet, personal experiences (includes pointers to resources)	"I was at a conference with Bates once, and he said…You can find the proceedings from the conference at http://www…"
	Responding to technical concerns	"If you want to include a hyperlink in your message, you have to…"

social presence, and ultimately, the establishment of a critical community of inquiry, is dependent upon the presence of a teacher" (p. 96).

In one of their follow-up studies, Anderson et al. (2001) defined teaching presence as "the design, facilitation, and direction of cognitive and social processes for purpose of realizing personally meaningful and educationally worthwhile learning outcomes" (p. 5). They provided indicators and examples for each of the three categories of teaching presence as shown in Table 2.

INTEGRATING TEACHING PRESENCE TO THE ASYNCHRONOUS COURSE

To promote an active learning community and enhance social presence in a text-based and asynchronous distance learning course, Yang and Maina (2004) applied Anderson et al.'s (2001) work of teaching presence by developing a systematic approach called "STEP." Figure 1 illustrates that STEP is essentially a cyclic process and the four components of STEP are interrelated

The Components of STEP Approach

The S in STEP stands for the *scaffolding* before starting new learning modules. The basic idea of scaffolding is "to gradually ease students into what are likely to be challenging tasks by creating a supportive structure to guide their work. In other words, as the educators, we would initially do some of the work for students" (Grabe & Grabe, 1998, p. 217). Students, especially those who participate in the course either with little experience in the textual and asynchronous distance learning environment, need to develop skills and understandings on this type of learning which has multiple threads with several discussions and interactions progressing simultaneously. To reduce the community anxiety and social distance among students, the following are strategies and actions that the instructor may take:

- Constructing an open discussion on the bulletin board by sharing his or her experience on distance learning and background of computer technology, and inviting students to participate in this activity. Since this activity is hosted at the beginning of

Figure 1. The STEP approach

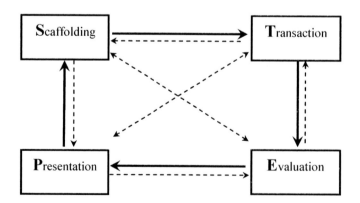

learning content, it helps in establishing a non-threatening atmosphere.

- On each learning module or topic, starting with presenting the related concepts/ knowledge and particular technological skills that students need to prepare their undertaking actual assignments/projects; providing resources links and examples; and encouraging students to reflect and discuss the possibilities for extending the ideas and skills into real world situations.
- Overall, organizing the learning sequences with each module, topic and assignment/ project building on the previous one(s) and making the level of difficulty a little higher than the one before.

Specifically, this scaffolding component encloses categories (indicators) of teaching presence which Anderson et al,(2001) defined, such as: design and organization (setting curriculum; designing methods), facilitating discourse (setting climate for learning; drawing in participants, prompting discussion), and direct instruction (presenting content/questions; injecting knowledge from diverse sources).

The T in STEP stands for the *transaction* during the learning process. An online asynchronous course brings some new challenges in learning process: on one hand, students have to deal with the lack of personal touches, non-verbal cues, and delayed responses; on the other hand, the instructor may carry off the real discussions among students if he or she merely acts as "sage on the stage" (Yang & Maina, 2004). Moore (1972) found that distance education was characterized by the amount of control exercised by the learner (dialogue) and the amount of control exercised by the instructor (structure). "Additional structure tends to increase distance (decreases community), and more dialogue tends to decrease distance (increase community)" (Rovai, 2002, p. 44). To meet these challenges and to keep students actively participating in learning activities and to reduce feelings of social isolation, the following are strategies and actions that the instructor may take:

- Using "private folder" or individual email serving as the "online office hours" to promptly respond to students' questions, and to privately acknowledge those students whose ideas have been posted without many or any response and feedback.
- Meanwhile, when common questions/concerns appear, interacting with students by posting answers and thoughts on the bulletin board or discussion area.

Below is an example of a message from the instructor used to encourage students on establishing

Figure 2. A message from the instructor

I truly believe that we have a great start on our class. So far, I enjoy what we are doing, and learn a lot from all of you. Even though I don't discuss quite often among our discussion (and plan to do this later on), I read and think your comments everyday. The reason I would use "On-line office hours" (through your private folder) to touch with you individually instead of jumping into discussion often -- I don't want to set any limitations or directions for our reactions. So, for those already started to discuss the issues of this module, let's keep up our good work:) for those somehow still "very quiet" there, please start to say something -- I know it's a little bit strange by using keyboard to communicate among us, but please feel free to do so. What do we lose anyway? We are all in the same boat now ☺

a socially responsive discourse with the course discussion in the early process of the course (see Figure 2).

Specifically, this transaction component encloses categories (indicators) of teaching presence which Anderson et al.,(2001) defined, such as: design and organization (establishing time parameters; utilizing medium effectively), facilitating discourse (seeking to reach consensus/understanding; encouraging, acknowledging, or reinforcing student contributions), and direct instruction (focusing the discussion on specific issues; diagnosing misconception; responding to technical concerns).

The E in STEP stands for the *evaluation* during and after each learning module. Periodically evaluating students' performances serves two ends: to remind inactive students to contribute ideas and/or react to others' contributions; and to reinforce interactive students continuing their journey on their knowledge and skills from emergent to mastery (Jonassen, 2000). Previous research on teacher immediacy has found that having a high regard for students' work, actions, or comments can subsequently contribute to affective, behavioral, and cognitive learning (Gorham, 1988; Gorham & Zakahi, 1990). Further, Rourke et al.,(2001) pointed out, "reinforcement is the object that fuels the development and maintenance of interpersonal interaction. Complimenting and acknowledging, and expressing appreciation are ways of communicating reinforcement in a text-based medium." From this perspective, the following are strategies and actions that the instructor may take:

- Privately sending every student a brief evaluation report to comment on the frequency and gravity of her or his postings.
- Meanwhile, publicly encouraging students to periodically summarize the discussion to avoid it becoming too fragmented or drifting off the theme.

Specifically, this evaluation component encloses categories (indicators) of teaching presence which Anderson et al.,(2001) defined, such as: design and organization (establishing time parameters; utilizing medium effectively), facilitating discourse (identifying areas of agreement/disagreement; encouraging, acknowledging, or reinforcing student contributions; assessing the efficacy of the process), and direct instruction (summarizing the discussion; confirming understanding through assessment and explanatory feedback).

The P in STEP stands for the *presentation* on outcomes. There are a variety ways to launch active and reflective learning. Providing opportunities for students to present their ideas, methods, and products is one of the most powerful ways. This is essential not only at the conclusion of a project, but also when the project grows. Presenting works/projects is an authentic activity that provides an enormous motivation for students (Grabe & Grabe, 1998; Wheatley, 1991; Yang, 2001). "Presentations, coupled with authentic outcomes and fairly explicit criteria for what counts as a good plan, can provide a strong incentive to prepare and revise" (Barron, Schwartz, Vye, et al.,1998, p. 286). Due to the nature of asynchronous learning, instead of the face-to-face synchronous presentation, the instructor may consider:

- Opening or providing the access to students' projects on the online course periodically.
- Encouraging students to share and compare their projects with projects generated by their classmates, which might inspire them to revise their project and communicate with peers further more.

Specifically, this presentation component encloses categories (indicators) of teaching presence which Anderson et al.,(2001) defined, such as: design and organization (establishing time parameter; establishing netiquette), facilitating discourse (encouraging, acknowledging, or reinforcing student contributions, drawing in participants and prompting discussion), and direct instruction (focusing the discussion on specific issues, injecting knowledge from diverse sources).

Case Study: The STEP on Social Presence

To assess the effectiveness of the STEP approach on social presence for online asynchronous learning, Yang (2006) collected and examined the final self-reports of students from spring, 2006 (n = 23) and summer, 2006 (n = 25), which were based on their own experiences in a graduate online asynchronous course *Multimedia and Internet for Educators* at the State University of New York at Oswego. In order to preserve anonymity and specification, an anonymous and voluntary student Social Presence Questionnaire (Lin, 2004) was also adapted and undertaken at the end of spring and summer, 2006, respectively. This questionnaire consisted of 12 items on which respondents reported their views of: (1) perception of the assistance of group activity to learning; (2) social comfort of expressing and sensing affect; and (3) social navigation. A seven-point scale was provided for each item in the questionnaire, with 7 representing a strong agreement and 1 representing a strong disagreement. Among the returned questionnaires, 17 out of 23 students' responses (74%) from spring 2006, and 19 out of 25 students' responses (76%) from summer 2006 were completed and usable.

Findings from students' final written reports and questionnaire reflected very positive student

Table 3. Respondents' perception of social presence

Factor	Spring 06 (N = 17)		Summer 06 (N = 19)	
	M	SD	M	SD
Perception of the assistance of group activity to learning				
I felt like I was a member of this class during the course activities	6.47	0.72	6.21	1.47
I felt comfortable participating in online group activities	6.41	1.06	6.53	1.43
I felt I came to know classmates via online group activities	5.29	1.26	5.47	1.22
The online group activities helped me accomplish the assignment with higher quality than if I were working alone	5.59	1.91	5.47	1.84
The online group activities helped me learn more efficiently than if I were working alone	5.59	1.84	5.58	1.68
Social comfort of expressing and sensing affect				
I felt comfortable expressing my feelings during the course activities	6.53	0.87	6.32	1.57
I felt comfortable expressing my humor (or if I could express any)	6.00	0.87	6.37	1.50
I was able to appreciate the humor of classmates	6.47	0.94	6.32	1.38
I was able to form distinct individual impressions of some classmates	5.71	1.86	6.05	1.08
Social navigation				
Actions by other classmates usually influenced me to do further work	5.71	1.49	6.16	1.17
Knowing that other classmates were aware of my work influenced the frequency and/or quality of my work	5.82	1.81	5.84	1.71
Knowing what other classmates did helped me know what to do	6.00	1.66	6.21	1.18

reactions in the effectiveness of utilizing the STEP approach to facilitate the online asynchronous course. Student responses related to use of the STEP approach for asynchronous online collaborative learning were extremely encouraging on the aspects of overall participation and satisfaction, perception of the assistance of group activity to learning, social comfort of expressing and sensing affect, and social navigation (see Table 3).

CONCLUSION

As Anderson et al. (2001) addressed, "teaching in online courses is an extremely complex and challenging function" (p. 3). "Filtered-cues" theorists consider the form of asynchronous text-based computer mediated communication (CMC) "lean" on interaction and "low" on social presence due to the lack of nonverbal cues.

This study yields findings of previous research related to teacher's role and teaching presence in the online learning environment and indicates the systematic approach with a variety of strategies should be designed and implemented for an asynchronous online course. In such a course, instructor's role should change from traditional face-to-face "lecturer" to "facilitator"/"moderator;" he or she should design and manage learning sequences, provide subject matter expertise, establish a positive learning environment, and facilitate active learning.

The findings of this study indicates that in order to establish social presence and active learning community for asynchronous text-based courses, the systematic approach with a variety of strategies should be designed and implemented. The effectiveness of STEP approach, which combines: the *scaffolding* before starting new learning topics; the *transaction* during the learning process; the *evaluation* during and after each learning topic; and *presentation* of outcomes online, has been approved in this study. Through this approach, students have perceived particularly positive on

the assistance of group activity to learning; social comfort of expressing and sensing affect; and social navigation.

It should be noted that much work remains to capture the dynamics that happen within online collaborative learning and social presence. For instance, the STEP approach presented in this study needs to be further examined in terms of generalizing to different courses.

ACKNOWLEDGMENT

The author wish to acknowledge the following for their support and contribution to this chapter: Dr. Sharon Kane, State University of New York at Oswego; Dr. Pamela Michel, State University of New York at Oswego; editors of this book and reviewers of this chapter.

REFERENCES

Anderson, T., Rourke, L, Garrison, D. R., & Archer, W. (2001). Assessing teaching presence in a computer conferencing context. *Journal of Asynchronous Learning Networks, 5*(2), 1-17.

Barron, B. J. S., Schwartz, D. L., Vye, N. J., Moore, A., Petrosino, A., Zech, L., & Bransford, J. D. (1998). Doing with understanding: Lessons from research on problem- and project-based learning. *The Journal of the Learning Sciences, 7*(3-4), 271-311.

Berge, Z. L. (1995). Facilitating computer conferencing: Recommendations from the field. *Educational Technology. 35*(1), 22-30.

Collins, M.P., & Berge, Z.L. (1997, March). *Moderating online electronic discussion groups.* Paper presented at the AERA Annual Conference, Chicago IL.

Davie, L. (1989). Facilitation techniques for the on-line tutor. In R. Mason & A. Kaye (Eds.),

Mindweave: Communication, Computers and Distance Education. Elmsford, New York: Pergamon Press.

Daft, R. L., & Lengel, R. H. (1984). Information richness: A new approach to managerial behavior and organizational design. In B. M. Staw & L. L. Cummings (Eds.), *Research in Organizational Behavior* (Vol. 6, pp. 191-233). Greenwich, CT: JAI Press.

Daft, R. L., & Lengel, R. H. (1986). Organizational information requirements, media richness, and structure design. *Management Science, 32*, 554-571.

Daft, R. L., Lengel, R. H., & Trevino, L. K. (1987). Message equivocality, media selection, and manager performance: Implications for information systems. *MIS Quarterly, 11*, 355-366.

Eastmond, D. V. (1992). Effective facilitation of computer conferencing. *Continuing Higher Education Review, 56*(1/2), 23-34

Feenberg, A. (1989). The written world: On the theory and practice of computer conferencing. In R. Mason and A. Kaye (Eds.), *Mindweave: Communication, computers and distance education.* Elmsford, New York: Pergamon Press.

Garrison, D. R., & Anderson, T. (2003). *E-learning in the 21ˢᵗ Century: A framework for research and practice.* London: Routledge Falmer.

Garrison, D. R., & Archer, W. (2000). *A transactional perspective on teaching and learning: A framework for adult and higher education.* Oxford, UK: Pergamon.

Garrison, D. R., Anderson, T., & Archer, W. (2000). Critical inquiry in a text-based environment: Computer conferencing in higher education. *The Internet and Higher Education, 2*(2-3), 87-105.

Gorham, J. (1988). The relationship between verbal teacher immediacy behaviors and student learning. *Communication Education, 37*, 40-53.

Gorham, J., & Zakahi, W. (1990). A comparison of teacher and student perceptions of immediacy and learning: Monitoring process and product. *Communication Education, 39*, 355-367.

Grabe, M., & Grabe, C. (1998). *Integrating technology for meaningful learning* (2ⁿᵈ ed.). Boston: Houghton Mifflin Company.

Gunawardena, C. N. (1995). Social presence theory and implications for interaction collaborative learning in computer conferences. *International Journal of Educational Telecommunications, 1*(2/3), 147-166.

Gunawardena, C. N., & Zittle, F. J. (1997). Social presence as a predictor of satisfaction within a computer-mediated conferencing environment. *The American Journal of Distance Education, 11*(3), 8-26.

Johansen, R., Vallee, J., & Spangler, K. (1988). Teleconferencing: Electronic group communication. In R. S. Cathcart and L. A. Samovar (Eds.), *Small group communication: A reader* 5ᵗʰ Ed. (pp. 140-154). Menlo Park, CA: Institute for the Future.

Jonassen, D. H. (2000). *Computers as mind tools for schools: Engaging critical thinking* (2nd Ed.). Upper Saddle River, New Jersey: Merrill.

Kerr, E. B. (1986). Electronic leadership: A guide to moderating online conferences. *IEEE Transactions on Professional Communications, 29*(1) 12-18.

Kerka, S. *Distance learning, the Internet, and the World Wide Web.* (ERIC Document Reproduction Service No. ED 395 214, 1996).

Kiesler, S., Siegel, J., & McGuire, T. W. (1984). Social psychological aspects of computer-mediated communication. *American Psychologist, 39*, 1123-1134.

Kremers, M. (1993). Student authority and teacher freedom. In B. Bruce, J. Kreeft Peyton, & T. Batson

(Eds), *Network-based classroom: Promises and realities* (pp 113-123). New York: Cambridge.

Lin, G. Y. (2004). Social presence questionnaire of online collaborative learning: Development and validity. In *Proceedings of the 27th AECT Annual Convention* (pp. 588-591). Bloomington, IN: Association for Educational Communications and Technology.

Lindlif, T. R., & Shatzer, M. J. (1998). Media ethnography in virtual space: Strategies, limits, and possibilities. *Journal of Broadcasting and Electronic Media, 42*(2), 170-189.

Mason, R. (1991). Moderating educational computer conferencing. *DEOSNEWS, 1*(19). Retrieved January 1, 2007, from http://www.ed.psu.edu/acsde/deos/deosnews/deosnews1_19.asp

Mehrabian, A. (1969). Some referents and measures of nonverbal behavior. *Behavior Research Methods and Instrumentation, 1*(6), 205-207.

Moore, M. G. (1972). Learner autonomy: The second dimension of independent learning. *Convergence, 5*(2), 76-88.

Palloff, R. M., & Pratt, K. (1999). *Building learning communities in cyberspace*. San Francisco: Jossey-Bass Publishers.

Paulsen, M. F. (1995). Moderating Educational Computer Conferences. In Z. L. Berge and M. P. Collins (Eds.), *Computer-mediated communication and the online classroom. Vol. 3: Distance learning* (pp. 81-90). Cresskill, NJ: Hampton Press.

Perse, E. I., Burton, P., Kovner, E., Lears, M.E., & Sen, R. J. (1992). Predicting computer-mediated communication in a college class. *Communication Research Reports, 9*(2), 161-170.

Richardson, J. C., & Swan, K. S. (2003). Examining social presence in online courses in relation to students' perceived learning and satisfaction. *Journal of Asynchronous Learning Networks, 7*(1), 68-88.

Rovai, A. A. (2002). A preliminary look at the structural differences of higher education classroom communities in traditional an ALN courses. *Journal of Asynchronous Learning Networks, 6*(1), 41-56.

Rourke, L., Anderson, T., Garrison, D.R., & Archer, W. (2001). Assessing social presence in asynchronous text-based computer conferencing. *Journal of Distance Education, 14*(2). Retrieved September 1, 2006, from http://cade.athabascau.ca/vol14.2/rourke_et_al.html

Salmon, G. (2000). *E-moderating: The key to teaching and learning online*. London: Kogan Page.

Sherry, L. (1996). Issues in distance learning. *International Journal of Educational Telecommunications, 1*(4), 337-365. Retrieved September 11, 2006, from http://carbon.cudenver.edu/~lsherry/pubs/issues.html

Short, J. A., Williams, E., & Christie, B. (1976). *The social psychology of telecommunications*. London: John Wiley & Sons.

Sproull, L., & Kiesler, S. (1986). Reducing social context cues: Electronic mail in organizational communication. *Management Science, 32*, 1492-1513.

Stacey, E. (2002). Quality online participation: establishing social presence. *Research in Distance Education 5: Revised papers from the 5th Research in Distance Education Conference* (pp. 138-153). Deakin University, Geelong.

Swinth, K. R., & Blascovich, J. (2002, October). *Perceiving and responding to others: Human-human and human-computer social interaction in collaborative virtual environments*. Paper presented at the 5th Annual International Workshop PRESENCE 2002, Porto, Portugal. Retrieved January 28, 2007, from http://www.temple.edu/ispr/prev_conferences/proceedings/2002/Final%20papers/Swinth%20&%20Blascovich.pdf

Tammelin, M. (1998). From telepresence to social presence: The role of presence in a network-based learning environment. In S. Tella (Ed.), *Aspects of media education: Strategic imperatives in the information age.* University of Helsinki. Retrieved September 14, 2006, from http://hkkk. fi/%7Etammelin/MEP8.tammelin.html

Trevino, L. K., Daft, R. L., & Lengel, R. H. (1990). Understanding managers' media choices: A symbolic interactionist perspective. In J. Fulk & C. Steinfield (Eds.), *Organizations and communication technology* (pp. 71-94). Newbury Park, CA: Sage.

Trevino, L. K., Lengel, R. H., & Daft, R. L. (1987). Media symbolism, media richness, and media choice in organizations. *Communication Research, 14,* 553-574.

Walther, J. B. (1992). Interpersonal effects in computer-mediated interaction: A relational perspective. *Communication Research, 19,* 52-90.

Walther, J. B. (1997). Group and interpersonal effects in international computer-mediated collaboration. *Human Communication Research, 23,* 342-369.

Wheatley, G. (1991). Constructivist perspectives on science and mathematics learning. *Science Education, 75,* 9-21.

Yang, H. (2001). Mission possible: Project-based learning preparing graduate students for technology. In C. Crawford et al. (Eds.), *Proceedings of Society for Information Technology and Teacher Education International Conference 2001* (pp. 2855-2857). Chesapeake, VA: AACE.

Yang, H. (2006, October). *STEP on social presence for online teaching and learning.* Paper presented at the AECT Annual Convention, Dallas, TX.

Yang, H., & Maina, F. (2004). STEP on developing active learning community for an online course. In C. Crawford et al. (Eds.), *Proceedings of Society for Information Technology and Teacher Education International Conference 2004* (pp. 751-760). Chesapeake, VA: AACE.

Chapter VIII
Transitioning from a Traditional Classroom to the Online Environment:
The SIMPLE Model

Barbara Wilmes
University of Central Arkansas, USA

Stephanie Huffman
University of Central Arkansas, USA

Wendy Rickman
University of Central Arkansas, USA

ABSTRACT

This chapter focuses on how faculty can effectively determine their technological needs as they move from the traditional classroom to an online teaching environment through strategic planning. SIMPLE is a technology planning model, which can be used by faculty and administrators to stair-step themselves through this transition period. SIMPLE is an acronym representing six areas which should be addressed when developing and implementing technology strategies: (1) student/instructor assessment, (2) inventory, (3) measurement, (4) planning, (5) leadership, and (6) evaluation. These six components represent common threads throughout the literature on the subject of technology planning, which were utilized to develop the SIMPLE model, and can be easily utilized to guide faculty.

CHAPTER OBJECTIVES

The reader will be able to:

- Understand the purpose of planning for technology integration within the curriculum
- Identify issues in transitioning to an online teaching environment
- Identify the need for technology planning
- Identify a technology planning model
- Determine their own technological needs in transitioning from a traditional classroom to an online teaching environment

INTRODUCTION

When addressing technology needs, it is imperative to remember that technology integration begins in the classroom with the teacher. Regardless of whether it is a traditional classroom or an online classroom, the need for technology planning is vital to success. If the fears of the faculty have not been alleviated, all the technology available will make no difference (O'Neil, 1995). The basic fears haunting the faculty can often effectively be dealt with by involving them in the technology planning process. Faculty will be more willing to undertake the changes that inevitability face them, if allowed to be jointly engaged in the technology planning process (Baule, 2001).

Today's students are veracious users demanding high-tech equipment, conveniences, and flexibility (Gordon, 2002). It is a given that educational institutions must provide quality hardware and software, yet it is a struggle. Faculty and programs wrestle to adapt the curriculum for the technology literate and to bridge the gap for those students who are in various stages of technological proficiency.

Tackling the enormous task of integrating technology in the classroom involves strategic planning; specifically, developing a technology plan. While many models are available for aid in technology planning as an instructor transitions from a traditional classroom to an online

Figure 1. SIMPLE model

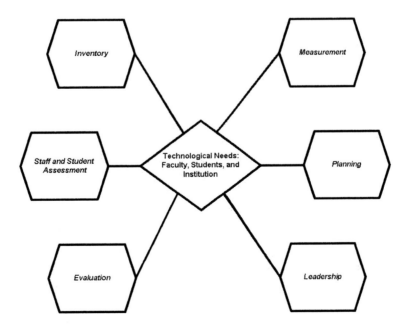

environment, all too often, faculty side step this fundamental building block. Sadly, they become frustrated resulting in finally giving up on teaching in an online format. The SIMPLE Model represents the best ideas and techniques for tackling the overwhelming job of planning for the technological needs of the online environment (see Figure 1).

THEORETICAL FRAMEWORK

SIMPLE is an acronym representing six areas which should be addressed in developing and implementing a technology plan. The six areas are: (1) student/instructor assessment, (2) inventory, (3) measurement, (4) planning, (5) leadership, and (6) evaluation (Huffman & Rickman, 2003). The SIMPLE technology planning model is a valuable tool for faculty transitioning from a traditional classroom to an online environment.

The principal theory of the SIMPLE model was based upon the importance of a thorough, multi-staged, comprehensive assessment and planning system. Research supports both the theory and the use of an on-going comprehensive assessment model for effective planning, teaching, and implementation of successful programs (Ryan & Cooper, 2004). A comprehensive assessment begins with a formative assessment that is used to collect initial data for planning, followed by implementation of the plan. Results are summarized through an evaluation to determine the effectiveness of the plan (Woolfolk, 2001). A pre-test (formative assessment) should include the use of assignments for faculty and students to determine where the participants are at prior to beginning instruction. A well-developed pre-assessment yields helpful information for the everyday use by the coordinator, instructor, and student (Mindes, 2007). Only after the pre-test has been conducted and analyzed, should the teaching begin. Instruction, whether in traditional classrooms or the online environment, is more

effective through careful planning. The formative assessment (pre-test) should yield information for planning what to teach, how to teach, to whom and when to teach various content and application skills (McAfee & Leong, 2002).

The formative assessment for transitioning to an online environment begins with the student and instructor element. It is considered best to extend a deliberate effort to determine the participants' [technological] skills and abilities (Popham, 1999). Likewise, all other elements of the SIMPLE model must receive an appraisal. Without the formative assessment model being applied to the (a) inventory (the hardware and software available), (b) measurement (what is currently being met and what is needed), (c) planning (input from all parties for all aspects of development), (d) leadership available and needed to be acquired (technology coordinator and specialists), and (e) evaluation (at the end of one cycle), a viable plan for transitioning to an online environment can not be established.

Novices to online instruction may miss the important step of a pre-test to determine the knowledge and skills of both the faculty and the students (Woolfolk, 2001). Without this necessary pre-assessment, the move to an online environment may fail due to the inherent weaknesses in each or any of the six elements of the SIMPLE model.

In using a multi-staged assessment theoretical model, after developing and implementing the SIMPLE model plan, on-going assessment data must be maintained, collected, and reviewed. Reflective decisions to modify the plan are made on aggregated information that delineates the performance of the plan. The plan for transitioning to an online environment may then be evaluated to move to an online environment and the results reviewed at any time thereafter.

The SIMPLE model was developed through an extensive review of research and literature on the subject of technology planning and assessment including the transition from a traditional classroom to an online environment spanning 11 years (1990-2001). A list of 81 books and journal articles was generated examining recent research on the topic of technology planning and its various aspects including learning environment transitions (i.e., traditional to online). Books and articles were selected for inclusion based on overall content. Each book and article was read and key topics were delineated. All topics were then grouped based on common themes (e.g., survey and questionnaire). If a theme appeared in 75% of the books and articles, then it was used to create the SIMPLE model. At the end of the process six major themes were generated: staff/student assessment, inventory, measurement, planning, leadership, and evaluation.

THE SIMPLE MODEL

Student/Instructor Assessment

In developing a technology plan, it is essential to first appraise the situation. Two types of assessment should be conducted. The initial assessment should determine the technological skills and abilities of the faculty and students. This assessment should include a hardware/software ability survey. It is vital to determine the skill level of *both* the instructor and the students, because this will directly impact future decisions in the planning process. Low-stakes student assignments can be built into courses early in the course to both assess skills and to develop skills needed to complete the course successfully.

While it is best practice to currently assess technology skills of students enrolled in online courses, it must be recognized that students bring with them a range of technological expertise ranging from minimal to highly proficient. In the future, however, there may be less of a need to assess college-level student skills for those enrolled in online courses because many, if not all high school graduates, may have been using

computer technology as early as preschool or primary school Thus, upon enrollment in online courses, they are familiar and comfortable with technology to embark on the tasks required.

Secondly, an assessment should determine what technology is needed to support an online curriculum, that is, a particular software that is efficient with communication (Voice over IP versus chat or discussion board), headphones with microphones, flat-screen monitors to reduce eye stress, and servers to provide storage for recorded class sessions. This assessment must address both present and future curricular technological deficiencies. From these instruments, a wealth of knowledge can be gleaned. Each assessment establishes a fundamental baseline for aiding instructors responsible for the planning process to delineate the gaps that currently exist (Anderson, 1996).

Inventory

Once the student/instructor assessment is addressed, a complete inventory of existing (in-house) hardware and software should be completed. From this process two questions should be answered:

1. What hardware and software is currently available for faculty and student use?
2. Based on the data collected from both the inventory and the curricular needs assessment, what must be purchased to maximize the success of both the instructors' and the students' transitioning process, as well as to meet their future needs?

Measurement

Measurement focuses on a spectrum of issues, such as: (1) measurement of current in-house media (hardware and software), (2) measurement of current and future curricular needs based on state, regional, and national technology standards,

(3) measurement of available new technologies, (4) measurement of standards (i.e., International Society for Technology in Education (ISTE), National Council for Accreditation of Teacher Education (NCATE), or other accrediting body), and (5) measurement of financial issues. In this instance, measurement is defined as "sizing up" or determining "what areas are being met verses what is actually needed." Applying this definition to each measurement issue sheds light onto pivotal areas where decisions must be made. The measurement element should be utilized in conjunction with both the faculty/student assessment. The inventory element includes the "measurement of current in-house media (hardware and software)." Fundamental measurement questions would target the following:

1. Does the current hardware and software meet the current needs of the Faculty and students? If not, where do the deficiencies lie?

2. What new technologies are available to target current deficiencies?

3. Is this inventory appropriate for the online environment, that is, both dissemination and retrieval of information and resources?

4. Is there a need to establish a minimum hardware and software standard for students? For faculty?

5. Does the current hardware and software meet the standards as outlined in state, regional, and national technology curriculum?

6. What funding and/or resources are available to meet the financial requirements?

Planning

In regard to planning, input from *all* parties (i.e., students, instructors, community members, and administration) involved is valued (O'Neil, 1995). Technology plans are usually developed for a

Figure 2. SIMPLE model technology planning form

SIMPLE Model Technology Planning Form: Instructor		
SIMPLE Planning Elements	*Issue*	*Comments*
Student & Instructor Assessment	Develop Instructor Survey	
	Develop Student Survey	
	Data Analysis: Survey Results	
Inventory Control	Hardware	
	Software	
Measurement	Develop Curricula Planning Instrument	
	State Standards	
	Regional Standards	
	National Standards	
	Data Analysis: Target Deficiencies	
Planning	Course Goals	
	Course Objectives	
	Professional Development	
	Funding Issues	
Leadership	Technology Support Specialist	
	Technology Coordinator	
	Development of Technology Leadership Skills: Classroom Teacher	
Evaluation	Data Analysis: Annual Evaluation	
	Report Deficient Areas	
	Revise Overall Technology Plan	
	Revise Timeline	

three or five year time span with major adjustments taking place at the end of the scheduled time period (Hoffman, 2002). The planning component includes: (1) outlining individual course goals and objectives, (2) development of technology goals and objectives accommodating the curricular agenda for courses (often these are addressed in faculty committees), (3) training for deficient technology areas—for both faculty and students, that is, orientation, one-day training, or on-going training, (4) funding issues—technology budget, grants, and community opportunities, and (5) becoming aware of institutional policy on technology development.

Professional development must target deficiencies outlined in the assessment instrument. Training through one-on-one mentoring with more technologically advanced peers is an inexpensive avenue for improvement of faculty technology skills. By knowing the collective strength of your faculty, departments can develop mentoring programs. What one person is good at, another may be deficient and vise versa; thus forming a natural symbiotic relationship. Professional conferences generally have two or three day workshops prior to general conference proceedings. Many benefit from attending early sessions targeting the technology specific workshops. Another option for professional development is attending a technology specific conference, such as ISTE, Association for Educational Communications and Technology (AECT), Association for Advancement of Computing in Education (AACE), Society for Information Technology and Teacher Education (SITE), and Ed Media World Conference on Educational Multimedia, Hypermedia, and Telecommunications.

There are a variety of different styles of planning forms available. Figure 2 characterizes a typical planning form based on the SIMPLE model.

Leadership

Leadership is the one area that is usually underdeveloped. Technology leadership should be a focal point on each level of the organization. Leadership begins in the classroom with the teacher (Hoffman, 1995). Classroom instructors have a hand on both the pulse of student and curricular needs. With guidance from the classroom, technology utilization blossoms into a fountain of ever flowing information. Problems arise when the instructor is afraid of change. Technology is change. When this particular problem arises, leadership issues weigh more heavily on the central administration. Administrators must see that technology support specialists and a technology coordinator are in place to work on hardware and software problems, as well as help in the creation of faculty technology training (Hoffman, 2002) and instructional design. This assistance is crucial in sustaining success.

Before throwing the faculty to the proverbial "techno wolves", that is, generation next students, adequate training must be supplied. Administrators' tossing money at a one-time, one to three day in-service does not equal adequate training. Dedication by the administration to provide comprehensive training on a yearly basis is the only viable option (Uebbing, 1995). It is essential that training not focus solely on hardware and software skills. The primary focus of any technology training is on the application process—in this case, integration of technology into the curriculum.

1. How can this piece of hardware or software be used to enhance the existing curriculum?
2. What hardware and software is needed to support the curriculum?
3. How will this hardware or software effect student learning?
4. What do I need to know and what do my students need to know in order to use this hardware or software effectively?

If technology integration is not the primary focus, then the technology becomes an add-on to the curriculum instead of an element of the curriculum (Fisher, 1995). This lack of integration oftentimes causes student frustration. Where tech support is limited, faculty must take up the case and lead. More can be accomplished by a handful of dedicated faculty than by an extensive consultant group. Leadership must sometimes come from within, such as the individual faculty member who takes initiative in seeking out help. A source often untapped is from other universities both nearby and within the system.

Once training has been initiated, a network of support must be put in place for the faculty. A fundamental part of the network is hiring a technology coordinator and a technology support specialist (Huffman & Rickman, 2003). The technology coordinator's chief set of functions is to seek out new sources of funding, to head-up the technology planning process, and to cultivate a training program including integration of technology and transition of learning environments. The technology support specialist's principle areas of concern are to maintain the hardware and software and to provide input in the purchasing and functionality of new hardware and software.

Along with placing these two individuals, a technology base must be established within the faculty. Members of the faculty need to be designated as additional technology support. The primary function is to help colleagues on a daily basis with curriculum development in relation to technology utilization. It is not the responsibility of these faculty members to know everything about technology, but simply to provide guidance and support. Over time, faculty fears will dissipate, if and only if they are involved in the technology planning process, are provided with adequate training, and a support staff is in place to help ensure success. Support staff is needed not only during the typical work day, but especially during evening and weekend hours when a number of online courses are often taught.

Administrators must be openly willing to change. Too many administrators maintain the philosophy "do what I say, not what I do." It is essential that each administrator lead by example, by improving their own technology skills and abilities. Technology leadership should also be as far reaching as to include student and community organizations as well as parents. These valuable groups can be a strong advocate, a source of funding and volunteers, and a wealth of technology knowledge and experience (Uebbing, 1995).

Evaluation

Finally, evaluation is the end of one cycle and the beginning of another. Every technology plan should allow for annual evaluation. Annual evaluation allows for minor adjustments in the overall plan (Baule, 2001). The evaluation process should address the goals and objectives of the technology plan, that is, have we met our goals and objectives for this year? Evaluation should also take place at each level of the organization (classroom, technology support staff, and administration). A thorough evaluation of the entire plan should be completed at the end of the planning cycle, thus allowing for any missed opportunities to be addressed during the next cycle.

SIMPLE MODEL SCENARIO

A good example of this process would be the following. A school or college currently offers distance education courses via compressed video, but is looking for a more efficient and less costly medium. It is known from student evaluations that there is much frustration on the students' part about the mode of communication. The dean supports a transition, but wants some data to support the costs of the transition.

Several options, such as course shells that provide secure chats and/or discussion board areas and Voice over IP (VoIP), are suggested.

After researching the skills needed to utilize such software, the faculty and students are assessed of their present skills and familiarity with such programs to determine the knowledge base. It is determined that both communities would be able to pick up the new mode of communication with a small amount of training.

Next, the college inventories the needs of both to determine what hardware, software, and training each group would need to implement this change of course delivery. For faculty, the needs are obvious: training and headphones with microphones as well as the software. The students would need training (usually the first night of class), headphones with microphones, software, and computer access at a certain quality level. The college or school would need to provide the software license, server storage, and training.

Out of the assessment, measurement, and inventory, a plan of implementation would then be derived. Costs, time, and method of transition would be recorded. While a person or committee would develop this document, ultimately the dean or administrative body would determine the initiation of the plan.

Once the plan is initiated, periodic evaluation to determine the success of the transition would be necessary. Periodic evaluation also aids in preventing the initiative from losing its focus, thus wasting time and resources.

INITIAL RESULTS

The SIMPLE model was successfully used from 2001-2005 for technology planning the Middle/Secondary Education and Instructional Technologies Department at the University of Central Arkansas. The results of the use of this model produced smooth transitions from traditional classrooms to online environments between academic years. Faculty had an established process fro requesting assistance and a department tech-

nology committee was established to support the administration and to provide leadership. Many faculty did not realize the model was being used, just that a new process was in place for handling technology planning. Some comments from the faculty follow:

- The overall environment seems more supportive.
- It is wonderful to just have new software and hardware without having to debate the merits.
- Upgrades are made without request.
- One-on-one training is an excellent way to support faculty.

CONCLUSION

Regardless of the approaches chosen to meet the needs of faculty and students; the organization must be dedicated to providing the equipment, software, and training needed to build the technology backbone for the programs it supports. Flexibility and convenience are essential for maintaining student and faculty morale. The best way to address these areas is through strategic planning. Technology is an essential component of every day life in the 21st century. When technology is used appropriately and wisely, instructors, students, and institutions are transformed. Often the technology planning process focuses on acquiring hardware and software. Entire scopes of avenues to benefit all areas of the curriculum and instructional modes are frequently overlooked. The SIMPLE Model provides a structure for developing a successful technology plan, as well as defining links between each component part. SIMPLE helps the planner maintain focus on the major issues, thus meeting the technological needs of faculty and students.

REFERENCES

Anderson, L. S. (1996). *Guidebook for developing an effective instructional technology plan*, (version 2). Mississippi State, MS: Mississippi State University.

Baule, S. M. (1995). Planning for technological support: Help! Why isn't the smiley face smiling? *Technology Connection, 2*(2), 12.

Fisher, F. (1995). *Growing healthy technology: a process for developing effective strategies to integrate education and technology.* Yakima, WA: Educational Technology Support Center 105.

Gordon, D. T. (2000). *The digital classroom: How technology is changing the way we teach and learn.* Boston: Harvard Education Letter.

Hoffman, B. (1995). Integrating technology into schools: Eight ways to promote success. *Technology Connection, 2*(6), 14-15.

Hoffman, R. (2002). Strategic planning lessons learned from a big-business district. *Technology & Learning, 22*(10), 26-38.

Huffman, S. P., & Rickman, W. A. (Spring, 2003). Keep it SIMPLE: Technology planning strategy.

In *Proceedings of Society of Information Technology and Teaching*, Albuquerque, NM: Spring 2003 International Conference.

McAfee, O., & Leong, D. J. (2002). *Assessing and guiding young children's development and learning* (3rd ed.). Boston: Allyn & Bacon.

Mindes, G. (2007). *Assessing young children* (3rd ed.). Upper Saddle River, NJ: Merrill/Prentic Hall.

O'Neil, J. (1995). Teachers and technology: Potential and pitfalls. *Educational Leadership. 53*(2), 10-12.

Popham, W. J. (1999). *Classroom assessment: What teachers need to know* (2nd ed.). Boston: Allyn & Bacon.

Ryan, K., & Cooper, J. M. (2004). *Those who can, teach* (10th ed.). Boston: Houghton Mifflin Company.

Uebbing, S. J. (1995). *Planning for technology.* The Executive Educator, *17*(11), 21-23.

Woolfolk, A. (2001). *Educational psychology* (8th ed.). Needham Heights, MA: Allyn & Bacon.

Chapter IX
A Pragmatic Framework for Promoting Interactivity in E–Learning

Haomin Wang
Dakota State University, USA

ABSTRACT

As e-learning keeps growing, an increasing amount of learning activities can be expected to take place through interactivity between the learner and e-learning materials. To better understand the processes and qualities of interactivity in e-learning, the chapter proposes a framework for analyzing and promoting interactivity from an information processing perspective. The framework consists of the dimensions of accessibility, information attributes of multimedia, learner control versus system control, hypermedia navigation, and cognitive engagement.

CHAPTER OBJECTIVES

The reader will be able to:

- Differentiate interactivity from interaction
- Describe ways to improve accessibility in e-learning
- Discuss effective use of multimedia to their respective advantages
- Discuss the interrelationships between learner control and system control
- Describe methods to facilitate learner navigation in hypermedia
- Describe strategies to foster cognitive engagement

INTRODUCTION

Interactivity is an appealing notion today. However, interpretations of interactivity remain fragmented, inconsistent, and rather messy (Rose, 1999). Interaction between human interlocutors is often mixed with interactivity between learners and learning materials. Many people use the two terms interchangeably. Some researchers feel that interaction between the learner and the learning material should be differentiated from interaction between human interlocutors (Kennedy, 2004; Gilbert & Moore, 1998; Sims, 2000). To distinguish the two constructs, we use the term interactivity to refer to the interaction between the leaner and the e-learning source, as distinguished from interaction between the learner and the instructor, or among learners themselves. Although many of the points discussed in the chapter can apply to interactivity with learning materials in general, the focus of the chapter is on interactivity with e-learning sources. E-learning source is defined as a combination of digital media, computer user interfaces, learning materials, domain knowledge base, and supporting software programs.

Interactivity and interaction can be differentiated in more than one dimension. A key differentiation is in the types of response and feedback. Response and feedback between human interlocutors are usually spontaneous and therefore unlimited in variability, whereas responses and feedback from e-learning sources are generally pre-designed or programmed, thus lacking spontaneity and limited in variability. Another differentiation is in the communication interfaces. Interaction between human interlocutors is mostly verbal and often vocal, enriched by paralinguistic features such as tone of voice, pitch and volume, body language, and facial expressions. On the other hand, interactivity between a learner and the e-learning source is facilitated mostly through digital media and electronic input and output devices.

As e-learning keeps growing, an increasing amount of learning activities can be expected to take place through the direct contact between the learner and the e-learning materials, rather than through direct interaction between the learner and the instructor. However, the interactive learning research community has not been able to provide adequate guidance yet for designers to promote interactivity. Very little research has been undertaken to actually determine what is happening during the interactive process (Sims, 2000). Most of the previous studies on interactivity have focused on user interfaces, learner responses, and system feedback (Schwier & Misanchuk, 1993; Sims, 1997). Few attempts have been made to analyze interactivity from an information processing perspective.

PERSPECTIVES OF INTERACTIVITY

With the advancement of digital technology, interactivity has come to be regarded by many as an innate attribute of instructional software (Rose, 1999) and interactivity is often described in terms of technology capabilities (Gilbert & Moore, 1998; Wagner, 1994, 1997). Computer-generated virtual reality allows the learner to experience simulated real-life situations, explore imaginary possibilities, and test "wild" hypotheses. Database-supported library systems can let the user search for desired information with far more effectiveness and efficiency. The Internet and World Wide Web have made it possible to pool computer resources around the world and build connections between distributed information nodes, allowing people to interact in a truly world-wide scope.

As technology capabilities grow, the issue of system control versus learner control becomes prominent. Constructivism tells us that learning is more likely to be active when the learner has control over the learning activities. Active learning generally leads to a greater depth and breadth of processing, which in turn leads to deeper and more durable learning. Learner control has been examined from various perspectives including: (a) content modality, (b) content coverage, (c) sequence of access and learning paths, (d) online help, and (e) opportunities to assess learning progress (Merrill, 1975; Sims, 1999).

Learner control and system control are inextricably coupled. While allowing some degree of learner control, an instructional source must be capable of certain system control, including taking learner input, assessing learner performances, providing appropriate feedback, adapting to changing needs, and advancing the learner in the right direction. The responses from the learner can provide further input for the instructional system to adjust content provision and learning paths to meet the learner needs. This reciprocal control-and-being-controlled relationship is a key attribute of interactivity.

A FRAMEWORK FOR DESIGNING INTERACTIVITY

A multitude of learning theories and models provide the grounds for designing and promoting interactivity. These theories and models include information processing, distributed cognition, cognitive flexibility, multiple intelligence, and usability. An e-learning source can be designed to interact with the learner at perceptual and conceptual levels. From an information processing perspective, interactivity logistically starts at the perceptual level through media and user interfaces. Different media have different information attributes and require different information processing skills. User-friendly media interfaces can facilitate learner perception and guide learner attention. Once the learner attends to the instructional content, the learner may study further into the topic or move away to search for some more relevant content. After the learner enters an "interactive conversation" with the content, cognitive engagement is a key to continuous productive interactivity.

Interactivity can be seen as a reciprocation of information presentation and information pro-

Figure 1. Dimensions of design to promote interactivity

Ensuring accessibility	• Optimizing the use of multimedia for easy access • Meeting accessibility requirements • Following standards and ensuring compatibility • Enhancing text legibility and readability
Using multimedia to facilitate perception	• Using realistic visuals to provide authentic learning context • Using analogous visuals to facilitate associative learning • Using organizational visuals to illustrate quantitative and spatial relationships • Using video to show action and motion
Supporting learner control and maintaining system control	• Designing intuitive interface controls with minimal interface interferences • Supporting information filtering and providing search capability • Providing both passive and productive input opportunities • Providing progressive learner assessment and adapting to learner needs
Facilitating hypermedia navigation	• Maintaining navigation consistency and content coherence • Providing immediate sensory feedback and dynamic context cues • Providing media options • Supporting alternative learning paths and multiple perspectives
Promoting cognitive engagement	• Activating learner prior knowledge • Stimulating cognitive curiosity • Fostering conceptual association, comparison, and elaboration • Providing cognitive modeling and scaffolding • Encouraging critical and reflective thinking

Figure 2. Layers of interactivity

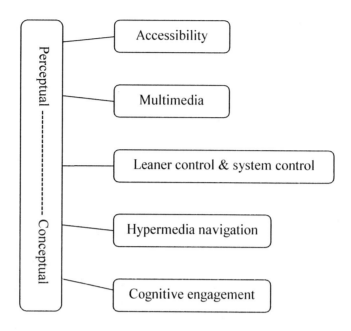

cessing between the learner and the e-learning source. In this chapter, interactivity is defined as a collective construct that includes learner access to learning materials, media information properties, user interface design, learner perception and action opportunities, system feedback in response to learner actions, and system adaptability. This chapter proposes a framework for analyzing and promoting interactivity from an information-processing perspective. The framework consists of the following dimensions: (a) ensuring accessibility, (b) using multimedia to facilitate information processing, (c) supporting learner control and maintaining system control, (d) facilitating learner navigation, and (e) promoting cognitive engagement (see Figure 1).

Interactivity takes place in a continuum of perceptual and conceptual processing (see Figure 2). In the media interface layer, perceptual functions play a primary role. In the cognitive engagement layer, conceptual processing plays a dominant role. Oftentimes, perceptual processing, affective reactions, and conceptual processing are interwoven. For instance, access difficulty can lead to user frustration, which in turn can affect the leaner's cognitive effectiveness.

Ensuring Accessibility

Accessibility is a preliminary condition for interactivity. Poor accessibility often results in little or no interactivity. For learners in the e-learning environment, accessibility is often perceived first of all as access speed: How fast a page or a content module can be retrieved over the Internet and displayed or played back on the learner's computer. Because multimedia files are typically large in file size and bandwidth-intensive to deliver, designers are advised to use multimedia only when multimedia are more effective than text in conveying the information. Compression and streaming technologies can be used to reduce file size to improve accessibility. Long audio and video clips may need to split into segments for easy access.

Accessibility also includes compatibility. Content should be displayed without distortion in different browsers and on different platforms. Compatibility is generally improved by following the Web standards for authoring and delivering content. Free validation tools are available online for compliance with the Web standards of HTML, XHTML, and Cascading Style Sheet (CSS).

In the United States, accessibility is not just a matter of user consideration, but a legal requirement. Section 508 of the Rehabilitation Act mandates that Web content delivered by any federally funded agencies and institutions must be accessible to individuals with disabilities. It requires that user interfaces should be designed in a way that can be navigated with a standard keyboard, and not dependent on pointing devices such as a mouse. Web pages should be designed so that critical information conveyed with color is also available without color. Text should be delivered in a format that can be processed by a screen reader, and text equivalent be provided for every non-text element. For graphics or image map regions, alt texts should be used to provide a description of what the image is about. For audio speeches, captions must be provided for hearing-impaired learners. For video presentations, audio narration should be provided to accommodate vision-impaired learners. When alternative equivalents cannot be provided for multimedia components, a text-only page with equivalent information or functionality should be made available. The content of the text-only page should be updated whenever the primary page changes. When electronic forms are to be submitted online, people should be able to use the keyboard, screen reader, and other assistive technology to access the information of the form and submit their input.

For text perception, there are two basic conditions that can affect accessibility and interactivity: legibility and readability. Legibility is first of all affected by foreground-background contrast. Adequate contrast generally requires dark text against light background or light text against dark background. Dark background should be used with caution on Web pages because the default colors of hyperlinks can be hard to see against a dark page background. Color contrast can also help highlight key points and distinguish certain parts of the page, such as headings, titles, and keywords. Text legibility can be further enhanced by appropriate variations of font type (serif versus sans serif) and size. On computer screens, serif fonts such as Times Roman are generally easier to view in size 12 or larger. If font size is 10 or smaller, sans serif such as Arial, Helvetica or Verdana is generally easier to view than serif fonts.

While legibility is about clarity of symbols, readability can be affected by text length, paragraphing, spacing, and page layout. By default, a Web page is displayed to the full width of a browser window. Some computer screen resolution can be as wide as 1,600 pixels or higher. Horizontal reading of continuous text lines across such width can be very tiring for the eye. A text line across a 1,400 pixel screen can contain over 110 characters or over 25 words. This is far more than the recommended length of text line between 50 and 70 characters, or roughly between 7 and 15 words. Exceedingly long lines of text can make it hard for the reader to correctly pick up the next line of text. A popular method to control text line length is to put text in a table and adjust the width of the table or the table cells. Another method is to use Cascading Style Sheet to allocate page space and control the widths of text blocks.

Readers are generally more tolerant of vertical scrolling than horizontal scrolling. It is therefore quite common to see pages that extend downward and require vertical scrolling. However, designers should be aware that some readers do not like scrolling and may skip any content below the visible part of the page. Many readers also tend to scan Web page content. There are some strategies to accommodate readers' tendency to scan page content: (a) breaking long text into paragraphs, (b) using advance organizers such as headings and topic sentences, and (c) using lists to group related items. Headings can significantly aid search, recall, and retrieval of information (Hartley, 2004), particularly helpful for students who had related prior knowledge (Wilhite, 1989). Readability can be affected by rhetoric and stylistic features as well, including sentence lengths, subordinate clauses, active voice versus passive voice, and the use of transitional words or phrases.

Using Multimedia to Facilitate Information Processing

Legibility and readability are for text presentations and processing. Along with text, graphics and other multimedia are widely used in e-learning materials. Different media have different information attributes and require different information processing skills (Mayer, 2001, Moreno & Mayer, 1999, Salomon, 1979). For example, what we can perceive from a weather forecast on television is not the same as what we get by listening to the same message on radio. Likewise, the perceptions we have when watching a movie based on a novel are usually different from the perceptions we get when reading the book. For an instructional designer, these information attributes can suggest important guidelines in developing course materials and designing learning activities to enhance information presentation, facilitate information processing, and promote interactivity. Kozma (1991) recommends taking advantage of media's cognitively relevant capabilities to complement the learner's cognitive abilities and skills.

For many people, visual rather than verbal representation is probably the most common form of multimedia. One of the basic elements of visual representation is color. Colors can convey information that is difficult or impossible to be coded verbally. Through human evolution, colors have acquired affective and cultural associations with the natural environment and social activities. Color preferences can vary with age, gender, seasons, and geographic locations. When designing color schemes for instructional materials, designers should consider the affective and cultural influences colors might have in relation to instructional context. For example, a warm color scheme may be more appropriate for active, dynamic, intense learning activities, whereas a cool color scheme might better fit more contemplative, reflective, thoughtful learning tasks. However, designers need to be careful in using colors to convey information. Section 508 requires that critical or primary information is not conveyed by color alone for vision-impaired users.

Compared with colors, graphics are generally more concrete and specific in their associations of meanings. Graphic functions can be categorized as: (a) decoration and perceptual enhancement, (b) realistic representation, (c) analogous and metaphoric representation, and (d) organizational representation. Lines, shapes, and space can be used to direct attention and allocate content through alignment, contiguity, orientation, and separation. Realistic pictures are generally used to represent contexts and scenes from real life, enhancing content authenticity and facilitating content mapping. The capability to show a scene as it appeared in real life makes realistic imagery a powerful medium to bring about affective impact. Most of us have experienced viewing a photo that was taken on a trip years ago and recalled many details of the trip. Such recollections usually do not occur as easily with verbal stimuli.

Although realistic depiction can generate a sense of authenticity, excessive realistic details can be a major hindrance in some cases. Irrelevant details can distract attention and obscure information focus. To highlight important points and minimize possible distractions, it is often necessary to be selective in graphic encoding. Selective encoding can make the most relevant parts stand out, eliminate interfering details, and emphasize characteristics. Selective encoding is often implemented in an analogous or metaphoric way for easier perception or more dramatic effects. A common form is cartoon.

Related to analogous images is organizational and spatial representation, often in the form of charts and diagrams to illustrate procedural and quantitative relationships. Application examples include: (a) pie chart to show proportional differences, (b) line chart to show developmental trend, (c) bar chart to show quantitative differences, (d) flowchart to illustrate procedures, (e) 3D chart to show multi-dimensional relationships, and (f) diagram to describe organizational structure.

A major limitation of static imagery is the inability to show action and motion. This is where video plays a role. Video can show continuously changing scenes and effectively demonstrate procedural and context-based events. Furthermore, through such techniques as montage, microscope, fast or slow motion, and zooming, video can be used to re-create and present scenes that we do not normally see in our daily life. For example, zooming can let us view an object or phenomenon from a micro level to a macro level, and vice verse. Video can compress time by taking snapshots, in intervals, of a long process, such as the formation of a hurricane or the growth of a plant. When the movie is played, the viewer can see the complete process in just a few seconds or minutes, whereas the actual process may have taken hours, days, or months. Video can also expand time by slow motion and can be very effective in demonstrating motor skills. Because the viewer of a video can be physically separate from the actual scene, video can be used to capture and represent scenes from remote or restricted areas, or scenes of hazardous or risky events. New video technology also allows us to capture and present scenes from multiple sites and present multiple scenes on the same screen simultaneously, creating a virtual community with multi communication channels.

Another use of video that many instructors find helpful is the capturing of screen actions to demonstrate applications on the computer, particularly procedural operations in rich visual interfaces. There are a number of software packages available for screen capturing. Some of them can record sound as well as capture screen action. The author can add annotation and voice narration afterwards. The author can also add callouts and graphics, and apply effects such as cursor and object highlighting.

Video files are larger in size than any other media and require a considerable amount of storage space and bandwidth to deliver. To make digital video accessible to users over the Internet, certain compression is needed. Because of delivery constraints, video over the Internet generally has to be relatively small in image size. Small text and fine visual details are typically hard to discern. Before making and putting a video online, designers should plan carefully what needs to be placed on the video. Another accessibility designers need to keep in mind is the accommodation for the hearing and vision impaired. For video that has speech, captions are needed to accommodate the hearing impaired. To convey the visual information to the vision impaired, audio description is needed.

If simulation rather than authentic imagery is needed, digital animation is often a better choice than video. For instance, a digital animation can effectively illustrate the water cycle of evaporation, condensation, precipitation, and percolation, or to simulate the traffic flow of a computer network by responding to varying data input and traffic conditions. By incorporating 3D graphics and allowing the user to interact with objects in ways similar to real world conditions, designers can create virtual reality (VR) simulations that can have application values for many professional fields, including aviation, architectural and interior design, business modeling, city planning, medicine, performing arts, and law enforcement. Virtual reality used to be rather costly to develop. Now, with rapid advancements in computing technology, there have been wide-spread endeavors to put VR into instructional use.

Audio and video are often integrated, but audio can be independent of video. Audio is an un-substitutable medium for music and language training, and an alternative medium to accommodate for the vision-impaired. Audio can also have affective appeal. The appeal and effectiveness of speech come largely from the non-verbal expressiveness and colloquialism that are available in speech, but hardly replicable in writing. The non-verbal expressions include variations in pitch, volume, intonation, tone, rhythm, and stress. Such variations can express attitude, feeling, and mood in ways that are difficult to convey or describe in writing.

Listening and reading involve different sensory channels. Audio messages can be combined with text or visuals to facilitate information processing without causing much cognitive overload. To let audio and text complement each other rather than compete against each other, a general recommendation is to avoid echoing text display with audio because simultaneous presentation of audio with redundant text may not be beneficial to information processing. Because sound is ephemeral, follow-up access and information retrieval can be an issue. Typical solutions are to make the recording available for replay or provide scripts as redundant copy of the content so that learners can selectively use these resources in a complementary or supplementary manner. If audio is used to convey critical or primary information, Section 508 of the Rehabilitation Act requires that transcripts be provided to accommodate the hearing impaired.

Another major constraint in listening to a speech is linearity. Because of the linear nature of a speech, many information processing strategies applicable to reading are not applicable to listening. For example, scanning and skimming are effective ways to get main ideas in reading, but not in listening, since the complete text is not available for perusal. Consequently, prediction plays a more important role in listening than in reading. To help the learner better follow a speech, it may be helpful to provide a text introduction with necessary background information to facilitate prediction and comprehension. For extended messages, providing pre-listening questions can guide the learners and help them focus on key points and prevent the problem of "not seeing the forest for the trees." If there are many colloquial expressions or jargons in the speech that may be unfamiliar to the students, designers may need to define or explain these items in the pre-listening activities. For a long recorded speech to be delivered over the Internet, it is generally a good practice to break the long speech into several segments. This would allow the audience to take short breaks between segments, or select particular parts to listen to or replay.

Facilitating Learner Control and Maintaining System Control

Interactivity is influenced by the amount of control available to the learner (Borsook & Higginbotham-Wheat, 1991; Robertson, 1998;). At the perceptual level, learner control can be exercised through customization of user interface including color scheme, font size, font type, page layout, and media options. At the conceptual level, learner control can be exercised through selection of learning paths, content coverage, access to external resources, and search options. Learner control and system control are inextricably coupled. The amount of control available to the learner is generally a function of the amount of control the system maintains. For example, the navigation design of the system basically determines the learning paths the learner can select.

An instructional program usually starts with an anticipation of user needs. The anticipation can be based on the system's knowledge of: (a) where the user has been (history-based), (b) how those places are related (prerequisite-based), and (c) what the user has shown to have understood (knowledge-based) (Eklund & Sinclair, 2000). Based on well-informed anticipation of learner needs, adaptive courseware can provide options in learning paths, monitor and assess learner performances, give feedback when needed, and adjust instructional content to meet the learner needs (see Figure 3). If the system does not have any existing data of a particular learner, the system can initialize interactivity by asking some diagnostic questions and assessing learner responses as the basis for further interactivity (De Bra, Brusilovsky, & Houben, 1999).

Learner response to instructional content is a direct reflection of interactivity. Learner responses can take many forms, including clicks on hyperlinks, selection of options on a Web form, data entry through a keyboard or stylus, or voice message through a microphone. When the learner selects among a set of given options, passive reaction or reflexive operation is more likely to occur. Furthermore, in selecting given options, the learner will not make any errors other than what is anticipated or given as choices. In contrast, learner productive output is in the learner's own language without the limitation of given choices by the instructional system. When the learner produces her or his own output, active thinking is more likely to occur, and the learner may make errors or responses that are not anticipated by the instructional system. Apart from productive input through Web forms, another important means to take learner input and provide system feedback is to build search capabilities into the instructional system. Search methods can include category browsing, criteria-based information filtering, and keyword search. Learner search behaviors can be useful indicators of the learner needs and provide the basis for the instructional system to adjust the instructional content and adapt to the learner needs.

To the learner, the quality of interactivity is often evaluated based on the type of feedback the instructional program can provide (Jonassen, 1988). Basic feedback from the instructional system can be immediate sensory feedback and dynamic context cues to suggest affordances or opportunities for learner actions (Gibson, 1986). System feedback can also be provided by adjusting

Figure 3. Dynamics of an interactive system

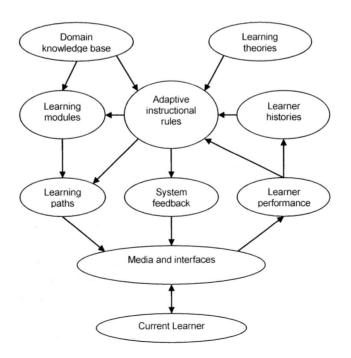

learning paths in response to learner performances and in evaluation of learner needs. More informative feedback can be given in short messages or progress reports, based the system's assessment of learner performance. System feedback can be categorized into the following: (a) acknowledgment, (b) elicitation, (c) guidance or orientation, (d) remedial action, (e) evaluation, and (f) suggestion for further action.

While allowing some degree of learner control, an instructional system must be capable of certain system control to maintain narrative coherence and keep learning on the right track. If the learner is frequently distracted by options and peripherals, narrative coherence may suffer (Plowman, 1996), especially when a specific learning sequence is desired. Narrative coherence could be difficult to maintain when external Internet resources are integrated into the course content. If a learner is led to an external website, distraction and digression may occur. A number of strategies can be used to minimize the possible distraction and digression. One strategy is to link to a specific content page or module rather than a general high-level page of a website. Another method is to give a brief description of the external resource and advise the learner to visit the external resource only if the learner wants to learn more about the resource.

Facilitating Learner Navigation

As described in the previous section, a good navigation structure is a key to promoting interactivity over learning paths. Navigation structure can be extremely flexible or restrictive. Linear paths are typically more restrictive and are often used in training procedural skills in a step-by-step manner. Tree-branching is less restrictive and generally provides alternative paths at each node along the learning paths. The learner needs to select a most desirable direction to proceed at each node, but can always return to a higher level to review and select a different path. Tree-branching is usually more appropriate for content that has a hierarchical structure and multiple levels of

content organization. More sophisticated adaptive courseware could use embedded loops with multiple branches, thus allowing more flexible learning paths.

In a flexible navigation structure, learners can traverse the content by selecting what is most relevant from among varied paths and multiple perspectives (Spiro, Feltovich, Jacobson, & Coulson, 1992). Dede (1996) succinctly describes hypermedia as user-controlled interactive technologies in which users can select paths in information navigation, and data can be delivered in multiple formats, including digital text, images, video, and sounds. Hypermedia can provide rich and realistic contexts for multi-channel content delivery, help focus learner attention on the relationship between content nodes, and encourage active, student-centered learning. As a facilitator of knowledge construction, hypermedia allows the learner to access a large knowledge base and seek out information that meets their particular needs, in terms of both prior knowledge and preferred learning style.

While hypermedia has great potential for providing flexible learning paths, there are also challenges in hypermedia navigation. Two commonly reported problems are learner disorientation and cognitive overload. To keep the learner well oriented in hypermedia navigation, a good navigation scheme should always give the user a sense of context within the learning environment, providing links to allow the user to move up to higher levels or down to lower levels in the content structure. A popular method is to use a "bread-crumb trail," which is a line of hyperlinks pointing to related nodes that are conceptually above and below the current node, or sequentially before and after the current node.

Consistency is another key factor in facilitating learner navigation and preventing disorientation. A consistent interface design can help learners quickly become familiar with the site organization. Consistency means predictability. Predictability can be driven by learner expectations and Web conventions, as well as consistent navigation, including the placement of side menus and the use of other navigation cues. For designers, there are two popular methods to help maintain interface consistency. The first method is to use Server Side Include (SSI) to embed a header or menu file in all related pages. The other method is to use a Cascading Style Sheet (CSS) to extend certain styles to all related pages. The primary advantage of using SSI and CSS is maintenance ease since any change or update made in the included file or the style sheet will be instantly reflected in all related pages, so that there is no need to change or update each individual page.

Promoting Cognitive Engagement

As discussed in the previous section, interactivity can be enhanced or constrained by the presence or absence of perceptual cues. At the conceptual level, content relevance is a fundamental attribute in promoting cognitive engagement and interactivity. Content relevance is usually directly linked to learner familiarity with topics or tasks, and is based on learners' prior knowledge and existing skills. Because learners have different prior knowledge, content relevance can be improved by providing alternative perspectives and varied learning situations. Learning acquired from multiple perspectives is more likely to be transferred to new settings (Brown, Collins, & Duguid, 1989; Salomon & Perkins, 1989; Spiro et al., 1992). Content relevance can also be promoted by building search capability into the instructional system. Search capabilities can include category browsing, criteria-based information filtering, and keyword search.

Figure 4. Promoting cognitive engagement

Activating prior knowledge and promoting content relevance	• Asking questions to activate learner prior knowledge • Providing background information • Providing search capabilities including criteria-based filtering and keyword search
Stimulating curiosity	• Presenting conflicting views • Presenting controversial issues • Challenging common assumptions
Promoting authentic learning	• Providing authentic context • Assigning authentic tasks
Encourage cognitive flexibility	• Encouraging multiple perspectives • Accommodating different learning styles
Providing cognitive modeling and scaffolding	• Asking preview questions or assigning preview tasks • Asking review questions or assigning review tasks • Asking questions or assigning tasks to encourage critical and reflective thinking • Providing just-in-time help • Enabling self assessment
Promoting knowledge integration	• Promoting associative learning • Promoting comparative analysis • Promoting elaborative learning

Alternative perspectives can help create a meaningful context for learning. However, a meaningful context does not have to start with familiar content. Curiosity can be stimulated through unusual topics, such as conflicting ideas or phenomena, a statement that challenges common assumptions, or a problem that calls for a solution. A most attractive topic or task would be one that the learner has some knowledge about, but still would like to learn more about. Bettex (1996) suggests four strategies to make instructional content interactive: (a) instructional content should confront learners with problem-solving situations; (b) for each activity, several suggestions will be provided to encourage knowledge construction and skill building; (c) instructional content should provide self-assessment activities, so that learners can evaluate their own progress, and (d) instructional content should be flexible and allow for ready modifications.

Once the learner is engaged into an interactive conversation with the content, cognitive modeling and scaffolding can be effective in continuing productive interactivity between the learner and the learning source. Davis and Linn (2000) propose three types of prompts to promote students' cognitive engagement: (a) *thinking ahead* prompts to urge learners to think about information needs and task structuring at the outset of the task, (b) *checking out understanding* prompts to ask learners to identify current knowledge gaps, and, (c) *thinking back* prompts to ask learners to reflect and think about what they might do differently next time.

Questioning is probably the most common, and often effective, method of cognitive modeling and scaffolding. Stimulating questions can lead students to: (a) critiquing based on diverse perspectives, (b) introspecting and retrospecting, (c) comparing and differentiating, and (d) elaborating by relating to personal experiences (Dillon, 1983, 1990). The placement of questions can be important. Some research indicate that factual questions when placed before passages

of relevant content often lead to specific learning, whereas general learning often occurs when similar questions are placed after the relevant passage (Allington & Weber, 1993; Hamaker, 1986; Hamilton, 1985).

CONCLUSION

As e-learning keeps growing, an increasing amount of learning activities can be expected to take place through the direct contact between the learner and the e-learning source. In this chapter, interactivity between the learner and the learning source was distinguished from interaction between human interlocutors. The differentiation is believed to be beneficial as it can help designers focus on the attributes and qualities of courseware that contribute to interactivity. These qualities include accessibility, media information attributes, hypermedia navigation, learner-system control, and cognitive engagement. This chapter proposed a pragmatic framework to serve as a model for analyzing and promoting interactivity in online learning.

Interactivity takes place at both perceptual and conceptual levels. Information processing is a function of both perceptual receptions of media symbols and conceptual interpretations of semantic messages. While perceptual interactivity is primarily at work in the layers of media and user interfaces, and conceptual interactivity mainly in the layers of navigation control and cognitive engagement, perceptual and conceptual functions are often interwoven and interdependent.

A primary perceptual condition for interactivity is accessibility. Without accessibility, there is no perception and no interactivity. Accessibility for the disabilities is a legal requirement in the United States, but has not received as much attention as it should. More people need to become aware of the importance of accessibility for e-learning. Accessibility is not just for the disabilities; it can benefit the general audience as well. Developers should keep accessibility in mind when designing media interfaces and developing content, including text legibility, readability, and optimal use of multimedia to their respective advantage. Appropriate use of media can enhance information presentation and facilitate information processing. Alternative media presentations can accommodate different learning styles, and alternative learning contexts can foster cognitive flexibility.

The provision of media options and alternative learning contexts encourages learner control over learning activities. Learner control is a direct reflection of interactivity. The amount of control available to the learner is usually a function of the amount of control the system maintains. To the learner, the quality of interactivity is often evaluated based on the level of adaptability and the type of feedback the system can provide. A customizable user interface and sensory feedback can promote interactivity at the perceptual level. Adaptive content provision and dynamic semantic feedback can advance interactivity at the conceptual level. Cognitive growth is the ultimate goal of interactivity. To be truly adaptive to learner needs, an instructional system should be able to identify learner needs and adjust the learning environment to meet the learner needs at both perceptual and conceptual levels.

FUTURE TRENDS

E-learning has every sign of a sustained boom. As digital technology becomes more portable and bandwidth becomes less of a constraint, multimedia applications are expected to prosper. With the increasing use of multimedia, accessibility will become a focus of attention. Making multimedia materials meet the requirements of Section 508 generally requires some training for course developers and usually takes a considerable amount of development time. Course developers would certainly hope that future multimedia authoring tools could include functions to automate the creation of alternative content equivalents. The need for content interoperability and resource sharing across platforms will grow. To promote world-wide resource sharing and ensure cross-platform compatibility, standards need to be adopted in using metadata for packaging and tagging learning objects. Courseware will be expected to be compliant with global standards such as SCORM and XML.

High level interactivity relies greatly on the adaptability of the courseware. With the integration of the domain knowledge base, learner profile database, and adaptable instructional rules, future courseware will be capable of customizing the learning environment and accommodating individual needs. For systematic management of learning resources and learner performance records, database and data mining will be extensively used. Artificial intelligence will be incorporated so that system actions can be triggered based on the instructional rules in response to learner actions and in evaluation of learner performances. Further research and development efforts are needed to study how instructional rules should be formulated with adequate flexibility to accommodate different learner needs and learning contexts. The primary goal of an adaptive system is to help the learner move forward in a zone of proximal development. Such a zone is never static. A major challenge is to build an instructional system that can interactively define this dynamic zone.

Even with the integration of learner profile database, knowledge base, adaptive instructional rules, and advanced artificial intelligence, it is a daunting task to design an instructional system that can keep a learner advancing without human diagnosis and intervention. Human intervention will still be needed at some points. Under what kind of circumstances is human intervention most likely to be needed? How should human intervention be best integrated? These would be issues to address and discuss in future studies.

REFERENCES

Allington, R. L., & Weber, R. (1993). Questioning questions in teaching and learning from text. In B. K. Britton, A. Woodward, & M. Binkley (Eds.), *Learning from textbooks: Theory and practice* (pp. 47-68). Hillsdale, NJ: Erlbaum.

Bettex, M. (1996). Textbooks: Prospects for the technological era. *EMI: ICEM conference report, 32*, 47-50.

Borsook, T., & Higginbotham-Wheat, N. (1991). Interactivity: What is it and what can it do for computer-based instruction? *Educational Technology, 31*(10), 11-17.

Brown, A. L., Collins, A., & Duguid, P. (1989). Situated cognition and the culture of learning. *Educational Researcher, 17*, 32-41.

Davis, E. A., & Linn, M. C. (2000). Scaffolding students' knowledge integration: Prompts for reflections in KIE. *International Journal of Science Education, 22*(8), 819-837.

De Bra, P., Brusilovsky, P., & Houben, G. J. (1999). Adaptive hypermedia: From systems to framework. *ACM Computing Surveys, 31*(4). Retrieved September 29, 2006, from http://portal.acm.org/

Dede, C. (1996). Emerging technologies and distributed Learning. *American Journal of Distance Education, 10*(2), 4-36.

Dillon, J. (1983). *Teaching and the art of questioning.* Bloomington, IN: Phi Delta Kappa Education Foundation, Fastback No. 194.

Dillon, J. (1990). *The practice of questioning.* London: Routledge.

Eklund, J., & Sinclair, K. (2000). An empirical appraisal of the effectiveness of adaptive interfaces for instructional systems. *Educational Technology and Society, 3*(4), 165-177.

Gibson, J. J. (1986). *The ecological approach to visual perception.* Hillsdale, NJ: Lawrence Erlbaum Associates.

Gilbert, L., & Moore, D.R. (1998). Building interactivity in web courses: Tools for social and instructional interaction. *Educational Technology, 38*(3), 29-35.

Hamaker, C. (1986). The effects of adjunct questions on prose learning. *Review of Educational Research, 56*(2), 212-242.

Hamilton, R. J. (1985). A framework for the evaluation of the effectiveness of adjunct questions and objectives. *Review of Educational Research, 55*(1), 47-85.

Hartley, J. (2004). Designing instructional and informational text. In D. Jonassen (Ed.), *Handbook of research on educational communications and technology* (pp. 917-947). Mahwah, NJ: Lawrence Erlbaum.

Jonassen, D. (Ed.). (1988). *Instructional design for microcomputer courseware.* Hillsdale, NJ: Lawrence Erlbaum.

Kennedy, G. (2004). Promoting cognition in multimedia interactivity research. *Journal of Interactive Learning Research, 15*, 43-61.

Kozma, R. B. (1991). Learning with media. *Review of Educational Research, 61*(2), 179-211.

Mayer, R. E. (2001). *Multimedia learning.* New York: Cambridge University Press.

Merrill, M. D. (1975). Learner control: Beyond aptitude/treatment interaction. *AV Communication Review, 23*, 217-226.

Moreno, R., & Mayer, R. E. (1999). Cognitive principles of multimedia learning: The role of modality and contiguity. *Journal of Educational Psychology, 91*, 358-368.

Plowman, L. (1996). Narrative, linearity and interactivity: Making sense of interactive multimedia. *British Journal of Educational Technology, 27*(2), 92-105.

Robertson, J. (1998). Paradise lost: Children, multimedia and the myth of interactivity. *Journal of Computer Assisted Learning, 14*(1), 31-39.

Rose, E. (1999). Deconstructing interactivity in educational computing. *Educational Technology, 39*(1), 43-49.

Salomon, G. (1979). *Interaction of media, cognition, and learning.* San Francisco: Jossey Bass.

Salomon, G., & Perkins, D. N. (1989). Rocky road to transfer: Rethinking mechanisms of a neglected phenomenon. *Educational Psychologist, 24*(2), 113-142.

Schwier, R., & Misanchuk, E. (1993). *Interactive multimedia instruction.* Englewood Cliffs, NJ: Educational Technology Publications.

Sims, R. (1997). Interactivity: A forgotten art? *Computers in Human Behavior, 13*(2), 157-180.

Sims, R. (1999). Interactivity on stage: Strategies for learner-designer communication. *Australian Journal of Educational Technology, 15*(3), 257-272.

Sims, R. (2000). An interactive conundrum: Constructs of interactivity and learning theory. *Australian Journal of Educational Technology, 16*(1), 45-57.

Spiro, R. J., Feltovich, P. J., Jacobson, M. J., & Coulson, R. L. (1992). Knowledge representation, content specification, and the development of skill in situation specific knowledge assembly: Some constructivist issues as they relate to cognitive flexibility theory and hypertext. In D. In & H. Jonassen (Ed.), *Constructivism and the technology of instruction: A conversation* (pp. 121-128). Hillsdale, NJ: Lawrence Erlbaum Associates.

Wagner, E. D. (1994). In support of a functional definition of interaction. *The American Journal of Distance Education, 8*(2), 6-26.

Wagner, E. D. (1997). Interactivity: From agents to outcomes. *New Directions for Teaching and Learning, 71*, 19-26.

Wilhite, S. C. (1989). Headings as memory facilitators: The importance of prior knowledge. *Journal of Educational Psychology, 81*, 115-117.

Chapter X
Online Interactions:
Comparing Social Network Measures with Instructors' Perspectives

Pedro Willging
University of La Pampa, Argentina

ABSTRACT

In the virtual environment created by asynchronous posting boards, e-mail lists, chat rooms, and other communication tools, it may not be easy for an instructor to detect communication problems among the participants. In this chapter, a research study where social network analysis (SNA) methods were applied to a sample of online classes to investigate interaction patterns and compare to instructors' perceptions is used to address social interactions in online environments. This study proves that SNA metrics and visualization of interactions are useful and potentially effective tools to analyze asynchronous online interaction patterns. The comparison of the results of a questionnaire administered to the instructors with the SNA results showed that the use of the SNA metrics and visualizations could reveal information the instructor is not aware of. Based on the findings from the study, recommendations for further research are provided. In the first part of this chapter, the importance of investigating interaction patterns in online environments is analyzed and basic SNA methodology is described. In the second part, the SNA methodology is utilized for analyzing online interactions.

CHAPTER OBJECTIVES

The reader will be able to:

- Understand the significance of investigating interaction patterns in online environments
- Learn about the SNA methodology applied to uncovering the patterning of people's interaction, through the analysis of archives of asynchronous online discussion boards from two different online courses
- Become familiar with the basic SNA methodology, which includes the use of visual instruments designed to produce images of the structure of the network, and computational tools which can help to analyze big amounts of social network data
- Evaluate the agreement between the SNA measured results in online interactions and the instructor's perceptions of students' performance
- Utilize the SNA methodology for analyzing online interactions

INTRODUCTION

Social interaction is necessary for successful online learning (Gillespie, 1998; Moore, 1989;). This interaction encourages students to get involved in their learning experience (Hillman, Willis, & Gunawardena, 1994), favoring the perception of a learning community that provides the feeling of belonging and connectedness. Swan and Shih (2005) contend that student satisfaction and success in online courses are related to social presence, that is, the degree to which the student feels affectively connected to the classroom community (Short, Williams, & Christie, 1976).

The amount and quality of interaction among students in online classes is a key indicator for assessing course and students' performances. Research reveals that students actively engaged in

collaborative learning achieve course objectives at a significantly higher level (Levenburg & Major, 2000) as the interaction process stimulates critical thinking (McCarthey & McMahon, 1992), and reduce students' anxiety while increasing their motivation (Hiltz, Coppola, Rotter et al., 2000). On the other hand, the loss of interaction among the participants can lead to isolation and attrition. Moody (2004), while referring to attrition rates in distance education, says: "Interaction increases retention" (p. 209).

In online courses, one of the most used tools is the electronic posting board, which allows discussion of class issues, exchange of ideas, and collaboration to solve class assignments. Students and instructors can post their comments and questions, read and analyze peer's reflections and opinions. Instructors of online courses usually encourage students to participate in the discussion boards for knowledge sharing. But, the amount of text messages generated in a semester for an active class can be difficult for the instructor to accurately assess student participation. Moreover, if students are required to contribute continuously for the duration of the course, the assessment becomes even more demanding.

While referring to evaluating online discussions, Ho (2002) says: "Apart from usage statistics and content analysis, I have not found other assessment procedures proposed within the research material surveyed" (¶ 22). These techniques, though, may not reveal relationship and interaction among participants.

This chapter explores new methodologies for analyzing participation and interaction in online environments. The research study investigated online courses using social network analysis (SNA) techniques and compared the results with instructors' perceptions in order to test the validity of the methodology. The study pointed to answer questions like:

- To what extent instructors' perceptions of what is happening in their online courses

match quantitative measures of these interactions?

- Are students with marginal participation in online classes being detected?
- What is the structure of the interactions?

This chapter asserts that SNA methodology is a valuable approach to evaluate online interactions and shows the procedures for using this approach. Providing instructors with alternative assessment tools for student participation in online discussion boards would help them to make better judgments and improve the accuracy in the evaluation of students' work.

BACKGROUND

Research Framework

As with traditional face-to-face classes, success in online learning is directly related to interaction among students and faculty, and students' sense of community or connectedness (Gunawardena, 1995; LaRose, & Whitten, 2000; Wegerif, 1998; Woods, & Ebersole, 2003). Discussion boards are frequently incorporated as a part of the instructional design of an online course. This reflects the belief that discussion and interaction between instructor and students, and between students, are keys to effective learning. Many sound pedagogical theories support the fundamental role of interaction in the act of learning. The conversation theory (Pask, 1975), the social development theory (Vygotsky, 1978), and Bandura's (1977) social learning framework postulate that learning and the development of cognition occur because of social interactions. The constructivist theory (Bruner, 1996) also puts the emphasis in learning as an active process, where instructor and student should engage in an active dialog for learning to happen.

Because of the importance of interaction in online discussion boards, different models and

techniques have been proposed to investigate social and cognitive aspects of learning in these environments. Content analysis techniques have been used in many research studies (Garrison, Anderson, & Archer, 2001; Gunawardena, Lowe, & Anderson, 1997; Henri, 1992; Howell-Richardson, & Mellar, 1996). Fahy, Crawford, and Ally (2001) employed a mix of a transcript analysis tool that they developed with social network theories to investigate exchange patterns in online conferencing. The content analysis methodology is a difficult and time consuming task, and since it is a retrospective analysis, requires that the researcher doing the analysis mentally recreates the discussion so the messages to have significance. This is a really arduous task to accomplish when analyzing big amounts of forum data.

Wu and Chen (2005) assessed student learning with automated text processing techniques that analyzed class messages produced in the online system by students and instructors. This model uses three measures: message length, message count, and keyword contribution to evaluate student participation. This assessment tool analyzes individual performances, but not group interactions.

Recently, Zhu (2006) explored the combination of SNA methods with qualitative content analysis to analyze participation, interaction, and learning in asynchronous online discussions. The study examined types of interaction and cognitive engagement in an online forum in social sciences courses. The applicability of SNA theory to the online environment has been already suggested by Garton, Haythornthwaite, and Wellman (1997):

When a computer network connects people or organizations, it is a social network. Just as a computer network is a set of machines connected by a set of cables, a social network is a set of people (or organizations or other social entities) connected by a set of social relationships, such as friendship, co-working or information exchange. (p. 1)

SNA has provided important applications for organizational behavior, inter-organizational relations, the spread of contagious diseases, mental health, social support, the diffusion of information, and animal social organization. It comprises a set of techniques used in recent studies related to electronic mediated interactions (Aviv, Erlich, Ravid, & Geva, 2003; Willging, 2004). In the studies of SNA related to learning situations, distribution of power and centrality in the network is often the focus of the analysis (Haythornthwaite, 1998; Martinez, Dimitriadis, Rubia et al., 2002). One of these studies (Cho, Stefanone, & Gay, 2002) found that, in Web-based communication, the most influential referrals are those who have been identified as powerful actors in the network. Global properties of the communication structure can efficiently assist instructors of online classes in assessing collaboration within the group. Cohesion, as characterized by SNA theory, can highlight isolated people and discover active subgroups and roles of the members in the communication structure. Reffay and Chanier (2003) designed an experiment, named *Simuligne*, where they measured cohesion of 40 distance learners involved in 10 weeks of activities that included different tools for virtual communication (e.g., discussion forums, e-mail, chat rooms, etc.). Using SNA concepts and theory, they computed communication graphs, cliques, and clusters of discussion forum graphs. They found that "cliques highlight the communication structure and the position of the agents for a given intensity of communication" (p. 352).

The social network created by students and instructors in an online course is sustained by knowledge exchange and interaction among its members. While interacting in this social network, students and instructors assume various roles.

The behavior of the members of a community, which is a complex social structure, is not random. The position in the social structure imposes upon the individuals that constitute it both privileges and constraints to their acting, and that defines

what is called their social role (Golder & Donath, 2004). In the online environment, as in the offline, people naturally tend to assume a variety of different characters and roles, whether by nature or by choice. These roles are essentially generalizations of characters, that is, a certain type of character that appears so often as to be nameable. White (2001) said:

Every community and online group is different. The purposes vary, the structures are different—and the people are different. But there are some common participation styles or patterns that have been observed. These can be helpful when you are trying to understand participation patterns in an online interaction space. Take note that for each style, there are attributes that can be seen as both positive and negative. (¶ 1)

As people rely more and more on electronic means for communication their experiences become more virtual and less tangible. These digital experiences are usually saved, recorded in hard drives or other electronic means, and therefore, the persistent data generated by online interactions could be traced and analyzed using methodologies like content analysis or thread analysis. However, these methods could be time consuming or overlook structural characteristics of the interactions. SNA techniques have been applied to a variety of problems, and they have been successful in uncovering relationships not seen with any other traditional method. Social and conversational patterns in online interactions can be understood by researchers if they use visualization techniques as visual aids (Viegas, Boyd, Nguyen et al., 2003). The use of SNA metrics, especially if supported with visualization software, could help to provide another view of online interactions.

SNA Theory and Definitions

SNA is a methodology to collect and analyze relational data. This methodology is focused on uncovering the patterning of people's interaction. Surveys, observations, interviews, and archival records are data sources SNA investigates. Archived e-mails, chat logs, and Web postings provide SNA with rich sources of information for analysis. SNA measures many structural characteristics of the network, like the existence of subgroups, the relative importance of individual actors, and the strength of the links (Wasserman & Faust, 1994).

While providing a complete treatment of the SNA theory and methodology is out of reach of this chapter, some basic definitions are needed to conceptualize a social network. The three essential components of a social network are: a set of nodes and arcs, a sociogram or graph (created with the nodes and arcs), and a sociomatrix. The nodes (also called actors) can be persons, organizations, or groups. The arcs are the relationships between the nodes, and the sociogram is the graphical representation of the network. In Figure 1, one of the first sociograms ever made is shown (Moreno, 1934, p. 32). In this graph, the nine circles represent babies (the nodes), and the arrows between them (the arcs) are present when a baby can recognize another one. The arcs are sketched with pointing arrows because in this case, the relationship is directed[1]. In undirected relationships, arcs are simply drawn with lines. The sociomatrix or adjacency matrix would keep the information about the links between the actors in a mathematical representation.

Density, centrality, and cohesion are some of the most important conceptual ideas derived from the SNA theoretical framework. Density is a widely-used concept in graph theory and measures the level of linkage among the nodes of a graph. In a complete graph, each node is connected directly to every other node. Density measures how much a graph differs from the state of completion. A point has two kinds of centrality measures: local and global. Local centrality measures how many connections a given point has and is calculated by the degree of the point. In directed graphs, it is relevant to talk about in- and out-degree. Global centrality measures the position of a point in the overall structure of the network. Freeman (1980) expresses global centrality in terms of geodesics (shortest distance between points). Those points, whose sums of geodesics to all other points are the smallest, are globally central.

Figure 1. Who recognized whom among a group of babies

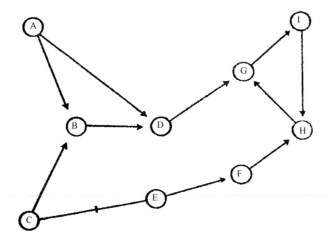

Another concept related to point centrality is that of betweenness, which measures the role of a point as intermediary. Some points may act as "brokers" or "gatekeepers" between groups of points, therefore playing an important role in the network. While density describes the general level of cohesion in a graph, the extent to which this cohesion is organized around particular focal points is measured by the centralization factor. The calculation of the centralization score will give a value between 0 and 1, with 1 achieved in a graph with "star" structure, and 0 for a complete graph. It may be useful to identify the structural center of the graph, which is a single point or a cluster of points that acts as the pivot of the whole graph. Then, it is possible to identify marginal and peripheral points, which have low centrality scores (Scott, 2000).

"One of the major concerns of social network analysis is the identification of cohesive subgroups of actors within a network. Cohesive subgroups are subsets of actors among whom there are relatively strong, direct, intense, frequent, or positive ties" (Wasserman & Faust, 1994, p. 249). For SNA theory, a group is a structure that can be discovered empirically by examination of patterns of interactions among members of a population. Those subsets of members that are highly interconnected constitute the groups (Garton, Haythornthwaite, & Wellman, 1997).

SNA Tools

SNA has two kinds of tools: visual and computational instruments. Visual instruments are designed to produce images of the structure of the network, while computational instruments, like UCINET (Borgatti, Everett, & Freeman, 1992) help to analyze big amounts of social network data (Freeman, Webster, & Kirke, 1998). Vladimir Batagelj and Andrej Mrvar (2003) developed Pajek, a software for analysis and visualization of large networks (thousands or even millions of vertices). The software MAGE was developed for molecular modeling by Richardson & Richardson (1992). This program produces elegant figures that can be manipulated in a 3-dimensional space. MAGE displays files in a special format, KIN images, which can be created using UCINET or Pajek software. Kinemage format and display were originally developed for visualizing biological molecules, but they are also useful for studying social, semantic, and ecological networks (Freeman, 2000; Johnson, Borgatti, Luczkovich, & Everett, 2001; Johnson, Richardson, & Richardson, 2002). Using MAGE it is possible to rotate, animate, and zoom in and out of the displays of the network representations in real time through a Java applet [2].

EVALUATING ONLINE INTERACTIONS

Instructors in traditional classrooms use social cues like sitting arrangements, voice intonations, and body language to evaluate (even unconsciously) the performance and motivation of students in their classes. But, in the virtual classroom, instructors have to rely on other measures to sense how the students are doing in the class. The learning management systems, used to deliver online learning, provide some information about student participation, like frequency of postings in the forums. The structural characteristics of the class (who is interacting with whom, for example), though, are usually not displayed. The SNA measures could help online instructors to model the interactions that take place in the virtual class. The results of a research study that compared SNA measures with instructor's views of online interactions are summarized and discussed in this section. The methodology deployed in the study is described first.

The questions guiding the study were: (1) to what extent the SNA measures are similar to instructor's view? (2) Can the SNA results be trusted? (3) In which ways can these indexes be used?

The Research Study Methodology

Sample

Archives of asynchronous online discussion boards from two different courses were analyzed. These archives come from two online courses, offered by an online master's degree program at the University of Illinois [3], which use the learning management system (LMS) WebBoard, BlackBoard, and Moodle for online discussion. The courses were chosen from the pool of available, saved archives of the master's program, and had to be courses in which students had been required to use the asynchronous space to complete class assignments involving discussions. The inspection of the syllabus and the recorded interactions, and consultation with the instructors in charge of the course were used to determine these conditions.

Data Collection

Records of the asynchronous interactions in the online classes are kept by the system used for its delivery in different ways. Most asynchronous posting boards will keep a graphic display showing who has posted a message and who replied to that message. The information displayed usually includes date and time stamps, e-mail address of the sender, subject title, how many times the message has been read, the body of the message, and other information.

The data collected for this study from those asynchronous data files were who sent the message and who replied to it. This information needed to be collected for each message in the online board. In addition to the archived online interactions, a questionnaire for instructors provided additional data for this study. The questionnaire included questions about interaction patterns of the class

as perceived by the instructor. The questionnaire contained items designed to elicit instructor's knowledge about the level of interaction in the class, the concentration of that interaction, and the perceived roles students played during the semester. The questionnaire asked also whether or not instructors were able to identify subgroups and required that the instructors reflect upon their own role in the online class interaction.

Procedure

The archived online discussions were processed as text files with standard spreadsheet software macros. The text files with the structural information were converted to adjacency matrices so as to apply the SNA metrics with UCINET, the software used to calculate the SNA measures.

The questionnaire for instructors was developed by the researcher using the SNA literature as a guide and was reviewed by four researchers to check for and improve internal validity. Instructors were asked to answer the questionnaire in the presence of the researcher, who provided clarification when necessary.

Data Analysis

Once the adjacency matrices were obtained, SNA calculations were made using UCINET. Density, centrality (degree, closeness, and betweenness), and cohesion analyses were made. The resulting tables from UCINET were analyzed and a report with the interpretation of these results was created for each class in the sample. The software programs UCINET, Pajek, and MAGE were used to visualize the group interactions. The reports of the SNA analysis for each case in the study and the visualizations created were presented to an expert in the field of SNA and interactions in online environments to check for accuracy in the analysis.

THE RESEARCH STUDY RESULTS AND DISCUSSION

The results of the questionnaire for instructors were compared to the results of the SNA calculations. These results are summarized in tables and discussed in this section of the chapter, which includes also some graphs depicting the online interactions (basically snapshots of 3D images).

The questionnaire was administered to the instructors of the courses that constituted the two cases in the study. Three questionnaires were completed by the instructor of Case 1, and the instructor and teaching assistant (TA) of Case 2. They were all very cooperative and showed interest in the study. The questionnaires/interviews were carried out during the last week of the fall semester and lasted between 15 to 25 minutes. The researcher observed as the questionnaires were completed and made notes of the comments made by the instructors during these interviews.

Before starting with the questionnaire items, the participants were asked about their experience with online teaching and asynchronous spaces in particular. For Class A, the TA had been working in two classes for one and a half years. She had used the LMS WebCT both as a student and a TA. The instructor of Class A had experience with online teaching for about four years. This instructor had used WebCT and First Class (another LMS) and teaches two classes a year at an accredited online university. The instructor of Class B had taught seven classes online already, using WebBoard as asynchronous space. All participants were experiencing Moodle for the first time. The results for each case are presented next.

Case 1

This course was taught during the fall semester, and is one of the last courses previous to graduation in the program. In this class, Moodle and live broadcasting audio were the main environments for class interaction. The asynchronous interaction was developed through the Moodle forums. In this class, the asynchronous space had forums where all class members could participate and forums where only team members could discuss. Most of the forum discussions were organized around weekly topics, but students could continue posting on topics that were initiated on previous weeks. The SNA metrics were calculated for different matrices of adjacency: the class open forums, the team forums, and all together. The total number of messages in the forums was 1270, of which 976 were posted in the open forums and 294 in the team forums. There were 26 participants including the instructor and one tech support graduate assistant. Twenty-two students were from the current cohort of the program, and two students were from a previous cohort.

In Table 1, a comparison between the instructor perceptions and the SNA metrics is displayed. For each item taken from the survey, the SNA result and the instructor answer are listed. Names of participants have been replaced by the code letter-number so to keep anonymity. The criteria to classify the course participants according to the SNA metrics are summarized in Table 2.

The comparison shows that the instructor perception of the level of interaction in this class matched the SNA calculation of the density. The instructor perceived the interaction as almost evenly distributed, and that is in agreement with the SNA calculations, which found moderate to low indexes for degree centrality. The instructor did not detect A8 and A9 as prolific students, and considered prolific three students (A1, A17, and A21) who posted less than average. The instructor identified one of the most replied students, and named A1, A4, and A22 as the most powerful members in this class. A4 matched the SNA calculations. A1 had high scores in two measures, so it can be said that it was powerful to a certain extent. A22 however, had very low scores in all the SNA measures.

There was some degree of agreement between the SNA report and the instructor's perception.

There was agreement in who were the most active/prolific members and the instructor spotted the single most isolated member in this group (A0). However, the instructor mentioned A7 as a bridge/broker, while its scores were very low in all measures. Also, A17 was named as "prolific" by the instructor while the out-degree as calculated by SNA was far below average.

The SNA measures and the visualizations showed very clearly the five subgroups that were assembled at the beginning of the semester (see Figure 2). The instructor perceived that he did

not dominate the discussion very often. He chose bridge/broker and promoter of interaction as the role he played in his class. This was in agreement with the SNA results as most of the SNA scores for the instructor indicated a moderate interaction.

Case 2

This course was taught during the fall semester, and it is half way through the completion of the program. A major piece of the course is a hands-on highly practical project in which students

Table 1. Comparison of questionnaire results and SNA metrics for case 1

Item	SNA metrics	Instructor questionnaire
Density of interaction	55%	Between 30% to 50%
Concentration of interaction	Moderate to low	Almost Evenly Distributed
Most prolific students	A3, A4, A6, A8, A9, A11, A13, A14, A16	A1, **A3, A4, A6, A11**, A12, **A13, A14, A16**, A17, A21
Most replied students	A1, A4, A6, A14, A16, A20	**A1**, A2, A17
Most "influential or powerful" students	A4, A6, A14, A16	A1, **A4**, A22
Role of students		
Star	A1, A4, A14	**A4**, A16
Prolific	A3, A4, A6, A8, A9, A11, A13, A14, A16	A1, **A3, A4, A6**, A12, **A13, A14, A16**, A17, A21
Isolate/lurker	A0, A7, A17, A19, A21, A24, A25	**A0**
Bridge/broker	A4, A6, A15, A16	A7
Subgroups	5	5
Instructor Role	bridge/broker	bridge/broker, promoter of interaction

Note: Bold font has been added to remark coincidences

Table 2. Criteria to identify participants' role according to SNA scores

Role label	Description	Related SNA metric
Consulted	Participant who others go to for advice or/and information	High *in-degree* score [4]
Star	Participant who attracted a lot of replies	Highest *in-degree* score
Bridge/broker	Participant who linked discussions, or/and tried to conciliate opinions, or/and connected information from one message to another	High *betweenness* score [5]
Prolific	Member who sent a lot of messages	High *out-degree* score [6]
Isolate/lurker	Participant with a marginal participation in the discussion	Low degree centrality (*out-* and *in-degree*) scores.
Influential or powerful	Participants who had a level of control of the interactions, in the sense of guiding conversations, making other members to react, produce replies, or generating divergent positions or groups	High scores in degree centrality (*out-* and *in-degree*), and *betweeness/closeness*.

Figure 2. Team forums activity visualization

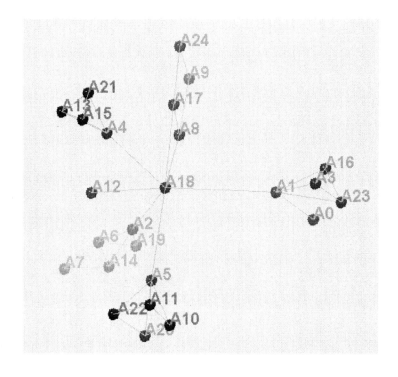

start to work early in the course. In this class, Moodle and Tapped-Inn (an online environment for synch and asynchronous interactions) were the main environments for class interaction. The asynchronous interaction was developed through the Moodle forums.

The forum discussions were organized in two weekly main topics. The total number of messages in the forums of this class was: 1037. There were 443 threads and 153 messages (start of a new thread) without reply. There were 30 participants; including two instructors (one professor and one TA) and one graduate student working as teach support. Twenty students were from the same cohort of the program, one student was from a previous cohort, and six students were on-campus students from other programs than the online masters program.

Table 3 shows the comparison between instructor and TA perceptions and the SNA metrics. The perception of the instructor about the level of interaction matched the SNA calculation of the density, but the TA over-estimated it. The TA perception regarding concentration of interaction matched the SNA calculations, which found a highly centralized network. The instructor instead perceived the interaction as not being very concentrated.

The instructor and the TA spotted the most prolific members in the course. Both the TA and the instructor named A10, a student whose postings were less than average. The instructor named A22 as a prolific member, but this student had an almost marginal participation in the forum (only 9 postings). The TA also mentioned A14 and A15 as prolific. Although these students both had not participated posting messages very often, they incited many replies from their peers.

A3 has been mentioned both by the TA and the instructor as the most replied member. There were two members, A8 and A13, which were not mentioned by the instructor or the TA. They ranked in third place as the most replied members in the course. The TA included in her list A25

and the instructor included A11, both of them got very few replies.

All but A8 have been spotted by the TA and the instructor as the most "influential or powerful" members in the course. The instructor and TA coincided in naming A10 as a powerful member, but the SNA measures do not give this student a higher rank.

There were similarities and differences in the roles assigned by the TA and the instructor to the students in this course. They both accorded in the roles of A6, A9, and A10. But they assigned quite opposite roles to A4 (star against lurker/isolate), and A14 (prolific against lurker/isolate). It seems that A7 activity has been gone unnoticed by the TA and the instructor as this student was classified as "don't know" by them both.

The SNA results and instructor's perceptions showed discrepancies regarding the role students played in the course. The TA identified 5 subgroups. The instructor named two subgroups that were already named by the TA. Three of those five subgroups were students that worked together in the final project of the course. The SNA cohesion analysis could not identify any sub-group in the course.

Regarding how often they dominated the discussions, the TA and the instructor answered in the opposite sides of the scale, with the TA choosing the Almost Always option. This was confirmed by the SNA metrics and visualizations where the TA is clearly dominant while the instructor played a more silent role in the asynchronous space.

As for their own perceived role, there was a fair agreement between the SNA results and instructors' perceptions of the role they played in the discussion forum. Figure 3 shows a representation produced with MAGE, which allowed the confirmation of many of the discussed results. A2 (the TA) is at the center of the stage in a quasi-star configuration, where A3, A6, A8, A13, and A16 are in the close circle, and the other nodes are connected all around in a satellite fashion. A19, A24, A26 and A28 certainly have a peripheral

Table 3. Comparison of questionnaire results and SNA metrics for case 2

Item		SNA metrics	Instructor	TA
Density of interaction		33%	Between 20% and 30%	More than 50%
Concentration of interaction		High	Not Very High	High
Most prolific students		A3, A4, A6, A8, A13	**A3, A6, A8**, A10, A22	**A3, A4, A6**, A10, A14, A15, A16, A19
Most replied students		A3, A6, A8, A10, A13, A14	**A3**, A4, A5, A11, A19, A22	**A3, A6**, A9, **A10**, A12, **A14**, A15, A16, A25, A29
Most "influential or powerful" students		A3, A6, A8, A13	**A3, A6**, A10, A11, A16, A26, A29	**A3**, A4, **A6**, A10, **A13**, A14
Role of students	Star	A3, A6, A8, A13	A4, **A6**, A9, A26	**A6**, A9, A10, A25
	Prolific	A3, A6, A8, A13	A5, A10, A11, A16, A19, A21, A22, A27	**A6**, A10, **A13**, A14
	Isolate/lurker	A9, A11, A15, A18, A19, A22, A24, A25, A26, A28	A14, **A15, A24**	A4, A23, **A24, A26**, A27
	Bridge/broker	A3, A7, A8, A13, A29	**A3**, A6, **A8**, A9, A10, **A13**, A28	A6, **A8**, A9, A16, A19, A25
Subgroups		none	2	5
Role	Instructor	Almost a lurker		Lurker/isolate
	TA	Star, prolific, bridge	Prolific, bridge, promoter	

participation in the discussion. Notice also how marginal A0 (the instructor) seems to be in this graph.

SUMMARY OF RESULTS AND DISCUSSION

Before getting into the discussion of the results, it has to be said that this study was not about evaluating the performance of the courses or their students and instructors. There has not been a preconceived idea of what a "good interaction pattern" should look like or what would be "good or bad" SNA measures for an online class. The study was about testing the usefulness of SNA metrics and comparing them to instructor's perceptions of online interactions. Whether a specific pattern of interaction or a set of scores for the SNA metrics are the desired ones would depend on course design, instructor and students'

expectations, or other reasons. A pattern of interaction that worked for a course may not work as well in another one. Instructors and students, as the participants of these interactions are the ones who can evaluate how satisfactory or not the experience was. They are the ones who can evaluate and judge if a particular kind of interaction did work for them.

The comparison of the results of the survey administered to the instructors with the SNA results showed that the use of the SNA metrics and visualizations can reveal information of which the instructor is not aware. Though, some of the discrepancies between the instructor perceptions and the SNA results can be attributed to the fact that the instructor's perceptions were made up not only with the asynchronous discussion forum interaction, but also with the whole set of activities developed in the class, which included synchronous interactions and other asynchronous communication.

The role analysis provided very interesting results. Although this was a rough first attempt of characterizing participants of online classes according to their behavior in it, it was revealing to see how dissimilar the perceptions of the instructors could be regarding students' participation in the class. The labels for the roles assigned to participants in the class were established by the researcher based on the literature; they should be refined and/or modified for future research. These labels are closely related to those used in previous sociology works where SNA has been used, with the addition of the online lexicon. Each participant in the course was classified into the roles according to her/his SNA scores. There was a role or participant category that was not considered at the beginning of the analysis, but that could be a useful one: the "typical" participant. The "typical" participant, unlike the "star" or the "isolate" who have their SNA scores lying at the top or at the end of the scale, would be a participant with scores close to the average in the SNA measures.

It seems that when the instructors do not assume the role of the "source" in the discussion (i.e., they have a moderate or peripheral participation) there will be a group of members that will assume the central role of the class. Although the small sample of this study makes difficult to generalize this inference, this is emphasizing again the importance of instructor behavior in molding the structure of the interactions.

The structures of the interactions in the two cases in this study were visibly different. One case had a star type of interaction while the other was an interconnected web kind of interaction. A powerful member takes control and directs the discussion in a course with a star type of interaction. When the instructor is that dominant member, the online discussion and instruction becomes instructor-controlled and centered. The interconnected web kind of interaction, on the other hand, is characterized by having multiple influential members that share bonds. Students and instructors in a course with this type of interac-

tion are more likely to share ideas, ask questions, or make suggestions on peers' comments in the online discussion board.

The differences in the structures of the interactions could be attributed to many reasons. Instructor presence in the online discussion is certainly one. The contributions of the instructors, if well-balanced and extended through the course semester, may encourage students' enthusiasm and engagement in the discussions. On the other hand, if the instructor takes a passive role in the discussion (absent or marginal) or does not provide guidance, students may lack motivation or direction for participating in the discussions. The same negative impact on students' willingness to participate can occur when the instructor takes a hyperactive role (for example, replying each message in the online forum, or making too many and lengthy interventions) because this can intimidate students.

Students' personality, academic maturity, technology literacy, and instructional design are other reasons that could contribute or deter the interactions. The online instructors can modify the patterns of interaction of online discussions by taking into account all these factors.

CONCLUSION

This chapter showed the application of the SNA methodology to evaluate online interactions, and how much agreement between the SNA measures of these interactions and the instructor's perceptions can be reached. Courses from an online master's degree program were used as cases in the study, which was the core of the discussion and used to show the techniques and test the validity of the approach. The results of the study described, indicate that the SNA techniques can provide with useful cues to instructors about the performance of their online courses.

If implemented as an additional teaching instrument, the methods that have been discussed so far might constitute a very useful tool to assist online instructors. Once the SNA metrics are calculated after automatically collecting the data from the discussion boards as it has been shown in this chapter, they can reduce instructor workload and keep track of students' contributions.

Although instructor qualitative perceptions can not be replaced by this automated assessment tool, it can collaborate with the instructor to judge students' participation in the asynchronous discussions more accurately. Human perception is extremely complex and can not be substituted by statistical or analytical information. However, SNA metrics can help red flag situations like marginalized students or dominant participants.

One of the instructors that had participated in the study said: "I have learned much about my patterns of responses also." Adding later, "I think this would be helpful to redirect discussion to students that were outliers if this could be used in a formative manner during the semester." The visual representations of the interactions, which can be made through the software and techniques demonstrated in this chapter, can work as devices to make participants (including the instructors) aware of their own social behavior in the online course.

The interactive visualizations created with the SNA software made "graphically evident" the SNA measures obtained from the forum data. This is a particularly important result as the visual representation of the SNA scores is a much more compact way to get a snapshot of the class activity. It is not hard to think that the visual representations would have an impact on how the "intangible" happenings in the virtual world are conceptualized by those who use them. Instructors or students who play and interact with those objects are very likely to see the online interactions with other perspective and make themselves meta-cognitive questions like: How centralized is this discussion? Who are the leaders in this forum? Who dominates the interaction? Or what is my own role in this forum?

If the SNA metrics and visual representations of the interactions are provided while the class

is taught, that could help to make interventions to avoid some students to become outliers or isolates. The possibility of early diagnosis of non-participants and the capability to monitor team interaction have been mentioned by the instructors in this study as the best features of these tools.

This research examined a methodology for analyzing social interactions in virtual environments and provided valuable insights on how students and instructors interact in an online discussion forum. Because of the importance of discussion forums in online education, it is important to make instructors aware that interaction in these environments does not occur naturally and is the result of facilitating factors instead. Instructors' interventions through social presence, instructional design, and moderator role are the elements that can modify and foster patterns of interaction and, therefore, impact positively on student learning and performance in the online course.

FUTURE RESEARCH DIRECTIONS

I wish the results of this study would provoke the discussion of new questions and issues related to interactions in online environments, like:

- What does a "good pattern" look like?
- If the class was successful (according to the instructor/students), what was its "shape" or SNA indexes?
- What do instructors want the SNA measures look like?
- What if the measures show little/no diversity?
- Do we want uniformity/homogeneity in these measures or do we want heterogeneity?

Based on the findings from this study, I see a number of ideas that could be followed in order to advance the applicability and understanding of SNA as it relates to online interactions. A possible subsequent path would be to work in the imple-

Figure 3. Snapshot of a 3D visualization of the class-interaction

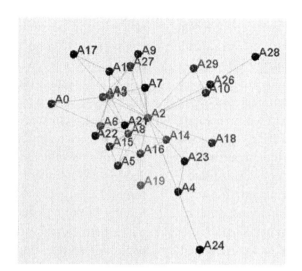

mentation of the necessary code so to provide a LMS with the SNA metrics and visualizations embedded in the system for the instructors and students to use them. Once the SNA metrics and visualizations are part of a LMS, it would be possible to see how instructors, students, and researchers can benefit from it.

To achieve the implementation of these tools into the LMS, there are many issues to be considered. During the development of this research, some issues such as the automatic collection of the relational data, the graphical display of the images, and the rules for simplification and manipulation of the data arose. The SNA metrics information and visualizations have to be presented to the instructors in a format that is easy to understand and communicate with clarity, precision, and efficiency. That must be done by taking out as much of the technical network language as possible, so to make it less overwhelming for instructors and students.

The survey that was created for the instructors to provide their perceptions about class interactions and student roles was the first attempt to design such an instrument. It was made without examples to take as models. The resulting instrument proved to be helpful in collecting valuable information, but it can certainly be improved.

Due to high attrition rates in distance education, especially relevant is the early identification of predictors of success or failure in online courses. The SNA metrics could be explored and investigated as such possible predictors.

The study discussed in this chapter applied the SNA methodology to analyze interactions in an asynchronous message board, which is one of the most used tool for communication in online courses, but not the only one. Chat, wikis, and blogs are other tools for group social interaction and collaboration in online environments. Further research can be done to investigate the applicability of the SNA techniques to chat, wikis and blogs or other tools for group social interaction and collaboration in online environments.

REFERENCES

Aviv, R., Erlich, Z., Ravid, G., & Geva, A. (2003). Network analysis of knowledge construction in asynchronous learning networks, *Journal of Asynchronous Learning Networks*, *7*(3). Retrieved April 23, 2004, from http://www.sloan-c.org/publications/jaln/v7n3/v7n3_aviv.asp

Bandura, A. (1977). *Social learning theory.* New York: General Learning Press.

Batagelj, V., & Mrvar, A. (2003). Pajek—Analysis and visualization of large networks. In M. Jünger, & P. Mutzel (Eds.), *Graph drawing software* (pp. 77-103). Berlin: Springer.

Borgatti, S. P., Everett, M. G., & Freeman, L. C. (1992). UCINET IV network analysis software. *Connections, 15,* 12-15.

Bruner, J. (1996). The *culture of education.* Cambridge, MA: Harvard University Press.

Cho, H., Stefanone, M., & Gay, G. (2002). Social network analysis of information sharing networks in a CSCL community. In: G. Stahl (Ed.), *Proceedings of Computer Support for Collaborative Learning (CSCL) 2002 Conference,* Jan. 7-11, Boulder, CO. (pp. 43-50). Mahwah, NJ: Lawrence Erlbaum.

Fahy, P.J., Crawford, G., & Ally, M. (2001). Patterns of interaction in a computer conference transcript. *International Review of Open and Distance Learning, 2*(1). Retrieved on December 18, 2006, from http://www.irrodl.org/content/v2.1/fahy.html

Freeman, L. C. (1980). The gatekeeper, pair dependency, and structural centrality. *Quality and Quantity, 14,* 585-592.

Freeman, L. C. (2000). Visualizing Social Networks. *Journal of Social Structure, 1*(1). Retrieved on December 11, 2004 from http://www.cmu.edu/joss/content/articles/volume1/Freeman.html

Freeman, L. C., Webster, C. M., & Kirke, D. M. (1998). Exploring social structure using dynamic three-dimensional color images. *Social Networks, 20,* 109-118.

Garrison, D.R., Anderson, T., & Archer, W. (2001). Critical thinking and computer conferencing: A model and tool to assess cognitive presence. *American Journal of Distance Education, 15*(1), 7-23.

Garton, L., Haythornthwaite, C., & Wellman, B. (1997). Studying online social networks. *Journal of Computer Mediated Communication, 3*(1). Retrieved September 23, 2002, from http://www.ascusc.org/jcmc/vol3/issue1/garton.html

Gillespie, F. (1998). Instructional design for the new technologies. *New Directions for Teaching and Learning, 76,* 39-52.

Golder, S. A., & Donath, J. (2004, September 19-22). *Social roles in electronic communities. Presented at Association of Internet Researchers IR 5.0.* Brighton, England. Retrieved May 12, 2005, from http://web.media.mit.edu/~golder/projects/roles/golder2004.pdf

Gunawardena, C. N, Lowe, C. A., & Anderson, T. (1997). Analysis of a global online debate and the development of an interaction analysis model for examining social construction of knowledge in computer conferencing. *Journal of Educational Computing Research, 17*(4), 397-431.

Gunawardena, C. N. (1995). Social presence theory and implications for interaction and collaborative learning in computer conferencing. *International Journal of Educational Telecommunications, 1*(2-3), 147-166.

Haythornthwaite, C. (1998). *Network structure among computer-supported distance learners: Multiple relations, multiple media, and time.* Retrieved March 11, 2003, from http://alexia.lis.uiuc.edu/~haythorn/LEEP3_2.html

Henri, F. (1992). Computer conferencing and content analysis. In A. R. Kaye (Ed.), *Collaborative learning through computer conferencing: The Najaden papers* (pp. 115-136). New York: Springer.

Hillman, D. C., Willis, D. J., & Gunawardena, C. N. (1994). Learner-interface interaction in distance education: An extension of contemporary models and strategies for practitioners. *The American Journal of Distance Education, 8*(2), 30-42.

Hiltz, S. R., Coppola, N., Rotter, N., Turoff, M., & Benbunan-Fich, R. (2000). Measuring the importance of collaborative learning for the effectiveness of ALN: A multi-measure, multi-method approach. *Journal of Asynchronous Learning Networks, 4*(2). Retrieved December 6, 2006, from http://www.sloan-c.org/publications/JALN/v4n2/v4n2_hiltz.asp

Ho, S. (2002). Evaluating students' participation in on-line discussions. In *Proceedings of AusWeb 2002, The Eighth Australian World Wide Web Conference,* Queensland, Australia. Retrieved December 5, 2006, from http://ausweb.scu.edu.au/aw02/papers/refereed/ho/paper.html

Howell-Richardson, C., & Mellar, H. (1996). A methodology for the analysis of patterns of participation within computer-mediated communication courses. *Instructional Science, 24,* 47-69.

Johnson, J. C., Borgatti, S. P., Luczkovich, J. J., & Everett, M. G. (2001). Network role analysis in the study of food webs: An application of regular role coloration. *The Journal of Social Structure, 2*(3). Retrieved September 2, 2004, from http://www.cmu.edu/joss/content/articles/volume2/Johnson-Borgatti.html

Johnson. J. C., Richardson, D. C., & Richardson, J. S. (2002, September). *Network visualization of social and ecological systems.* Paper presented at the Russian-American Workshop on Studies of Socio-Natural Co-Evolution from Different Parts of the World, Academgorodok, Siberia.

LaRose, R., & Whitten, P. (2000). Re-thinking instructional immediacy for web courses: A social cognitive exploration. *Communication Education, 49,* 320-338.

Levenburg, N. M., & Major, H. T. (2000). Motivating the online learner: The effect of frequency of online postings and time spent online on achievement of learning goals and objectives. In *Proceedings of the International Online Conference On Teaching Online in Higher Education.* Indiana University-Purdue University: Fort Wayne.

Martinez, A., Dimitriadis, Y., Rubia, B., Gomez, E., Garrachon, L., & Marcos J. A. (2002, Jan. 7-11). Studying social aspects of computer-supported collaboration with a mixed evaluation approach. In Stahl, G. (Ed.), *Proceedings of Computer Support for Collaborative Learning (CSCL) 2002 Conference,* Boulder, Colorado (pp. 631-632). Mahwah, NJ: Lawrence Erlbaum,

McCarthey, S. J., & McMahon, S. (1992). From convention to invention: Three approaches to peer interactions during writing. In R. Hertz-Lazarowitz & N. Miller (Eds.), *Interaction in cooperative groups.* New York: Cambridge University Press.

Moody, J. (2004). Distance education. Why are the attrition rates so high? *The Quarterly Review of Distance Education, 5*(3), 205-210.

Moore, M. G. (1989). Three types of interaction. *The American Journal of Distance Education, 3*(2), 1-6.

Moreno, J. L. (1934). *Who shall survive? Foundations of sociometry, group psychotherapy, and sociodrama.* Washington DC: Nervous and Mental Disease Publishing Co.

Pask, G. (1975). *Conversation, cognition, and learning.* New York: Elsevier.

Reffay, C., & Chanier, T. (2003). How social network analysis can help to measure cohesion in collaborative distance-learning. In B. Wasson, S. Ludvigsen, & U. Hoppe (Eds.), *Computer-supported collaborative learning, designing for change in networked learning environments.* In *Proceedings of the International Conference on Computer Support for Collaborative Learning 2003* Dordretch, *(Vol. 2* pp. 343-352). The Netherlands: Kluwer Academic Publishers.

Richardson, D. C., & Richardson, J. S. (1992). The kinemage: A tool for scientific communication. *Protein Science 1,* 3-9.

Scott, J. (2000). *Social network analysis: A handbook.* Second edition. London: Sage Publications.

Short, J. A., Williams, E., & Christie, B. (1976). *The social psychology of telecommunications.* New York: John Wiley & Sons.

Swan, K., & Shih, L. F. (2005). On the nature and development of social presence in online course discussions. *Journal of Asynchronous Learning Networks, 9*(3), 115-136.

Viegas, F. B., Boyd, D., Nguyen, D. H., Potter, J., & Donath, J. (2003). Digital artifacts for remembering and storytelling: *PostHistory and social network fragments.* Retrieved March 21, 2004, http://web.media.mit.edu/~fviegas/papers/posthistory_snf.pdf

Vygotsky, L. (1978). *Mind in society.* Cambridge, MA: Harvard University Press.

Wasserman, S., & Faust, K. (1994). *Social network analysis: Methods and applications.* New York: Cambridge University Press.

Wegerif, R. (1998). The social dimension of asynchronous learning networks. *Journal of Asynchronous Learning Networks, 2*(1). Retrieved July 23, 2003, from http://www.aln.org/alnweb/journal/vol2_issue1/wegerif.htm

White, N. (2001). *Community member roles and types.* Retrieved August 12, 2006, from http://www.fullcirc.com/community/memberroles.htm

Willging, P. A. (2004). Using social network analysis to study teamwork dynamics. In T. N. Garavan, E. Collins, M. J. Morley, R. Carbery, C. Gubbins, & L. Prendeville (Eds.), *Proceedings of the Fifth UFHRD/AHRD Conference.* University of Limerick, Ireland.

Woods, R., & Ebersole, S. (2003). Social networking in the online classroom: Foundations of effective online learning. *EJournal, 12-13*(1). Retrieved August 28, 2003, from http://www.acs.ucalgary.ca/ejournal/archive/v12-13/v12-13n1woods_print.html

Wu, Y. B., & Chen, X. (2005). Assessing student learning with automated text processing techniques. *Journal of Asynchronous Learning Networks, 9*(3). Retrieved November 12, 2006, from http://www.sloanc.org/publications/jaln/v9n3/v9n3_wu.asp

Zhu, E. (2006). Interaction and cognitive engagement: An analysis of four asynchronous online discussions. *Instructional Science, 34*, 451-480.

ENDNOTES

[1] A relationship between two nodes can be directed or undirected. For example, the relationship *recognizes* is directed because if baby A *recognizes* baby B, this does not imply that baby B *recognizes* baby A. The relationship *has the same father as*, on the other hand, is undirected because if baby A *has the same father as* baby B, then baby B *has the same father as* baby A.

[2] A Java applet is a small piece of software programmed with Java (cross-platform programming language developed by Sun Microsystems).

[3] This program was designed in a *cohort style* of learning, that is, all students in the group take the same courses at the same time.

[4] The students who received many replies to their messages would have a high *in-degree* score.

[5] The students who tried to moderate the discussion would have a high *betweenness* score.

[6] The students who sent many messages would have a high *out-degree* score.

Chapter XI
Implications of Anonymity in Cyber Education

Bobbe Baggio
Advantage Learning Technologies, USA

Yoany Beldarrain
Florida Virtual School, USA

ABSTRACT

This chapter explores the pros and cons of anonymity in cyber education and discusses possible ethical and social implications for online learning. It evaluates both sides of the anonymity issue and presents strategies that may help cyber educators and instructional designers safeguard academic integrity. The educational implications include concern for authenticity and academic integrity, and the dynamics found in social presence. This chapter discusses pertinent policy while analyzing anonymity's potential for limiting and monitoring academic freedom and the social benefits it brings. Strategies are suggested to enhance social presence by planning for interaction through the instructional design process. The far-reaching effects of anonymity within online educational settings and group dynamics have immediate and long term implications for instruction and learning.

CHAPTER OBJECTIVES

The reader will be able to:

- Understand the educational implications of anonymity in cyber education
- Understand how the enactment of policies attempt to protect individuals as well as institutions
- Identify the main two ways in which academic integrity breaches may occur in online courses.
- Evaluate different strategies that may be used to safeguard academic integrity.

INTRODUCTION

The topic of anonymity in cyber education presents ethical concerns as well as benefits. The privacy offered by the anonymity of cyberspace can influence a person's level of isolation. This is a risk that online learners take and which instructional designers must minimize by planning for interactions that increase social presence. Anonymity also brings about the added concerns of academic integrity and authenticity. This chapter will explore ethical and social implications of anonymity in cyber education.

Anonymity affects class discussions, emerging online identities, and interpretations. This brings a new freedom for learners or instructors who do not want to feel categorized, such as those with a physical disability who could be perceived negatively (Lance, 2002). The benefits of anonymity also create challenges. Constructivist learning theories support online instructional modeling strategies that may help enhance social presence and thus reduce the feelings of remoteness.

While some individuals may actually prefer seclusion, most online learners either choose or are required to actively participate in the course. New social norms are developed within the course room as students get to know each other through interactions. These norms require that individuals use new communication skills (Kerka, 1996). Monitoring within the online environment is also a necessary task for instructors and administrators alike. E-learning platforms, such as WebCT, not only let instructors monitor how learners are using the course room, but also offer features for administrators to go behind the scenes and assess the effectiveness of the instructor.

There is a dichotomy in a technological society: on one hand, anonymity is one of the characteristics of technology; on the other hand, evolving technologies are making anonymity increasingly less evident. Misconduct and improper use of the Internet have prompted governments around the globe to seek regulation and control over the anonymity inherent in Web-based communications. The online community, including distance learners, is affected by these policies and/or lack of them.

Anonymity is the capability to act in private. Privacy means the ability to act without being known or isolated from the invasion of others. In years past, choosing not to reveal one's name or writing with a pseudonym enabled anonymity. Through anonymity, individuals have the freedom to think and express their ideals, even if these ideals may not be in favor politically or socially. It also offers protection from ridicule and retribution. Being unreachable though, has other consequences (Nissenbaum, 1999). Some of these consequences include identity theft, lack of authenticity, and lack of personalization. Anonymity may also exaggerate fear and isolation.

Cyber culture may present a false sense of online security. While the learners hold that their interactions are private and secure, the reality is that everything is traceable. The ability to track, profile, trace, and categorize are inherent in the media. It is inescapable that in order for data to travel to a designation around the world it must know where to go. "Most of society is not equipped to understand what is going on underneath the shiny, glossy surface of the World Wide Web.

While it appears that most of the Internet makes it possible for us to lose contact with our bodies and assume some ethereal cyber presence, the amount of surveillance also possible is surprising" (Herman & Swiss, 2000, p.148).

Improvements in telecommunications and mobile learning, as well as the continuing development of alternative technologies to deliver education, are creating a climate of digital access that has more user entry points daily. The kinds of issues surrounding anonymity and the way theses issues influence cyber education are difficult to pin down. According to the National Research Council, the observations we make today will not only be different from observations in the past, but will be changed by the events in the future (Kettler, Klensin, Medin et al., 2001). On the other hand, good policies cannot be developed unless a constant conversation is taking place regarding the issues faced by distance educators, especially those who are part of online learning communities. As national boundaries disappear, the international concern for safeguarding individuals and their information from possible misuse also grows (Karmaker, 2002). The protection afforded by policy varies not only by nation, but also by economic sector. Educational institutions in the United States are affected primarily by the Family Educational Rights and Privacy Act of 1974 (FERPA) and the Uniting and Strengthening America By Providing Appropriate Tools Required To Intercept and Obstruct Terrorism (U.S. Patriot) Act, which will be discussed in the next section.

In order to plan for cyber education successfully, it is critical that the issues confronting the extended cyber space community are understood (Kettler et al., 2001). The term cyber education will be used throughout this chapter when referring to online teaching and learning. The implications of anonymity are far-reaching in cyber education, and instructional designers will need to focus on ways to create engaging online courses while maintaining accountability for students and instructors.

PROTECTION AFFORDED BY POLICY

The meaning of anonymity today is not the same as it was as 25 years ago. The concept becomes obscure in a society that is electronically capable of sending information around the world in nanoseconds and has implications far beyond those of just remaining nameless. Anonymity takes on new a meaning when technologies make it possible to trace people or access networks in ways that World Wide Web pioneers never imagined. Security breaches are a real concern for institutions and governments, which have enacted policies and laws to protect the rights of individuals, and protect themselves from intruders.

Security breaches are an unpleasant reality for educational institutions as well as businesses. In a 2005 report to Congress, it was revealed that about half of all security breaches in the U.S. happen within higher education settings (Tehan, 2005). Many major U.S. universities such as Indiana University, Michigan State University, and California State University among many others, have experienced security breaches that have put at risk of exposure confidential information residing in the school's server. Personal information, such as social security numbers and bank accounts, has been accessed by hackers and virus infections have threatened entire networks.

While the institutions at risk may have taken great steps to remedy this situation, one can not help but wonder how much information from anonymous surveys and confidential documents is actually out there. Certainly one way to minimize security breaches is to let technology correct the problem. Technologies have been developed to deter the loss of privacy and anonymity, which include firewalls, Web browsers that can deny loading personal information, and Platform for Privacy Preferences (P3P) that allow Websites to communicate their privacy practices to end users (Wenning, 2006). Regulation through the enactment of laws is another approach (Spinello, 2003).

In 1960, the Supreme Court passed a law declaring privacy as a separate right. The federal government has since passed several laws upholding this right including the Privacy Act of 1988 (Adamson & Mietus, 2000). This Privacy Act has 11 Information Privacy Principles (IPPs) and 10 Nation Privacy Principles (NPP) that apply to government agencies, the states, health care, and the private sector. The federal government has also passed a host of additional legislations to address data mining, matching, and telecommunications (Office of the Privacy Commissioner, 2006). As educational initiatives move into this dimension of cyberspace, personal privacy is affected, thus influencing the anonymity inherent in distance education.

Even though Internet use policies warn users of the open nature of the Internet, caution should still prevail. The Privacy Rights Clearinghouse Document "Privacy in Cyber Space: Rules of the Road for the Information Super Highway" states "there are virtually no online activities or services that guarantee an absolute right of privacy" (Academic Senate of California Community Colleges, 1999).

U.S. vs. Europe: Policy on Internet Anonymity

The European Union has taken a stronger stance than the United States to assure privacy and anonymity on the Internet. Because of the global reach of cyber education, it is interesting to examine the diverging paths taken by these entities. While the United States has relied on a "hands off" policy and self regulation, Europe has passed laws to protect privacy and the individual directly.

The United States' stance is founded on the belief that market regulation and self-policing by technology tools is the best way. Instead of sweeping policy regarding the issues of privacy and anonymity of Internet data, the United States has taken the approach of regulating specific industries. Laws such FERPA offer control and protection in situations where sensitive data could

be compromised (Spinello, 2003; United States Department of Education, 2006).

Europe has taken an opposite approach. The European Union has chosen to directly regulate the privacy rights of the individual across all sectors. The legislation covers the next generation of Internet protocol and requires the maintenance of proper confidentiality with respect to location, actual data, and information trafficking (British Parliament, 2000). This initiative empowers users to take control of safeguarding their own personal information. The major problem with this policy is that it is not supported by the technologies currently available for Internet communications. The current protocol gives away the location and traffic information when a user accesses the Internet. What is important is the philosophical underpinning behind the laws.

FERPA vs. U.S. PATRIOT Act

In an attempt to protect citizens from unforeseen terrorist attracts, the U.S. government has enacted laws that make monitoring easier. While these laws may mean well, they have impacted the ability for individuals to take shelter in anonymity. The U.S. Patriot Act, although amended, may have limited academic freedom and diversity of perspective. These limitations come about the heightened concerns for protecting national security at a time when expressing divergent opinions publicly may be construed as a threat. Only a good balance of different views can ensure freedom of academic pursuit. The problem is compounded in a digitally connected world of traceable information and profiling.

The importance of protecting the privacy of online learners may be seldom discussed, but the consequences may be brought to light under the U.S. Patriot Act (Kettler et al., 2001). Because of the implications of this act, face-to-face, as well as online, learners may have to make politically correct displays of opinion and interests, or they could potentially experience the inquisition of government officials. It could be argued that this type of limitation may warn off the pursuit of academic freedom. Interactions within the virtual course room for example, are easily identified and traced, thus potentially discouraging intellectual discourse and difference of opinion if placed in the wrong hands. These interactions could be e-mails, blogs, wikis, discussion postings, or written assignments that could include subversive political thoughts.

FERPA provides a tough standard for the review of educational records by third parties. Prior to September 11, 2001, few third party inquiries required release of student records. Only a court subpoena or pursuit of a subpoena could disclose student records. In Gonzaga University and Roberta S. League v. John Doe (Supreme Court of the United States, 2001), the rights guaranteed under FERPA were somewhat diminished, as the case restricted the threat of exposing a learner's private record to loss of federal funding. With the federal government given easy access to a student's records and undermining privacy rights in enforcing FERPA, the privacy of student records is vulnerable (American Civil Liberties Union, 2001).

Policies enacted in Europe and the United States affect the educational sector as well as other sectors which rely on the Internet (Spinello, 2003). Cyber education could be affected by the methods used to empower the users to determine which information is communicated and allow them to select control of their anonymity. As cyber educators take into consideration how the different policies impact educational practices, taking a balanced approach to anonymity remains a challenge.

ETHICAL IMPLICATIONS OF ANONYMITY IN THE ONLINE LEARNING ENVIRONMENT

In addition to traditional ways of securing the individual's information, educational institutions must now monitor the quality of their online programs and ensure the authenticity of student work. The feelings of "distance" inherent in anonymity may tempt some individuals to cheat (Burgoon, Stoner, Bonito, & Dunbar, 2003). This realization has cyber educators seeking to secure assessments in an effort to validate the grades they issue. Two ways to possibly deter ethical infractions are through monitoring the learning environment and implementing certain design strategies to enhance authenticity of student work.

Just like there are rules for driving on roads and highways, it is necessary to have guidelines for navigating and interacting within online environments. Shea (1994) introduced 10 core rules of Netiquette. Although these were developed for commercial application, they apply to all cyber communications.

These include:

- Remember to be human
- Adhere to the same standards of behavior online, that you would follow in real life
- Know where you are in cyberspace
- Respect other people's time and bandwidth
- Make yourself look good online
- Share expert knowledge
- Help keep the flame wars under control
- Respect other people's privacy
- Don't abuse your power
- Be forgiving of other people's mistakes

These 10 core rules have served as a bare minimum in cyber courtesies. The legal status of anonymity on the Internet is unanswered and debatable. Yet, basic guidelines such as these 10 Netiquette rules may help set ethical boundaries to help safeguard academic integrity and reinforce an online learner's sense of presence in the course.

Authenticity of student work and sense of presence may well be influenced by the level of anonymity experienced. Every learner is required in most asynchronous and blended courses to participate in online discussions and assignment postings. These discussions and assignment postings reveal the person's name but not the physical cues that help form an opinion about the individual. Therefore, in this semi-anonymous environment there is both safety and concern. Threaded discussions, for example, are captured digitally and can be retained for extended periods of time. Academic institutions, such as Baker College (Heberling, 2002), archive entire online courses for quality control. A student's interaction patterns can be analyzed for any particular purpose and opinions can be formed based on the patterns found.

The level of anonymity may affect student contributions and feedback. Because of the permanent and visible characteristics of posting information online, many students, for example, may hesitate to share unpopular ideas. One way to protect against fear of retribution is to provide anonymity to the learners. Because discussions are so critical to learner exchange and communications in cyber space, developing interesting and robust exchanges is desirable.

While instructors are not in the business of judging students, they must monitor their course room interaction and the quality of their discussion postings, which is often a large component of their grade. Instructors and peer learners are bound to form unintentional misunderstandings and misconceptions if the social constraints of anonymity are not removed by purposely creating safe online learning environments.

In Pursuit of Academic Integrity

The lack of identity brings to light serious issues about how we distinguish, handle, and negotiate identifying information. Having authentic records is critical to cyber education, the credibility of entire educational institutions rides on the ability to prove who did what work. Authenticity then becomes an interdependent of anonymity. In face-to-face settings, anonymity is generally

indistinguishable if the norms are followed and socially acceptable behaviors are adhered. In cyberspace, the observance of mainstream and socially acceptable behaviors are mainstay. The counterweight to anonymity is accountability, thus safeguarding academic integrity is of utmost importance to cyber educators.

Anonymity is seen as undesirable when it becomes an enabler for fraud or deception, yet the need for accountability creates ambiguity and concern. Minor educational implications include tracking when and how long a student has accessed the virtual classroom, documenting interaction and "surfing" patterns, and personal tendencies or preferences. Major implications can include tracking subversive political views or actions that are perceived to be threatening. While the latter is a provocative thought, academic institutions may be more interested in curtailing plagiarism than following radical points of view. Academic integrity is mainly breached in two ways: when students plagiarize from Internet or other written sources and when students have someone else do their online assignments or assessments.

The problems that cause students to cheat are the same in face-to-face and online classrooms; for example, a student may feel pressured to produce an essay he did not have time to write, or maybe he did not understand the topic covered (Christe, 2003). Anonymity can be wrongfully used in ways that would be more evident in the face-to-face classroom, such as having someone else take the exam. Nonetheless, educators are responsible for safeguarding the authenticity of assignments and assessments and may do so utilizing specific tools and strategies

Tracking student access to a course can provide important information to the instructor. For example, if the student has spent little time in the course, or has not navigated to the appropriate lessons, yet produces high quality assessments for those lessons, a flag of concern is raised. In this case, the student may be getting information from someone who has previously taken the same course.

In the online environment, distance and anonymity may tempt a student to bend socially accepted norms. Although tracking personal tendencies and preferences could possibly be mishandled, instructors may gather clues as to the writing and communication style of their students. When an instructor knows students as individuals, she or he is better prepared to notice any sudden changes in a person's writing or communication style that may indicate some one else has completed the assignment.

The most common type of academic integrity breach may be plagiarism. Cheating online is often seen as easier both psychologically and technologically. Academic institutions, however, rely on services such as *Turnitin.com.* to identify and curtail such behavior. Equipped with search engines, these companies can scan Web-published documents, online books, and their own repertoire of previously scanned documents, to find any matching content. This technology has empowered cyber educators to easily detect plagiarized work.

Instructional designers can employ different strategies that enhance authenticity and promote honesty in the virtual classroom. Attention must be paid to assessments and appropriate monitoring. The consequence of ignoring academic integrity in the online environment is a threat to online credibility (Christe, 2003). Authentication is only as valid as the morality of the person accessing the information (Rezmierski & Soules, 2000).

Designing for Authenticity

In a midst of frustration and a sense of urgency, distance educators are looking to the instructional designer to provide added security and authenticity in the online course room. Anonymity should remain part of the environment if it indeed protects privacy and promotes academic freedom. This must be balanced with the need to have a secure environment free of security or academic integrity breaches. Teachers and learners must be protected from anonymity concerns that compromise work, their identity, or their validity (Rezmierski & Soules, 2000). Two strategies that may help cultivate academic integrity are to create meaningful assessments (Olt, 2002) and monitor student activities.

Good assessment tools are fundamental to ensuring the quality of online learning. Carefully selected and crafted, these tools can support the positive aspects of anonymity online and decrease the impact of the negative. Using multiple techniques and selecting various methods that evaluate students in an authentic manner may foster academic integrity.

These techniques include synchronous activities such as virtual presentations, debates, position statements, or interviews. Another approach might be to craft questions that are broad enough to be authentic and allow the learner to apply the knowledge to their life and their world. These techniques may also have the side effect of not only diminishing the "need" to cheat, but also facilitating transfer by internalizing the knowledge gained. Although these synchronous assessment strategies are a departure from the more popular multiple choice tests, they still do not guarantee that the person participating is indeed the student enrolled.

Overall, instructors and designers should strive to design assessments and assignments that are meaningful, require mastery of the subject matter, and call for real-world applications. Thus cyber educators can focus on the process instead of the product. If the designers make the assessments a learning experience and add variety and meaning, the learner is more likely to see the assessments as meaningful and less likely to cheat (Rowe, 2004).

Several other things can be done to help minimize cheating in online assessments and curtail plagiarism. Expectations and consequences for breaching academic integrity should be communicated to learners at the beginning of the course. The instructor may also use monitoring tools within the Learner Management System (LMS) to track student activity. If such monitoring tools are available, they should be used to monitor participation, times, and duration (Christe, 2003). Other strategies include: (1) changing the assessment each time the course is offered, (2) using a larger pool of questions for the assessment, (3) conducting oral assessments via phone, and (4) monitoring student communication. These strategies may be helpful but are not without weaknesses and challenges.

Course design and instructional methods can make a critical difference in reducing the negative effects of anonymity online and supporting the positive attributes. The classroom should be supportive and impartial. Communications and interactions can enhance collaboration and sharing, and minimize remoteness. Designers and instructors need to meet the increasing ethical challenges of assessment in online education. The biggest challenge is awareness and acceptance of the problems brought about by technologies and the temptations afforded by anonymity.

SOCIAL IMPLICATIONS OF ANONYMITY THAT IMPACT EDUCATION

The social implications of anonymity are evident in the interactions of online learners. Student-student as well as student-instructor interactions display clues to the level of anonymity as well as the type of emergent persona chosen by each individual. Proper interactions provided by instructional design and modeling can help create safe environments where learners are encouraged to participate in academic discourse. Activities should be designed to support authenticity and help instructor and learners build a learning community.

The potential to experiment and explore different perspectives is at the heart of online teaching and learning. The anonymity of teaching and learning in cyberspace supports the experience of leaving one's culture and wandering into another, or experimenting with one's sense of identity and returning home safe and sound. It also supports the freedom that is responsible for challenging and shifting perspectives and encouraging appreciation for differences, while valuing members of the learning community as independent thinkers (Chester & Gwynne, 1998; Rheingold, 1994).

Social presence is a way of defining our place in cyberspace. Heim (1992) implies that interactions in cyberspace are a way of defining our sense of reality. Kennedy (2000, p.13) defines cyberspace as the "cultural space in cyberculture" where "subjective empowerment, pleasure, play, and creative connection(s)" occur. Social positioning in cyberspace becomes one of questioning the subjective and pre-subjective elements of the encounter. Whether it is through course management systems, e-mail, bulletin boards or the Web, encounters in cyberspace rely on positioning through discourse. In cyberspace, each learner is at equal distance from the learning stimuli. It is only the learner's perception of closeness and intimacy, which is influenced through interactions that provides a sense of presence and social identity (Gunawardena, 1995).

Current educational epistemology supports the theories of constructivism. Constructivist theorists Cote (1996) and McAdams (1998) support the theory that each individual has some control over the development of his or her identity. An online learner's identity is constructed through a combination of social forces and the learner's ability to navigate through these powers (Cote). Online identity is often put together through the use of language as a text through which identity is constructed and maintained. Reality is then born through narrative assumptions that help shape identities (McAdams).

Constructivist theory has greatly influenced how collaborative learning is applied in the online environment and supports the concept that thinking is grounded in social and physical experiences. Knowledge is constructed by interactions with others and the learning environment. Constructivist pedagogy asserts that knowledge is constructed by the learner through meaningful interactions and this can lead to substantial learning gains (Jonassen, 1999).

In a constructivist environment, learners and instructors do not exist independent of each other, nor can knowledge transfer be measured by an end-of-unit test. Each learner has a host of responses applicable to a situation depending on progression, cognitive processes, and resources. There are qualities inherent in meaningful and engaging constructivist learning environments, which can be applied to understand the why and how individuals engage in an activity (Jonassen & Rohrer-Murphy, 1999). These qualities include use of active, constructive, collaborative, intentional, complex, contextual, conversational, and reflective environments (Jonassen, 1999; Jonassen & Rohrer-Murphy, 1999). Where many instructional designers fall short is not effectively integrating these aspects into a distributed learning environment (Morice, 2002).

Building environments that support multiple perspectives and authentic examples can support collaboration and the construction of knowledge through social negotiations. Learning environments that support the active construction of knowledge must also foster social presence and trust. The promotion of social presence may be a significant factor in instructional effectiveness and collaborative learning.

Minimizing Perceived Instructor Authority: Benefit or Detriment?

Because these Internet communications lack the initial social and emotional cues that are provided in face-to-face environments, there is an initial feeling of anonymity. This allows introverted learners to participate in discussions and share feelings in ways they may not be able to do in face-to-face classrooms. This same distancing also creates equality between professors and students by eliminating things like standing in front of the class and divesting the professor of some authority. Learners feel a greater sense of anonymity and therefore empowerment to express ideas and open discussions, which leads to a changing role for the instructor. The role is certainly more of a facilitator and less of an expert; it breaks down the authority structure and opens up channels of communication.

Disarming the traditional lecturer of some perceived authority has its own social implications. For instance, traditional societies that have long valued and respected educators will find it inappropriate for a student to address the instructor by the first name or question the grade received on an assignment. Placing the instructor at a more equal level with the student can potentially undermine the instructor's authority, especially when the student is frustrated about something that could otherwise have been resolved in a face-to-face environment (DeVries & Lim, 2003). Instructors and designers must take this aspect of anonymity into consideration, as it can impact the way learners from different cultural backgrounds interact with the instructor.

Equalizing instructor and learner roles can bring benefits to building online learning communities. Online learning communities are the framework that facilitates the exchange of social information as well as reinforcement of key concepts learned. Wegerif (1998) agrees that learning communities provide the social dimensions necessary for learners to be successful in asynchronous learning environments.

The Emergence of a New Persona

This initial sense of anonymity and freedom gives way to a different feeling, as individuals experience the emergence of a new online identity. The acknowledgement that ones' style and presence can be easily identified by the consistencies expressed in writing and the ideas and attitudes that have not only been captured but also preserved over time. Anonymity may also affect the quality of comments offered in communications by students. Peer accountability and anonymity can affect the degree to which learners communicate with each other as well as the quality of these communications.

Asynchronous learning environments create a new dimension for learner interaction. New patterns of social interactions emerge as students take on their new online identity. Gender differences can play a huge role in the way a learner interacts within a course room (Rovai & Baker, 2005). Rovai and Baker found that female online learners felt more connected during their learning experience. But how does interaction relate to anonymity?

The feelings of anonymity will impact the student's interaction patterns. If females tend to feel more connected, this could mean that females deal differently with the feelings of anonymity than males. Further research is needed to investigate the relationship between anonymity and interaction as they are impacted by gender. Recent research shows that there are personality factors which may influence a person's inclination to follow norms or be academically dishonest. Etter, Cramer and Finn (2006) found that students who perceived sensation-seeking behaviors to be acceptable, were at a higher risk of breaching academic integrity, yet cheating in church-affiliated institutions versus traditional institutions was very similar.

Earlier studies in online learning showed contradictory conclusions in regards to anonymity. Kiesler, Seigel and McGuire (1984) suggested that anonymity would minimize gender differences. But, Herring (2000) insisted that gender-based communication styles carry over into electronic environments. Herring bases his claim on research showing that males who tend to be more aggressive face-to-face, also displayed the same behaviors in online environments, such as listserves.

Meanwhile, the women tended to be more assertive in male-dominated groups. Herring found a myriad of gender differences that are visible in online environments; thus, he believes that true anonymity is very hard to achieve.

Deindividuation: Setting "Self" Free

Deindividuation is the psychological state of mind that causes a person to become less inhibited and less self-evaluative (Postmes, Spears, & Lea, 1998). Postmes et al.'s social identity model of deindividuation (SIDE) targets the interaction of online learners as individuals and as members of a learning community. They found that computer-mediated communications did not free individuals from being influenced by social norms or pressures. This is contrary to the idea that anonymity only brings freedom of expression.

Other researchers, such as Scott (1999), have concluded that when a person's identity is salient or emergent, the person is less likely to follow the group norms. But, when a more social identity emerges, the person is more likely to follow group norms and feel part of the social structure. He contends that the same anonymity that causes students to become uninhibited creates social salient identities that in turn increase the stereotypical behaviors of those individuals. In other words, when we identify ourselves with a group, we are likely to behave according to the group's norms. The effects of depersonalization on group dynamics are astounding. When learners are depersonalized, their individuality is less salient, thus they bond with the group, giving way to the emergence of stereotypes (Postmes et al., 2002).

The power of culture is also a factor to consider. Individualistic cultures influence the way learners from that particular culture identify themselves. Jetten, Postmes, and McAuliffe (2002) found that people from individualistic cultures, like in North America, tend to have low identifiers, in contrast to cultures that value collectivism.

Collectivist cultures, such as those from Asia, show high identifiers, but follow the salient group norms, more so than low identifiers. This reveals how cultural background influences a learner's interactivity and feelings of anonymity.

The question as to whether asynchronous learning environments are better at sustaining anonymity poses a concern for designers who are being asked to do just that. Research has shown that computer mediated communications are not necessarily asynchronous. Wegerif (1998) cites the example of frustrated students and instructors having to sort through an extensive list of messages after being a short time away from the course room. The first challenge is to provide a sense of community for learners of both individualistic as well as collectivist tendencies while the second challenge is to design learning environments that encourage learners to actively participate.

Designing for Interaction

From the instructional design standpoint, the positive aspects of anonymity can possibly be nurtured while deterring fraud or deception. Courses may be created to include activities that support learner-learner and learner-instructor communications, foster collaboration, and fight isolation. The more connected the learners feel to each other and to their instructor the less likely they are to cheat and or be successful at it (Burgoon et al.,2003).

Face-to-face interactions have the effect of immediacy as the results of unethical and improper behaviors are immediately conveyed. On the other hand, online interactions can establish a mental distance that may make individuals feel more distant from ramifications (Rowe, 2004). Overtime, though, and with established guidelines, this psychological detachment can be reduced. Cheating is a genuine concern for cyber educators. Pressure to get good grades and lack of knowledge on how to address cheating may contribute to even more academic infractions (Gearhart, 2001).

Instructional designers have the responsibility of modifying instructional design models to ensure that different types of interaction are built into the course for diverse purposes. Best practices in the field should include those that have set guidelines for dealing with plagiarism, building online communities, and planning and organizing to implement learning theories that promote interaction. Message boards, IM, chats, blogs, wikis, and social networking software are just some of the tools that can be used to foster interaction in the course room. These tools help enhance social presence and build a sense of community. Many of these technologies already have built-in features to password protect and trace published content, thus providing other ways to monitor academic integrity.

Design frameworks should support building good and close relationships between instructors and learners as well as encourage direct and regular communication. Multiple communication methods enhance social presence and reduce the negative effects related to anonymity, such as remoteness. Furthermore, such interactions should purposely take into account differences in gender, culture and individual preferences.

Gunawardena (1995) conducted a study that indicates participants in online conferences ce-rate social presence by projecting their identities and building online communities. In order to encourage collaboration and interactive learning, it is important that learning environments are conducive to the creation of social and individual presence. Building social cohesiveness requires that instructional designers build interactive learning environment where learners feel comfortable choosing the level of anonymity and where instructors encourage and respect freedom of expression. Recognition and acknowledgement of learner presence by the instructor as well as developing protocols, etiquette and expectations will also enhance interactions and communications, thus potentially decreasing the desire to cheat.

Building an online community is as important as dealing with ethical infractions. Ethical guidelines must be practiced and enforced daily (Campbell, 2001). Palloff and Pratt (1999) stipulate that there is no online course without a learning community. It would then be logical to say that a learning community cannot exist without interactivity. Yet, these communities must be built with academic integrity as the foundation.

Planning and organization are pillars for building interaction among learners as well as between learner and instructor. There are a myriad of other skills and responsibilities that stem from planning, such as facilitating collaborative groups; choosing questioning strategies (Cyrs, 1997) and applying the most pedagogically sound practices that fit the objectives.

Cyber educators are responsible for creating a student-centered environment that encourages interaction for different purposes. According to Wagner (1997), there can be interaction for the purpose of increasing participation, developing communication, enhancing retention, supporting learner control/self-regulation, and interaction to receive feedback or clarification. Another important purpose of interaction is to increase motivation, which is a big factor of learner success in distance education.

Sims (2000) cites four dimensions that should be taken into account when assessing learning theories for the purpose of identifying how they promote interactivity:

1. **Learners:** The who of the learning process
2. **Content:** The what of the learning process
3. **Pedagogy:** Tthe how of the learning process
4. **Context:** The when and where of the learning process

Seasoned cyber educators understand the need for interactivity. As Pelz (2004) puts it, "interactivity is the heart and soul of effective asynchronous learning."

Two defining elements of online learning are the creation of learner identity and social presence. Learner identity can not be addressed in cyberspace without including the balancing act innate in anonymity. The opacity of cyberspace invites the learner to play with identity and build multiple selves (Turkle, 1997). The culture of cyberspace must be advanced with an open and eclectic approach to instructional design and modeling.

CONCLUSION

Anonymity in cyber education presents ethical concerns as well as benefits that must be taken into consideration when designing online courses. The privacy offered by the anonymity of cyberspace is threatened by the technological advancements that make possible the access to personal information. Online learners take the risk of having their ideas and thoughts exposed, thus it is the duty of instructional designers, instructors, and educational institutions to create a safe haven for scholarly discourse.

Anonymity affects class discussions, emerging online identities, and interpretations. But, at the same time, there are new dimensions, such as group dynamics, that affect the quality of discussions. New social patterns and norms emerge, as learners tend to identify themselves with their cultural background or relate to specific group behaviors. The tendency is to prefer either individualism or collectivism; such preferences will dictate how a person will blend in a group situation that is deindividualized.

Gender differences, once believed to equalize computer-mediated communication, emerge in asynchronous and synchronous learning environments. Furthermore, online courses cannot be successful without a learning community, and a learning community cannot exist without interactivity. Only by understanding this relationship can cyber educators realize the impact of anonymity.

There is now a heightened awareness on the part of governments and educational institutions on the need to protect personal privacy and anonymity. This awareness has prompted legislations such as the FERPA and Patriot Act in the United States. While these initiatives are meant to protect, they may set back the intellectual exchange of ideas, especially those with political connotations. Political tensions around the globe aggravate the problems with privacy already faced by cyber educators. The European Union has taken a different approach than the United States, leading the way in the enactment of laws that directly protect consumers. Only time will tell how the rest of the world will deal with these issues. Educational institutions face the challenge of maintaining data secure from intruders, as well as safeguarding the academic integrity of online programs.

In the mean time, cyber educators and instructional designers must evaluate implementation choices that build interactivity in online courses without compromising a learner's self-identity or the institution's academic integrity. By carefully balancing anonymity and identity, cyber educators have the task of creating online learning environments where students can safely exchange ideas that promote cultural understanding; a daunting task in a world that craves diplomatic dialogue.

REFERENCES

Adamson, J.E., & Mietus, N. J. (2000). *Law for business and personal use* (15th ed.). Cincinnati: International Thompson Publishing.

Academic Senate of California Community Colleges. (1999). *Academic freedom, privacy, copyright and fair use in a technological world.* Retrieved November 17, 2006, from ERIC ED482188.

American Civil Liberties Union. (2001, October). *How the anti-terrorism bill puts student privacy at risk.* Retrieved December 28, 2006, from http://www.aclu.org/natsec/emergpowers/12479leg20011023.html

British Parliament. (2000). Freedom of information act 2000. Retrieved June 5, 2006, from http://www.opsi.gov.uk/acts/acts2000/20000036.htm

Burgoon, J., Stoner, M., Bonito, J., & Dunbar, N. (2003, January). *Trust and deception in mediated communication.* 36th Hawaii International Conference on Systems Sciences. Retrieved August 10, 2007, from http://csdl2.computer.org/comp/proceedings hicss/2003/1874/01/187410044a.pdf

Campbell, E. (2001). Let right be done: Trying to put ethical standards into practice. *Journal of Education Policy, 16*(5), 395-411.

Chester, A., & Gwynne, G. (1998). Online teaching: Encouraging collaboration through anonymity. *Journal of Computer Mediated Communication.* Retrieved September 30, 2006, from http://jcmc.indiana.edu/vol4/issue2/chester.html

Christe, B. (2003) Designing online courses to discourage dishonesty: Incorporate a multilayered approach to promote honest student learning. *Educause Quarterly, 4,* 54-58.

Cote, J. E. (1996). Identity: a multidimensional analysis. In G.R. Adams, R. Montemayor, & T.P. Gullotta (Eds.) *Psychosocial development during adolescence: progress in developmental contextualism. Advances in adolescent development.* Newbury Park, CA: Sage.

Cyrs, T. E. (1997, Fall). Competence in teaching at a distance. In T.E.Cyrs, (Ed.), *New directions for teaching and learning, 71,* (pp. 15-18). Jossey Bass.

DeVries, J., & Lim, G. (2003, November 7-11). Significance of online teaching vs. face-to-face: similarities and differences. *E-Learn 2003, World Conference on E-Learning in Corporate,*

Government, Healthcare and Higher Education. Retrieved December 28, 2006, from http://ole. tp.edu.sg/courseware/teaching_guide/resources/ article/TP%20Staff/F2FandOnline.pdf

Etter, S., Cramer, J. J., & Finn, S. (2006, Winter). Origins of academic dishonesty: Ethical orientations and personality factors associated with attitudes about cheating with information technology. *Journal of Research on Technology Education, 39*(2), 133-155.

Gearhart, D. (2001). Ethics in distance education: Developing ethical policies. *Journal of Distance Learning Administration*: State University of West Georgia, Distance Learning Center. Retrieved June 7, 2006, from http://www.westga. edu/~distance/ojdla/spring41/gearhart41.html

Gunawardena, C. N. (1995). Social presence theory and implications for interaction and collaborative learning in computer conferences. *International Journal of Educational Telecommunications, 1*(23), 147-166.

Heberling, M. (2002, Spring). Maintaining academic integrity in online education. *Journal of Distance Learning Administration, 5*(1). Retrieved December 27, 2006, from http://www.westga. edu/~distance/ojdla/spring51/heberling51.html

Heim, M. (1992). The erotic ontology of cyberspace. In M. Benedikt (Ed.), *Cyberspace: First steps.* Cambridge: MIT Press.

Herman, A., & Swiss, T. (Eds.). (2000). *The world wide web and contemporary culture theory.* New York: Routledge.

Herring, S. C. (2000, Winter). Gender differences in CMC: Findings and implications. *The CPSR Newsletter, 18*(1), 3-11. Retrieved June 6, 2006, from http://www.cpsr.org/prevsite/publications/ newsletters/issues/2000/Winter2000/herring. html

Jetten, J., Postmes, T., & McAuliffe, B. (2002). We're all individuals: Group norms of individu-alism and collectivism, levels of identification, and identity threat. *European Journal of Social Psychology, 32,* 189-207.

Jonassen, D. (1999). Designing constructivist learning environments. In C.M. Reigeluth (Ed.), *Instructional-design theories and models Vol. II: A new paradigm of instructional theory* (pp. 215-239). Mahwah, NJ: Lawrence Erlbaum.

Jonassen, D., & Rohrer-Murphy, L. (1999). Activity theory as a framework for designing constructivist learning environments. *Educational Technology, Research & Development, 47*(1), 61-79.

Karmaker, N. L. (2002). *Online privacy, security and ethical dilemma: A recent study.* Association for the Advancement of Computing in Education, ERIC IR021765.

Kennedy, B. (Ed.). (2000). *The cybercultures reader.* New York: Routledge.

Kiesler, S., Seigel, J., & McGuire, T. W. (1984). Social psychological aspects of computer-mediated communication. *American Psychologist, 39*(11), 1123-1134.

Kerka, S. (1996). *Distance learning, the Internet and the World Wide Web.* Retrieved May 8, 2006 from http://www.cete.org/acve/docgen.asp?tbl=digests&ID=21

Kettler, A., Klensin, J.C., Medin, M., Partridge, C., Schutzer, D., et al. (2001). *The Internet's coming of age, Vol. 2005.* Washington, DC: National Academy Press.

Lance, G.D. (2002). Distance learning and disability: A view from the instructor's side of the virtual lectern. *Information Technology & Disabilities, EASI,* (Vol.8). Retrieved May 8, 2006 from http:// www.rit.edu/~easi/itd/itdv08n1/lance.htm

McAdams, D. P. (1998). *Power, intimacy, and the life story: Personalogical inquiries into identity.* New York: Guilford.

Morice, J. (2002). *Lights and wires: Effective e-learning.* Paper to the World Conference on Educational Multimedia, Hypermedia & Telecommunications, Denver, CO.

Nissenbaum, H. (1999). The meaning of anonymity in an information age. In A. Spinello & H. T. Tavani (Eds.), *Readings in cyberethics* (2nd ed.), (pp. 450-461). Sudbury, MA: Jones and Bartlett Publishers.

Office of the Privacy Commissioner. (2006). *Federal privacy law.* Retrieved September 29, 2006, from http://www.privacy.gov.au/act/

Olt, M. R. (2002) Ethics and distance education: strategies for minimizing academic dishonesty in online assessment. *Journal of Distance Learning Administration.* Retrieved October 16, 2006, from http://www.westga.edu/~distance/ojdla/fall53/olt53.html

Palloff, R. M., & Pratt, K. (1999). *Building learning communities in cyberspace: Effective strategies for the online classroom.* San Francisco: Jossey-Bass.

Pelz, B. (2004, June). (My) Three principles of effective online pedagogy. *Journal of Asynchronous Learning Networks, 8*(3), 33-46. Retrieved December 27, 2006, from http://www.sloan-c.org/publications/JALN/v8n3/v8n3_pelz.asp

Postmes, T., Spears, R., & Lea, M. (1998). Breaching or building social boundaries? SIDE-effects of computer-mediated communication. *Communication Research, 25,* 689-715.

Postmes, T., Spears, R., & Lea, M. (2002). Inter-group differentiation in computer-mediated communication: Effects of depersonalization. *Group Dynamics, 53*(6), 3-16.

Rezmierski,V., & Soules, A. (2000) Security, anonymity: The debate over user authentication and information access. *Educause Review, March-April,* 22-30. Retrieved December 27,

2006, from http://www.educause.edu/ir/library/pdf/ERM0022.pdf

Rheingold, H. (1994). *The virtual community: Finding connection in a computerised world.* London: Secker & Warburg.

Rovai, A. P., & Baker, J. D. (2005, Spring). Gender differences in online learning. *Quarterly Review of Distance Education, 6*(1), 31-45. Retrieved June 6, 2006, from EBSCO Full text Database.

Rowe, N. (2004). Cheating in online student assessment: Beyond plagiarism. *Journal of Distance Learning Administration.* Retrieved September, 23, 2006, from http://www.westga.edu/%7Edistance/ojdla/summer72/rowe72.html

Scott, C. R. (1999). Communication technology and group communication. In L.R. Frey, D.S. Gouran, & M.S. Poole (Eds.), *The handbook of group communication theory and research* (pp.432-472). Thousand Oaks, CA: Sage.

Shea, V. (1994). *Netiquette.* Retrieved June 7, 2006, from http://www.albion.com/netiquette/corerules.html

Sims, R. (2000). An interactive conundrum: Constructs of interactivity and learning theory. *Australian Journal of Educational Technology, 16*(1), 45-57. Retrieved May 17, 2006, from http://www.ascilite.org.au/ajet/ajet16/sims.html

Supreme Court of the United States. (2001, October). *Gonzaga University and Roberta S. League v. John Doe.* Case No. 01-679. Retrieved December 28, 2006, from http://www.aclu.org/FilesPDFs/gonzaga.pdf

Spinello, R. A. (2003). Cyberethics; morality and law in cyberspace (2nd Ed.). Sudbury, MA: Jones and Bartlett Publishers, Inc.

Tehan, R. (2005, December). Personal data security breaches: Context and incident summaries. *CRS Report for Congress.* Retrieved December 28, 2006, from http://digital.library.

unt.edu/govdocs/crs//data/2005/upl-meta-crs-8258/RL33199_2005Dec16.pdf

Turkle, S. (1997). *Life on the screen: Identity in the age of the internet.* New York: Touchstone.

United States Department of Education. (2006). *Family Educational Rights and Privacy Act (FERPA).* Retrieved December 28, 2006, from http://www.ed.gov/policy/gen/guid/fpco/ferpa/index.html

Wagner, E.D. (1997, Fall). Interactivity: From agents to outcomes. In T.E. Cyrs, (Ed.), *New Directions for Teaching and Learning, 71,* 19-26. Jossey Bass.

Wegerif, R. (1998). The social dimensions of asynchronous learning networks. *Journal of Asynchronous Learning Networks, 2*(1), Retrieved June 7, 2006, from http://www.sloan-c.org/publications/jaln/v2n1/v2n1_wegerif.asp

Wenning, R. (2006, December). *Platform for privacy preferences (P3P) project.* Retrieved September 29, 2006, from http://www.w3.org/P3P/

Section III
Online Instructional Modeling:
A Multi-Disciplinary Perspective

Chapter XII
The Relationship of Online Gaming and Feedback Type in Facilitating Delayed Achievement

Brian Cameron
Pennsylvania State University, USA

ABSTRACT

Instructional gaming has historically been used as a means of rehearsal and motivation. A majority of research in this area has attempted to identify the most effective method of rehearsal that maximizes student achievement and minimizes information loss over a specified time period. A few studies have suggested that instructional gaming environments have the ability to provide corrective feedback and reinforcement of previously taught information. The author investigates whether or not instructional online and computer gaming and the use of different forms of feedback produce a significant difference in improving delayed retention of different instructional objectives.

CHAPTER OBJECTIVES

The reader will be able to:

- Understand the major theories on instructional gaming and feedback type as they related to the achievement of different learning objectives
- Identify the relationship between instructional gaming and feedback type
- Define the role of instructional gaming and feedback in the enhancement of delayed retention

INTRODUCTION

According to Gagne (1985), people learn in incremental and predictable ways. He argues that external instructional events can be arranged in order to facilitate internal learning processes (Gagne, Briggs, & Wagner, 1988). However, in real life learning situations, where learning often occurs incrementally, the use of innovative instructional techniques is often limited. Feedback has been viewed as a critical element in the learning process, effecting learning in a variety of ways. In the late 1960s, the dominant position on feedback suggested that post response information acted as a type of "reinforcer," functioning to increase the probability of a correct response occurring at some later time (Kulhavy, & Stock, 1989). This position developed from the association of feedback and operant psychology (Skinner, 1958).

Operant psychology has as its foundation the "law of effect," which states that if a behavior is followed by a pleasant or desired response, it is likely to occur in the future. If the response is followed by an unpleasant response or less desirable response, it is less likely to occur in the future. In this view of feedback as a reinforcer, errors are ignored and attention is paid only to correct responses. Therefore, the operant approach does not provide a means to correct errors. Support for

the feedback-as-reinforcement idea declined when studies began to suggest that feedback's main function was to provide corrective information and information-processing theories began to gain wider acceptance (Anderson, Kulhavy, & Andre, 1972; Bardwell, 1981; Barringer & Gholson, 1979; Kulhavy, 1977; Roper, 1977).

Feedback is defined as any of the numerous procedures that are used to tell a learner if an instructional response is right or wrong (Kulhavy, 1977). Basically, feedback has two primary functions; that of verification and elaboration (Kulhavy & Stock, 1989). Feedback can also motivate a learner (Wagner & Wagner, 1985). Lee, Smith, and Savenye (1991) have defined three major types of feedback: knowledge of response (KOR), knowledge of correct response (KCR), and elaborative feedback. Knowledge of response feedback informs the learner of whether his or her response is correct or incorrect (Lee, 1985). For example, KOR feedback after an incorrect response might state, "No, that is incorrect."

Knowledge of correct response feedback informs the learner of the correct answer regardless of the learner's response (Lee, 1985). For example, KCR feedback after a correct or incorrect answer might state, "No, the correct answer is…" or, "Yes, the correct answer is…" Elaborative feedback informs the learner whether or not his or her response is correct and also gives the learner additional information regarding the correct response (Clariana, 1993). According to Schimmel (1983), examples of elaborative feedback vary greatly and may include step-by-step solutions to an incorrectly answered problem, general review feedback, and knowledge of correct response feedback with additional information such as text or graphics.

The Role of Instructional Gaming and Computer Games

Gaming has been used in education throughout history. Rieber and Noah (1997) have noted that instructional gaming is one of the earliest forms of instructional technology. The concept of instructional gaming is defined as any training format that involves competition and is rule-guided (Jones, 1987). This definition is consistent with that of other authors in the area. Competition in computer-based games may entail attempting to achieve the best overall score (Laveault & St. Germain, 1997). Several researchers have suggested that instructional gaming methods, used in a practice setting, can motivate learners. Thiagarajan (1988) has advocated the use of games in many instructional settings and suggested that the use of instructional gaming provides extrinsic motivation for iterative practice (Thiagarajan, 1976). Instructional games provide high-motivational approaches for reinforcement of already taught skills, concepts, and information (Malone, 1980, 1981). Keller (1987a) suggested that the use of gaming in instruction may enhance student attention and motivation.

Several authors have suggested that instructional gaming methods actively involve students and thereby increase motivation by generating enthusiasm, excitement, and enjoyment (Coleman, 1968; Ernest, 1986; Rakes & Kutzman, 1982; Wesson, Wilson, & Mandlebaum, 1988). When motivation is a concern, instructional games are often utilized for rehearsal learning environments. Instructional games are capable of delivering various forms of feedback in an immediate and direct manner. According to Oliver, Omari, and Herrington (1998), many computer-based instructional games are designed for individual students working separately on computers.

With the advent of the World Wide Web, educational organizations are investing significantly in the development of online learning environments. Yet there are mixed reports about the effectiveness of these environments. Online learning has long been plagued by high dropout rates due to lack of motivation and low student satisfaction. Current research in this area focuses on strategies for motivating learners in this new instructional environment (Jasinski & Thiagarajan, 2000).

The Importance of Motivation

Motivation is defined as "an impetus to act." Research has suggested that this impetus is not stable for different learners. Motivation is different from individual to individual. According to the ARCS Model (Keller, 1984), there are four general requirements to be met in order for people to be motivated to learn, and there are practical strategies to use in achieving each of the four requirements (Table 1).

The first requirement of this model is to obtain and sustain the student's attention. In the learning process, a student's attention has to be directed

Table 1. Components of the ARCS model (Adapted from Keller, 1984)

Major Categories	Definitions
Attention	Capturing the interest of learners; stimulating the curiosity to learn
Relevance	Meeting the personal needs/goals of the learner to effect a positive attitude
Confidence	Helping the learners believe/feel that they will succeed and control their success
Satisfaction	Reinforcing accomplishment with reward (internal and external)

to the appropriate cues. Before attention can be directed, it has to be acquired. After this has been accomplished, it is important to show the student the relevance of the material presented. Before learners can be motivated to learn, they will have to believe that the instruction is related to important personal goals or motives.

After relevance has been successfully established, students may still not be properly motivated due to too little or too much confidence or expectancy for success. They could have fears of the topic or situation that prevent them from learning effectively or at the other extreme, they might be overly cocky and overlook important details in the learning activities. For these reasons, it is important to design learning materials and environments that establish an appropriate level of confidence in regard to the learner's expectancy for success.

In order to have a continuing desire to learn, the student must have a sense of satisfaction with the process or results of the learning experience. Satisfaction can result from extrinsic and intrinsic factors. Extrinsic factors include opportunities for advancement, certificates, or other material rewards. Intrinsic factors are often overlooked but can be very powerful. These factors include feelings of self-esteem and achievement that result from successfully completing a learning activity.

The ARCS model has been applied to computer-based instructional gaming environments to help improve the motivational aspects of the instruction. Keller (1987b) found that games increase student motivation when they contain elements of the ARCS model, such as competition and goal setting and suggested that the use of games could help solve the attrition problem that often accompanies self-paced instructional programs.

The Importance of Delayed Retention

Learning is defined by Gagne (1988) as the ability to identify with, retain, organize, and apply information. Lindsay and Norman (1977, p. 337) stated "… the problem in learning new information is not getting the information into memory; it is making sure that it will be found later when it is needed." It is imperative that instruction prepares learners in such a way so as to promote the long-term retention of information. Information is much more valuable if it can be remembered and not just utilized and then forgotten. By developing innovative rehearsal methods that can facilitate the delayed retention of information, the field of instructional design may be enhanced.

According to Dwyer and Dwyer (1985), the depth of information processing is facilitated by rehearsal of the stimulus in short-term memory. The researchers argued that the type and intensity of the rehearsal methods utilized can impact student achievement by maximizing the transference of the stimulus into long-term memory. This view is consistent with that of other researchers and suggests that the quality and quantity of rehearsal methods can help learners identify, retain, organize, and apply information. Dwyer and Dwyer (1987, p. 264) also indicated, "…all levels of depth of information processing are not equally effective in facilitating student achievement of different instructional objectives."

Dual Coding Theory (Paivio, 1971) provides an account of how visually and verbally presented material might be integrated within the learner's working memory during learning. This theory suggests that information may be transferred and retained into long-term memory if the information is presented using text and graphics formats. Research has supported the contention that learning is positively affected by presenting text and illustrations together (Bernard, 1990; Glenberg &

Langston, 1992; Guri-Rozenblit, 1988; Purnell & Solman, 1991; Reed & Beveridge, 1986, 1990).

Gagne (1988) stated that contiguity, repetition, and reinforcement play important roles in fostering learning. It would seem reasonable to speculate that if instructional gaming and feedback properties were combined into one rehearsal sequence, learning may be enhanced. Specifically, providing content repetition in varied contexts and motivational reinforcement may produce optimum performance of specified learning objectives over an extended period of time. In order to determine an optimal format for feedback in an instructional gaming environment, further investigation is warranted.

According to Orbach (1979), instructional games generally ignore the fact that people have different cognitive styles and different motivations for learning. Andrews and Goodson (1980) reviewed more than 40 instructional design models and indicated that most of the instructional design models investigated did advocate some form of target population analysis. However, most of these models did not present a strong rationale or means for assessing particular learner characteristics. This may offer some insight on the lack of research in this emerging area of instructional design.

GAMING, FEEDBACK, AND THE LEARNING PROCESS

The field of instructional technology has experienced dramatic growth in the research and development of multimedia learning environments. This growth has been especially pronounced in computer-based and web-based learning environments (Jonassen, 1988, 1991; Marsh & Kumar, 1992; Rieber, 1996b; Yoder, 1994,). Instructional designers are struggling to find innovative ways to exploit computer-based and online learning environments while remaining consistent with widely accepted learning theories and beliefs about how people learn. (Hannafin, 1992; Rieber,

1996b). According to Gagne (1977), carefully designed instructional programs may relieve the learner's processing burden by performing processing activities for the learner. This analysis is conducted in relation to each state of the learning process as outlined by Gagne et al. (1988).

Oxford and Crookall (1988) have asserted that instructional games can be used to foster the development of several learning strategies. These learning strategies include: affective strategies (anxiety reduction and self-encouragement), organizational strategies (paying attention, self-evaluation, and self-monitoring), compensatory strategies (guessing meaning intelligently and using synonyms to represent an unknown precise expression), memory strategies (grouping, imagery, and structured review), and others. According to Jacobs and Dempsey (1993), the use of instructional feedback in a gaming environment may assist learners in becoming more responsible for their own learning process and in the achievement of instructional goals. Mory (1991) indicated that feedback promotes learning during instruction by providing students with information about their performance. Both feedback and instructional games have the capacity to function as advanced organizers for future encounters with the subject matter, due to their ability to inform the learner of objectives, to provide learning guidance, and to suggest meaningful organization of the instructional content. Moreover, graphic organizers have been found to facilitate comprehension and immediate recall (Boothby & Alvermann, 1984).

An instructional game, as defined by Jones (1987), is any training format that involves competition and is rule-guided. A well-designed instructional game must develop confidence in success by generating positive expectancies (Jonassen, 1988; Keller, 1979). Research has indicated that instructional gaming has the intrinsic ability to develop the learner's confidence in determining his or her own destiny. Furthermore, research has shown that as the learner's self-concept improves, cognitive learning increases (Coleman, 1967; Olliphant, 1990). In computer-based instructional gaming environments, feedback can be easily provided so that the learner may quickly evaluate his or her progress against the goals of the game (Rieber, 1996b). In addition to providing appropriate feedback, a well-designed instructional game should be based on specific instructional objectives (Atkinson, 1977; Jacobs & Baum, 1987; Orbach, 1979).

One of the most important components of feedback is its ability to give the learner information about whether or not the learner's action resulted in the expected outcome (Norman, 1988, 1993; Rieber, 1996a). There are numerous research studies that have indicated that the greatest effect of feedback is its ability to correct inaccurate information (Anderson, Kulhavy, & Andre, 1971; Kulhavy & Anderson, 1972; Tait, Hartley, & Anderson, 1973). Keller and Suzuki (1987) proposed that learners evaluate outcomes against their own expectations. Research conducted by Kulhavy and his associates has provided a basis for a hypothesis that corrective feedback should be personally relevant to the learner and tailored to the learner's expectancy for success.

Research has indicated that several factors may influence the effectiveness of feedback in computer-based instruction. The first factor relates to the degree to which feedback provides the student with useful information about the appropriateness of the student's response. Gilman (1969) asserted that providing the learner with a statement of correct response was essential to the effectiveness of knowledge of correct response feedback. Cohen (1985) suggested that informational feedback has its greatest effect after incorrect responses.

A second factor in the effectiveness of feedback in computer-based instruction is the need for immediate feedback (Waldrop, Justin, & Adams, 1986). There is conflicting research on the use of immediate feedback rather than delaying the feedback message. Operant psychologists would predict that learning would be facilitated by immediate feedback. Some researchers have indicated

that delaying the feedback message facilitates both acquisition and retention of a learning task (Bardwell, 1981; Gaynor, 1981; Roper, 1977).

Other researchers have asserted that immediate feedback appears to be the most effective when the task involves discrimination learning, acquisition of knowledge, or when the student is having difficulty achieving mastery of the material (Carter, 1984; Cohen, 1985; Kulhavy & Anderson, 1972). Malone (1981), advocated the use of immediate feedback in instructional gaming situations in order to keep the student's attention and motivation high, to promote sensory curiosity, and keep the student informed of his progress in the game. Gredler (1995) indicated that poorly designed feedback in computer-based instructional gaming environments can produce negative learning effects. In one example, a little man jumps up and down and waves his arms after an incorrect answer. Instead of answering the questions with the correct answers, the students in the study answered randomly, in hopes of seeing the little man jump up and down.

Attention Acquisition

According to Anderson (1970), optimal learning occurs when a learner's cognitive processes are fully engaged. According to Gagne (1985), attention can be commanded by using an abrupt stimulus change or appealing to the learner's interests. Keller's theory of motivation, known as the ARCS model, includes the following components: attention, relevance, confidence, and satisfaction. Each of these elements is necessary to ensure learner motivation (Keller, 1979, 1983, 1984). The model grew from a macro-theory of motivation and instruction developed by Keller (1983). It is grounded in expectancy value theory which assumes that "... learners engage in an activity if it is perceived to be linked to the satisfaction of personal needs (the value aspect), and if there is a positive expectancy for success (the expectancy aspect)" (Keller, 1987a, pp. 2, 3).

While learning theories and instructional models often differ on how to best enhance learning, most of these theories and models include practice as a primary component of instruction and learning (Gagne, 1985; Gropper, 1983; Merrill, 1983). Designing effective instructional activities that provide opportunities that motivate learners to practice is one of the great challenges of instructional design. Theoretical support for instructional gaming comes from many sources. The theory of intrinsic motivation (Malone, 1981) is by far the dominant source of support for instructional gaming. This theory suggests that intrinsic motivation in an instructional gaming context is comprised of an optimal relationship between fantasy, challenge, curiosity, and control (Malone, 1981; Malone & Lepper, 1987b).

Instructional games are attractive to learners because they offer a simple and creative means of providing high-level motivation, clear and consistent goals, and sustained interactivity (McVay, 1980). Research has indicated that instructional games have the intrinsic ability to focus attention more effectively than traditional methods of instruction (Coleman, 1967; Thiagarajan 1988). Orbach (1979) has suggested that instructional games with feedback that provides information concerning the results of performance can increase student motivation and achievement. Alessi (1991) asserted that feedback, in the form of text or graphics, may help to focus a learner's attention and increase motivation.

Some research studies have suggested that student interest can persist for longer periods of time in a gaming situation, as compared to traditional instructional methods, if the learner has a high level of interest in the game (Dill & Doppelt, 1963; Neideffer & Evans, 1981). However, other authors have indicated that interest will decrease as the novelty effect of a game wanes (Greenlaw & Wyman, 1973; Lepper, 1985; Lepper & Gilovich, 1982; Molcho, 1988). Both Keller (1983, 1987b) and Brophy (1987) have suggested that variability and novelty should be included in instruction to increase student attention and motivation. Most of today's computer-based instructional games are designed for individual students working separately on computers. The individual nature of computer-based instructional gaming has not changed much with the advent of the World Wide Web and web-based distance education (Oliver et al., 1998).

Retrieval to Working Memory

Malone (1980, 1981) suggested that relevance is one of the most important factors in facilitating retrieval in instructional gaming. The competition inherent in instructional games and the proper use of feedback can facilitate the relevance of the game to the learner (Malone, 1981). A well-designed instructional game must connect instruction to important needs and motives of the learner (Jonassen, 1988; Keller, 1979). Research has indicated that informational feedback that is based on the learner's pre-existing experiences may be more easily recalled than other forms of feedback (Hull, 1986).

Several authors have suggested that rehearsal serves the dual purpose of maintaining items in short-term, working memory and transferring information about the items to a more permanent long-term memory (Atkinson & Shiffrin, 1968; Waugh & Norman, 1965). Craik and Lockhart (1972) have suggested that the level at which information is processed determines how much is retained. Researchers have theorized that there are two broad categories of rehearsal: maintenance and elaborative (Bransford, 1979; Craik & Watkins, 1973; Lindsay & Norman, 1972). Maintenance rehearsal can facilitate the transfer of informational stimuli into long-term memory. "Maintenance rehearsal is the type used to retain a telephone number to use it" (Dwyer & Dwyer, 1987, p. 264).

Maintenance rehearsal has been shown to be effective in facilitating short-term memory (Craik & Watkins, 1973). However, research has indicated that for encoding and long-term retention to occur, elaborative rehearsal must be utilized (Murray & Mosberg, 1982). "Maintenance rehearsal provides the opportunity for elaborative rehearsal to take place" (Murray & Mosberg, 1982, p. 283). Elaborative rehearsal provides for the processing of information at the appropriate level and for encoding for later retrieval. Dwyer and Dwyer (1987) suggested that if the interaction between the learner and the intended information can be extended, transfer to long-term memory will occur.

With respect to feedback, research has indicated that the use of immediate feedback in most instructional settings facilitates the transfer of information into long-term memory (Kulik & Kulik, 1988). Knowledge of correct response feedback has been shown to be more effective in facilitating retention than knowledge of results feedback (Gilman, 1969; Roper, 1977). A comparison of three types of feedback in concept learning by Waldrop, Justin, and Adams (1986) supported similar findings in Gilman's and Roper's studies that knowledge of correct response feedback with elaborated feedback is superior to simple knowledge of results feedback in facilitating retention of information. Clariana (1993) also found elaborative feedback more effective than knowledge of correct response and knowledge of response feedback at facilitating delayed retention. In general, there is an inconsistent pattern of results with elaborative feedback, with some studies showing no effect on delayed retention (Kulhavy & Stock, 1989).

Material Presentation/Selective Perception

The dual coding theory states that learner interactions with words and pictures will activate encoding systems in different ways. The dual coding theory predicts the picture superiority effect based on two assumptions (Kobayashi, 1986). First, the dual coding theory suggests the additive effects of verbal and visual codes. The theory indicates that the chances of retrieval are doubled if information is coded both verbally and visually. The second assumption of the theory is that mental processing is activated in very different ways by words and pictures. Pictures are believed to have a much greater likelihood of being coded both visually and verbally while words are less likely to be coded visually (Paivio, 1971, Paivio & Clark, 1986). Rieber (1996a) used the dual coding theory to suggest that the use of visual feedback in instruction increases transfer and retention.

The use of imagery is considered to be a useful technique for enhancing long-term memory (Meyer & Ober-Reynolds, 1988). The importance of the relevance of the imagery and the ability of the imagery to attract and hold the learner's attention should not be underestimated. Research has indicated that, as the number of irrelevant stimuli dimensions increase in the learning situation, the number of errors committed by the learners also increase (Dwyer, 1972; Hunt, 1962; Walker & Bourne, 1961). The use of bizarre images used in conjunction with relevant instructional materials has been shown to enhance memory over time (Iaccino et al., 1988).

Using a meta-analysis, Kulik and Kulik (1988) showed that the delay of feedback presentation is beneficial to learners only under controlled conditions and that immediate feedback is recommended for most educational purposes. Also using a meta-analysis, Schimmel (1983) found that the amount of information contained in feedback was not related to feedback effects and that feedback was more effective in computer-based instruction than in traditional programmed instruction. Interestingly, Kulik and Kulik (1988) reported that most feedback research with computer-based instruction concentrates on feedback related to testing instead of instructional materials presentation.

Encoding into Long-Term Memory Storage

Research has shown that learner guidance facilitates the encoding of information into long-term memory. There are many methods that can be used to guide learning. The use of questions, feedback, and hints has been widely used in instruction to provide meaningful organization of the content to facilitate the encoding, retention, and recall of facts, concepts, and rules.

Instructional gaming can serve as an effective rehearsal activity and feedback can function as a rehearsal tool by facilitating the organization and retention of instructional content (Dwyer & Dwyer, 1985; Orbach, 1979). Rieber and Noah (1997) argued that instructional gaming alone may not be adequate to encourage deeper levels of information processing and learning that the learner can transfer beyond the gaming context. The authors found that graphical feedback may foster information encoding, retention, and transfer. Because of their unique qualities, instructional games are often employed as effective methods of rehearsal in learning environments where motivation is a concern. Instructional games are capable of delivering various forms of feedback in an immediate and direct manner.

Kulhavy and Anderson (1972) suggested that feedback plays a major role in the encoding of information and delayed retention. In addition, instructional games have been shown to facilitate learning as proficiently as traditional methods of practice (Klein & Freitag, 1991). Research has indicated that instructional games that require repeated responses to specific information improve delayed retention by producing increased attention to information that enhances the encoding of information to long-term memory (Anderson & Faust, 1973; Anderson & Biddle, 1975; Andre, 1979; 1987; Hamaker, 1986).

Riding and Rayner (1998) indicated that cognitive style may influence how a learner organizes and represents information. Research has suggested that instruction presented in a self-paced format may facilitate information acquisition and retention by allowing the learner to utilize his or her own learning and retrieval strategy (Dwyer & Dwyer 1985; Dwyer & Dwyer 1987). This implies that learner characteristics, such as cognitive style, will determine the amount of hinting and feedback involved in the guidance of the learner, "...the best practical solution may sometimes be to apply learning guidance a little at a time and allow the learner to use as much as he needs" (Gagne et al., 1988, p. 188).

Intellectual skills can be classified into the following categories: facts, concepts, principles, and problem solving (Gagne, 1965). As a result of there being different types of information, Bloom (1956) theorized that there are also different types of learning (knowledge, comprehension, application, analysis, synthesis, and evaluation). Because there are different types of information and different types of learning, research has indicated that different feedback strategies should be employed to facilitate different types of learning (Carter, 1984; Dwyer, 1978). According to Andre and Thieman (1988), most feedback research has utilized achievement tests that tested only for factual learning. The few studies that have been conducted on concept/principle acquisition have produced inconclusive learning and retention results. In a meta-analysis, Bangert-Drowns, Kulik, Kulik, and Morgan (1991) suggested that current feedback research may be "too simple or specific" (p. 234). The authors called for future research that examines feedback in more complex environments that involve higher learning outcomes.

According to Smith and Ragan (1993), few researchers have attempted to investigate the differences in feedback needs for different types of learning and for different learning styles. The vast majority of feedback studies have dealt with verbal information (Schimmel, 1983). Char (1978) examined the effect of both informative feedback versus no feedback for concept and rule learning environments. He found that informative feedback significantly improved the retention of both verbal and higher-order information.

In most cases, increase in dimensionality has been shown to increase information processing (Dwyer, 1978; Hsia, 1968). Long-term memory has been shown to be facilitated by activities that employ multiple senses (Olliphant, 1990). This position is supported in feedback research. In general, feedback that employs multiple senses had been shown to increase information processing and improve retention (Rieber, 1990, 1996a; Kulhavy, White, Topp, Chan, & Adams, 1985). In this manner, instruction can be made more effective as it is made more adaptive.

Rieber (1990) argued that despite advances in educational technology, research is inconclusive on how to design computer-based instruction using words and pictures. Carr, McCauley, Sperber, and Parmelee (1982) suggested that a common semantic code is available that can represent the meaning of either a picture or a word. A body of research has asserted that student learning is affected positively by presenting text and illustrations together (Bernard, 1990; Glenberg & Langston, 1992; Guri-Rozenblit, 1988; Purnell & Solman, 1991; Reed & Beveridge, 1986, 1990). With respect to visualization, Rieber, Smith, Al-Ghafry et al.,(1996) indicated that graphical feedback used in an instructional gaming situation produces less learner frustration and faster game completion time than does text-only feedback.

Ausel and Bieger (1989) examined the effect of adding visuals to textual instructions on the immediate and delayed recall of information. They found that the use of visuals alone appeared to produce faster recall of information than text alone, which produced the slowest recall of information in the short-term. However, text alone appeared to produce faster recall of information in the long-term. The authors attributed this facilitation of long-term information retention to the duration of interaction with the information, which appeared to have produced a deeper level of information processing.

Reinforcement

Many researchers have purported the importance of reinforcement in the learning process. "One must be highly aware of the after-effects of the learning event and their important influence on determining exactly what is learned. In other words, at a minimum, there should be feedback concerning the correctness or the degree of correctness of the learner's performance" (Gagne et al., 1988, p. 188). According to Schimmel (1983), one of the functions of feedback is to assist learners in monitoring their understanding. This monitoring may lead students to re-study or seek help on points where feedback has identified errors.

Corrective feedback is considered to be the most essential aspect of mastery learning. Mastery learning environments with corrective feedback have shown tremendous success in improving motivation, achievement, and retention (Daines, 1982). Elliot (1988) proposed that "...feedback and knowledge of results are often associated with direct gains in performance" (p. 110). Peeck et al. (1985) found that awareness of initial errors through the use of immediate informative feedback was indeed helpful. However, Driscoll and Dempsey (1987) found that, although learners who received feedback performed better than those not receiving feedback, the type of feedback employed (correct answer only, elaborated, forced repetition, and forced processing) did not make a difference.

Instructional games alter the reinforcement structure of the classroom because they provide a motivational opportunity for students to earn reinforcement. Because winning is a powerful reinforcer, instructional games must be designed carefully so that inappropriate strategies are not learned (Gredler, 1995). The impact of peer comparison in instructional gaming, by players comparing their progress and overall success in the game in relation to their opponents, offers another aspect of feedback to be considered. This type of behavior is inherent to single-user computer gaming environments where the players strive to achieve the high score and beat previously set scores. A successful instructional game must manage reinforcement by providing satisfying consequences (Jonassen, 1988; Keller, 1979). Jacobs and Dempsey (1993) suggested that a varied schedule for reinforcement in instructional gaming (e.g., the accumulation of points) may increase learner satisfaction and increase motivation.

Enhancement of Retention and Transfer

Research has shown that varied contexts for the cuing and retrieval of the instructional content can enhance retention and transfer. This can be best assured by "...setting some variety of new tasks for the learner—tasks that require the application of what has been learned in situations that differ substantially from those used for the learning itself ... Ingenuity on the part of the teacher is called for in designing a variety of novel 'application' situations for the purpose of ensuring the transfer of learning" (Gagne et al., 1988, p. 190). There is evidence that instructional games may improve retention and transfer. Molcho (1988) indicated that instructional games can promote retention and the ability to transfer to new domains. In a meta-analysis, Pierfy (1977) found that retention was significantly better with instructional gaming versus conventional methods of instruction.

There appears to be an interesting effect of emotion on immediate and delayed retention. Research has indicated that recall of highly arousing emotional associations is significantly greater for delayed retention than for neutral associations (Parkin, Lewinsohn, & Folkhard, 1982). Furthermore, the recall of highly arousing emotional associations was found to be significantly lower for immediate retention than for neutral associations. These findings suggest that the anticipation of a correct answer to a particular question can invoke such an emotional association during game play.

Research has revealed that the use of feedback increases retention (Pridemore & Klien, 1995). The use of various feedback types in instruction has been studied for decades with few conclusive results (Kulhavy & Stock, 1989). In some feedback studies, feedback forms containing more information generally produced higher retention and instructional performance (Albertson, 1986; Collins, 1987; Hannafin, 1983). In other studies, the increase in the amount of information had no significant effect on retention and learning performance (Corbett & Anderson, 1990; Hodes, 1985; Merril, 1987). In general, studies that have examined the type and amount of information contained in feedback have not produced very consistent results (Kulhavy, 1977; Schimmel, 1983).

CONCLUSION

Based on the insights gained from conducting this research, the following recommendations are made concerning future research in the field:

* There is a need to examine the role of cognitive styles in relation to instructional gaming environments. According to Orbach (1979), instructional games generally ignore the fact the people have different cognitive styles and different motivations for learning. Messick (1976) identified 19 cognitive styles and associated learning style inventories.
* There is a need to examine other forms of feedback that are possible in online gaming environments such as video and sound.
* There is a need to examine the impact on delayed retention of increased learner interaction with the game and with other online game players.

The field of instructional technology has experienced dramatic growth in the research and development of online learning environments in recent years. (Yoder, 1994; Rieber, 1996b). Instructional designers are struggling to find innovative ways to exploit computer-based and online learning environments while remaining consistent with widely accepted learning theories and beliefs about how people learn. (Hannafin, 1992; Rieber, 1996b). Although research has indicated that both the type and intensity of rehearsal methods employed does have an effect on depth of information processing (Dwyer & Dwyer, 1985), the effect of different types of feedback in online educational gaming environments has yet to be conclusively determined.

Andrews and Goodson (1980) reviewed more than 40 instructional design models and indicated that most of the instructional design models investigated did not present a strong rationale or means for assessing particular learner characteristics. Furthermore, Jonassen (1988) cited the lack of solid instructional design models for use in computer-based courseware design. "The characteristics of good instructional games provided by Malones's work, and the other psychological effects noted provide designers with some useful guidelines for designing instructional courseware. Courseware designers may have difficulty with them for two related reasons. First, they are not comprehensive, and second, they are not presented in the context of a developmental model with which they are likely to be familiar. They do not emerge from the instructional developmental field and are not associated with any well-known courseware or instructional development process" (Jonassen, 1988, p. 399). This situation persists today in the fields of online instructional design and online instructional game design, both of which are still in their infancy. As a result, there are many possibilities for meaningful future research.

REFERENCES

Albertson, L. M. (1986). Personalized feedback and cognitive achievement in computer-assisted instruction. *Journal of Instructional Psychology, 13*, 55-57.

Anderson, R. C. (1970). Control of student mediating process during verbal learning and instruction. *Review of Educational Research, 40*(3), 349-369.

Anderson, R. C., & Biddle, W.B. (1975). On asking people questions about what they are reading. In G. Bower (Ed.), *Psychology of Learning and Motivation* (Vol. 9, pp. 96-132). New York: Academic Press.

Anderson, R. C., Kulhavy, R.W., & Andre, T. (1971). Feedback procedures in programmed instruction. *Journal of Educational Psychology, 62*, 148-56.

Anderson, R., Kulhavy, R., & Andre, T. (1972). Conditions under which feedback facilitates learning from programmed lessons. *Journal of Educational Psychology, 63,* 186-188.

Anderson, R. C., & Faust, G. W. (1973). *Educational Psychology.* New York: Dodd, Mead.

Andre, T. (1979). Does answering higher-level questions while reading facilitate productive learning? *Review of Educational Research, 49*(2), 280-318.

Andre, T. (1987). Questions and learning from reading. *Questioning Exchange, 1*(1), 47-86.

Andre, T., & Thieman, A. (1988). Level of Adjunct Question, Type of Feedback, and Learning Concepts by Reading. *Contemporary Educational Psychology, 13*(3), 296-307.

Andrews, D. H., & Goodson, L. A. (1980). A comparative analysis of models of instructional design. *Journal of Instructional Development, 3*(4), 2-16.

Atkinson, F. D. (1977). Designing simulation/gaming activities: A systems approach. *Educational Technology, 17*(2), 38-43.

Atkinson, R. C., & Shiffrin, R. M. (1968). Human memory. A proposed system and its control processes. In K. W. Spence & J. T. Spence (Eds.), *The Psychology of Learning and Motivation* (Vol. 2, pp. 89-195). New York: Academic Press.

Ausel, D., & Bieger, G. R. (1989). The durability of picture text procedural instructions for individuals with different cognitive styles. In *Proceedings of Selected Research Papers presented at the Annual Meeting of the Association for Educational Communications and Technology*, Dallas, TX.

Bangert-Drowns, R. L., Kulik, C.-L. C., Kulik, J. A., & Morgan, M. (1991). The instructional effect of feedback in test-like events. *Review of Educational Research, 61*(2), 213-238.

Bardwell, R. (1981). Feedback: How does it function? *Journal of Experimental Education, 50*(1), 4-9.

Barringer, C., & Gholson, B. (1979). Effects of type and combination of feedback upon conceptual learning by children: Implications for research in academic learning. *Review of Educational Research, 49*(3), 459-478.

Bernard, R. M. (1990). Using extended captions to improve learning from instructional illustrations. *British Journal of Educational Technology, 21*, 215-225.

Bloom, B. S. (1956). *Taxonomy of Educational Objectives: Book 1 Cognitive domain.* New York: Logman Publishing Company.

Boothby, P. R., & Alvermann, D. E. (1984). A classroom training study: The effects of graphic organizer instruction on fourth grader's comprehension. *Reading World, 23*(4), 325-37.

Bransford, J. D. (1979). *Human cognition: Learning, understanding, and remembering.* Belmont, CA: Wadsworth Publishing Company.

Brophy, J. (1987). Synthesis of research on strategies for motivating students to learn. *Educational Leadership, 45*(2), 40-48.

Carr, T. H., McCauley, C., Sperber, R. D., & Parmelee, C. M. (1982). Words, pictures, and priming: on semantic activation, conscious identification, and the automaticity of information processing. *Journal of Experimental Psychology: Human Perception and Performance, 8*(6), 757-777.

Carter, J. (1984). Instructional learner feedback: A literature review with implications for software development. *The Computing Teacher, 12*(2), 53-55.

Char, R. O. (1978). The effect of delay of informative feedback on the retention of verbal information and higher-order learning, for college students. (Doctoral dissertation, Florida State University, 1978). Dissertation Abstracts International, 40, 748A.

Clariana, R. B. (1993). The effect of item organization and feedback density using computer-assisted multiple-choice questions as instruction. *Journal of Computer-Based Instruction, 20*(1), 26-31.

Cohen, V. B. (1985). A Re-examination of feedback in computer based instruction: Implications for instructional design. *Educational Technology, 25*(1), 33-37.

Coleman, J. S. (1967). Learning through games. *National Education Association Journal, 56*(1), 69-70.

Coleman, J. S. (1968) Social processes and social process simulation. In S. Boocock & E. O. Schild (Eds.), *Simulation games in learning* (pp. 29-54). Beverly Hills: Sage.

Collins, A. (1987). Implications of cognitive theory for instructional design: Revisited. *Educational Communications and Technology Journal, 36*(1), 3-14.

Corbett, A.T., & Anderson, J.R. (1990). *The effect of feedback control on learning to program with the Lisp tutor. In Proceedings of the 12th Annual Conference of the Cognitive Science Society* (pp. 796-803). Hillsdale, NJ: Lawrence Erlbaum Associates.

197

Craik, F. I., & Lockhart, R. S. (1972). Levels of processing: a framework for memory research. *Journal of Verbal Learning and Verbal Behavior, 11*, 671-684.

Craik, F. I. M., & Watkins, M. J.(1973). The role of rehearsal in short-term memory. *Journal of Verbal Learning and Verbal Behavior, 12*, 599-607.

Dill, W. R., & Doppelt, N. (1963). The acquisition of experience in a complex management. *Management Science, 10*(3), 0-4.

Driscoll, M. P., & Dempsey, J. V. (1987). *Developing and testing a method for enhancing concept learning in computer-based instruction.* Paper presented at the annual meeting of the Association for Educational Communications and Technology, Atlanta, GA.

Dwyer, F. M. (1972). *A guide for improving visualized instruction.* State College, PA: Learning Services.

Dwyer, F. M. (1978). *Strategies for improving visual learning.* State College, PA: Learning Services.

Dwyer, C. A., & Dwyer, F. M. (1985). The effect of visualized instruction and varied rehearsal and evaluation strategies (verbal and visual) in facilitating students' long-term retention on tests measuring different instructional objectives. *Journal of Visual Languaging, 5*(2), 15-27.

Dwyer, C. A., & Dwyer, F. M. (1987). Effect of depth of information processing on student's ability to acquire and retrieve information related to different instructional objectives. *Programmed Learning and Educational Technology, 24*(4), 264-279.

Elliot, J. L. Jr. (1989). A review of the literature on the relationship between motivational techniques and academic achievement. *Dissertation Abstracts International, 49*(07), 1737.

Ernest, P. (1986). Games: A rationale for their use in the teaching of mathematics in school. *Mathematics in School, 15*(1), 2-5.

Gagne, R. M. (1965). *The conditions of learning.* New York: Holt, Rinehart and Winston, Inc.

Gagne, R. M. (1977). *The conditions of learning* (3rd ed.). New York: Holt, Rinehart and Winston.

Gagne, R. M. (1985). *The conditions of learning and theory of instruction* (4th Ed.). New York: Holt, Rinehart & Winston.

Gagne, R.M., Briggs, L.J., & Wagner, W.W. (1988). *Principles of instructional design* (3rd ed.). New York: Holt, Rinehart and Winston.

Gaynor, P. (1981). The effect of feedback delay on retention of computer-based mathematical material. *Journal of Computer-Based Instruction, 8*(2), 28-34.

Gilman, D. (1969). Comparison of several feedback methods for correcting errors by computer-assisted instruction. *Journal of Educational Psychology, 60*(6), 503-508.

Glenberg, A.M., & Langston, W.E. (1992). Comprehension of illustrated text: Pictures help to build mental models. *Journal of Memory and Language, 31*(2), 129-151.

Gredler, M. (1995). Program evaluation. New York: MacMillan.

Greenlaw, P. S., & Wyman, F. P. (1973). The teaching effectiveness of games in collegiate business courses. *Simulation & Games, 4*(3), 259-294.

Gropper, G. L. (1983). A behavioral approach to instructional prescription. In C.M. Reigeluth (Ed.), *Instructional-design theories and models: An overview of their current status* (pp. 101-161). Hillsdale, NJ: Lawrence Erlbaum.

Guri-Rozenblit, S. (1988). The interrelationship between diagrammatic representations and verbal explanations in learning from social science text. *Instructional Science, 17*(3), 219-234.

Hamaker, C. (1986). The effects of adjunct questions on prose learning. *Review of Educational Research, 56*(2), 212-242.

Hannafin, M. J. (1983). The effects of systematized feedback on learning in natural classroom settings. *Educational Research Quarterly, 7*(3), 22-29.

Hannafin, M. J. (1992). Emerging technologies, ISD, and learning environments: Critical perspectives. *Educational Technology Research & Development, 40*(1), 49-63.

Hodes, C. L. (1985). Relative effectiveness of corrective and non-corrective feedback in computer assisted instruction on learning and achievement. *Journal of Education Technology Systems, 13*(4), 249-254.

Hsia, H. J. (1968). Output, error, equivocation, and recalled information in auditory, visual, and audiovisual information with constraint and noise. *Journal of Communications, 18*(4), 325-353.

Hull, J. G. (1986). *Exploring the connections between self, cognition, and behavior.* Summary of paper presented at the 94th annual convention of the American Psychological Association, Washington, DC.

Hunt, E. B. (1962). *Concept learning.* New York: Wiley.

Iaccino, J. F., Dvorak, E., & Coler, M. (1989). Effects of bizarre imagery on the long-term retention of paired associates embedded within variable contexts. *Bulletin of the Psychonomic Society, 27,* 114-116.

Jacobs, R. L., & Baum, M. (1987). Simulation and games in training and development: Status and concerns about their use. *Simulation and Games, 18*(3), 385-394.

Jacobs, J. W., & Dempsey, J. C. (1993). Simulation and Gaming: Fidelity, Feedback, and Motivation.

In J. C. Dempsey & G. C. Sales (Eds.), *Interactive Instruction and Feedback* (pp. 197-227). Englewood Cliffs, NJ: Educational Technology.

Jasinski, M., & Thiagarajan, S. (2000). Virtual games for real learning: learning online with serious fun. *Educational Technology, 40*(4), 61-63.

Jonassen, D. H. (1988). *Instructional designs for microcomputer courseware.* Hillsdale, NJ: Lawrence Erlbaum Associates.

Jonassen, D.H. (1991). Evaluating constructivist learning. *Educational Technology, 31*(9), 28-3.

Jones, K. (1987). *Simulations: A handbook for teachers and trainers.* London: Kogan Page.

Keller, J. M. (1979). Motivation and instructional design: A theoretical perspective. *Journal of Instructional Development, 2*(4), 26-34.

Keller, J.M. (1983). Motivational design of instruction. In C.M. Reigeluth (Ed.), *Instructional-design theories and models: An overview of their current status* (pp. 386-434). Hillsdale, NJ: Lawrence Erlbaum.

Keller, J. M. (1984). Use of the ARCS model of motivation in teacher training. In K.E. Shaw (Ed.), *Aspects of educational technology XVII: Staff development and career updating* (pp. 140 - 145). New York: Nichols Publishing Company.

Keller, J. M., & Suzuki, K. (1987). Use of ARCS motivation model in courseware design. In D.H. Jonassen (Ed.) *Instructional designs for microcomputer courseware* (pp. 409-434). Hillsdale, NJ: Erlbaum.

Keller, J.M. (1987a). Development and use of the ARCS model of instructional design. *Journal of Instructional Development, 10*(3), 2-10.

Keller, J.M. (1987b). Strategies for stimulating the motivation to learn. *Performance and Instruction, 26*(8), 1-7.

Klein, J.D., & Freitag, E. (1991). Enhancing motivation using an instructional game. *Journal of Instructional Psychology, 11*(2), 111-116.

Kobayashi, S. (1986). Theoretical issues concerning superiority of pictures over words and sentences in memory. *Perceptual and Motor Skills, 63*(October), 783-792.

Kulhavy, R. W., & Anderson, R. C. (1972). Delay-retention effect with multiple-choice tests. *Journal of Educational Psychology, 63*(5), 505-512.

Kulhavy, R. W. (1977). Feedback in written instruction. *Review of Educational Research, 47*(1), 211-232.

Kulhavy, R. W., & Stock, W. (1989). Feedback in written instruction: The place of response certitude. *Educational Psychology Review, 1*(4), 279-308.

Kulhavy, R. W., White, M.T., Topp, B. W., Chan, A. L., & Adams, J. (1985). Feedback complexity and corrective effectiveness. *Contemporary Educational Psychology, 10*, 285-291.

Kulik, J. A., & Kulik, C. C. (1988). Timing of feedback and verbal learning. *Review of Educational Research, 58*(1), 79-97.

Laveault, D. & St-Germain, M. (1997). Factors of success of simulations and games: A systemic approach to the evaluation of an organization's impact on the user. *Simulation & Gaming, 28*(3), 317-336.

Lee, O. M. (1985). The effect of type of feedback on rule learning in computer-based instruction. *Dissertation Abstracts International, 46*(04), 955.

Lee, D., Smith, P. L., & Savenye, W. (1991). The effects of feedback and second try in computer-assisted instruction for rule-learning task. In *Proceedings of selected research papers. Association for Educational Communications and Technology Research and Theory Division*, (pp. 441-32). Orlando, FL.

Lepper, M. R. (1985). Microcomputers in education. *American Psychologist, 40*(1), 1-18.

Lepper, M. R., & Gilovich, T. (1982). Accentuating the positive: Eliciting generalized compliance from children through activity-oriented requests. *Journal of Personality and Social Psychology, 42*, 248-259.

Lindsay, P. H., & Norman, D. A. (1972). *An introduction to psychology.* New York: Academic Press, Inc.

Lindsay, P. H., & Norman, D. A. (1977). *Human information processing.* New York: Academic Press.

Malone, T. W. (1980). What makes things fun to learn? A study of intrinsically motivation computer games. (Doctoral dissertation, Stanford University Graduate Board). *Dissertation Abstracts International, 41*(5B).

Malone, T. (1981). Toward a theory of intrinsically motivating instruction. *Cognitive Science, 5*(4), 33-369.

Malone, T. W., & Lepper, M.R. (1987b). What makes computer games fun. *Byte, 6*(12), 258-277.

Marsh, E. J., & Kumar, D. D. (1992). Hypermedia: A conceptual framework for science education and review of recent findings. *Journal of Educational Multimedia and Hypermedia, 1*(1), 25-37.

McVay, P. (1980, June 23-25). *Tapping the appeal of games in instruction.* Proceeding of the National Educational Computing Conference, Norfolk, Virginia.

Merril, J. (1987). Levels of questioning and forms of feedback: Instructional factors in courseware design. *Journal of Computer-Based Instruction, 14*(1), 18-22.

Merrill, M. D. (1983). Component display theory. In C.M. Reigeluth (Ed.), *Instructional-design theories and models: An overview of their current status* (pp. 279-333). Hillsdale, NJ: Lawrence Erlbaum.

Messick, S. (1976). Personality consistencies in cognition and creativity. In S. Messick (Ed.), *Individuality in learning* (pp. 4-22). San Francisco: Jossey-Bass.

Meyer, G. R., & Ober-Reynolds, S. (1988). *How to create and conduct a memory enhancement program.* Paper presented at the 34th annual meeting of the American Society on Aging, San Diego, CA.

Molcho, M. (1988). The effects of traditional instruction and game strategies on teaching selected typing skills to junior-high school students with moderate to severe handicaps through computer-assisted instruction (CAI) (Doctoral dissertation, Temple University Graduate Board). *Dissertation Abstracts International, 50*(02A), 347.

Mory, E. H. (1991). The use of informational feedback in instruction: implications for future research. *Educational technology research and development, 40*(3), 5-20

Murray, F. B., & Mosberg, L. (1982). Cognition and memory. In Mitzel, H.E. (ed.) *Encyclopedia of Educational Research* (fifth edition). New York: The Free Press.

Neideffer, J. D., & Evans, S. H. (1981, June 17-19). *Games people play: Development of a method to assess interest in instructional games.* Paper presented at the 3rd National educational Computing Conference, North Texas State University, Denton, Texas.

Norman, D. A. (1988). *The psychology of everyday things.* New York: Basic Books.

Oliver, R., Omari, A., & Herrington, J. (1998). Exploring student interactions in collaborative world wide web computer-based learning environments. *Journal of Educational Multimedia and Hypermedia, 7*(2/3), 263-87.

Olliphant, J. A. (1990). *From research to reality: activities and strategies that work.* Paper presented at the annual meeting of the Pacific Northwest Council on Foreign Languages, Portland, OR.

Orbach, E. (1979). Simulation games and motivation for learning: A theoretical framework. *Simulation & Games, 10*(1), 3-40.

Oxford, R., & Crookall, D. (1988). Simulation/gaming and language learning strategies. *Simulations and Games, 19*(3), 349-353.

Paivio, A. (1971). *Imagery and verbal processes.* New York: Holt, Rinehart, and Winston.

Paivio, A., & Clark, J. A. (1986). The role of topic and vehicle imagery in metaphor comprehension, *Communication and Cognition, 19*(3), 367-387.

Parkin, A. J., Lewinsohn, J., & Folkhard, S. (1982). The influence of emotion on immediate and delayed retention: Levinger & Clark reconsidered. *British Journal of Psychology, 73*(3), 389-393.

Peeck, J. E. A. (1985). Effects of informative feedback in relation to retention of initial responses. *Contemporary Educational Psychology, 10*(4), 303-13.

Pierfy, (1977). Comparative simulation game research: Stumbling blocks and steppingstones. *Simulation and Games, 8*(2), 255-68.

Pridemore, D.R., & Klien, J.D. (1995). Control of Practice and Level of Feedback in Computer Based Instruction. *Contemporary Educational Psychology, 20*(4), 444-4449.

Purnell, K. N., & Solman, R. T. (1991). The influence of technical illustrations on students' comprehension in geography. *Reading Research Quarterly, 26*(3), 277-299.

Rakes, T. A., & Kutzman, S. K. (1982). The selection and use of reading games and activities. *Reading Horizons, 23*(1), 67-70.

Reed, D. J., & Beveridge, M. (1986). Effect of text illustration on children's learning of a school science topic. *British Journal of Educational Psychology, 56,* 294-303.

Reed, D. J., & Beveridge, M. (1990). Reading illustrated science texts: A microcomputer based investigation of children's strategies. *British Journal of Educational Psychology, 60,* 76-87.

Riding, R., & Rayner, S. G. (1998). *Cognitive styles and learning strategies.* David Fulton Publisher, London

Rieber, L. P. (1990). Animation in computer-based instruction. *Educational Technology Research and Development, 38*(1), 77-86.

Rieber, L. P. (1996a). Animation as feedback in a computer-based simulation: Representation matters. *Educational Technology Research & Development, 44*(1), 5-22.

Rieber, L. P. (1996b). Seriously considering play: Designing interactive learning environments based on the blending of microworlds, simulations and games. *Educational Technology Research & Development, 44*(2), 43-58.

Rieber, L. P., & Noah, D. (1997). *Effect of gaming and visual metaphors on reflective cognition within computer-based simulations.* Paper presented at the Annual Conference of the American Educational Research Association (AERA), Chicago, IL.

Rieber, L. P., Smith, M., Al-Ghafry, S., Strickland, W., Chu, G., & Spahi, F. (1996). The role of meaning in interpreting graphical and textual feedback during a computer-based simulation. *Computers and Education, 27*(1), 45-58.

Roper, W. J. (1977). Feedback in computer-assisted instruction. *Programmed Learning and Educational Technology, 14*(1), 43-49.

Schimmel, B. J. (1983). *A meta-analysis of feedback to learners in computerized and programmed instruction.* Paper presented at the annual meeting of the American Educational Research Associa-

tion, Montreal. (ERIC Document Reproduction Service No. 233 708)

Skinner, B. F. (1958). Teaching machines. *Science, 128,* 969-977

Smith, P. L., & Ragan, T. J. (1993). Designing instructional feedback for different learning outcomes. In J.V. Dempsey & G.C. Sales, (Eds.), *Interactive instruction and feedback* (pp. 75-193). Englewood Cliffs, NJ: Educational Technology.

Tait, K., Hartley, J. R., & Anderson, R. C., (1973). Feedback procedures in computer-assisted arithmetic instruction. *British Journal of Educational Psychology, 43*(2), 161-71.

Thiagarajan, S. (1976). Using games to improve human performance: Some general approaches & specific examples. *Improving Human Performance Quarterly, 4*(3), 84-95.

Thiagarajan, S. (1988). A personal philosophy of performance technology. *Performance & Instruction, 27*(5), 6-7.

Wagner, W., & Wagner, S. (1985). Presenting questions, processing responses, and providing feedback in CAI. *Journal of Instructional Development, 8*(4), 2-8.

Waldrop, P. B., Justin, J. E. III, & Adams, T. M. II, (1986). A comparison of three types of feedback in a computer-assisted instruction task. *Educational Technology, 26*(11), 43-45.

Walker, C. M., & Bourne, L. E. (1961). The identification of concepts as a function of amount of relevant and irrelevant information. *American Journal of Psychology, 74*(3), 410-417.

Waugh, N. C., & Norman, D. A. (1965). Primary memory. *Psychological Review, 72*(2), 89-104.

Wesson, C., Wilson, R., & Mandlebaum, L. H. (1988). Learning games for active student responding. *Teaching Exceptional Children, 20*(2), 12-14.

Yoder, S. (1994). Math, microworlds, and hypermedia. *The Computing Teacher, 21*(8), 18-20.

Chapter XIII
Cognitive–Adaptive Instructional Systems for Special Needs Learners

Bruce J. Diamond
William Paterson University, USA

Gregory M. Shreve
Kent State University, USA

ABSTRACT

This chapter provides a perspective on the problems, challenges, and unique opportunities faced by instructors and designers of information technology in helping students who are differently-abled learn more effectively in online environments. The proposed solution is provided in the form of a cognitive-adaptive instructional system. This system provides menu-driven adaptive options or online assessments that evaluate a student's cognitive and sensory needs. These needs are translated into cognitive-sensory profiles, which are linked to compensatory and remedial actions. These actions render content automatically and dynamically in ways that provide adaptations that compensate for a student's special-needs while complementing their strengths.

CHAPTER OBJECTIVES

This chapter should help the reader:

- Better understand the nature and extent of the problems faced by special needs learners
- Better understand the interrelationships between cognitive and sensory impairments and their potential impact on participation in online learning communities
- Understand the importance of integrating adaptive instructional capabilities into online instructional models
- Understand the key technical concepts underlying the cognitive-adaptive instructional system and identify potential applications

INTRODUCTION

Recent decades have seen significant advances in the design and implementation of hardware and software for delivering online and computer-assisted instruction. Educational applications of information technology are increasingly integrated into a diverse array of devices, from personal digital assistants and cell phones, to laptop and desktop computers. They are deployed in a dizzying variety of forms, ranging from broadband distance learning to CD-based instruction and digital textbooks. Information technology is increasingly the primary instructional vehicle for a number of application areas including basic skills training in companies, educational telemedicine, military training, and, of course, the delivery of K-12 and college curricula.

At the same time that this technological infrastructure is developing, our understanding of the pedagogy of online and computer-assisted instruction is rapidly increasing. As a result, more and more individuals participate successfully in innovative learning environments that are partially or wholly computer-based and increasingly delivered online. As we learn more about how students learn online, we can develop increasingly sophisticated and effective instructional models to inform and guide more effective instructional information system design. One population at risk in this new digital learning environment is students who have inherited or acquired cognitive and sensory impairments. These impairments may interfere with a student's ability to access and learn subject matter in both traditional and in digital information rich environments. These special needs students will challenge our ability to translate educational and cognitive remediation theory into practice and into the design of more intelligent online educational technology systems.

Therefore, the goal of this chapter is to provide a context and rationale for the need to develop and use adaptive instructional systems in order to help students, especially those with learning disabilities (LDs) or deficiencies in basic skills or academic achievement, to learn more effectively. In order to achieve the goal of providing effective online instruction to diverse user populations, a cognitive-adaptive instructional system that uses adaptive hypermedia is proposed. The ways in which this system can be used to accommodate a diverse range of cognitive and sensory impairments and skill deficiencies will be described. In explaining how this system can be implemented, new Web-based information technologies will be discussed. In addition, examples of online applications of adaptive models will be provided in order to demonstrate that such a practice-based system can help meet the learning needs of special students.

BACKGROUND

Special needs individuals at risk in digital learning environments are of all ages and at all developmental stages. They become cognitively "differently-abled" due to the effects of aging, accidents (e.g., traumatic brain injury), disease, or specific developmental or inherited neurological conditions. Many of these individuals are often left behind in traditional classroom environments. The failure to provide for their information processing and learning needs in online and other digital environments will only widen an educational and social participation gap that already threatens their full inclusion in 21st century life. If we do not address the problems and special needs of such differently-abled users, we will help promote the development of a generation of digitally disenfranchised individuals who are not able to participate equitably in technology-mediated educational, cultural, social, and economic communities. The effectiveness with which issues relating to the accessibility and utility of digital environments by the differently-abled are addressed will critically impact the role that information technology will play for these populations now and in the future.

Instructional models and information architectures for learners with special needs must provide mechanisms that dynamically adapt the information delivery interface as well as the organization and presentation of instructional content to the learner's unique cognitive-sensory impairment profile. Such "cognitive-adaptive" instructional information systems have the potential to optimize information delivery for such users and maximize the efficacy of instruction to the greatest extent possible. A significant issue in online instructional modeling for special needs populations will be creating adaptive online instructional systems that integrate clinical and educational evaluations of a learner's cognitive and sensory impairments with instructional heuristics. These heuristics will then drive specific adaptive and "compensatory" information system behaviors at the human computer-interface.

Learning Disabilities in Context

Cognitive-adaptive instructional systems must be understood against the background of an increasing use of digital resources for educational purposes and an increasing population of special needs learners with low academic achievement, basic skill deficiencies, and learning disabilities associated to cognitive impairment. The impact of digital information delivered via the Internet to all students is dramatic. Ninety seven percent of 12- to 18-year-olds use the Internet, with 61% reporting the Internet "very" or "extremely" important as an information source compared with 60% for books and 58% for newspapers (UCLA, 2002). Moreover, "having access to the Internet and its rich resources…is having a positive impact on student achievement" (eSchool News, 2003).

However, the number of students diagnosed or classified with specific learning disabilities has also increased by 34% since 1990-91 (OSEP, 2001). Learning disabilities can occur in one or more areas of language development, reading, memory, mathematics, reasoning, and problem solving. Impairments contribute to lower levels of school achievement than would be expected based on intelligence. The prevalence of LDs in the United States is estimated to be up to 6% of the school children aged 6-18 (Lewitt & Baker, 1996), translating into approximately six million children. Given that 11 million children and adults have learning disabilities, it is one of our most prevalent developmental disabilities (Reiff & Gerber, 1994). Overall, learning disabilities cost the nation an estimated $50 billion in the 1999-2000 school year alone (Chambers, Parrish, & Harr, 2000). Fifty one percent of students receiving special education services in public schools have learning disabilities (OSEP, 2001), and almost one in three college freshmen with disabilities report a learning disability (Henderson, 1995). The National Istitute of Child Health and Human

Development (NICHD) longitudinal studies indicate that of children who are reading-disabled in the third grade, 74% remain reading disabled at the end of high school. In other words, learning disabilities can impact performance in and out of the classroom throughout a person's lifetime.

Educational models for dealing with special-needs students are sometimes driven by instructional, diagnostic, and assessment techniques that emphasize deficits rather than the creative abilities and resources special needs learners already possess. Talents and abilities are simply not recognized. The interventional efficacy of deficit-oriented techniques is low (Coles, 1987; Poplin, 1988a, 1988b). As early as 1983, Gardner widened our view of intelligence to include the idea of "multiple intelligences" (e.g., linguistic, logico-mathematical, musical-rhythmic, visual-spatial, bodily-kinesthetic, interpersonal, and intra-personal). Among students with learning disabilities, four areas of multiple intelligence strength have emerged: conceptual writing, divergent thinking, computer aptitude, and musical ability. In divergent thinking skills, LD students are at least as able as students with no learning disabilities (NLD), as measured by the test of divergent thinking and the test of divergent feeling. In some cases, LD students have scored higher than their NLD counterparts on measures of figural and verbal creativity, such as the Torrance test of creativity and the alternative uses test (Tarver, Ellsworth, & Rounds, 1980). Stone, Poplin, Johnson, and Simpson (1992), reported no difference between elementary school LD and NLD students with LD students actually scoring higher than NLD students on many of these measures.

These areas of multiple intelligence strength, especially computer aptitude, create a promising foundation for educational intervention models for special needs learners using computer-assisted and online technology. On tests of computer aptitude that do not require complex linguistic skills, such as the computer aptitude, literacy, and interest

profile (Poplin, Drew, & Gable, 1984), Hearne, Poplin, Schoneman, and O'Shaughnessy (1988) reported that students with LD had computer "aptitudes" equivalent to those of their non-disabled counterparts with no gender differences noted. This is relevant to cognitive-adaptive systems, as it suggests that having learning disabilities due to cognitive-sensory impairments will not necessarily preclude a student from using and benefiting from instructional systems. However, as computer systems are increasingly used in online learning environments, more complex cognitive operations and skills will be needed in order to effectively use these learning tools.

Cognitive Impairments, Learning Styles, and Instructional Technology

The development of adaptive instructional systems can be especially challenging in certain populations (i.e., older people) because they are less likely to have computer experience (Czaja & Sharit, 1998) and may lack the knowledge and skills required for interacting with computer search engines (Morrell, Mayhorn, & Bennett, 2000). Acquired neurological injuries, developmental conditions, or declines in memory and reasoning skills due to aging can all adversely impact online information-seeking (Park, 1999) and digital library searching (Rousseau, Jamieson, Rogers, et al., 1998), resulting in less efficient search strategies (Mead, Spaulding, Sit, et al., 1997). Czaja, Sharit, Ownby, Roth, and Nair (2001) reported relationships between search and retrieval performance in older participants and cognitive abilities (e.g., processing speed, memory, and verbal speed). Westerman, Davies, and Glendon (1995) reported that older participants were slower than their younger counterparts in retrieving information (perhaps attributable to difficulty in recalling previous links and page information). Moreover, participants with low spatial ability also took longer in retrieving information. These challenges are not restricted to the elderly. Younger people (e.g., college students) with a variety of learning disabilities can exhibit similar impairments in information processing, working memory, and attention (Henderson, 1995). Glisky and Schachter (1988) demonstrated that by using self-paced and vanishing cue techniques even individuals with profound memory impairments could learn how to use computer-based systems (although they might not remember the specific learning episode afterwards).

The areas of memory, attention, executive function, information processing, and higher-order thinking skills are emphasized in the cognitive-adaptive approach because these cognitive domains involve skills that mediate student success in school-related tasks that require information manipulation and processing. In other words, these skills are used in reading and textbook comprehension, attending to class lectures, writing and thinking effectively, and using instructional and information technology tools. Thus, effective approaches for modeling user behavior in impaired individuals should involve educational and clinical assessments of these cognitive domains and result in compensatory actions whose effectiveness can be demonstrated empirically to have an effect on the performance of learning behaviors.

Helping Special Needs Students Learn: Meeting the Challenge

The challenge is that the cognitive impairments that impede students' academic progress in the classroom can also impede their ability to effectively use more complex information technology tools and resources. However, as previously stated, we can build on some of the demonstrated strengths in computer use exhibited by special learners, but we must also be cognizant of the challenges. For example, school-aged children with mild to moderate learning disabilities exhibit impairments in working memory compared to children of average ability. Impairment is more

severe with increases in task and content complexity (Bayliss, Jarrold, Baddeley, & Leigh, 2005). The generalized working memory deficit in LD students has been attributed to storage constraints in the executive system (Swanson, 1993). Inefficient decoding and word recognition skills during the reading process can also reduce attention and memory resources, with comprehension impeded by poor verbal recall (Stothard, 1994). Problems in speed of processing, processing verbal and visual-spatial material, organizing information, and multi-tasking can have a devastating impact on functioning both in and out of the classroom, but especially in the use of complex information displays and user interfaces.

TOWARDS THE SOLUTION

If special needs learners are going to be able to use information systems in educational contexts, including digital libraries, learning object repositories, and widespread educational technology delivery systems such as Blackboard, WebCT and Vista, we must develop systems that are adaptive enough to respond to specific learning disabilities. Educational materials and information delivery systems are generally not designed to meet these special needs. If an instructional application for learners with cognitive impairments and sensory impairments is properly designed, it should be able to quickly and effectively provide personalized information display and educational content packaging. This information would be reflective of the learner's cognitive strengths as well as their impairment profile so that the learning environment can fully or partially compensate for deficiencies in cognition through dynamic system adaptation of content and display. The following sections provide a more technological discussion of current information technologies that will be used to design and build a more flexible and adaptive instructional system.

Accessibility and Adaptive Systems: Current Technologies

The impetus underlying the development of cognitive-adaptive instructional systems is that implementation of compensatory information delivery techniques will enhance educational outcomes for learning-disabled users. Recent developments in the core Web protocols and data formats including the extensible markup language (XML), cascading stylesheets (CSS), extensible stylesheet language (XSL), scalable vector graphics (SVG), and the synchronized multimedia integration language (SMIL) have provided a technological infrastructure capable of supporting innovative new information delivery systems for learning disabled populations with cognitive impairment.

Many of these protocols (XML, SVG, SMIL) are "markup languages." A markup language is a way of using simple text-embedded codes to describe the structure and semantics of documents. XML, for instance, provides a generic mechanism for describing the content of almost any kind of document, while SVG is oriented toward describing, creating, and controlling the appearance of online graphics. SMIL allows for the integration of multimedia properties with XML and SVG documents. Documents containing markup codes can also be attached to "stylesheet languages" (CSS, XSL) that provide instructions that tell computers how to handle and display the contents of a marked-up document. A basic objective of markup languages is the separation of content from display. A document's content may be described just one time using XML, but then presented in multiple different presentation formats simply by assigning new stylesheets to it. In addition to greater flexibility in the presentation and display of documents, a new level of interactivity and dynamism can be added to digital documents through the use of the "document object model"(DOM). The DOM is an Internet browser technology that allows for the attachment

of server and client-side scripts (small programs) to documents. For example, the DOM allows an instructional designer to assign a script creating a popup message to a section of a document. The message would appear whenever a mouse is moved or clicked over the section. The combination of scripts and DOM can dynamically access and update the content and structure of HTML (hypertext markup language) and XHTML (extensible hypertext markup language) and XML documents. The new World Wide Web Consortium (W3C) XML-Events specification makes the online document interface even more dynamic, providing for the association of specific DOM document behaviors with XML-based markup languages and content, thereby separating document content from scripting.

These technologies for separating content from on-screen behavior, presentation, and display can be used to specify how to render underlying content markup for multiple information appliances and multiple user groups "on the fly." The modality specifications (which information appliance) and presentation specifications (organization and appearance) for the document are provided at the moment the document is invoked. The document perceived by the user at the human-computer interface is "rendered" dynamically in real time. This on the fly capability is particularly critical in the development of adaptive online systems since it allows for the dynamic tailoring of Web content to individual needs.

Many of the new protocols also include so-called accessibility features. For instance, the newest CSS specification includes several accessibility features such as dynamically generated content, aural stylesheets, and access to alternative representations of content that could be used to great effect with differently-abled populations. One interesting example of how current online technology helps address users with special needs is the W3C recommendation XHTML+Voice Profile that combines the VoiceXML markup language with XHTML and XML-Events to allow voice output from Web pages and voice reaction to page events. If these technologies are used in combination with cognitive adaptive models, they offer the instructor the capability to alter content, presentation, and pedagogy in flexible ways that respond to individual student needs, strengths and weaknesses. Taken together, it seems clear that the foundation for more accessible and adaptive systems has been established.

A Global Perspective

In fact, there are a number of initiatives that have tried to address the issues of online information accessibility for those with cognitive and sensory impairments. For instance, in addressing the needs of those with sensory impairments the CAPS (Communication and Access to Information for Persons with Special Needs) project of the European Union's Directorate for Telecommunications, Information Industries and Innovation focused on visual (reading) impairment by providing broader access to digitally distributed documents, especially newspapers, books, and public information. The follow-up HARMONY (Horizontal Action for the Harmonization of Accessible Structured Documents) project tried to improve the quantity and quality of documents accessible to the reading impaired by focusing on standardization issues, for example, population needs and compensatory actions that could or should be taken by information systems.

The Federal Government of the United States is also increasingly committed to improving the accessibility of information technology and Web-based information (i.e., Section 508 guidelines from the Architectural and Transportation Barriers Compliance Board of the U.S. Federal Government). In addition, the World Wide Web Consortium has launched a large-scale Web Accessibility Initiative (WAI), and there have been numerous calls for information system and software design to subscribe to "universal design" principles—the notion that design methods can be

developed and applied so as to make "products, communications, and the built environment" more usable by more people (Aslaksen, 1997). The W3C recognizes accessibility barriers for the deaf, the blind and those with physical disabilities, and argues that "people with cognitive or neurological disabilities may have difficulty interpreting Web pages that lack a consistent navigation structure or that lack visual signposts" (Chisholm, Vanderheiden, & Jacobs, 2001).

This is an implicit recognition that the next step in online document design and online instructional modeling is to deal with the more "invisible" cognitive impairments associated with learning disabilities. Over the last decade, the hypertext markup language-based World Wide Web has become the nation's premiere educational resource. However, using simple HTML documents as educational tools poses serious accessibility problems, particularly if documents need to be displayed using alternate modalities (Flammia, 1997). The mere digitization of documents does not ensure their accessibility or utility. Solving accessibility problems can involve difficulties in any number of areas including extracting content from format (a necessary first step in alternative presentation) and exerting finer more dynamic control over non-textual content (audio, video, images). New technologies, such as XML and XSL, provide more opportunity for overcoming these obstacles to accessible design than simple HTML can offer.

While the European initiatives have focused on visual processing impairments, they emphasized two important issues with broader implications for cognitive-adaptive design: (1) the increasing "digitization" of information previously delivered in document form (including Braille for the vision impaired) has created online accessibility problems, and (2) the need to develop standard protocols and formats for representing and displaying digitized information.

Developing and Implementing Cognitive-Adaptive Instructional Systems

The great potential of cognitive-adaptive systems derives from the integration of advances in applied cognitive and clinical neuroscience with recent developments in online information technology. What design considerations need to be addressed in order to combine these two areas of research to benefit special need populations?

We argue that information can be made more accessible if several conditions are satisfied in the information delivery system: (1) educational content is separated from presentation and display information and stored as "user neutral" learning objects in an object library, (2) there are methods for acquiring and protocols for representing relevant cognitive impairment data in XML-based cognitive user profiles, (3) there are standard protocols for attaching cognitive user profiles to sets of adaptive and compensatory actions that systems should make when rendering educational content at the human-computer interface, and (4) appropriate online technologies exist for implementing the adaptive actions implied by the profiles.

Design Elements of a Cognitive-Adaptive Instructional System

The recent appearance of World Wide Web Consortium standard core protocols like XML and XSL makes a learning-adaptive Web increasingly possible by satisfying the previously mentioned fourth condition. It remains only to satisfy the first three conditions. The first design element of a cognitive-adaptive system involves the creation of learning objects via decomposition and metadata description. Learning objects have several unique characteristics: (1) they are atomic and self-contained, decomposed from objects of greater complexity, (2) they are reusable "in multiple contexts for multiple purposes," (3) they can be recombined to create larger, more complex structures including lessons, courses and curricula, and (4) they are described with metadata about their educational function, physical characteristics, semantic content, and other relevant properties (Chitwood, 2005). Once created, learning objects are stored in an object library (OL) as a set of elementary resources capable of dynamic recombination with other objects under the influence of the rules of an instructional model.

Some objects may already be atomic, with little or no internal structure and may not be decomposable into smaller information units. In these cases, it is sufficient to describe the resource, for example, a particular image, with metadata and store in the object library. Many other existing instructional objects, on the other hand, are information containers, with both a complex semantic structure and a complex internal "document" organization. That is, they are structurally and semantically decomposable. An example of educational content that would have to be decomposed for use in a cognitive-adaptive system might be an online biology lesson whose organizational structure would consist of headings, paragraphs, figures, tables, and graphics, and whose content would have to be decomposed into special vocabulary or terminology, concepts, concept relations, proper names, and a myriad of other semantic properties and relationships.

Even as the educational materials are stripped of formatting information to become as user and culture-neutral as possible for display purposes (Cannataro, Cuzzocrea, Mastroianni et al., 2002), they are enriched with both educational metadata and content description metadata. Educationally relevant metadata can be provided by an object schema such as the IEEE LTSC 1484.12 Learning Object Metadata (LOM) protocol. This metadata specification provides a rich set of descriptors for describing the core characteristics of the resource (identifier, title, author, description) as well as a wide range of other characteristics from rights management through educational uses, to technical information. The LOM specification also provides a rich annotation mechanism to allow users of the library to add commentary to the resource record as well as a relationship mechanism that allows any given LOM-described resource to be linked to other resources (Shreve & Zeng, 2003).

Content Description

Content description of the objects in an object library can be accomplished with metadata derived from existing or custom domain-specific semantic markup languages. The domain specific markup languages chosen to describe content elements in a cognitive-adaptive system would be dependent, once again, on the pragmatics of object library use, that is, what the library's user communities expect to do with the resources and what functions they expect the resources to serve. The tag names, attributes, and document type descriptions or schema provided by a markup language directly reflect a domain-specific semantics and pragmatics. Markup languages are the single most important way that an explicit semantics can be applied directly to natural language and multimedia resources (Shreve & Zeng, 2003). Cognitive-adaptive systems will undoubtedly leverage many existing semantic (content) markup languages, depending on the field of the educational materials to be delivered (for instance, MathML the mathematics markup language or GML (geography markup language). Markup languages to represent the user profiles and other elements of the cognitive-adaptive system will have to be borrowed or customized.

User Profiles: Determining Individual Learning Needs

Assuming an object library is successfully created, the next step in designing a cognitive-adaptive system would involve acquiring and storing user models or profiles. Current research in adaptive hypermedia systems (De Bra, 1999), user modeling (Brusilovsky, 1994; Fink, Kobsa, & Schreck, 1997; Hothi & Hall, 1998), and Web accessibility (Velasco & Mohamad, 2002) has provided useful guidance in designing systems to make instructional content more accessible to learning disabled students. This research emphasizes the importance of coupling user profiles with adaptive information system design. Current adaptive approaches typically modify navigation support and document content for individuals or target populations based on a user model most often developed empirically by observing patterns of use and browsing behavior (De Bra, Brusilovsky & Houben, 1999; Wu, de Kort, & De Bra, 2001). However, because this approach implicitly presumes that cognition is within normal limits, it cannot account for and differentiate user behaviors that are due to cognitive impairment, as opposed to simple preference or idiosyncratic work style.

We propose an approach based on specifying a set of empirically-derived "best practice" adaptations (a *prescription*, if you will), offered by cognitive and educational remediation experts after evaluating the results of educational and neuropsychological assessments. This prescription can (and should) be later refined with a customization wizard and modified with data gained from the empirical observation of the actual behavior of cognitively impaired user-learners.

It is not uncommon for sensory impairments to be dealt with by information system actions based on user profiles. For instance, "visual profiles" for low-vision computer users meet the need to account for visual impairments of acuity, contrast sensitivity, color perception, and field of view when designing human-computer interfaces (Jacko, Rosa, Scott, et al., 2000). Although existing systems can use profiles to alter elements of the user interface including site navigation, organization, and content to support visually impaired users, more flexibility, and innovation is needed in order to remediate less visible cognitive impairments. Few if any studies have focused on building systems that integrate more complete and complex cognitive impairment user profiles with online information systems.

Successful cognitive-adaptive systems are dependent on robust user profiles to generate the parameters for determining the specific compensatory modifications to be made at the computer-human interface, for example, the architecture of the presentation or display, as well as to control the re-packaging of educational content delivered in digital documents. Cognitive user profiles could be based on combinations of online and in-person clinical and educational assessments of learners diagnosed with cognitive impairments and specific learning disabilities. The assessments, consisting of neurocognitive and educational screens, will measure, among other capacities, memory, executive function, and cognitive information processing. The assessments could also include measures of mood, anxiety, computer aptitude, and creative or divergent thinking.

Automated User Profile Development

A significant issue in the design of adaptive systems is determining exactly what remedial or compensatory actions to take for a given set of impairments and how to derive the actions and their representations in a practical, automatic manner. Initial test systems will have to rely heavily on standard educational and clinical empirical research with prototypes in the hope of gathering data that can be used to establish principles that would enable systems to do online assessment, generate user profiles, and then automatically generate action models.

User profile acquisition could be accomplished by the development of a modeling wizard to acquire additional user cognitive/sensory impairment data from online dialogs and/or browser modeling and represent it in a machine-usable XML-based metadata format. The wizard could elicit educational and clinical profile information to supplement the data collected in off-line assessments. The wizard would also process the data in off-line assessments and convert it to XML data. The profiles generated by the wizard provide a basis for determining optimal adaptive information delivery and display. The wizard might also include some "exemplars" of differently presented or formatted online information to gauge user reactions and preferences. An important research objective will be to determine the optimal requirements and content for a cognitive profile wizard including the correct mixture of cognitive-sensory assessment and exemplar presentation.

The results of neurocognitive and educational assessments would be stored in an XML-based user profile, using, where possible, data elements derived from the clinical document architecture (CDA) (Health Level Seven, 2002). In cases where appropriate data elements do not exist, they would be developed as subsets or extensions to the CDA. In any case, an ongoing area of research in cognitive-adaptive systems will be working with the neurocognitive and educational assessment community to develop a markup language to represent the relevant data.

The representation and storage of user profiles are well discussed in the literature (Fink, Kobsa, & Schreck, 1996; Kules, 2000; Velasco & Mohamad, 2002) and a variety of approaches are offered. We adopt the broad model described by Velasco and Mohamed, who suggest storing user profiles as XML schema, with the exception that we specify CDA conformance. The authors also suggest merging user information with device information in a single schema that follows, where possible, the guidelines for device profiles.[1]

Action Models and Compensatory Action Heuristics

Once a user profile is generated from an assessment battery, it remains to specify the set of adaptive compensatory actions the system should take for specific configurations of impairment or skill deficiency. The pairing of neurocognitive assessments with information system action is a complex scenario referred to as a cognitive-adaptive "action model" and characterizes the relationship between cognitive impairment and remedial or compensatory system actions (Diamond, Shreve, & Johnston, 2001).

The heuristics of the cognitive-adaptive action model are represented as rules. In the database they are stored as XML statements that express the relationship between configurations of educational assessments and compensatory action in general production rule form: **IF** *this-educational-result* **THEN** *this-adaptive-action*. The head of the rule is an XML- expressed cognitive impairment pattern and the tail is a set of actions also expressed in XML, including attachment to XML-Event behaviors, CSS, XSL and other stylesheet render-

ing technologies. The use of production rules for this purpose is an adaptation model as described by Cannataro and his colleagues (2002).

The action recommendations in the action models are linked to specific adaptive system actions via the adaptive control language (ACL), (i.e., the set of conventions that express the production rules). The heuristics underlying the action models are stored in cognitive adaptation (CA) and sensory adaptation (SA) databases that contain action instructions describing generic system actions and adaptations addressing impairments in a variety of cognitive/sensory domains. These adaptations provide instructions for how learning objects are to be expressed, organized, configured, formatted, and manipulated for the benefit of a specific class of user impairments or disabilities. There are also instructions that inform the system how to react to particular events in the document/user interface.

Figure 1. Schematic of an adaptive system

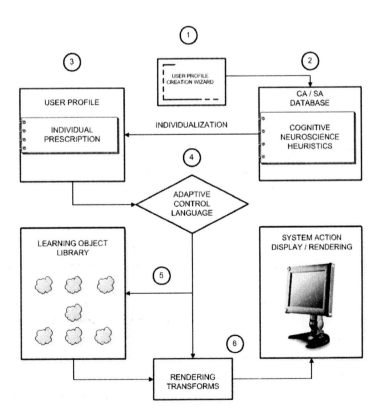

The ACL connects the results of the cognitive profiles generated by the user profile wizard to the adaptive heuristics of the CA/SA databases and to the set of educational objects (resources) to be displayed. The heuristics are expressed by the ACL at the system level by XSL (eXtensible Stylesheet Language) transformations of XML-based object/action representations derived from the CA/SA databases as modified by the profile wizard. The ACL produces system responses such as reorganization of the user interface; changes in rate of presentation of visual materials; dynamic selection, presentation, and linking of content; alteration in the configuration and organization of "information units;" and so on.

Taken together, the ACL specifies the relationship between cognitive, sensory or functional impairment and remedial or compensatory system actions (Diamond, Shreve, Bonilla, et al., 2003; Diamond et al., 2001). To the extent that users with similar impairments may require similar adaptations, it should be possible to group adaptive rules into categories reflective of clusters of recommended actions for particular user groups, creating what Brusilovsky has called user stereotypes (1996). To this point there has been little attempt in the user modeling community to address automated mechanisms for deriving adaptation models appropriate for complex cognitive and sensory impairment conditions. Other approaches that could be applied include deriving stereotypes (Rich, 1979) and inferring dynamic modeling rules from the data using acquisition heuristics as discussed by Ardissono and his colleagues (Ardissono, Console, & Torre, 1999).

Compensatory Actions, Cognition, and Educational Applications

Individuals with short-term memory impairments, for instance, could be expected to experience difficulty in memory of previously-visited links or for the content of dropdown menus and their submenus. A CA-stored instruction for such

cases would spell out the "performance implications" of this class of impairment and detail the general system steps that could be taken, such as alternative presentations for links or dropdown menu information.

In order to help improve learning and accessibility, the relationships between impairments and the ability to use an information system need to be delineated. Diamond et al. (2003) demonstrated that there are important relationships between the severity and nature of cognitive impairments and the ability to use information technology. The most important finding in their study was that while all participants learned how to use a telerehabilitation system (referred to as the VRC or Virtual Rehabilitation Center), the rate of learning or the number of "trials to acquisition" varied among participants with traumatic brain injuries. Individuals who needed more trials to acquisition were more impaired in visuo-spatial construction, reasoning-similarities and language repetition. Interestingly, 50% of those individuals who required fewer trials to acquisition and 75% of those who required more trials to acquisition exhibited impairments in memory. Thus, memory impairments were pervasive, but memory alone did not account for all of the differences in learning and accessibility.

The relationship between identified areas of cognitive impairment and performance on the VRC may be due to the implicitly normative information architecture of the VRC and other internet and computer-based systems that require impaired users with deficits in working memory and executive function (e.g., reasoning and organization) to process and store visual and auditory information (i.e., text, graphics, embedded or streaming audio and video) using displays that are ill-suited to them. Overall, the authors found that impairment in cognitive domains reflecting visual-spatial integration, memory, language processing, and executive-type functions inhibited learning efficiency and accessibility. The work underscored the need to link system design intended for differently-abled populations to individualized adaptations and compensatory actions.

Recent research has supported the contention that adaptations informed by clinical and educational assessments can be effective in improving task performance. Diamond, DeLuca et al. (2000) showed that using special software individualized processing speeds could be computed and used to help older adults achieve levels of performance accuracy that did not significantly differ from that of younger adults. These results demonstrated that a cognitive neuroscience-derived software tool could be used to help suggest efficacious compensatory actions that enhanced the ability of seniors with moderate cognitive and sensory impairments due to age, to process information more efficiently. Similar optimal processing speeds could be integrated into computer-based learning systems so that information could be presented to student users in ways that enhance their processing and performance accuracy.

The REY-organizational and extended memory (R-OEM) protocol (Diamond, DeLuca, & Kelley, 1997) used an "executive prosthetic" (i.e., a cognitive assistive technique) that helped individuals with learning and executive impairments learn and recall complex visual information. This assistive technique helped enhance performance. It did so, by first guiding the decomposition of text, images, and graphics into simpler, more atomic elements, and then providing organizational structures or schemas for re-organizing the graphic and textual information in new ways that more effectively tap explicit and implicit memory. Generally, the decomposition of complex objects or behaviors, with the subsequent reintegration and synthesis of the parts into a whole, increases instructional effectiveness in treatment subjects and predicts the magnitude of treatment outcomes for higher-order cognitive functions (Swanson, 1999). In clinical tests, the R-OEM generated alternative displays of information that allowed amnesiacs to retain information over a 30-minute delay, a performance comparable to that of non-amnesiacs (Diamond et al., 1997).

In a cognitive-adaptive information system, analogues of R-OEM-based techniques could be used to implement a stylesheet-based "executive function" facilitator that displays complex text and images dynamically by building them up from simpler graphic and textual elements. These decomposed learning objects, stored as XML data, could then be rendered by an XSL stylesheet to produce a synchronized multimedia integration language (SMIL) document where relative positioning, and attributes and tags such as *begin* and <sequence>, as well as SMIL events (begin event, end event) could be manipulated to dynamically construct more complex presentations according to the results of the protocol. SMIL presentations, essentially dynamically constructed multimedia presentations, could dynamically present information in the manner prescribed by an R-OEM-type informed representation schema.

Another example of adaptive, computer-based techniques derived from cognitive and clinical neuroscience work are the auditory threshold serial addition test (ATSAT), visual threshold serial addition test (VTSAT) and the dual task (DT) protocol (Diamond et. al., 1997; Diamond, DeLuca, et al., 2000). These protocols quantify processing speed while controlling accuracy and they have been implemented with clinical populations (stroke, traumatic brain injury, chronic fatigue syndrome, and multiple sclerosis). These programs measure speed and accuracy and determine the optimum speeds at which both visual and auditory information can be presented while maintaining a given level of performance accuracy. Dual task software is used to measure a subject's ability to process simultaneous streams of information presented in both the visual and auditory modes. Taken together, these programs assesses the impact of the single and dual processing of information streams on working memory, sustained attention, accuracy of performing arithmetic operations, and on reaction time. These techniques could be used to enhance a user's processing speed and accuracy by incrementally altering the computed optimum speeds and stimulus parameters of, for instance, the presentation of text online or the speed at which voice or video information is displayed. In other words, information could be both visually and aurally presented at individualized and optimized speeds of presentation, thus enhancing processing efficiency. The dynamic adaptation of a display, including speed/duration of text, graphic, or auditory information display could be controlled by using XSL stylesheets to generate multimedia SMIL documents and then controlling the value of the SMIL *duration* attribute for individual page elements to control how long they appear on the screen.

Adaptive action models based on semantic activation techniques also arise out of research in the fields of neuropsychology and behavioral neurology (i.e., prosopagnosia and visual agnosia, or the inability to recognize familiar faces and objects, respectively). Diamond and his colleagues describe another adaptive approach using the semantic activation protocol (SAP) protocol, where faces or objects drawn from similar semantic categories helped enhance and activate aware memory in a prosopagnosic patient (Diamond, Valentine, Mayes, & Sandel, 1994). In this research, it was shown that clustering faces/objects according to semantic categories induced a sense of familiarity and recognition. Similar types of semantic activation techniques could be used in educational systems to optimize learning and memory.

For example, a cognitive-adaptive information system could enhance memory for images and objects by visually clustering or navigationally linking information stored in XML-based semantic network representations or content schema. Using XSL stylesheet-generated SMIL documents, items could be dynamically clustered in visual regions of a presentation using the SMIL <layout>, <root-layout> and <region> tags. Similarly, semantic categories (semantic information would have to be stored in the content schema) could be used to organize links between dynamically created displays to capitalize on semantic similarity.

Perceptual priming protocols can also play a role in cognitive-adaptive systems. These protocols are based on the observation that information (words or images) that have been previously experienced can exert an effect on subsequent behavior or physiology (Diamond et al., 1994). Thus, while the specific learning episode may not be remembered, information can still be encoded and subsequently alter performance (i.e., perceptual fluency) (Johnston, Dark, & Jacoby, 1985). Improvement in performance as a result of prior exposure can be measured by reaction time protocols that indicate changes in saliency of learning (i.e., faster reaction time with learning) or faster relearning of material. In a cognitive-adaptive system, a priming reaction time (PRT) protocol could be used to measure the saliency of implicit and explicit learning as well as the speed of making perceptual-semantic decisions by determining if RT decreases or information processing speed increases following instruction. The results could be used to create XSL-generated "priming pages" for important content elements, which over repeated presentation and display could assist special needs learners in representing and storing information.

There are also modality-based processing differences between individuals that have an important bearing on the design of adaptive systems for the cognitively impaired learner. Some individuals display faster visual versus auditory processing speed and some display reverse patterns (Diamond et al., 2000). A cognitive-adaptive system could provide modality-specific options. Similar content could be presented as text, as image, or as speech using the relevant multimedia SMIL tags and attributes. For instance, using the SMIL <parallel> tag, parallel text and voice streams could be simultaneously presented in a document and selection between modalities could be offered to the user.

An Online Educational Scenario

Clearly, a variety of tools and technologies are currently available for use in online instructional communities. These technologies, implemented in a cognitive-adaptive instructional system, can significantly enhance the responsiveness and adaptability of online learning environments to special needs students. Systems could allow instructors to provide dynamic control over most aspects of an online display, including: (a) speed and duration of information unit presentation; (b) organizational structure or layout of the page; (c) placement and clustering of visual or typographic elements; (d) sequence of presentation of visual elements; (e) adaptive navigation and linking to other content/displays; (f) graphic or typographic features: size, color, font, and so on; (g) modality: text, image, voice, and (h) dynamic selection of page elements from underlying content. The system could also alter the rate at which information is presented; select memory and executive prosthetics; and alter the manner in which content and learning objects are to be expressed, organized, configured, formatted, and manipulated. The following is an example of an online scenario:

A student who is taking an online course in biology has had a mild brain injury. The current topic is the concept of *action potential* (AP). This topic includes information involving a variety of constituent concepts described in text (e.g., ion movements, resting potential, electrophysiological and concentration gradients, threshold of excitation, depolarization, hyper- polarization, and channels/gates), numerical and statistical information (tables, calculations), and visual material (images, movies, animations). The events that constitute the AP process occur in a specified sequence, and the event is usually described in narrative and then illustrated schematically in the typical textbook or Webpage. This static and normative presentation might not be the optimal display for a brain-injured student.

However, if the AP lesson document is first decomposed and described using an XML-based markup language, it would be possible to gain control of the appearance and presentation of the material in the lesson down to the level of individual words, sentences, paragraphs, illustrations, text, images, tables, and animations. This enhanced level of control could be used to optimize the individual learning experience if then connected to individual user profile information. The user profile information would allow: (a) for system presentation adaptations that would dynamically organize the visual and textual material in the lesson in ways that would compensate for executive dysfunction (i.e., deconstructing information into simpler units); (b) compensate for visual-conceptual integration deficits (i.e., simpler arrangement and sequencing of information via alternative schematics or custom animations); (c) alter the modality of textual presentation in order to compensate for reading disorders (i.e., use auditory-based text); (d) alter the rate of information presentation (visual and auditory) in order to compensate for slower processing (often observed in individuals with learning disabilities and brain injury) or ; (e) provide linkages to specially designed learning objects with built-in memory cues (i.e., clustering of semantically-related objects) to compensate for deficiencies in working memory. Overall, control over these elements would provide a range of compensatory and remedial actions to help improve the educational performance of students with special needs.

CONCLUSION

Adaptive information systems provide an opportunity to broaden the participation of certain classes of differently-abled populations in learning environments that depend heavily on information technology, such as Web-based and distance learning. The challenges in developing instructional models for online adaptive systems serving special needs learners with cognitive and sensory impairments are considerable. The instructional models must deal not only with the diverse learning problems such users confront in "traditional" classroom environments, but also with the new challenges presented by online instruction. Adaptive systems must integrate new online technologies in ways that provide unique opportunities to enhance individual instruction and learning through the use of highly personalized pedagogical models.

Adaptive online instructional systems achieve the goal of personalizing the content and delivery of information to the needs of individual learners by integrating educational and clinical evaluations of a user's cognitive and sensory impairments with instructional heuristics. The combination of specialized heuristics and clinical assessment data drives specific adaptive "compensatory" information system behaviors at the human computer-interface. Such adaptive interfaces act dynamically to modify information architecture and display in ways that address higher level cognitive processing deficiencies as well as altering formatting and presentation in order to address sensory-based needs. Using adaptive information systems to deliver educational content and services can make online learning environments and communities more accessible to individuals with inherited or acquired learning problems.

The implementation of an adaptive approach to instructional modeling offers a number of additional advantages. It affords both instructor and students a great deal of flexibility. The approach is practical and cost-effective from a technology standpoint. That is, the system can be implemented on any information system that implements the core World Wide Web (W3C) data formats and protocols. Because content is not rigidly linked to format, once heuristics and cognitive user profiles are developed, instructional content of all types can be automatically and dynamically adapted to an individual user's special needs.

Overall, the cognitive-adaptive approach we have described enhances and expands our understanding of how computer-assisted and online instructional systems can be more effectively designed for special needs learners. As such, it makes a new contribution to an important area of online instructional modeling for special populations. Cutting-edge, cross-disciplinary work will help inform the development of instructional models that enable cognitively impaired learners to acquire, remember, and manipulate information more effectively. Such systems will broaden the participation of this underrepresented group in education and in knowledge-based communities. In this age of global communication, educators have an obligation to equip as many individuals as possible with the tools that will allow them to participate in the educational, social, and political fabric of contemporary societies. By integrating adaptive instructional system concepts into the broader area of online instructional modeling, we can help empower differently-abled individuals to more fully use information technology and participate in an increasingly global educational community.

FUTURE RESEARCH

Future research must address a number of multidisciplinary issues involving clinical research with special populations, accessible information system design, and models of online instruction for special needs learners. Scholars in cognitive neuroscience, neuropsychology, and online and special education need to conduct empirical research focusing on information technology usage and the human-computer interface. The research should detail how cognitive and sensory deficits associated with a variety of inherited and acquired neurological and learning disorders might be mitigated by adapting the organization, navigation, and display of digital information in specific ways. Clinical insights into the mechanisms, course, and impact of learning and sensory deficits are needed in order to develop more effective remedial and compensatory strategies for employment in adaptive information systems. Research should especially be directed at developing more valid, reliable, and economical online assessments of cognitive and sensory deficits that are accompanied by appropriate age, education and culturally-adjusted norms. These assessments must be represented in a markup language format that can be integrated with rule-based instructional heuristics that act to guide a system's adaptive responses. Adaptive system designers need to communicate more effectively with brain and behavior scientists and educational and rehabilitation specialists in order to translate research advances from diverse fields into effective heuristic algorithms that would satisfy a wide array of special user needs. Software application researchers must continue to develop standard software mechanisms, using available Web-based protocols and markup languages such as XML and XSL, to integrate clinical findings and assessments, compensatory heuristics, and adaptive system action. Application research needs to focus on the goal of incorporating "universal access" principles that will help foster greater inclusiveness and system accessibility for special needs user by allowing for the creation of localized, personalized information system interaction and display. Finally, empirically based, randomized placebo controlled (RPC) trials need to be developed and executed in ecologically valid environments in order to evaluate the efficacy of adaptive models and identify areas of future research and development.

ACKNOWLEDGMENT

The authors wish to acknowledge Amy C. Moors for her editorial assistance.

REFERENCES

Ardissono, L. Console, L., & Torre, I. (1999). *Exploiting user models for personalizing news presentations.* Paper presented at the 8th International World Wide Web Conference. Retrieved December 11, 2002, from http://wwwis.win.tue.nl/asum99/ardissono/ardissono.html

Aslaksen, F., Steinar, B., Bringa, O., & Heggem, I. (1997). *Universal design planning and design for all.* Retrieved December 11, 2002, from www.independentliving.org/ docs1/nscd1997.html

Bayliss, D., Jarrold, C., Baddeley, A., & Leigh, E. (2005). Differential constraints on the working memory and reading abilities of individuals with learning difficulties and typically developing children. *Journal of Experimental Child Psychology, 92*(1), 76-99.

Brusilovsky, P. (1994). Methods and techniques of adaptive hypermedia. *User Modeling and User-Adapted Interaction, 4,* 21-45.

Brusilovsky, P. (1996). Methods and techniques of adaptive hypermedia. *User Modeling and User-Adapted Interaction, 6*(2-3), 87-129.

Cannataro, M., Cuzzocrea, A., Mastroianni, C., Ortale, R., & Pugliese, A. (2002). *Modeling adaptive hypermedia with an object-oriented approach and XML.* Paper presented at the 2nd International Workshop on Web Dynamics. Retrieved December 11, 2002, from http://www.dcs.bbk.ac.uk/~ap/pubs/webDyn2Report.pdf

Chambers, J. G., Parrish, T., & Harr, J. J. (2002). *What Are We Spending on Special Education Services in the United States, 1999-2000.* Advance Report #1, Special Education Expenditure Project (SEEP). Washington, DC: U.S. Department of Education, Office of Special Education Programs.

Chisholm, W., Vanderheiden, G., & Jacobs, I. (Eds). (2001). Web content accessibility guidelines 1.0. *Interactions, 8*(4), 35-54. Retrieved from http://portal.acm.org/citation.cfm?id=379550

Chitwood, K. (2005). *Learning objects: Making a difference in teaching and learning.* 20th Annual Conference on Distance Teaching and Learning. Retrieved December 11, 2002, from University of Wisconsin: http://www.uwex.edu/disted/conference/Resource_library/proceedings/04_1078.pdf

Coles, G. (1987). *The learning mystique.* New York: Fawcett Columbine.

Czaja, S. J., & Sharit, J. (1998). The effect of age and experience on the performance of a data entry task. *Journal of Experimental Psychology: Applied, 4*, 332-351.

Czaja, S. J., Sharit, J., Ownby, R., Roth, D., & Nair, S. (2001). Examining age differences in performance of a complex information search and retrieval task. *Psychology & Aging, 16*(4), 564-579.

De Bra, P. (1999). *Design issues in adaptive web-site development.* Paper presented at the 8th International World Wide Web Conference. Retrieved December 11, 2002, from http://wwwis.win.tue.nl/asum99/debra/debra.html

De Bra, P., Brusilovsky, P., & Houben, G. (1999). Adaptive hypermedia: From systems to framework. *ACM Computing Surveys, 31*(4).

Diamond, B. J., DeLuca, J., & Kelley, S. (1997). Executive functions and memory impairments in patients with aneurysms of the anterior communicating artery. *Brain, 120*, 1015-1025.

Diamond, B. J., DeLuca, J., Rosenthal, D., Vlad, R., Davis, K., Lucas, G., & Richards, J. (2000). Aging: Information processing speed and modality-specific effects. *International Journal of Rehabilitation and Health, 5*(1), 55-64.

Diamond, B., DeLuca, J., Rosenthal, D., Vlad, R., Davis, K., Lucas, G., & Richards, J. (2000). Information processing in younger versus older adults: Accuracy versus speed. *International Journal of Rehabilitation and Health, 5*(1), 55-64.

Diamond, B. J., Shreve, G., & Johnston, M. (2000). Telerehabilitation: A web-based "virtual rehabilitation center." Archives in Physical Medicine and Rehabilitation, *81*(12), 16-17.

Diamond, B. J., Shreve, G., & Johnston, M. (2001, October). *The virtual rehabilitation center: Testing user friendliness.* Paper presented at Kessler Medical Rehabilitation Research and Education Corporation, Kessler Conference Center, West Orange, NJ.

Diamond, B. J., Shreve, G., Bonilla, J., Johnston, M., Morodan, J., & Branneck, R. (2003). Cognition, telerehabilitation and user-accessibility, Special Issue on Telerehabilitation. *NeuroRehabilitation, 17*, 1-7.

Diamond, B. J., Valentine, T., Mayes, A., & Sandel, M. (1994). Evidence of covert recognition in a prosopagnosic patient. *Cortex, 30*, 377-393.

eSchool News Online. (2003). Retrieved December 11, 2002, from www.eschoolnews.com

Fink, J., Kobsa, A., & Nill, A. (1996, October). *User-oriented adaptivity and adaptability in the AVANTI Project.* Paper presented at the conference "Designing for the web: Empirical studies," Redmond, WA.

Fink, J., Kobsa, A., & Schreck, J. (1997). *Personalized hypermedia information provision through adaptive and adaptable system features: User modeling, privacy and security issues.* Proceeding of the workshop "Adaptive Systems and User Modeling on the World Wide Web," 6th International Conference on User Modeling, 1997. Chia Laguna, Sardinia.

Flammia, G. (1997). XML and style sheets promise to make the Web more accessible. *IEEE EXPERT, 12*(3), 98-99.

Gardner, H. (1983). *Frames of mind*. New York: Basic Books.

Glisky, E., & Schacter, D. (1988). Long-term retention of computer learning by patients with memory disorders. *Neuropsychologia, 26*(1), 173-178.

Health Level Seven, Inc: The clinical document architecture. (2002). Retrieved December 11, 2002, from http://www.hl7.org

Hearne, J. D., Poplin, M., Schoneman, C., & O'Shaughnessy, E. (1988). Computer aptitude: An investigation of differences among junior high students with learning disabilities and their non-learning-disabled peers. *Journal of Learning Disabilities, 21*, 489-492.

Henderson, C. (1995). *College freshmen with disabilities: A triennial statistical profile*. Washington DC: American Council on Education, HEATH Resource Center. (ERIC Document Reproduction Service No. ED387971)

Hothi, J., & Hall, W. (1998, June). An evaluation of adapted hypermedia techniques using static user modeling. In *Proceedings of the Second Workshop on Adaptive Hypertext and Hypermedia, (pp. 45-50)*. Pittsburgh, USA.

Jacko, J. A., Rosa, R. H., Scott, I., Pappas, C. J., & Dixon, M. A. (2000). Visual impairment: The use of visual profiles in evaluations of icon use in computer-based tasks. *International Journal of Human-Computer Interaction, 12*(1), 151-164.

Johnston, W., Dark, V., & Jacoby, L. (1985). Perceptual fluency and recognition judgments. *Journal of Experimental Psychology: Learning, Memory, & Cognition, 11*(1), 3-11.

Kules, W. (2000). *User modeling for adaptive and adaptable software systems*. Retrieved December 11, 2002, from University of Maryland, College Park, Department of Computer Science Web site at http://www.otal.umd.edu/uuguide/wmk/

Lewitt, E., & Baker, L. (1996). Child indicators: Children in special education. *The Future of Children, 6*(1), 139-152.

Mead, S., Spaulding, V., Sit, R., Meyer, B., & Walker, N. (1997). Effects of age and training on world wide web navigation strategies. In *Proceedings of the Human Factors and Ergonomics Society 41st Annual Meeting, (pp. 152-156)*.

Morrell R., Mayhorn C., & Bennett J. (2000). A survey of world wide web use in middle-aged and older adults. *Human Factors, 42*(2), 175-82.

OSEP: Office of Special Education Programs. (2001). *Twenty-third Annual Report to Congress on the Implementation of the Individuals with Disabilities Education Act*. Retrieved December, 8, 2003, from http://www.ed.gov/offices/OSERS/OSEP/Products/OSEP2001AnlRpt

Park, D. C. (1999). The basic mechanisms accounting for age-related decline in cognitive function. In D.C. Park & N. Schwartz (Eds.), *Cognitive aging: A primer* (pp. 3-22). Philadelphia, PA: Psychology Press.

Poplin, M., Drew, D., & Gable, R. (1984). *Computer aptitude, literacy, and interest profile*. Austin, TX: PRO-ED.

Poplin, M. (1988a). Holistic/constructivist principles of the teaching and learning process: Implications for the field of learning disabilities. *Journal of Learning Disabilities, 21*, 401-416.

Poplin, M. (1988b). The reductionistic fallacy in learning disabilities: Replicating the past by reducing the present. *Journal of Learning Disabilities, 21*, 389-400.

Reiff, H., & Gerber, P. (1994). Social/emotional and daily living issues for adults with learning disabilities. In P.J. Gerber & H.B. Reiff (Eds.),

Learning disabilities and adulthood, (pp. 72-81.)

Rich, E. (1979). User modeling via stereotypes. *Cognitive Science, 3,* 329-354.

Rousseau, G., Jamieson, B., Rogers, W., Mead, S., & Sit, R. (1998). Assessing the usability of online library systems. *Behaviour & Information Technology, 17,* 274-281.

Shreve, G., & Zeng, M. L. (2003). Integrating resource metadata and domain markup in an nsdl collection. In *DC-2003: Proceedings of the International DCMI Metadata Conference and Workshop* (pp. 223-229). Seattle, Washington.

Stothard, S. (1994). The nature and treatment of reading comprehension difficulties in children. *Reading development and dyslexia.* Retrieved September 16, 2006, from PsycINFO database.

Stone, S., Poplin, M., Johnson, J., & Simpson, O. (1992). *Non-traditional talents of the learning disabled: Divergent thinking and feeling.* Unpublished manuscript, Claremont Graduate School.

Swanson, H. (1993). Working memory in learning disability subgroups. *Journal of Experimental Child Psychology, 56,* 87-114.

Swanson, L. (1999, May). *Intervention research for students with learning disabilities: A meta-analysis of treatment outcomes.* Paper presented at the meeting of Keys to Successful Learning: A National Summit on Research in Learning Disabilities, Washington, D.C.

Tarver, S., Ellsworth, P., & Rounds, D. (1980). Figural and verbal creativity in learning disabled and non-learning-disabled children. *Learning Disability Quarterly, 3,* 11-18.

UCLA Center for Communication Policy. (2003). *Surveying the digital future: the UCLA Internet report, year three, UCLA Center for Communication Policy.* Retrieved May 12, 2003, from UCLA Center for Communication Policy Web site: http://www.ccp.ucla.edu/pdf/UCLA-Internet-Report-Year-Three.pdf

Velasco, C., & Mohamad, Y. (2002, May). *Web services and user/device profiling for accessible internet services provision.* Paper presented at CSUN's Seventeenth Annual International Conference: "Technology and Persons with Disabilities." Los Angeles.

Westerman, S. J., Davies, D. R., Glendon, A. I., Stammers, R. B., & Matthews, G. (1995).

Age and cognitive ability as predictors of computerized information retrieval. *Behaviourand Information Technology, 14,* 313-326.

Wu, H., de Kort, E., & De Bra, P. (2001). A reference architecture for adaptive hypermedia systems. In *Proceedings of the 12th ACM Conference on Hypertext and Hypermedia,* (pp.141-150). Århus, Denmark.

ENDNOTE

[1]   As given in the W3C guidelines for Composite Capability/Preference Profiles at http://www.w3.org/TR/1999/NOTE-CCPP-19990727.

Chapter XIV
Challenges and Solutions in the Delivery of Clinical Cybersupervision

Kenneth L. Miller
Youngstown State University, USA

Susan M. Miller
Kent State University, USA

ABSTRACT

Supervision is both a special case of instruction and a critical aspect of professional development. The ongoing development of Web-based infrastructures and communication tools provides opportunities for cybersupervision. Advantages of cybersupervision for counselor training include opportunities to provide location-independent, "live" supervision of counseling sessions in which: (a) evaluative feedback is communicated in "real time" using text or graphical modalities; (b) audio evaluative feedback is digitally recorded in "real time" for post-session playback; and, (c) weekly, hour-long, supervision sessions are conducted using either synchronous (e.g., multifeatured video conferencing, chat room) or asynchronous (video recording, email) Web-based communication tools. Challenges to quality online supervision include communicating critical supervisor characteristics, developing an effective supervisor/supervisee online relationship, insuring requisite personal dispositions and computer skills, implementing a theoretical model of supervision, and resolving legal and ethical problems. Authors examine these advantages, challenges, and solutions in the context of two online supervision/instructional models for training counselors (i.e., professional counselors, psychologists, clinical social workers, and psychiatrists) and discuss the generalizability of the cybersupervision model for professional training in a variety of fields that include medicine, law, and education.

CHAPTER OBJECTIVES

The reader will be able to:

- Identify advantages, challenges, and solutions related to the delivery of online clinical supervision/instruction
- Apply methods of two supervision theories in the delivery of cybersupervision
- Understand how synchronous and asynchronous communication tools can be used to facilitate the development of clinical skills through the delivery of online supervision
- Draw conclusions regarding the value of cybersupervision for clinical and other professional training and development

INTRODUCTION

Supervision is a critical aspect of training and development for professionals in a variety of fields. It is a process by which a highly skilled or master practitioner observes and evaluates the performance of a novice with the goal of promoting the development of requisite knowledge and skills for competent practice. One can scarcely imagine a psychotherapist or medical doctor providing services to patients without benefit of supervision during their training programs. Yet, supervision is a costly and time consuming process that frequently strains the financial and human resources of organizations charged with these responsibilities. These costs are incurred as supervisors take time from routine duties that generate income for businesses and organizations to provide supervision that does not typically produce income. Supervisors are also frequently required to provide supervision services at remote locations that require compensation for travel time and mileage. Taken together, these challenges create circumstances that may limit both the quantity and quality of supervision.

Supervision of clinical work typically occurs during the middle to later stages of graduate education of future mental health professionals. Students will have completed didactic coursework (i.e., theories, clinical methods/techniques, ethical/legal issues) and are ready to apply this knowledge in direct services to clients in a practicum or internship setting. In most cases, clinical programs are affiliated with a counseling clinic so that students' (i.e., supervisees') first introduction to counseling occurs in a highly-structured environment. Viewing sessions from an observation room, the course instructor (i.e., supervisor) carefully observes supervisees' performances and session dynamics, and intervenes when necessary. This initial practicum experience is usually followed in subsequent semesters by field placements or internships in a variety of mental health, hospital, community agency, and/or school settings. Internship supervision is typically provided by an on-site supervisor on a weekly basis and by a university supervisor at less frequent intervals.

What should be evident from this brief description of clinical supervision is that it is a special case of instruction. In order to provide clinical supervision, laws in many states mandate that counselors complete specialized training and earn a supervision credential. During this training, counselors are typically taught to provide supervision using two to three major supervision models (with specialized training in alternative models). What they learn, in fact, are different instructional models for providing supervision. Each model corresponds to a particular theoretical perspective and instructional methodology, which determine supervision goals, supervisor roles, and learning outcomes.

BACKGROUND

The capacity to supervise counseling sessions has changed dramatically as new technologies have provided more sophisticated communication options. Early supervision utilized an observation room in which a supervisor could observe a limited number of counseling sessions through one-way mirrors. The supervisor communicated to the student-counselor by knocking on the door and providing feedback or suggestions. This *knock on the door* approach is still used, but has generally been replaced by the use of technologies to facilitate communication from the supervisor to the supervisee (i.e., student-counselor). These included installation of telephones and video cameras in counseling rooms and multiple television monitors in an observation room, which increased the number of sessions that can be readily supervised. This configuration permitted supervisors to provide live, evaluative feedback via telephone installed in the counseling room (i.e., *telephone call-in*), a low-tech approach, or through a mid-level technology approach called *bug-in-the-ear*. For the latter method, the student-counselor received feedback from the supervisor through an audio ear-bud.

Research findings suggest that supervisory interruptions are not as disruptive as might be expected (Champe & Kleist, 2003). Supervisees have reported that live supervisory feedback is beneficial, especially when the supervisor is perceived as flexible and supportive. Moorhouse and Carr (1999) found a tentative relationship between frequent and complex supervisory feedback using the telephone call-in method and client cooperation. Although research findings reveal that student-counselors approach the supervisory experience with some anxiety, Mauzey, Harris, and Trusty (2000) reported that neither the phone-in method nor the bug-in-the-ear method increased the anxiety or anger levels during live supervisory sessions.

A relatively new, and potentially much less intrusive, supervision approach is called *bug-in-the-eye* (BITE: Klitzke & Lombardo, 1991). Computers in an observation room are linked to monitors located in counseling rooms. Supervisors send live evaluative text-based or iconographic messages to monitors that are positioned in the counseling rooms so that only the counselor/supervisee can read the screen. Because the supervisee controls when he or she reads the message on the computer screen, bug-in-the-eye technology may facilitate greater integration of supervisory feedback without distractions that can impede the normal flow of the counseling process (Gallant, Thyer, & Bailey, 1991; Klitzke & Lombardo, 1991) and in a manner that is efficient and timely (Liddle, 1991; McCollum & Wetchler, 1995).

One of the first attempts of what was to become known as bug-in-the-eye technology involved linking two computers to provide live supervision in a basic counseling skills course (Neukrug, 1991). Student-counselors (i.e., supervisees) participated in counseling role-plays with student-clients. Supervisory feedback provided during these role-plays included general positive statements about the supervisee's performance (i.e., "good") as well as comments directed at targeted performance areas. Neukrug reported that the supervisees readily mastered use of the system.

"Bug-in-the-eye feedback can be text or icon-based" (see Miller, Miller, & Evans, 2002 for more details). Text-based feedback may include directives such as, "Ask the question again," or "Explore the client's emotional response to her divorce." This feedback may also include positive statements such as, "Good job of confronting client on this issue," or specific recommendations for language use such as, "Say to the client, 'You feel angry and betrayed.'" Supervisors may use text-based feedback to focus on immediate concerns (e.g., "Determine if the client has a plan to commit the murder, an identified victim, and the means to carry it out.") or on broader issues after observing session dynamics over longer time periods (e.g., "You are responding to the client from a position of powerlessness and fear...BE MORE ASSERTIVE.").

Icon-based feedback is designed as graphical shorthand for communicating complex ideas.

Examples of iconic messages include the image of a downward pointing arrow to communicate the need for the supervisee to explore the current issue in greater depth and the image of a judge's gavel to communicate that the supervisee is communicating in a judgmental manner. In order to insure immediate and accurate interpretation of iconic messages during counseling sessions, prior training is required.

A complex system of bug-in-the eye supervision was installed by the first author when he served as director of the University Counseling Center/Community Counseling Clinic at Youngstown State University. Wall-mounted computer monitors were installed in six counseling rooms in the clinic and each monitor was connected to a laptop computer in an observation room (see Miller, Miller, & Evans, 2002 for details). Supervisees in a first counseling practicum were exposed to three modes of supervisory feedback (i.e., telephone-call-in, bug-in-the-ear, and bug-in-the-eye) as part of a qualitative study. At the end of the semester, supervisees participated in structured interviews to assess perceptions of their supervisory experience. Feedback from the first students to use the BITE technology was positive: they reported a preference for bug-in-the-eye technology over bug-in-the-ear supervision, were comfortable using the technology, and thought that the use of BITE increased their confidence as they worked with clients. These findings are consistent with those of Scherl and Haley (2000) who reported that their trainees preferred BITE technology over knock-on-the-door and telephone call-in approaches.

Although live supervision has many advantages, the most popular supervisory method has remained the post-supervisory review (Champe & Kleist, 2003). For this approach, counseling sessions are either audiotaped or videotaped and the supervisor later reviews the session with the supervisee. However, newer technologies now provide the opportunity to combine some of the advantages of live supervision with the review

method. While viewing a live session through an observation window or via a computer monitor, analog or digital recordings of the supervisor's feedback can be overlaid on the video recording of the session or can be saved simultaneously in a sound file. This method has been called the audio track overlay protocol (ATOP) (Evans, Miller, & Miller, 2005). With little modification, this system can also be used to provide supervision at a distance.

This abbreviated history of technology used in clinical supervision reveals that the enhanced communications options afforded by new technologies have been adapted for use in the supervision process. Supervisors have used these new technologies to modify the methods and timing of supervision. What has remained common to all of these approaches is the assumption that the supervisor and supervisee communicate in the same location. Only recently has the option of providing supervision that is location-independent been a viable option. This phenomenon may be do to the fact that some counselor educators view the computer, and more recently the Internet, as more appropriate for the dissemination of didactic or content information, rather than a method for teaching skills based and practicum/internship courses (Wantz, et al., 2003). It is worthwhile to discuss the context in which online supervision has evolved.

Beginning in the early 1990s, the delivery of online instruction promised increased university enrollments and decreased faculty costs. University administrators responded by encouraging faculty to develop online courses. In 2003, Wantz, et al. conducted a comprehensive survey of counseling programs to determine the nature and extent to which online learning opportunities were part of the curriculum. The final sample consisted of faculty from 127 counseling programs (out of 416 who received the survey). Less than half of the programs (42%, n = 53) included some type of online distance learning: 23 programs offered blended courses (i.e., online plus a face-to-face component); 11 programs offered courses that were entirely online; and 12 programs offered both blended and full online courses.

Respondents were also asked whether they conducted "supervision and consultation with practicum and internship counselor trainees via distance learning" (p. 336). Thirty-eight percent reported that they did. What is not clear from the reported findings is the number of programs in which the online element was used for supervision rather than for general consultation, the number of programs that used live or post-sessions formats for online supervision, and the types of Web-based communications and other technologies that were used. The number of faculty who did not offer online supervision courses should be understood in light of their expressed concerns regarding the suitability of the Internet to deliver courses designed to teach clinical skills. The delivery of supervision via the Internet is a relatively new phenomenon and is known by a variety of names that include online supervision, e-supervision, or cybersupervision. The latter term became popular following the introduction of the term, cybercounseling. Coursol (2004) defined cybersupervision as the use of "...Internet videoconferencing to enhance the supervision of student counselors" (p. 83), although she also discusses the use of e-mail for on-going contact.

The National Board of Certified Counselors (NBCC) uses the term WebCounseling, which is defined as "the practice of professional counseling and information delivery that occurs when client(s) and counselor are in separate or remote locations and utilize electronic means to communicate over the Internet" (Bloom, 1997, p. 1). Descriptions of cybercounseling (i.e., the direct delivery of counseling services to a client using the Internet) are readily available due to the popularity and availability of online counseling (Chester & Glass, 2006). Since cybersupervision is a much newer phenomenon, there are fewer descriptions available. The previously mentioned article by Miller et al. (2002) described a bug-in-the-eye

technology system that can be adapted for online supervision. Coursol (2004) identified minimum hardware and software requirements for an online BITE system. Brown (2000) reported on the use of the Internet by faculty in three programs (counselor education, school psychology, and school social work) at the University of North Carolina at Chapel Hill to communicate with students at off-campus field sites for purposes of staffing and treatment planning.

Myrick and Sabella (1995) described what they called *e-mail supervision* that was offered in the school counseling program at the University of Florida. Students were placed at elementary, middle, and high schools for practicum and internship experiences. They participated in individual and group supervision and were supervised by both an on-site counselor and a faculty member. Supervisees communicated with their supervisor via e-mail to describe a case or to ask for assistance. When appropriate, a case was sent via e-mail to the supervision group, which consisted of other practicum/internship students. It is worth it to note the fact that a case was sent to members of the International Counselor Network and the Counselor Education and Supervision Network, thereby substantially enlarging the volume and diversity of feedback to the supervisee. Authors reported positive supervisee reactions to the use of written versus spoken words. Emails could be saved and reviewed. Because of the need to use precise language, authors indicated that the written word seemed to have a "powerful effect" (p. 6). Reported limitations of this model included omission of information due to the time required for typing versus speaking and the absence of nonverbal cues in written feedback.

As revealed by information presented in this section, computer technologies have generated effective, efficient, and cost-effective modalities to provide clinical supervision. When these technologies are used in conjunction with the distributed communications capabilities of the World Wide Web, unique options and advantages are created for the delivery of online supervision. The following scenario is presented to illustrate the advantages of online supervision:

Imagine that you are a counselor supervisor on a journey by train to present a paper at a regional conference. Three hours into your trip, your laptop computer alarm sounds to remind you that, in 15 minutes, two of your supervisees (Stacey and Lawrence) will be conducting counseling sessions at the university's counseling clinic that is now 200 miles from your present location. Before you left campus, you assured both supervisees that you would provide "live" supervision of their counseling sessions. You boot your wireless laptop and login to the password protected network and digital cameras in predetermined counseling rooms at the clinic. Displayed at the perimeter of the laptop monitor are thumbnail images of the two counseling rooms at the clinic.

As Stacey's counseling session begins, you click on the thumbnail image of her counseling room, which fills the center of your laptop computer's screen. For the next several minutes, you observe Stacey's counseling session in real time. With the aid of headphones, you hear counselor-client dialogue with digital clarity. After observing the session for 10 minutes, you determine that the Stacey needs to confront the client more directly on her failure to comply with her treatment plan to reduce her depressive symptoms. You open a password-protected, Internet-based, instant messaging program and prepare such feedback. After composing your feedback, you depress a series of keystrokes to send it instantly to a flat-screen monitor mounted in the counseling room so that only Stacey can view your feedback. From your laptop, you observe the message flash onto her monitor. You note by her head nod that Stacey has received the feedback and immediately depress a key combination to retrieve the message screen back to your computer in preparation for additional feedback. As you continue to observe

the session, you open a secure, Web-based audio recording file on the university server that is simultaneously video recording the counseling session. This audio recording file enables you to attach a voice recording to the session in real time (i.e., synchronized to the video recording). Using the microphone on your laptop computer, you record several strategies for dealing with client resistance and instruct Stacey to read two journal articles on this topic in preparation for your regularly-scheduled, weekly, one-hour supervision session.

On the alternate thumbnail image, you observe that Lawrence's counseling session has begun. You click on this image, which fills the center of your computer screen while the thumbnail image of Stacey's counseling session remains visible at the perimeter of your monitor. After observing the second session for five minutes, you determine that Lawrence is flirting with the client as she makes inappropriate sexual overtures. Using the same Internet-based, instant messaging program, you send an immediate directive to Lawrence to stop flirting with the client and, for emphasis, include a graphic of a large red stop sign in this message. You then retrieve the message screen in preparation for additional feedback. As you continue to observe Lawrence's session, you open the same secure, Web-based audio recording file on the university server that is simultaneously video recording the counseling session. This audio recording file enables you to attach a voice recording to the session in real time (i.e., synchronized to the video recording). Using the microphone on your laptop computer, you remind Lawrence of both legal and ethical prohibitions against such behavior with clients and require him to write a 10-page paper on this topic for submission via e-mail attachment in two days. After insuring that Lawrence has responded appropriately to this directive, you click on the thumbnail image of the Stacey's counseling session and continue to provide live supervision. You use this procedure to alternate between sessions, insuring that both counselors are receiving high quality, live supervision with immediate evaluative feedback.

At the end of each counseling session, you send text messages to Stacey and Lawrence informing them of the need to review both the digital video and audio files of their counseling sessions now stored on the university server in preparation for regular "live," weekly, one-hour supervision sessions with them. Using a multi-featured video conferencing program, you complete the live supervision sessions at regularly scheduled times.

CHALLENGES AND SOLUTIONS

There are a number of issues involved in providing effective cybersupervision. We have conceptualized these as challenges for which solutions can be generated. As noted at the beginning of the chapter, we will examine five challenges in the provision of cybersupervision: (a) communicating critical supervisor characteristics; (b) developing an effective supervisor-supervisee online relationship; (c) insuring requisite personal dispositions and computer skills; (d) implementing a theoretical model of supervision; and, (e) resolving legal and ethical problems. This is not an exhaustive list of challenges, although these are some of the most compelling.

Communicating Critical Supervisor Characteristics

Supervisees are more likely to implement supervisory feedback if they believe that the supervisor possesses expertness, trustworthiness, and attractiveness (Dorn, 1984). Rickards (1984) attempted to isolate the relationship between attributions made by supervisees and verbal interactions during face-to-face supervision. He found that negative feedback to supervisees and negative comments made by supervisees were negatively associated with supervisees' positive attribute ratings of supervisors. A positive relationship was found between supervisee statements that "ask for information, opinions, or suggestions," and attributions of supervisor attractiveness. This and similar studies reveal the need to study processes by which supervisees make attributions about their supervisors in online environments. Research findings on computer-mediated communication reveal that individuals communicate differently online than in face-to-face situations.

Strengths of cybersupervision include the use of Web-based communication tools that permit supervisor-supervisee interactions that are independent of location and time. Asynchronous communication modes such as e-mail permit time for both parties to reflect on written communications and make thoughtful responses (Harper, 1999). However, the absence of nonverbal cues in e-mail communications may limit a supervisee's ability to form accurate attributions regarding a supervisor. Without access to a supervisor's facial cues, gestures, and tone of voice, a supervisee can easily exaggerate and distort negative supervisory feedback that can lead to inaccurate supervisor attributions. Similarly, a supervisor may be unable to detect a supervisee's expression of anxiety or frustration (Kanz, 2001) or notice the degree to which a supervisee is resistant to suggestions or directives (Mallen, Vogel, & Rochlen, 2005). This may lead the supervisor to respond inappropriately or inaccurately to the supervisee and may cause the supervisee to make misattributions regarding the supervisor's expertness and trustworthiness. One solution for problems generated by the absence of visual communication cues is the use of video conferencing. Other strategies are discussed in the following section.

Developing an Effective Supervisor-Supervisee Relationship

Although attributions of expertness, trustworthiness, and attractiveness are necessary, they are not sufficient for the establishment of a successful supervisor/supervisee relationship. For supervision to be effective, the supervisor and supervisee must establish a working alliance. Mallen, Vogel, and Rochlen (2005) suggested that the development of such an alliance may take longer in online environments.

Due to the absence of research on cybersupervision, literature on cybercounseling provides some insight into the development of effective counselor-client online relationships. In text-based environments it is difficult to detect a client's emotional state, to demonstrate empathy, or use non-verbal encouragers (Harper, 1999; Mallen, Vogel, & Rochlen, 2005). In their review of cybercounseling, Mallen, Vogel, Rochlen, and Day (2005) reported mixed findings from three studies on the development of successful counselor-client relationships in face-to-face versus online environments: Cohen and Kerr (1998) and Cook and Doyle (2002) found no differences in the development of a therapeutic relationship between face-to-face and computer-mediated counseling, but Hufford, Glueckauf, and Webb (1999) found that teenage clients reported better relationships in face-to-face sessions. Day and Schneider (2000) reported no differences in the relationship between counselors and clients in audiotaped, videotaped, and face-to-face sessions as perceived by an external set of raters. Interviews with participating counselors revealed mixed feelings about distance technology: some counselors felt hindered in development of the therapeutic relationship but other counselors preferred the computer-mediated format.

Mallen and Vogel (in Mallen, Vogel, & Rochlen, 2005) found that student-counselors who interacted with a client using synchronous chat formed gender-stereotyped impressions of their clients. Unknown to the student-counselor, the client was a research confederate and the reported gender of the client was randomly manipulated. The importance of this finding is that in the absence of sufficient information during counseling interactions, individuals may engage in stereotypical thinking. This dynamic may also

occur during cybersupervision in the absence of a video component or face-to-face interactions between the supervisor and supervisee.

One technique used to compensate for the absence of nonverbal cues is emotional bracketing, a concept developed by Murphy and Mitchell as part of an e-mail-based counseling practice they called therap-e-mail (Collie, Mitchell, & Murphy, 2000). Along with the content of the communication, when appropriate, the counselor or client inserts a description of their feelings by the use of brackets. Murphy and Mitchell also developed a set of strategies they call presence techniques. One such technique, descriptive immediacy, involves the counselor describing his or her non-verbal behavioral reactions. The goal of this descriptive narrative is to bring the counselor and client into the same virtual space, thus deepening the online therapeutic relationship. Although these techniques were developed to overcome the absence of nonverbal cues in text-based online counseling, the strong parallels between cybercounseling and cybersupervision suggest that these same strategies would be useful for developing working alliances between a supervisor and supervisee.

It is important to note the similarity between Murphy and Mitchell's emphasis on the role that "presence" plays in forming counselor-client relationships, and the general problem of establishing social presence during online instruction discussed in the chapter by Snelbecker, Miller, and Zheng (2008). The cybersupervisor's responsibilities are to teach clinical skills; assess supervisee knowledge, attitudes, and performance; communicate feedback; and challenge irrational thinking. Broadly defined, these are the responsibilities of any teacher. Online "presence" techniques used to promote a therapeutic relationship between counselors and clients and working alliances between supervisors and supervisees can be generalized to the development of a teaching-learning relationship between teachers and students.

Insuring Requisite Personality Dispositions and Computer Skills

Implicit in the previously discussed challenges is the assumption that supervisors and supervisees possess the necessary dispositions and computer skills to be fluent in an online environment. Although research using the Myers-Briggs Type Indicators (MBTI) has revealed the personality types of effective counselors in face-to-face settings, authors have noted that MBTI indicators are unknown for effective online counselors (e.g., Harris-Bowlsbey, 2000). Research suggests that warmth, genuineness, and empathy are essential characteristics of successful counselors and by extension, successful supervisors (Parrott, 2003). It is not yet known how these dispositional characteristics affect the choice to engage in cybersupervision. It may be that as more counseling professionals use technology to provide clinical services, perceptions of cybercounseling will change, thereby attracting students who possess dispositions necessary to work effectively in an online environment. What is unknown is the degree to which these individuals will be successful counselors. Given the unknowns about dispositional characteristics and use of the Internet for counseling and supervision, counselor educators and program administrators should stay alert to interaction effects between students' dispositions and success in cybersupervision.

A related challenge is insuring that supervisors and supervisees are computer literate and competent in the use of online technologies. Participants should be adept at using hardware (e.g., video cam), software telecommunication and utility programs (e.g., chat, email), and be familiar with limitations of online communication. The profession has taken steps to resolve this challenge. The Association for Counselor Education and Supervision (ACES, 1999) has established Technical Competencies for Counselor Education Students: Recommended Guidelines for Program Development. These guidelines should result in the development of new technology intensive courses in counselor training programs, more technology-based assignments in existing courses, and competencies designed to insure that trainees possess abilities to communicate effectively using written text (Alleman, 2002). Counseling students can and should take responsibility for developing these competencies by enrolling in technical courses and online workshops and by obtaining information on cybercounseling (Mallen, Vogel, & Rochlen, 2005).

Implementing a Theoretical Model of Supervision

A fourth challenge is for supervisors to adapt and implement a theoretical model of supervision using a Web-based approach. This is a significant challenge in light of the fact that considerable knowledge and skill are required to execute a theoretical approach even in face-to-face supervision. This problem is exacerbated by the complexity of the supervision process that typically requires supervisors to: teach clinical skills; assess supervisee knowledge, attitudes, performance, and responses; effectively communicate evaluative feedback; challenge irrational thinking and clinical limitations; and, offer a supportive learning environment. Each supervision model delineates the extent to which these and other tasks must be accomplished.

Three primary categories of supervision models are used in counselor training and include developmental, psychotherapy-based, and integrative models. Other categories include supervision-specific models, transgenerational models, purpose-systematic models, and postmodern models of family supervision (Haynes, Corey, & Moulton, 2003). Each category includes specific models that posit unique supervisory roles, responsibilities, and methods for the delivery of effective supervision. For purposes of this chapter, we will discuss two specific supervision models: (a) the cognitive-behavioral model from the psychotherapy-based category; and, (b) the integrated developmental model (Stoltenberg, Mc-Neill, & Delworth, 1998) from the developmental category. These models were selected because of their popularity and common use in clinical supervision and because they represent divergent approaches to the supervision process with diverse solutions for Web-based applications.

The Cognitive-Behavioral Model

Cognitive-behavioral therapy (CBT) focuses on the influence of thoughts/beliefs on both emotions and behaviors (Haynes et al., 2003). A primary goal of cognitive-behavioral supervision is to teach specific techniques and to correct supervisees' inaccurate beliefs about the use of CBT in their work with clients. Supervision sessions are typically highly structured and are designed to educate the supervisee. A fundamental purpose of cognitive-behavioral supervision is help the supervisee understand how her or his beliefs regarding counseling ability influence her or his performance in counseling. In this process, supervisees translate what they have learned in supervision to their work with clients (Haynes et al., 2003).

Liese and Beck (1997) specified nine steps that provide the structure for a cognitive-behavioral supervision session. These steps are designed to parallel those that occur in cognitive-behavioral therapy, specify the supervisor's roles, and provide useful information for adapting this model for Web-based supervision. Haynes et al., (2003) delineate the nine steps:

1. **Check-in:** The supervisor asks the supervisee how she or he is doing.
2. **Agenda setting:** The supervisor encourages careful preparation for the supervision session by asking the supervisee to provide a focus.
3. **Bridge from the previous supervision session:** The supervisor asks the supervisee

to focus on learning from the previous session.

4. **Inquiry about previously supervised therapy cases:** The supervisor asks the supervisee to review successes and problems with cases previously discussed.
5. **Review of homework since the previous supervision session:** This may include reviews of assigned readings or progress in using specific techniques with clients.
6. **Prioritization and discussion of agenda items:** The supervisor focuses on a review of the supervisee's recorded therapy sessions using role plays to teach new skills.
7. **Assignment of new homework:** Based on information gleaned in the supervision session, the supervisor assigns homework designed to help the supervisee develop knowledge and skills in cognitive-behavioral therapy.
8. **Supervisor's capsule summaries:** The supervisor reflects on important issues to provide a focus for supervision.
9. **Elicit feedback from the supervisee:** The supervisor solicits feedback throughout the session with the goal of helping the supervisee recognize gains in knowledge and skills.

This structure clearly identifies the primary role of the cognitive-behavioral supervisor as a teacher. This role is consistent with the identification of supervision as a special case of instruction. Features of and communication tools available for use on the World Wide Web make is possible to adapt the instructional aspects of the cognitive-behavioral supervision model for the provision of cybersupervision. Because live video conferencing most closely approximates face-to-face interaction, we recommend it as the primary tool for delivery of cybersupervision. Using the nine-step process and assuming the use of a multi-featured, live video conferencing program, these features and sample tools are described following.

1. **Check-in:** Because it is critical for the supervisor to assess the supervisee's appearance, affect, and psychological readiness to engage in supervision, this step is best accomplished using a synchronous communication tool such a live video conferencing that permits access to both verbal and non-verbal behaviors in real time.

2. *A*genda setting: The supervisor requests that the supervisee prepare for the live video conference by emailing a proposed session agenda prior to the supervision session.

3. **Bridge from the previous supervision session:** Prior to the cybersupervision session, the supervisor assigns the supervisee to review digital video recordings of two counseling sessions completed by the supervisee during the previous week, prepare a two-page text document in which she discusses knowledge and skills gained during these sessions, and to upload this document into the live video conference for comment and discussion.

4. **Inquiry about previously supervised therapy cases:** Consistent with the request made in Step 3, the supervisor assigns the supervisee to create and save digital video files that reflect three examples of her most effective work and three examples of her least effective work during counseling sessions completed by the supervisee over the past two months. During the cybersupervision session, these digital files are uploaded and jointly reviewed for discussion and evaluative feedback.

5. **Review of homework since the previous supervision session:** During the previous cybersupervision session, the supervisor assigned the supervisee to create a 15-minute digital video in which she demonstrates a new counseling technique. During the current cybersupervision session, this digital video is uploaded and both supervisor and supervisee evaluate her performance.

6. **Prioritization and discussion of agenda items:** During the cybersupervision session, the supervisor uploads and reviews two, 15-minute digital video segments of counseling sessions completed by the supervisee during the previous week. Both the supervisor and supervisee are able to view the uploaded video using a multifeatured video conferencing program. The supervisor evaluates the supervisee's clinical performance by focusing on opportunities to teach new skills.

7. *A*ssignment of new homework: During the cybersupervision session, the supervisor uses the capabilities of the multi-featured video conferencing program to access a jointly viewed Website in which a targeted counseling skill in the use of cognitive-behavioral therapy is demonstrated on digital video. Upon completion of the video review, the supervisor assigns the supervisee to create a 10-slide Microsoft PowerPoint presentation that highlights critical aspects of this cognitive-behavioral approach for uploading and joint review at the next cybersupervision session.

8. **Supervisor's capsule summaries:** The supervisor digitally records the cybersupervision session during which she reflects on important issues for the supervisee to consider in the coming week. The supervisor asks the supervisee to review the digitally recorded cybersupervision session and to prepare brief responses to each summary for discussion at the next session.

9. **Elicit feedback from the supervisee:** The supervisor solicits feedback throughout the cybersupervision session and asks her to share additional feedback via email before the next session.

The process and online communication tools do not reflect a comprehensive approach to cybersupervision. They are cited as examples of how online supervision can be provided effectively and efficiently from a cognitive-behavioral theoretical perspective.

The Integrated Developmental Model

The integrated developmental model (IDM) (Stoltenberg et al., 1998) posits that supervisees pass through a sequence of three developmental stages that reflect varying levels of professional competence and which suggest corresponding supervisory roles and responsibilities. At Level 1, the supervisor provides structure and support to encourage the supervisee's autonomy and self-awareness. As the supervisee develops more autonomy (Level 2), the supervisor shares more responsibility with the supervisee, creates appropriate clinical and personal challenges, and promotes a focus on process issues. At Level 3, the supervisor provides collegial supervision by encouraging the supervisee to structure supervision sessions and by reinforcing professionalism and competence. Stoltenberg et al., (1998) identified eight clinical practice domains that serve as the basis for assessing the supervisees' developmental levels:

1. Intervention skills competencies
2. Assessment techniques
3. Interpersonal assessment
4. Client conceptualization
5. Individual differences
6. Theoretical orientation
7. Treatment plans and goals
8. Professional ethics (Haynes et al., 2003)

Through the lens of the IDM, developmental processes are ongoing, but not necessarily linear. Supervisees may demonstrate a high level clinical competence in the provision of family counseling, but possess limited skill in working with individuals. Additionally, newly learned skills may decay if not practiced regularly. Consequently, the roles and responsibilities of supervisors and supervisees will vary from session to session based upon an assessment of the supervisee's developmental level in a particular clinical practice domain.

The goal of supervision using an IDM approach is to help supervisees develop clinical competence through performance assessments in the eight domains of clinical practice identified above. This approach requires the IDM supervisor to assume primary roles as an assessor (to determine supervisees' developmental levels) and developmental specialist (to promote professional development in a manner consistent with current developmental level). Although theoretically distinct from the cognitive-behavioral model, the roles adopted by the IDM supervisor are consistent with the identification of supervision as a special case of instruction. Instructors are responsible for assessing and promoting the novice's development of learners.

Communication tools available for use on the World Wide Web make is possible to adapt the IDM for the provision of cybersupervision. As noted above, live video conferencing most closely approximates face-to-face interaction. Therefore, we recommend it as the primary tool for delivery of cybersupervision. Assuming a Level 1 stage of development (i.e., supervisor provides structure, direction, and support) and use of a multifeatured, live video conferencing program, we will describe sample communication tools and techniques used in IDM cybersupervision for assessing and promoting development in eight clinical practice domains.

1. **Intervention skills competencies:** The supervisor uploads two digital videos of counseling sessions completed by the supervisee during the previous week. He additionally uploads a "Clinical Skills Evaluation Form," that can be viewed and completed online by both supervisor and supervisee. Following a 15-minute review of each digital video, the supervisor asks the supervisee to evaluate his performance on each clinical skill and provides evaluative feedback on each self-rating.

2. **Assessment techniques:** The supervisor assigns the supervisee to conduct an intake assessment interview that includes a mental status examination. During the following cybersupervision session, the supervisor uploads the digital interview file, jointly reviews it with the supervisee, and comprehensively evaluates the supervisee's performance in conducting these assessments.

3. **Interpersonal assessment:** The supervisor assigns the supervisee to complete and save two personality tests available on the World Wide Web. Before the cybersupervision session, the supervisor accesses and scores the completed tests. During the session, the supervisor uploads the digital files that contain the scored tests and provides interpretations to the supervisee as they relate to the congruence of his personality profile with profiles of professional counselors.

4. **Client conceptualization:** The supervisor assigns the supervisee to write an eight-page, comprehensive case conceptualization paper for a client the supervisee has seen for four months and to send it by e-mail prior to the next cybersupervision session. The supervisor evaluates the case conceptualization paper and uploads it during the next session, at which time they jointly review the paper and his feedback.

5. **Individual differences:** The supervisor assigns the supervisee to complete readings and visit three Websites that provide detailed information on Hispanic, Asian, and Eastern European cultures. He then requires the supervisee to create three digital videos in which he demonstrates culturally-sensitive practices in counseling three classmates who represent each cultural group. At the following session, the supervisor uploads and evaluates the supervisee's performance as they jointly review each video.

6. **Theoretical orientation:** The supervisor assigns the supervisee to create a Microsoft PowerPoint presentation in which he contrasts and compares basic tenets and counseling techniques associated with psychodynamic, cognitive-behavioral, and Gestalt counseling theories. At the next cybersupervision session, the supervisor uploads the PowerPoint file, asks the supervisee to present the content, and provides evaluative feedback.

7. **Treatment plans and goals:** During the cybersupervision session, the supervisor uploads digitally saved treatment plans created by the supervisee over the preceding six months. As each plan is jointly reviewed in chronological order, the supervisor provides evaluative feedback on the appropriateness and comprehensiveness of identified goals and behavioral objectives as they relate to diagnoses.

8. **Professional ethics:** The supervisor directs the supervisee to observe a one-hour digital video of a counseling session conducted by the supervisee with a client, who was later reported to be a "former girlfriend." He assigns the supervisee to review the codes of ethics of three national counseling organizations and to specify standards that he violated in each ethical code in a ten-page paper to be e-mailed before the next counseling session. During the cybersupervision session, the supervisor uploads both the digital video and assigned paper, which are jointly reviewed and discussed.

Resolving Legal and Ethical Problems

A range of potential ethical and legal problems face online counselors and online supervisors. A unique aspect of clinical supervision is that supervisors are legally and ethically responsible for the actions of supervisees. This vicarious liability of supervisors poses special risks in the delivery of cybersupervision.

The limitations of providing cybersupervision at remote sites become obvious when a client reveals plans to harm self or others. As previously noted, the absence of sufficient information and visual cues in an online format may lead the cybersupervisor to misinterpret or underestimate the client's potential for harm. In order to address this problem, the cybersupervisor should develop a protocol for online interventions in emergent situations that involve the use of explicit questions and procedures.

Privileged communication, confidentiality, and privacy are at the core of the counseling process. Although technological safeguards, such as firewalls, password protection, and encryption, increase the likelihood that online counseling communications will be confidential, breaches of these security measures are less than uncommon. Consequently, online clients and supervisees must be informed that although appropriate precautions may have been implemented to protect online communications, supervisors cannot guarantee confidentiality. The ability to save emails, other narrative communications, and audio or video files is useful from a clinical perspective. However, these same storage capabilities create opportunities for breaches of confidentially through unauthorized access and legal processes.

Jurisdiction is a problem frequently mentioned with regard to online counseling. State laws vary, but the trend is to assume that jurisdiction resides in the client's home state (reported in a 2006 interview with John Bloom (ACA Ethics Revision Task Force member) conducted by David Kaplan (ACA Chief Professional Officer). This issue influences the delivery of cybersupervision as supervisees complete practicum/internship experiences in states where the supervisor is not licensed.

The counseling profession is guided by a code of ethics. Practitioners must adhere to the standards of conduct prescribed in these codes or face sanctions by the profession. Because cybersupervision is a relatively new practice, there are no current technology codes to cover its practice. This challenge will be addressed as cybersupervision processes and techniques are explicated in the professional literature. This information will be used to create standards designed to protect the confidentiality and appropriate use of online supervision communications and to insure the competent delivery of cybersupervision

The American Counseling Association Code of Ethics was revised in 2005 to include a substantial section on technology (see Bloom interview previously mentioned). The code addresses some of the challenges we noted in this subsection: the need for encrypted communication to maintain client privacy and the use of passwords to protect client confidentiality. The first professional organization to provide substantial guidance regarding online counseling was the National Board of Certified Counselors (NBCC). In 1997 NBCC published standards for WebCounseling (Bloom, 1997), which were later revised (NBCC, 2005). An affiliated organization, the Center for Credentialing and Education established the Distance Counselor Credential (DCC) for counselors who successfully complete a two-day training course on distance counseling. Detailed information regarding technology-related ethical codes are available on the organization's Website and in the literature (e.g., Layne, & Hohenshil, 2005; Mallen et al., 2005; Shaw & Shaw, 2006).

CONCLUSION

Supervision is a specialized form of instruction. Cybersupervision is a specialized form of online instruction. As technological infrastructures continue to emerge that support its use, clinical supervisors will be required to demonstrate proficiency in the use of online supervision models. The authors have attempted to address this need by describing how cybersupervision can be delivered using divergent theoretical perspectives and practices. They have further identified challenges and solutions in the delivery of cybersupervision.

The primary advantages of clinical cybersupervision are opportunities to: (a) provide immediate, corrective, supervisory feedback during live counseling sessions from remote locations; (b) conduct regular, weekly, one-hour supervision sessions using a multifeatured video conference program from remote locations; (c) use a host of synchronous and asynchronous Web-based communication tools to facilitate the supervision/instructional process; (d) save time, money, and human resources, thereby enhancing the efficiency of supervision.

Challenges to the use of cybersupervision include: (a) difficulties in communicating supervisor characteristics that are necessary for the development of an effective supervisor/supervisee working relationship; (b) insuring that supervisees possess requisite dispositions and computer skills; (c) implementing a theoretical model of supervision in an Web-based format; and, (d) resolving technological, legal, and ethical problems unique to the online supervision format. Although these challenges may temporarily slow its expansion, the advantages of cybersupervision insure its implementation not only in clinical training programs, but also in the majority of university-based professional preparation programs throughout the world in the twenty-first century.

FUTURE TRENDS

Despite the challenges posed by cybersupervision, the advantages of this instructional medium virtually assure its growth. The ongoing development of Web-based infrastructures and communication tools, ease of remote access to clinical practice situations, and savings in time, money, and human resources will contribute to its popularity and widespread use. However, like all innovative practices, the development of cybersupervision

will pose unique dilemmas and problems. In the section below, we delineate the dynamics of these advantages and limitations in a discussion of future trends in cybersupervision.

Trend 1: The Future Will Witness Ongoing Development of Internet Infrastructures and Communication Tools That Support Cybersupervision

Since its inception, efforts to enhance communication structures and capabilities of the Internet have been unceasing. Spurred by needs of the military, business, education, and a variety of other entities, Web-based communications have evolved from simple text-based messages, to the transmission of graphics, video, multifeatured video conferencing, and a host of other options. Because Internet-based communications are vital to infrastructures that support modern societies, the tools that enhance such communications will continually be refined. All of these developments will support and sustain the use of cybersupervision.

Trend 2: Cybersupervision Will Become the Norm for Counselor (and all Professional) Training

The twenty-first century will witness sustained growth in Internet-based counselor training and supervision as political leaders, policy makers, and administrators at Institutions of Higher Education (IHEs) realize the cost effectiveness of these options. Larger numbers of students will be enrolled in fewer university programs that will be taught by fewer faculty at lower costs. The implementation of cyber teaching and cybersupervision will be heralded by politicians as necessary steps to insure equal access to a university education and to reduce tax burdens. University administrators will support the expansion of these initiatives as dwindling tax revenues create pressures for efficiency and fiscal accountability.

In response to these developments, professional organizations have developed technology standards as well as standards for online counseling and supervision. The result is that counseling program curricula will be revised to insure that students possess computer skills necessary to communicate in multiple electronic formats with instructors, understand legal and ethical issues associated with confidential online communications, complete on-line assignments and tests, and respond to cybersupervision feedback.

Trend 3: Ease of Access to the Internet will Create more Opportunities for Unauthorized Access to Confidential Communications

The first two trends will generate needs for additional legal and ethical mandates to protect Internet-based, confidential communications. Because confidentiality is a cornerstone of clinical service, legislative bodies and professional organizations will draft increasingly restrictive laws and ethical standards regarding the use of instruction that employs confidential communications (e.g., Internet-based supervision). Computer chip manufacturers and software engineers will be required to design systems that defeat attempts at such access and subsequent breaches of confidentiality. Growth in the use of Web-based counseling programs may be limited by the ability to insure confidential communications, through technological, legal, or legal interventions.

Firewalls, password-protection, and encryption technologies are used to protect sensitive or confidential information transmitted via the Internet. However, these safeguards can be, and have been, compromised. As the volume of confidential communications swells in a new era of online instruction and cybersupervision, technology-based measures that guarantee secure communications must be developed.

Legislatures in a few states have created statutes to control the transmission of confidential, Web-based, counseling communications. However, because cybercounseling and cybersupervision are in their infancy, legislators often lack sufficient information to create effective laws. Several professional counseling organizations (i.e., American Counseling Association, American Psychological Association, Association for Counselor Education and Supervision, National Board for Certified Counselors) have revised current or developed new ethical standards designed to protect the confidentiality of Web-based counseling communications. Fewer standards have been established to protect confidential communications in the provision of cybersupervision.

Trend 4: Cybersupervision will Become the Instructional Medium of Choice in a Wide Variety of Professional and Nonprofessional Applications.

Although this chapter has focused on advantages and challenges of cybersupervision in the clinical training of counseling professionals, the benefits of this instructional medium insure that it will be used across multiple disciplines. Supervisors in the fields of medicine, law, education, and a host of others will use the remote access and instantaneous feedback features of cybersupervision to monitor trainees' work in the delivery of services to patients, clients, and students. For example, medical supervisors will work from the convenience of their offices to observe and provide live, immediate corrective feedback to interns and residents as they conduct medical examinations, diagnose patient conditions, and prescribe medications in hospitals across the street and across the country. Supervisors of law interns will remotely access mock trials being conducted at affiliated universities or justice centers, provide instantaneous performance feedback that affords opportunities to correct mistakes, and offer additional commentary on performance via use of ATOP technology discussed previously. Teacher supervisors will use cybersupervision to observe and provide in vivo performance feedback to student teachers working in public schools from the instructional environment of their university classrooms. In this way, both supervisors and students enrolled in teacher education programs will benefit from the use of this instructional approach.

Supervisors and trainers in nonprofessional settings, such as construction and industry, will also use cybersupervision to provide immediate information and feedback without the expense and inconvenience of travel to worksites. For example, as civil engineers in New York City redesign a complex bracket for refitting a bridge girder in Seattle, Washington, the procedures for installing the new bracket will be provided via cybersupervision. A digital recording of the installation procedure will be played for site supervisors and ironworkers at the worksite and opportunities for live questions and answers will be provided via live videoconference. Live video of the new installation will be viewed by engineers in New York and immediate procedural feedback will be provided.

REFERENCES

Association for Counselor Education and Supervision (1999). *Technical competencies for counselor education students: Recommended guidelines for program development.* Retrieved November 30, 2006, from http://www.acesonline.net/competencies.htm

Alleman, J. R. (2002). Online counseling: The internet and mental health treatment. *Psychotherapy: Theory/Research/Practice/Training, 39,* 199-209.

American Counseling Association (2005). *ACA code of ethics.* Alexandria, VA: Author.

Bloom, J. W. (1997). *NBCC webcounseling standards.* Originally appeared in *Counseling Today.* Retrieved November, 30, 2006, from http://members.tripod.com/TCP_2/TCP_2/nbcc_stn.htm

Brown, D. (2000). The Odyssey of a technologically challenged counselor educator into cyberspace. In J. W. Bloom & G. R. Walz (Eds.), *Cybercounseling and cyberlearning: Strategies and resources for the millennium* (pp. 51-64). Alexandria, VA: American Counseling Association and CAPS with ERIC Counseling and Student Services Clearinghouse.

Champe, J., & Kleist, D. M. (2003). Live supervision: A review of the research. *The Family Journal: Counseling and Therapy for Couples and Families, 11,* 268 - 275.

Chester, A., & Glass, C. A. (2006). Online counseling: A descriptive analysis of therapy services on the internet. *British Journal of Guidance & Counseling, 34,* 145-160.

Cohen, G. E., & Kerr, B. A. (1998). Computer-mediated counseling: An empirical study of new mental health treatment. *Computers in Human Services, 15*(4), 13-26.

Collie, K. R., Mitchell, D., & Murhpy, L. (2000). Skills for online counseling: Maximum impact at minimum bandwidth. In J. W. Bloom & G. R. Walz (Eds.), *Cybercounseling and Cyberlearning: Strategies and Resources for the Millennium* (pp. 219-236). Alexandria, VA: American Counseling Association and CAPS with ERIC Counseling and Student Services Clearinghouse.

Cook, J. E., & Doyle, C. (2002). Working alliance in online therapy as compared to face-to-face therapy: Preliminary results. *CyberPsychology & Behavior, 5,* 95-105.

Coursol, D. (2004). Cybersupervision: Conducting supervision of the information superhighway. In G. R. Walz & C. Kirkman (Eds.), *CyberBytes: Highlighting compelling uses of technology in counseling* (pp. 83-85). (ERIC Document Reproduction Service No. ED478221)

Day, S. X., & Schneider, P. (2000). The subjective experiences of counselors in face-to-face, video, and audio sessions. In J. W. Bloom & G. R. Walz (Eds.), *Cybercounseling and cyberlearning: Strategies and resources for the millennium* (pp. 203-218). Alexandria, VA: American Counseling Association and CAPS with ERIC Counseling and Student Services Clearinghouse.

Dorn, F. J. (1984). Using social influence theory in the supervision of mental health counselors. *American Mental Health Counselors Association Journal, 6*(2), 173-179.

Evans, W., Miller, K. L., & Miller, S. M. (2005, October). *Enhancing live clinical supervision through the use of audio.* Poster session made at the National Association of Counseling Educators and Supervisors, Pittsburgh, PA.

Gallant, J. P., Thyer, B. A., & Bailey, J. S. (1991). Using bug-in-the-ear feedback in clinical supervision: Preliminary evaluations. *Research on Social Work Practice, 1*(2), 175-187.

Harper, S. G. (1999). *Counseling and the internet.* Retrieved November 30, 1999, from http://www.findarticles.com

Harris-Bowlsbey, J. (2000). The internet: Blessing or bane for the counseling profession? In J. W. Bloom & G. R. Walz (Eds.), *Cybercounseling and cyberlearning: Strategies and resources for the millennium* (pp. 39-50). Alexandria, VA: American Counseling Association and CAPS with ERIC Counseling and Student Services Clearinghouse.

Haynes, R., Corey, G., & Moulton, P. (2003). *Clinical supervision in the helping professions: A practical guide.* Pacific Grove, CA: Thomson: Brooks/Cole.

Hufford, B. J., Glueckauf, R. L., & Webb, P. M. (1999). Home-based, interactive videoconferencing for adolescents with epilepsy and their families. *Rehabilitation Psychology, 44*(2), 176-193.

Kanz, J. E. (2001). Clinical-supervision.com: Issues in the provision of online supervision. *Professional Psychology: Research and Practice, 32*, 415-420.

Kaplan, D. (2006, October). Ethical use of technology in counseling [CT Online – Ethics update]. *Counseling Today Online.* Retrieved December 7, 2006, from http://www.counseling.org

Klitzke, M. J., & Lombardo, T. W. (1991). "A bug-in-the-eye" can be better than "bug-in-the-ear": A teleprompter technique for on-line therapy skills training. *Behavior Modification, 15*, 113-117.

Layne, C. M., & Hohenshil, T. H. (2005). High tech counseling: Revisited. *Journal of Counseling & Development, 83*, 222-226.

Liddle, H. A. (1991). Training and supervision in family therapy: A comprehensive and critical analysis. In A. S. Gurman & D. P. Kniskern (Eds.), *Handbook of family therapy* (Vol. 2, pp. 638-697). New York: Brunner/Mazel.

Liese, B. S., & Beck, J. S. (1997). Cognitive therapy supervision. In C. E. Watkins Jr. (Ed.), *Handbook of psychotherapy supervision* (pp. 114-133). New York: John Wiley & Sons.

Mallen, M. J., Vogel, D. L., & Rochlen, A. B. (2005). The practical aspects of online counseling: Ethics, training, technology, and competency. *The Counseling Psychologist, 33*, 776-818.

Mallen, M. J., Vogel, D. L., Rochlen, A. B., & Day, S. X. (2005). Online counseling: Reviewing the literature from a counseling psychology framework. *The Counseling Psychologist, 33*, 819-871.

Mauzey, E., Harris, M. B. C., & Trusty, J. (2000). Comparing the effects of live supervision interventions on novice trainee anxiety and anger. *The Clinical Supervisor, 19*, 109-120.

McCollum, E. E., & Wetchler, J. L. (1995). In defense of case consultation: Maybe "dead" supervision isn't all that dead after all. *Journal of Marital and Family Therapy, 21,* 155-166.

Miller, K. L., Miller, S. M., & Evans, W. J. (2002). Computer-assisted live supervision in college counseling centers. *Journal of College Counseling, 5*(2), 187-192.

Moorhouse, A., & Carr, A. (1999). The correlates of phone-in frequency, duration and the number of suggestions made in live supervision. *Journal of Family Therapy, 21,* 241-249. Retrieved November 30, 2006, from Academic Search Premier database.

Myrick, R. D., & Sabella, R. A. (1995). Cyberspace: A new place for counseling. *Elementary School Guidance & Counseling, 30,* 35-44.

National Board for Certified Counselors. (2005 copyright) *Standards for the practice of Internet counseling.* Retrieved November, 30, 2006, from http://www.nbcc.org/webethics2

Neukrug, E. S. (1991). Computer-assisted live supervision in counselor skills training. *Counselor Education & Supervision, 31,* 132-138.

Parrott, L. III. (2003). *Counseling and psychotherapy.* Pacific Grove, CA: Brooks/Cole.

Rickards, L. D. (1984). Verbal interaction and supervisor perception in counseling supervision. *Journal of Counseling Psychology, 31,* 262-265.

Scherl, C. R., & Haley, J. (2000). Computer monitor supervision: A clinical note. *The American Journal of Family Therapy, 28,* 275-282.

Shaw, H. E., & Shaw, S. F. (2006). Critical ethical issues in online counseling: Assessing current practices with an ethical intent checklist. *Journal of Counseling & Development, 84,* 41-53.

Snelbecker, G. E., Miller, S. M., & Zheng, R. (2008). Function relevance and online design. In R. Zheng & P. Ferris (Eds.), *Understanding online instructional modeling: Theories and practice.* Hershey, PA: Information Science Reference.

Stoltenberg, D. D., McNeill, B., & Delworth, U. (1998). *IDM supervision: An integrated developmental model for supervising counselors and therapists.* San Francisco: Jossey-Bass.

Wantz, R. A., Tromski, D. M., Mortsolf, C. J., Yoxtheimer, G., Brill, S., & Cole, A. (2003). Incorporating distance learning into counselor education program: A research study. In J. W. Bloom & G. R. Walz (Eds.), *Cybercounseling and cyberlearning: An encore.* (ERIC Document Reproduction Service No. ED 481146).

Chapter XV
Online Integration of Information Literacy in an Environmental Management Systems Course

Michael F. Russo
Louisiana State University, USA

Sigrid Kelsey
Louisiana State University, USA

Maud Walsh
Louisiana State University, USA

ABSTRACT

Recognizing the value, as expressed by the Association of College and Research Libraries Information Literacy Competency Standards for Higher Education, of incorporating information literacy instruction into a subject discipline, LSU Libraries partnered with the instructor of an environmental management course to develop online information literacy instruction with direct tie-ins to the subject matter of the course. This chapter discusses the results of that effort, including the advantages and problems encountered.

CHAPTER OBJECTIVES

The reader will be able to:

- Appreciate the importance of placing IL instruction within the context of a disciplinary course
- Appreciate the connections between IL and online learning
- Comprehend the value and importance of cooperation between information professionals, such as librarians, and course instructors relative to IL instruction
- Apply ACRL standards of information literacy to any subject discipline

INTRODUCTION

A recent paper published as part of the MacArthur Foundation's five-year, $50 million *Digital Media and Learning* initiative asserts that the Internet has resulted in a cultural change, making ours a new kind of "participatory culture," one in which sharing creations, informal mentoring, and other forms of social connections have fewer boundaries (Jenkins et al., 2006, p. 3). The paper asserts that potential benefits of this culture include peer-to-peer learning and acquiring valuable skills for students as they enter the workplace. Jenkins maintains that policy and pedagogical interventions should take place to address concerns brought about by the change in culture, naming 11 skills needed to succeed in the new participatory culture. Several of these skills, built upon traditional literacy and research skills, complement the American Library Association's (ALA) information literacy (IL) skills.

New Jersey Institute of Technology librarian Richard T. Sweeney asserts that the "Net generation," or "millennials" will change the way in which professors teach (Carlson, 2005), noting that the current generation reads less but prefers video, audio, and interactive media. Bleed reports that by age 21, the "average students will have spent 10,000 hours on video games; sent or received 200,000 e-mails; talked for 10,000 hours on a cell phone; and read for under 5,000 hours" (Bleed, 2005). Computer-mediated communication (CMC) has brought about a shift in communication from the written to the oral. So as communication, an integral piece of literacy, evolves, and so does the meaning of literacy. Literacy in today's world requires having the ability to communicate in these changing digital environments.

The American Library Association has identified "21st Century Literacy" as one of five key action areas for fulfilling its mission. The ALA's Website states that, "helping children and adults develop skills they need to fully participate in an information society—whether it's learning to read or explore the Internet—is central to that mission" (American Library Association, 2001). "Information Literacy," "Digital Media and Learning," and "21st Century Literacy" are contemporary terms conveying how traditional values of literacy apply to the cultural changes brought about by the Internet.

Libraries—public, academic, school, or any type—play an essential role in developing the critical thinking skills for effective online learning in students, as well as promoting unique online teaching models to teach these very skills. The connections between online learning and the LSU e-struction program are twofold: first, the program itself is a model of online teaching, second, and perhaps more important, the skills imparted through the e-struction program are the very skills that are more important now than ever for online learners; in short, the program teaches the students how to be effective online learners.

The goals of the e-struction program are to introduce participants to a range of multidisciplinary online library resources and to introduce them to the basic concepts of information literacy (as defined by the Association of College and Research Libraries (ACRL)). The program comprises a series of lessons, in text form, e-mailed to the participants. Each week's lesson introduces a new resource or concept and provides the participants with information on content, access, and search strategies for the product. In addition, each e-mail message has a link to an online assignment for the students to complete. The e-struction program serves as a unique online learning model in several ways. While delivering lessons through e-mail is not a new idea, this program allows a course teacher to integrate a component of information literacy into his/her class without taking away from class time. Further, the purpose of the material itself is to cultivate skills and reasoning for effective online learning in all situations.

While the broad topic of the program is "agriculture," the information literacy skills taken away by the students can be applied in any online learning context. Adaptable for any discipline or level of teaching, the agriculture e-struction program at LSU can serve as a paradigm for any college or university wishing to incorporate information literacy into the classroom to effect strong online learning and literacy skills in students.

BACKGROUND

Critical thinking and educated judgments about the sources of information have always been important skills to impart to students. However, with a growing amount of information and a growing ease of access to it, it can be argued that these information literacy skills are more crucial than ever. In 1989, in the United States, 53,446 books were published (Simora, 1991). The same year, 1,403 television stations were on the air, transmitting to 98.2% of American households, while over 9,000 radio stations sent their signals to 99% of U. S. homes (U.S. Census Bureau, 1992). That year, 85.1% of Americans acknowledged reading newspapers (U.S. Census Bureau, 1990) and the telecommunications industry produced over 9,000,000 cordless telephones (U.S. Census Bu-

reau, 1992). And Internet use—well, that was not to appear as a government statistic until 1997. In 1989, information and the media which dispersed it were proliferating at a quantum pace, and the end was nowhere in sight.

1989 was also the year the Presidential Committee on Information Literacy of the American Library Association submitted its final report. The report, issued in response to "the ever-growing tidal wave of information" (American Library Association, 1989), emphasized the importance of process over rote learning, problem solving over textbooks, and critical thinking over lectures as ways of managing this information surge. In essence, the committee advocated teaching people how to learn as a way of mastering the relentless onslaught of information in their daily lives.

Flash forward to the new millennium. Not only do the media of 1989 continue to thrive, but information consumers now have even more media options spewing information at them. Blackberries, iPods, video phones, satellite radio and TV with hundreds of channels, hand-held computers, downloadable entertainment, and Internet (with the inevitable profusion of blogs and wikis) that can be accessed wirelessly in coffee shops all produce an information tsunami that makes the "tidal wave" of 1989 look like a ripple.

Besides the onslaught of information and increasing numbers of ways in which to obtain it, the lines differentiating the types of information are blurring. A growing trend toward open access journals and Google-like search engines will affect the traditional "information literacy" methods for distinguishing authority, reliability, and other measures of quality. Advice offered by librarians from a few years back, that searching the Internet will not yield quality peer-reviewed journal articles, no longer holds true. Google Scholar, open access, and initiatives and movements of the like have changed that. The lines blur further as traditional library online catalogs attempt to emulate search engines like Google's and Amazon's. Federated search engines promoted by academic research libraries search a variety of publications and Web sites simultaneously, presenting information from many sources on a single interface.

However one chooses to analogize this information overload matters little. What is important is the desperate need to manage this growing phenomenon. It has become increasingly recognized by information professionals, such as librarians, that this situation calls for a sensible strategy that will equip the consumers of information, like students, with the discrimination and control they need to make information work for them and not the other way around. In a university setting, this discrimination is key to the students' academic success. The principles of information literacy (as this strategy has come to be known) have evolved through a process of discussion among information professionals and have been put forward as necessary aids for handling the information deluge. Nevertheless, the end goal of information literacy will remain the same: to impart to students critical thinking skills regarding the information they use.

The ACRL Information Literacy Competency Standards for Higher Education posit that information literacy instruction is most effective when integrated into the disciplinary courses at all levels. Stated another way, "If students are to develop information literacy, including subject matter autonomy, the context in which they are learning must allow and encourage them to act as autonomous information users" (McDowell, 2002). In the e-struction program, the online teaching model allowed for the material to be integrated into the context of the university course.

If, as the ACRL standards assert, "developing lifelong learners is central to the mission of higher education institutions," then it should be the business of the university to be sure that students go into the world with "the intellectual abilities of reasoning and critical thinking" that are central to the idea of information literacy. And, if practitioners of a specific discipline are to

have those intellectual abilities, then the obvious route to that destination is through integration of online learning and information skills into the disciplinary courses. Further, today's tech-savvy students must be prepared to be lifelong *online* learners, in the classroom and in settings beyond school. Although today's students are comfortable with new technology, the need to apply traditional literacy skills, such as discretion and the ethical use of information, to online learning, is crucial.

The developmental arc has led from stand alone, but general, library skills training (in the form of one-time instruction sessions, self-guided tutorials, or even brief credit courses) to the subject-specific, yet still segregated, research class. The ACRL standards have pushed disciplinary courses and the research training required by them closer together, until we have reached an evolutionary plateau whereby information professionals and subject faculty are working together to produce meaningful information literacy instruction within the context of the discipline under review.

Many institutions have woven information literacy instruction into the fabric of host courses. The University of Arizona, for example, in response to state accreditation standards, has infused some of its engineering courses. Researchers there felt context was key to effective information literacy (IL) instruction. Per the results of a pre-survey, it was found that only 26% of systems and industrial engineering seniors recalled the unincorporated mandatory library research training they had received as freshmen. Thus, the Arizona researchers concluded, "The most effective way to educate is to teach in the context of real-life situations and real problems" (Williams, Blowers, & Goldberg, 2004).

Cardiff University in the United Kingdom has integrated IL instruction into its undergraduate law course, Legal Foundations, trying to avoid the "bolted-on" effect of much of information literacy instruction. In doing so, they have moved research instruction "from a bibliographic orientation towards a greater concentration on the process of finding and using information" (Jackson, 2005).

In 2000, the Division of Business and Enterprise of the University of South Australia sought to encourage the inclusion of information literacy skills training in disciplinary courses, beginning with its eight first-year division core courses. Their endeavor started at the program level, working through eight course coordinators. Through a process of interviews and analysis of course descriptions, investigators found a number of factors working against the inclusion of information literacy in its core business courses including some fundamental stumbling blocks such as information literacy not being a course objective and course design simply not allowing for inclusion of IL instruction. Nevertheless, information literacy was acknowledged as important enough for the author to recommend persistence in encouraging teaching staff "to embed information literacy into teaching of courses as opposed to 'add-on' approaches or specialist courses teaching information literacy outside the context of the course content" (Feast, 2003).

AGRICULTURE E-STRUCTION

The LSU Libraries' experience teaching information literacy totally incorporates the two needed components identified for success: the context-relatedness and the partnership between teaching faculty and information professionals. Its model exemplifies the first component in that the very skills it teaches are integral for success in the class research project. Partnering with a teaching faculty member of the course allows the librarians to tailor the lessons and information to the course research project requirements. Additionally, the program addresses a commonly-voiced concern of teaching faculty that they are reluctant to surrender class time to anything other than the

specific subject matter of the course. Thus, unlike the efforts previously described, our effort to infuse information literacy took the form of brief, online lessons and exercises. Implementing an online teaching model allows a librarian to address Information Literacy in more depth than a guest lecture, yet does not take away any class time from the primary course instructor.

The first faculty member to contact the libraries about this program was an environmental management systems faculty member. The partnership enabled the librarians to learn the goals and objectives of the department's curriculum and determine a highly specific context in which to introduce the information literacy. The environmental management systems curriculum at Louisiana State University is designed to prepare students for a career in environmental management and for further study in the sciences, law, medicine or business. Students in the environmental management systems curriculum receive training in the basic and social sciences that underlie complex environmental issues as well as in-depth preparation in one of three areas of concentration in environmental management. The college of agriculture, which houses the program, has identified communication skills as critical for its graduates based on feedback from employers and graduate programs. One of the key goals of the environmental management systems program is that students be able to demonstrate proficiency in oral and written communication relating to environmental management. In order to meet this goal, core classes in the curriculum require that students research environmental issues and prepare one or more written reports.

However, like many science majors (Firooznia & Andreadis, 2006; Mangurian, Feldman, Clements, & Boucher, 2001), environmental management students have difficulty locating and using scientific information resources. With few exceptions, students in both introductory and upper-level classes have difficulties at several stages of the writing assignments: identification of an appropriate topic, location of information, and evaluation of sources of information. Those in the library see the evidence of this each time a student sheepishly seeks help finding articles or books or awkwardly tries to explain their research thesis. Those in the classroom see it in research papers that rely on dubious Web sites as their only sources. Many of these difficulties arise from the problem that the students are not effective online learners. Effective online learning and research in today's library requires students be able to access online catalogs, indexes, and databases, to understand field searching, and Boolean operators, and finally, to be able to evaluate and use the information they retrieve.

Most students are not aware of the library resources, including databases, the online catalog, and reference services (and in some cases, the actual location of the library!). Students use Internet search engines extensively, but are not able to discriminate among types of Websites nor are they able to evaluate the reliability of sources, a phenomenon common among college students (Brown, Murphy, & Nanny, 2003). Many students are unaware of the difference between primary and secondary sources of information, and regard trade news magazines as the equivalent of peer-reviewed journals. The need for improved information literacy to facilitate online learning amongst environmental management students led to the request for asynchronous library instruction tailored to specific course needs. The online agriculture information literacy instruction program was a simple response to address these basic needs.

While nesting information literacy within a course's context is ideal in principle, practical issues and problems must be taken into consideration to make it work, such as the form of the instruction, how extensive and deep the instruction should be, and how much of the course could be devoted to information literacy instruction in terms of the students' efforts. The more information literacy instruction can be integrated into the normal class work, rather than as a separate element, the less it takes away from the class assignments. An ideal integration would teach the information literacy concepts with the other class materials, with final research papers exhibiting that the students are information literate and competent online learners.

The information literacy standards, promulgated by the ACRL in January of 2000, are intended to guide and inform instructional design, rather than to dictate it. In other words, it is not essential that every single standard be taught. Nevertheless, ideal information literacy instruction will meet each standard so that the student comes away with a full appreciation of the meaning and use of information and the processes employed to create, store, and disseminate it. Because the librarian is often responsible for the information literacy portion of a course while the teaching faculty is responsible for the subject matter of the course, combining the two takes close cooperation and collaboration between information professionals (librarians) and teaching faculty, and complete integration is not always possible. With complete integration of all of the ACRL standards of information literacy being at times impractical, information professionals must take their opportunities as they find them and exploit them to the extent possible. In some cases, this will mean emphasizing only some ACRL information literacy standards, while leaving some out altogether. In the case of LSU Libraries' environmental management course, the basics of information literacy were addressed, but teaching them in great depth was not possible. Nonetheless, the program provides a foundation for further online learning and development.

These issues were worked out in consultation with the course professor. It was already agreed that the information literacy instruction would be entirely online. The librarians would not invade the classroom to impart info-wisdom to the students; nor would the classroom instructor stop the flow of course content to enlighten students how this information could be ferreted out through library resources. Information literacy instruction would take place in tandem with course content, outside of class time, thereby capitalizing on a chief advantage of online learning: that is, the asynchronous communication of the lessons allowed the students, librarians, and teaching faculty to work together free from time and space constraints.

The Libraries' agricultural information resources specialist together with the Libraries' instruction specialist created the instruction and assessment instruments. They generated a list of topics, including appropriate databases that students of this subject would find most useful for their current course work and important for more advanced work and online learning in the field. (See Table 1 below).

Limitations on the amount of credit to be given the students, and the amount of time expected of the students, for the e-struction portion of the class constrained the librarians from going into as much detail as they might have liked, so the program was unable to address the complete range of ACRL information literacy standards. However, the program was able to introduce the students to important concepts and ideas, to form a basis for further online learning and discovery.

ACRL standard one states "The information literate student determines the nature and extent of the information needed." Traditionally, in a discipline course, this is determined by the course instructor, who may set minimum standards for the number and types of sources that can be used to complete a research project. The course instructor also might provide guidance as to the appropriate level of research, for example, scholarly versus popular, books versus articles. Because the class is at an introductory level, the research skills acquired will be useful as students are later required to gather and present information for assignments in upper-level classes. The information literate student will be able to apply this skill in future settings, in the workplace, and when seeking information online.

Standard two was the simplest to deal with, as it encompasses mere mechanics. As stated, "The information literate student accesses needed information effectively and efficiently."

Students were told, in each lesson, of the scope and focus of each of the several databases covered in the course. For example, in the lesson on the CAB Direct database, students were informed that:

CAB Direct contains 46 electronic abstract journals—examples of the abstract journals include

Table 1. Relationship between lesson time frame, material, and ACRL information literacy standards

Week 1	Standard One (preparing to search for information)	
Week 2	Online Catalog	Standard Two (access information effectively and efficiently) and Three (is able to evaluate information)
Week 3	Agricola	
Week 4	CabDirect	
Week 5	Cambridge Scientific Abstracts	
Week 6	Web of Science	
Week 7	Wrap up of sources covered, how to find out about more sources	Standards Four (uses information effectively) and Five (uses information ethically and legally)
Week 8	Final exam	

Sugar Industry Abstracts, Agroforestry Abstracts, Maize Abstracts, Rice Abstracts, and Seed Science Abstracts. CAB Direct is an excellent database to search for literature abstracts in all areas of the agricultural sciences.

Additionally, students learned the database included "over 4 million records and indexed over 3,500 titles not covered in Web of Knowledge" database. This same type of information was imparted relative to each of the databases covered by the instruction. Students also had to be instructed in the basics of accessing the databases. Knowing about a specific resource for information is one thing, knowing where to find that resource is another, so basic information, such as which links on the library Web page to click, was also included in the instruction. Thus, the simple act of reading would put students in possession of a most important weapon in their information arsenal—where to find certain kinds of information. Further, students learned that specialized databases and research tools exist to facilitate their online learning; there is more to finding information than searching the Internet.

Each lesson also covered basic searching techniques, some peculiar to specific databases, including the use of keywords as well as Boolean and proximity operators. With the location of the information trove secure, students now had the shovel they needed to unbury the information they sought. These skills as well, translate to future online learning settings for the students.

Standard Three—"The information literate student evaluates information and its sources critically and incorporates selected information into his or her knowledge base and value system"—is the most difficult concept to teach students who are interested primarily in getting through their assignments as quickly as possible. Frequently, students seeking help with research in the library will inform librarians that they need a certain number of sources, and it does not matter what they are.

While the narrative e-struction supplied the students with some information concerning database contents that might help them evaluate which electronic databases are appropriate for their needs, there was not otherwise any place for teaching evaluation specifically. Our first assessment instrument (20 questions on CAB Direct) included a few questions such as: Which of these would be the most authoritative article for a senior level research paper on the taste and smell of bread?

A. "Slow start a weekend breakfast should be leisurely, hearty, and sweet." Sheryl Julian and Julie Riven. *The Boston Globe*, February 29, 2004, Sunday, Third Edition, Pg. 29.

B. "Making bread the new-fashioned way". *Consumer Reports*, December, 1995, Vol. 60, No. 12; Pg. 799.

C. NBC News Transcripts, Sunday Today (9:00 AM ET) - NBC, November 2, 2003 Sunday, 1166 words, Rose Beranbaum discusses bread recipes from her book "The Bread Bible," Campbell Brown.

D. Sensory analysis of whole wheat/soy flour breads. Shogren, R. L., Mohamed, A. A., and Carriere, C. J. *Journal of Food Science, 2003, Vol. 68, No. 6, pp. 2141-2145.*

This question requires several things of the student. First, the student has to understand that this question speaks to the issue of evaluation, that he or she must make a value judgment. Second, he or she must understand that this judgment has to be based on at least a cursory comprehension of the article's substance as derived from the article abstract. Third, he or she must know enough of the mechanics of the database under review to be able to look up each of these articles and find the abstract within the record. This question and others like it were ultimately dropped from the assessment at the request of the classroom instructor as requiring too much work for the paltry payoff in terms of the credit the students would earn.

Instead, the course instructor wanted to focus more on standard two, with more practice searching incorporated into the lesson. So, more mechanical questions replaces the evaluation questions, which, though limiting the depth of exposure to information literacy, nevertheless allowed of a certain breadth with respect to the one ACRL standard most students fret over—how to find information. For example:

Which search yields the fewest results?

A.   wild turkey
B.   "wild turkey"
C.   wild near/1 turkey
D.   wild and turkey

The effective (standard four) and ethical (standard five) use of information were primarily addressed through the research assignment given by the course instructor. Students were required to submit a written paper that synthesized and evaluated information gathered through their literature research. The legal and ethical use of information was emphasized as an important component of academic honesty. Specific guidelines by the LSU dean of students were discussed in class and included in instructions for the paper assignment. So while these two standards were not part of the supplemental online program, they were in fact integrated into the course.

EVALUATION

Though IL e-struction was a conscious collaboration between librarians and course instructor with an eye toward integrating IL instruction into the curriculum, it nevertheless still had the feel of being "tacked on." This feeling is the result of at least two things that might be—indeed, ought to be—changed for future editions.

While the asynchronous communication of the material removed the IL instruction in time and space from the rest of the course, this advantage

of online teaching may have created a problem of perception within the students. Although it was integrated into the course over a period of several weeks, the e-mail and online format suggested that it was separate. Thus, students may have concluded that if the material was not important enough to devote class time to, then it was not really that important. Hinting at this attitude were test results, indicating that some students selected the same answer for every question, playing the odds and, in the easiest way possible, trying to get whatever fraction they could of the five percent of the grade made up by the information literacy component.

Online teaching presents another difference from face-to-face communication that could remedy the problem previously mentioned: that of identity. The students in the e-struction class were aware that the lessons and assignments were coming from librarians, and not their course professor, but the e-struction course could be tailored in such a way so that the students are not aware that it is taught by anyone other than the course professor. Moving the assignments to the course management system used by the professor, and sending the e-mail messages from that system would make the librarians anonymous—in fact synonymous—with the course professor. The authors predict that the students would put more effort into the assignments in this case. Additionally, the five percent that the e-struction contributed to the students' final grades did not impose any great ponderousness upon the enterprise, and the authors predict that increasing the grade value of the e-struction assignments would also encourage the students to make a better effort.

Besides putting more value on IL in terms of the final grades, it might be more to the point to make it a respectable percentage of the rubric that applies to grading the research project, which, in this case, was 15 percent of the final grade. Indeed, some thought might be given to increasing the value of the research paper, inasmuch as it would constitute evidence of comprehension of all five

ACRL standards. Additionally, if students understand that achieving a high level of information literacy will help their research throughout their college careers and beyond that, they may value it more than if they look at it as an incidental library assignment. Therefore, the teaching faculty can help pique interest and respect by emphasizing this point.

CONCLUSION

Information professionals need to continue to develop innovative ways in which to provide information literacy through online learning to technologically savvy students. Collaboration with teaching faculty is essential for effectively modeling the instruction for individual classes, and to ensure that the students will use the instruction.

Yet, while the methods of communicating information have rapidly changed, the basic literacy skills of analyzing, synthesizing, and evaluating, taught for centuries, remain integral to the formation of information literate students. In fact, as information becomes more accessible, boundaries broaden, new conduits of information develop, these literacy skills are more important than ever, and the information professionals of the future will find new ways in which to teach the students to think critically about the information they find. Librarians have realized for years that the library is no longer confined within library walls. They are already reaching out through the Internet, classroom lectures, and numerous other ways.

FUTURE TRENDS

In 2005, approximately 21.8 million subscribers activated wireless services, bringing the number of wireless subscribers to more than 200 million (International Data Group, 2005). By 2009, $75.5 billion of DVD content will likely be produced, compared to $33 billion in 2004 (Bleed, 2005), and 12.3 million U.S. households will listen to podcasts by 2010 (Bleed, 2005). The ways in which information is communicated are changing rapidly; students have a world of information in their reach with a few clicks of a computer mouse, cell phone, or iPod. Information in a wireless world is available anywhere, anytime, no longer confined within library walls, or even tethered to a computer.

Higher education, immersed in tradition, is sometimes slow to be moved by the outside world. Not always responsive to societal change, it must nevertheless recognize the impacts technology has in order to prepare its graduates for careers in a digital world where online learning is critical to success. The 21st Century Workforce Commission reports that "In the near future, every American job will be radically affected by applications of information technology. New jobs and career paths will be created, and old jobs will either be eliminated or significantly transformed. And, as never before, there will be a premium on American workers who are able to read and understand complex material, think analytically, and use technology efficiently" (21st Century Workforce Commission, 2000, p.8).

Professors face challenges when attempting to cover class materials as well as teach the students how to use the information available to them. Students will access information in the fastest, easiest way possible, which usually does not include trips to the library, or even a visit to the library home page. Effective online models like the LSU E-struction model incorporate information literacy into a class without taking class time away from the primary professor. Models like this will be invaluable to professors wishing to instruct their Net Generation students to be literate in the digital world. Information professionals are able to reach out to students in a digital environment that the students relate to. Librarians already are using blogs, really simple syndication (RSS), and other digital tools to help teach students traditional literacy skills in a new digital age.

Indeed, the digital world has provided a new sphere of information but at the same time a new sphere in which to teach the same literacy skills. The world of information and communication is evolving, and so must the ways in which we teach. Analysis, synthesis, and evaluation of information, in short, critical thinking, has been the crux of literacy skills for centuries, and will continue to be so. "Information Literacy" is a comparatively recent term for these age old skills, and while the buzzwords for them may change and the ways in which we teach them will evolve, the basic skills for critical thinking and making educated judgments about information that define literacy will remain in tact. In fact, these literacy skills are becoming ever more critical as the formats of information become more diverse and the venues broaden. Students must be more discerning than ever when choosing information resources.

REFERENCES

21st Century Workforce Commission. (2000). A nation of opportunity: building America's 21st century workforce. *Washington, D.C: National Alliance of Business.* Retrieved September 29, 2006, from http://purl.access.gpo.gov/GPO/LPS5258

American Library Association. (1989) American Library Association Presidential committee on information literacy: Final report. *Presidential Committee on Information Literacy.* Retrieved September 29, 2006, from http://www.ala.org/ala/acrl/acrlpubs/whitepapers/presidential.htm

American Library Association. (2001) 21st century literacy @ your library. *ALA Action (1).* Retrieved September 29, 2006, from http://www.ala.org/ala/ourassociation/governingdocs/keyactionareas/lit-action/literacybrochure.htm

Association of College and Research Libraries. (2000). *Information Literacy Competency Standards for Higher Education.* Retrieved September 29, 2006, from http://www.ala.org/ala/acrl/acrl-standards/informationliteracycompetency.htm

Bleed, R. (2005). Visual literacy in higher education. *ELI Explorations* (August 2005). Retrieved September 29, 2006, from http://www.educause.edu/ir/library/pdf/ELI4001.pdf

Brown, C., Murphy, T. J., & Nanny, M. (2003). Turning techno-savvy into info-savvy: Authentically integrating information literacy into the college curriculum. *Journal of Academic Librarianship, 29,* 386-398.

Carlson, S. (2005). The net generation goes to college. *The Chronicle of Higher Education, 52*(7), A34-A37.

Feast, V. (2003). Integration of information literacy skills into business courses. *Reference Services Review, 31*(1), 81-95.

Firooznia, F., & Andreadis, D. K. (2006). Information literacy in introductory biology. *Journal of College Science Teaching, 35*(6), 23-27.

International Data Group (IDC). (2005, October 5) With nearly 12 billion instant messages each day, IM is growing into a serious business collaboration tool, IDC finds. Retrieved May 25, 2006, from http://www.idc.com/home.jhtml

Jackson, C. (2005, February). Integrating information literacy into an undergraduate law course. Paper presented at the UKCLE seminar on teaching and learning for legal skills trainers, 16 February 2005. http://www.ukcle.ac.uk/resources/biall/jackson.html

Jenkins, H., Clinton, K., Purushotma, R., Robinson, A. J., and Weigel, M. (2006). *Confronting the challenges of participatory culture: Media education for the 21st Century.* Retrieved December 12, 2006, from http://www.digitallearning.macfound.

org/atf/cf/%7B7E45C7E0-A3E0-4B89-AC9C-E807E1B0AE4E%7D/JENKINS_WHITE_PA-PER.PDF

Mangurian, L., Feldman, S., Clements, J., & Boucher, L. (2001). Analyzing and communicating scientific information. *Journal of College Science Teaching, 30*(7), 440-445.

McDowell, L. (2002). Electronic information resources in undergraduate education: An exploratory study of opportunities for student learning and independence. *British Journal of Educational Technology, 33*(3), 255-266.

Simora, F. (Ed.). (1991). *The Bowker annual library and book trade almanac* (36 Ed.). New Providence, NJ: R. R. Bowker.

U. S. Census Bureau. (1990). *Statistical abstract of the United States 1990* (110 Ed.). Washington, DC: Bureau of the Census.

U. S. Census Bureau. (1992). *Statistical abstract of the United States 1992* (112 Ed.). Washington, DC: Bureau of the Census.

Williams, B., Blowers, P., & Goldberg, J. (2004). Integrating information literacy skills into engineering courses to produce lifelong learners. Retrieved June 9, 2006, from http://www.asee.org/acPapers/2004-2405_Final.pdf

Compilation of References

21st Century Workforce Commission. (2000). A nation of opportunity: building America's 21st century workforce. *Washington, D.C: National Alliance of Business.* Retrieved September 29, 2006, from http://purl.access.gpo.gov/GPO/LPS5258.

Academic Senate of California Community Colleges. (1999). *Academic freedom, privacy, copyright and fair use in a technological world.* Retrieved November 17, 2006, from ERIC ED482188.

Adamson, J.E., & Mietus, N. J. (2000). *Law for business and personal use* (15th ed.). Cincinnati: International Thompson Publishing.

Age and cognitive ability as predictors of computerized information retrieval. *Behaviour and Information Technology, 14,* 313-326.

Aiken, R. M., & Snelbecker, G. E. (1991). Hindsight: Reflections on retaining secondary school teachers to teach computer science. *Journal of Research on Computing in Education, 23*(3), 444-451.

Alleman, J. R. (2002). Online counseling: The internet and mental health treatment. *Psychotherapy: Theory/Research/Practice/Training, 39,* 199-209.

American Civil Liberties Union. (2001, October). *How the anti-terrorism bill puts student privacy at risk.* Retrieved December 28, 2006, from http://www.aclu.org/natsec/emergpowers/12479leg20011023.html

American Counseling Association (2005). *ACA code of ethics.* Alexandria, VA: Author.

American Library Association. (1989) American Library Association Presidential committee on informa-

tion literacy: Final report. *Presidential Committee on Information Literacy.* Retrieved September 29, 2006, from http://www.ala.org/ala/acrl/acrlpubs/whitepapers/presidential.htm.

American Library Association. (2001) 21st century literacy @ your library. *ALA Action (1).* Retrieved September 29, 2006, from http://www.ala.org/ala/ourassociation/governingdocs/keyactionareas/litaction/literacybrochure.htm

Anderson, L. S. (1996). *Guidebook for developing an effective instructional technology plan,* (version 2). Mississippi State, MS: Mississippi State University.

Anderson, T. (2004). *Teaching in an online learning context.* New York: Oxford University Press.

Anderson, T., Rourke, L, Garrison, D. R., & Archer, W. (2001). Assessing teaching presence in a computer conferencing context. *Journal of Asynchronous Learning Networks, 5*(2), 1-17.

Anderson, T., Rourke, L., Garrison, D., & Archer, W. (2001). Assessing teaching presence in a computer conferencing context. *Journal of Asynchronous Learning Networks, 5*(2), 1-17.

Ardissono, L. Console, L., & Torre, I. (1999). *Exploiting user models for personalizing*

Askham, P. (1997). Workplace learning: Removing the barriers. In R. Hudson, S. Maslin-Prothero, & L. Oates, (Eds.), *Flexible learning in action case studies for higher education.* (pp. 67-72). London: Kogan Page.

Aslaksen, F., Steinar, B., Bringa, O., & Heggem, I. (1997). *Universal design planning and design for all.* Retrieved

December 11, 2002, from www.independentliving.org/docs1/nscd1997.html

Association for Counselor Education and Supervision (1999). *Technical competencies for counselor education students: Recommended guidelines for program development.* Retrieved November 30, 2006, from http://www.acesonline.net/competencies.htm

Association of College and Research Libraries. (2000). *Information Literacy Competency Standards for Higher Education.* Retrieved September 29, 2006, from http://www.ala.org/ala/acrl/acrlstandards/informationliteracycompetency.htm.

Ausubel, D. (1963). *The psychology of meaningful verbal learning.* New York: Grune and Stratton.

Aviv, R., Erlich, Z., Ravid, G., & Geva, A. (2003). Network analysis of knowledge construction in asynchronous learning networks, *Journal of Asynchronous Learning Networks, 7*(3). Retrieved April 23, 2004, from http://www.sloan-c.org/publications/jaln/v7n3/v7n3_aviv.asp

Ayersman, D. J. (1995). Introduction to hypermedia as a knowledge representation system. *Computers in Human Behavior, 11*(3-4), 529-531.

Azar, B. (1999). Crowder mixes theories with humility. *APA Monitor, 30*(10), 18.

Baer, W. S. (2000). Competition and collaboration in online distance learning. *Information, Communication & Society, 3*(4), 457-473.

Ball, M. J., & Snelbecker, G. E. (1982). Overcoming resistances to telecommunication innovations in medicine and continuing medical education. *Computers in Hospitals, 3*(4), 40-45.

Ball, M. J., & Snelbecker, G. E. (1982). Physicians' perceptions of present and future computer usage. *Hospital Information Management, 2*(3), 12-16.

Ball, M. J., & Snelbecker, G. E. (1983). How physicians in the U.S. perceive computers in their practice. In *MedInfo 1983: Proceedings of the Forth World Conference on Medical Informatics, Part 2* (pp. 1169-1172).

Ball, M. J., Snelbecker, G. E., & Schechte, S. L. (1985). Nurses' perceptions concerning computer uses before and after computer literacy lecture. *Computers in Nursing, 3*(1), 23-31.

Bandura, A. (1977). *Social learning theory.* New York: General Learning Press.

Barrett-Leonard, G.T. (1959). *Dimensions of perceived therapist response related to therapeutic change.* Unpublished doctoral dissertation, University of Chicago.

Barron, B. J. S., Schwartz, D. L., Vye, N. J., Moore, A., Petrosino, A., Zech, L., & Bransford, J. D. (1998). Doing with understanding: Lessons from research on problem- and project-based learning. *The Journal of the Learning Sciences, 7*(3-4), 271-311.

Barrows, H. (1996). Problem-based learning in medicine and beyond: A brief overview. In L. Wilkerson, & W. Gijselaers (Eds.), *New directions for teaching and learning.* San Francisco: Jossey-Bass Publishers.

Batagelj, V., & Mrvar, A. (2003). Pajek — Analysis and visualization of large networks. In Jünger, M., Mutzel, P., (Eds.) *Graph drawing software* (pp. 77-103). Berlin: Springer.

Baule, S. M. (1995). Planning for technological support: Help! Why isn't the smiley face smiling? *Technology Connection, 2(2),* 12.

Bayliss, D., Jarrold, C., Baddeley, A., & Leigh, E. (2005). Differential constraints on the working memory and reading abilities of individuals with learning difficulties and typically developing children. *Journal of Experimental Child Psychology, 92(*1), 76-99.

Bednar, A. K., Cunningham, D., Duffy, T. M., & Perry, J. D. (1992). Theory into practice: How do we link? In T. M. Duffy & D. H. Jonassen (Eds.), *Constructivism and the technology of instruction* (pp. 17-34). Hillsdale, NJ: Lawrence Erlbaum.

Berge, Z. L. (1995). Facilitating computer conferencing: Recommendations from the field. *Educational Technology. 35*(1), 22-30.

Beyth-Marom, R., Saporta, K., & Caspi, A. (2005). Synchronous vs. asynchronous tutorials: Factors affecting students' preferences and choices. *Journal of Research on Technology in Education, 37*(3), 245-262.

Biggs, J. (1987). *Student approaches to learning and studying.* Melbourne: Australian Council for Educational Research.

Bleed, R. (2005). Visual literacy in higher education. *ELI Explorations* (August 2005). Retrieved September 29, 2006, from http://www.educause.edu/ir/library/pdf/ELI4001.pdf

Bliss, J. (1994). From mental models to modeling. In H. Mellar, J. Bliss, R. Boohan, J. Ogborn, & C. Tompsett (Eds.), *Learning with artificial worlds: Computer based modeling in the curriculum.* London: The Falmer Press.

Bloom, B. (1981). *All our children learning.* New York: McGraw-Hill.

Bloom, J. W. (1997). *NBCC webcounseling standards.* Originally appeared in *Counseling Today.* Retrieved November, 30, 2006, from http://members.tripod.com/TCP_2/TCP_2/nbcc_stn.htm

Bodie, G. D., Powers, W. G., & Fitch-Hauser, M. (2006). Chunking, priming, and active learning: Toward an innovative and blended approach to teaching communication related skills. *Interactive Learning Environments, 14,* 119-136.

Boettcher, J. V. (1999). Cyber course size: Pedagogy and politics. *Syllabus, 12*(8), 42-43.

Borgatti, S. P., Everett, M. G., & Freeman, L. C. (1992). UCINET IV network analysis software. *Connections, 15,* 12-15.

Bransford, J., Sherwood, R., Hasselbring, T., Kinzer, C., & Williams, S. (1990). Anchored instruction: Why we need it and how technology can help. In D. Nix, & R. Spiro (Eds.), *Cognition, education and multimedia.* Hillsdale, NJ: Erlbaum Associates.

British Parliament. (2000). Freedom of information act 2000. Retrieved June 5, 2006, from http://www.opsi.gov.uk/acts/acts2000/20000036.htm

Brown, C., Murphy, T. J., & Nanny, M. (2003). Turning techno-savvy into info-savvy: Authentically integrating information literacy into the college curriculum. *Journal of Academic Librarianship, 29,* 386-398.

Brown, D. (2000). The Odyssey of a technologically challenged counselor educator into cyberspace. In J. W. Bloom & G. R. Walz (Eds.), *Cybercounseling and cyberlearning: Strategies and resources for the millennium* (pp. 51-64). Alexandria, VA: American Counseling Association and CAPS with ERIC Counseling and Student Services Clearinghouse.

Brown, J. S., Collins, A., & Duguid, P. (1989). Situated cognition and the culture of learning. *Educational Researcher, 18*(1), 32-42.

Bruner, J. (1966). *Toward a theory of instruction.* Cambridge, MA: Harvard University Press.

Bruner, J. (1996). The *culture of education.* Cambridge, MA: Harvard University Press.

Bruning, R. H., Schraw, G. J., & Ronning, R. R. (1999). *Cognitive psychology and instruction.* Upper Saddle River, NJ: Prentice Hall, Inc.

Brusilovsky, P. (1994). Methods and techniques of adaptive hypermedia. *User Modeling and User-Adapted Interaction, 4,* 21-45.

Brusilovsky, P. (1996). Methods and techniques of adaptive hypermedia. *User Modeling and User-Adapted Interaction, 6*(2-3), 87-129.

Bryant, K., Campbell, J., & Kerr, D. (2003). Impact of web based flexible learning on academic performance in information systems. *Journal of Information Systems, 14*(1) 41-50.

Buber, M. (1965). *Between man and man.* New York: Macmillan.

Buhrmester, D., Furman, W., Wittenberg, M. T., & Reis, H. T. (1988). Five domains of interpersonal competence in peer relationships. *Journal of Personality and Social Psychology, 55,* 991-1008.

Burbules, N. (1993). *Dialogue in teaching: Theory and practice.* New York: Teachers College Press.

Burgoon, J., Stoner, M., Bonito, J., & Dunbar, N. (2003, January). *Trust and deception in mediated communication*. 36th Hawaii International Conference on Systems Sciences. Retrieved August 10, 2007, from http://csdl2. computer.org/comp/proceedings hicss/2003/1874/01/187410044a.pdf

Campbell, E. (2001). Let right be done: Trying to put ethical standards into practice. *Journal of Education Policy, 16*(5), 395-411.

Cannataro, M., Cuzzocrea, A., Mastroianni, C., Ortale, R., & Pugliese, A. (2002). *Modeling adaptive hypermedia with an object-oriented approach and XML*. Paper presented at the 2nd International Workshop on Web Dynamics. Retrieved December 11, 2002, from http://www. dcs.bbk.ac.uk/~ap/pubs/webDyn2Report.pdf

Carlson, S. (2005). The net generation goes to college. *The Chronicle of Higher Education, 52*(7), A34-A37.

Carr, S. (2000). As distance education comes of age, the challenge is keeping the students. *Chronicle of Higher Education, 46*(23), A39-41.

Carroll, J. (1963). A model of school learning. *Teachers College Record, 64*, 723-733.

Caspi, A., & Gorsky, P. (2006). The dialogic behavior of Open University students. *Studies in Higher Education, 31*(6), 735-752.

Caspi, A., Gorsky, P., & Chajut, E. (2003). The influence of group size on non-mandatory asynchronous instructional discussion groups. *The Internet and Higher Education, 6*(3), 227-240.

Chambers, J. G., Parrish, T., & Harr, J. J. (2002). *What Are We Spending on Special Education Services in the United States, 1999-2000* Advance Report #1, Special Education Expenditure Project (SEEP). Washington, D.C.: U.S. Department of Education, Office of Special Education Programs.

Champe, J., & Kleist, D. M. (2003). Live supervision: A review of the research. *The Family Journal: Counseling and Therapy for Couples and Families, 11*, 268 - 275.

Chen, Y. (2001). Transactional distance in world wide web learning environments. *Innovations in Education and Teaching International, 38*(4), 327-338.

Chen, Y. (2001). Dimensions of transactional distance in World Wide Web learning environment: A factor analysis. *British Journal of Educational Technology, 32*(4), 459-470.

Chen, Y., & Willits, F. (1998). A path analysis of the concepts in Moore's theory of transactional distance in a videoconferencing learning environment. *The American Journal of Distance Education, 13*(2), 51-65.

Chester, A., & Glass, C. A. (2006). Online counselling: A descriptive analysis of therapy services on the internet. *British Journal of Guidance & Counseling, 34*, 145-160.

Chester, A., & Gwynne, G. (1998). Online teaching: Encouraging collaboration through anonymity. *Journal of Computer Mediated Communication*. Retrieved September 30, 2006, from http://jcmc.indiana.edu/vol4/issue2/chester.html

Chisholm, W., Vanderheiden, G., & Jacobs, I. (Eds). (2001). Web content accessibility guidelines 1.0. *Interactions, 8*(4), 35-54. Retrieved from http://portal.acm. org/citation.cfm?id=379550

Chitwood, K. (2005). *Learning objects: Making a difference in teaching and learning*. 20th Annual Conference on Distance Teaching and Learning. Retrieved December 11, 2002, from University of Wisconsin: http://www. uwex.edu/disted/conference/Resource_library/proceedings/04_1078.pdf

Cho, H., Stefanone, M., & Gay, G. (2002). Social network analysis of information sharing networks in a CSCL community. In: G. Stahl (Ed.), *Proceedings of Computer Support for Collaborative Learning (CSCL) 2002 Conference*, Jan. 7-11, Boulder, CO. (pp. 43-50). Mahwah, NJ: Lawrence Erlbaum.

Christe, B. (2003) Designing online courses to discourage dishonesty: Incorporate a multilayered approach to promote honest student learning. *Educause Quarterly, 4*, 54-58.

Clark, R. (1983). Reconsidering research on learning from media. *Review of Educational Research, 53,* 445-460.

Clark, R. C., & Mayer, R. E. (2003). *E-Learning and the science of instruction.* San Francisco, CA: Jossey-Bass/Pfeiffer.

Cobb, P. (1994) Where is the mind? Constructivist and sociocultural perspectives on mathematical development. *Educational Researcher, 23*(7), 13-20.

Cohen, J. (1977). *Statistical power analysis for the behavioral sciences* (Rev. Ed.). New York, NY: Academic Press.

Cohen, J., Cohen, P., West, S. G., & Aiken, L. S. (2003). *Applied multiple regression/correlation analysis for the behavioral sciences* (3rd Ed.). Mahwah, NJ: Erlbaum.

Colella, V. (2000). Participatory simulations: Building collaborative understanding through immersive dynamic modeling. *The Journal of the Learning Sciences, 9*(4), 471-500.

Coles, G. (1987). *The learning mystique.* New York: Fawcett Columbine.

Collie, K. R., Mitchell, D. & Murhpy, L. (2000). Skills for online counseling: Maximum impact at minimum bandwidth. In J. W. Bloom & G. R. Walz (Eds.), *Cybercounseling and Cyberlearning: Strategies and Resources for the Millennium* (pp. 219-236). Alexandria, VA: American Counseling Association and CAPS with ERIC Counseling and Student Services Clearinghouse.

Collins, A. (1988). *Cognitive apprenticeship and instructional technology.* (Technical Report No. 6899). BBN Labs Inc., Cambridge, MA.

Collins, M.P., & Berge, Z.L. (1997, March). *Moderating online electronic discussion groups.* Paper presented at the AERA Annual Conference, Chicago IL.

Collison, G., Elbaum, B., Haavind, S., & Tinker, R. (2000). *Facilitating online learning: Effective strategies for moderators.* Madison, WI: Atwood.

Colwell, J., & Jenks, C. (2004). *The upper limit: The issues for faculty in setting class size in online courses.* Paper presented at the Teaching Online in Higher Education 2004 Conference, Online.

Connor, K., & Day, R. (1988). *Class size: When less can be more.* Sacramento, California: Senate Office of Research, State of California.

Cook, J., & Powers, W. G. (in press). A case study on strengthening workforce training outcomes. *Training and Management Development Methods.*

Cost, D. L., Bishop, M. H., & Anderson, E. S. (1992). Effective listening: Teaching students a critical marketing skill. *Journal of Marketing Education, 14,* 41-45.

Cote, J. E. (1996). Identity: a multidimensional analysis. In G.R. Adams, R. Montemayor, & T.P. Gullotta (Eds.) *Psychosocial development during adolescence: progress in developmental contextualism. Advances in adolescent development.* Newbury Park, CA: Sage.

Coursol, D. (2004). Cybersupervision: Conducting supervision of the information superhighway. In G. R. Walz & C. Kirkman (Eds.), *CyberBytes: Highlighting compelling uses of technology in counseling* (pp. 83-85). (ERIC Document Reproduction Service No. ED478221)

Cowan, N., Chen, Z., & Rouder, J. N. (2004). Constant capacity in an immediate serial-recall task: A logical sequel to Miller (1956). *Psychological Science, 15,* 634-640.

Cronin, P. (1997). *Learning and assessment of instruction.* Retrieved from http://www.cogsci.ed.ac.uk/~paulus/Work/Vranded/litconsa.htm

Cyrs, T. E. (1997, Fall). Competence in teaching at a distance. In T.E.Cyrs, (Ed.), *New directions for teaching and learning, 71,* (pp. 15-18). Jossey Bass.

Czaja, S. J., & Sharit, J. (1998). The effect of age and experience on the performance of a data entry task. *Journal of Experimental Psychology: Applied, 4,* 332-351.

Czaja, S. J., Sharit, J., Ownby, R., Roth, D., & Nair, S. (2001). Examining age differences in performance of a complex information search and retrieval task. *Psychology & Aging, 16*(4), 564-579.

Daft, R. L., & Lengel, R. H. (1984). Information richness: A new approach to managerial behavior and organizational design. In B. M. Staw & L. L. Cummings (Eds.), *Research in Organizational Behavior* (Vol. 6, pp. 191-233). Greenwich, CT: JAI Press.

Daft, R. L., & Lengel, R. H. (1986). Organizational information requirements, media richness, and structure design. *Management Science, 32*, 554-571.

Daft, R. L., Lengel, R. H., & Trevino, L. K. (1987). Message equivocality, media selection, and manager performance: Implications for information systems. *MIS Quarterly, 11*, 355-366.

Datamonitor. (2004, July 14). *E-learning in education.* Retrieved July 1, 2006, from http://www.datamonitor.com

Davie, L. (1989). Facilitation techniques for the on-line tutor. In R. Mason and A. Kaye (Eds.), *Mindweave: Communication, Computers and Distance Education.* Elmsford, New York: Pergamon Press.

Day, S. X., & Schneider, P. (2000). The subjective experiences of counselors in face-to-face, video, and audio sessions. In J. W. Bloom & G. R. Walz (Eds.), *Cybercounseling and cyberlearning: Strategies and resources for the millennium* (pp. 203-218). Alexandria, VA: American Counseling Association and CAPS with ERIC Counseling and Student Services Clearinghouse.

De Bra, P. (1999). *Design issues in adaptive web-site development.* Paper presented at the 8th International World Wide Web Conference. Retrieved December 11, 2002, from http://wwwis.win.tue.nl/asum99/debra/debra.html

De Bra, P., Brusilovsky, P., & Houben, G. (1999). Adaptive hypermedia: From systems to framework. *ACM Computing Surveys, 31*(4).

Dean, P., Stahl, M., Sylwester, D., & Pear, J. (2001). Effectiveness of combined delivery modalities for distance learning and resident learning. *Quarterly Review of Distance Education, 2*, 247-254.

DeLacey, B. J., & Leonard, D. A. (2002). Case study on technology and distance in education at Harvard Business School. *Educational Technology & Society, 5*, 13-28.

Derntl, M., & Motschnig-Pitrik, R. (2005). The role of structure, patterns, and people in blended learning. *Internet and Higher Education, 8*, 111-130.

DeVries, J., & Lim, G. (2003, November 7-11). Significance of online teaching vs. face-to-face: similarities and differences. *E-Learn 2003, World Conference on E-Learning in Corporate, Government, Healthcare and Higher Education.* Retrieved December 28, 2006, from http://ole.tp.edu.sg/courseware/teaching_guide/resources/article/TP%20Staff/F2FandOnline.pdf.

Dewey, J. (1916). *Democracy and education.* Toronto: The Macmillan Co.

Diamond, B. J., DeLuca, J., & Kelley, S. (1997). Executive functions and memory impairments in patients with aneurysms of the anterior communicating artery. *Brain, 120*, 1015-1025.

Diamond, B. J., DeLuca, J., Rosenthal, D., Vlad, R., Davis, K., Lucas, G., & Richards, J. (2000). Aging: Information processing speed and modality-specific effects. *International Journal of Rehabilitation and Health, 5*(1), 55-64.

Diamond, B. J., Shreve, G., & Johnston, M. (2000). Telerehabilitation: A web-based "virtual rehabilitation center." *Archives in Physical Medicine and Rehabilitation, 81*(12), 16-17.

Diamond, B. J., Shreve, G., & Johnston, M. (2001, October). *The virtual rehabilitation center: Testing user friendliness.* Paper presented at Kessler Medical Rehabilitation Research and Education Corporation, Kessler Conference Center, West Orange, NJ.

Diamond, B. J., Shreve, G., Bonilla, J., Johnston, M., Morodan, J., & Branneck, R. (2003). Cognition, telerehabilitation and user-accessibility, Special Issue on Telerehabilitation. *NeuroRehabilitation, 17*, 1-7.

Diamond, B. J., Valentine, T., Mayes, A., & Sandel, M. (1994). Evidence of covert recognition in a prosopagnosic patient. *Cortex, 30*, 377-393.

Diamond, B., DeLuca, J., Rosenthal, D., Vlad, R., Davis, K., Lucas, G., & Richards, J. (2000). Information processing in younger versus older adults: Accuracy versus speed. *International Journal of Rehabilitation and Health, 5*(1), 55-64.

Dillenbourg, P., & Self, J. A. (1995). Designing human-computer collaborative learning. In C. O'Malley(Ed.), *Computer supported collaborative learning*. Berlin, Germany: Springer.

Dochy, F., Segers, M., Van de Bossche, P., & Gijbels, D. (2003). Effects of problem-based learning: A meta-analysis. *Learning and Instruction, 13*(5), 533-568.

Dorn, F. J. (1984). Using social influence theory in the supervision of mental health counselors. *American Mental Health Counselors Association Journal, 6*(2), 173-179.

Drennan, J., Kennedy, J., & Pisarski, A. (2005). Factors affecting learner attitudes toward flexible online learning in management education. *The Journal of Educational Research, 98(6)* 331-338.

Driscoll, M. P. (2000). *Psychology of learning for instruction, 2nd Ed.* Needham Heights, MA: Pearson Education.

DuCharme-Hansen, B. A., & Dupin-Bryant, P. A. (2005). Distance education plans: Course planning for online adult learners. *TechTrends, 49*(2), 31-39.

Duchastel, P. (1998). Prolegomena to a theory of instructional design. *Online ITFORUM presentation and archived discussion*. Retrieved January 15, 2007, from http://itech1.coe.uga.edu/itforum/paper27/paper27.html.

Duffy, T. M., & Cunningham, D. J. (1996). Constructivism: Implications for the design and delivery of instruction. In D. Johassen (Ed.), *Handbook of research for educational communications and technology* (pp. 170-198). New York: Simon and Schuster Macmillan.

Dunning, L. (1997). Don't lecture me about flexible learning! Being flexible in the delivery of an undergraduate education studies module. In R. Hudson, S.

Maslin-Prothero, & L. Oates, (Eds.), *Flexible learning in action case studies for higher education.* (pp. 17-21). London: Kogan Page.

Eastmond, D. V. (1992). Effective facilitation of computer conferencing. *Continuing Higher Education Review, 56*(1/2), 23-34

Egbert, J. (1993). Group support systems for computer assisted language learning. In L. M. Jessup & J. S. Valacich (Eds.), *Group support systems: New perspectives.* (pp. 294-310). New York, NY: Macmillan.

Erickson, H. L. (2001). *Stirring the head, heart, and soul: Redefining curriculum and instruction, 2nd Ed.* Thousand Oaks, CA: Corwin Press Inc.

eSchool News Online. (2003). Retrieved December 11, 2002, from www.eschoolnews.com

Etter, S., Cramer, J. J., & Finn, S. (2006, Winter). Origins of academic dishonesty: Ethical orientations and personality factors associated with attitudes about cheating with information technology. *Journal of Research on Technology Education, 39*(2), 133-155.

Evans, W., Miller, K. L., & Miller, S. M. (2005, October). *Enhancing live clinical supervision through the use of audio*. Poster session made at the National Association of Counseling Educators and Supervisors, Pittsburgh, PA.

Fahy, P. J., Crawford, G., & Ally, M. (2001). Patterns of interaction in a computer conference transcript. *International Review of Open and Distance Learning, 2*(1). Retrieved on December 18, 2006, from http://www.irrodl.org/content/v2.1/fahy.html

Feast, V. (2003). Integration of information literacy skills into business courses. *Reference Services Review, 31*(1), 81-95.

Feenberg, A. (1989). The written world: On the theory and practice of computer conferencing. In R. Mason and A. Kaye (Eds.), *Mindweave: Communication, computers and distance education.* Elmsford, New York: Pergamon Press.

Feltovich, P. F., Coulson, R. L., & Spiro, R. F. (2001). Learners' (mis)understanding of important and difficult concepts. In K. D. Forbus & P. J. Feltovich (Eds.), *Smart machines in education: The coming revolution of educational technology* (pp. 349-375). Menlo Park, CA: AAAI/MIT Press.

Fernback, J. (2003). The nature of knowledge in web-based learning environments. *Academic Exchange Quarterly, 7*(4), 28-32.

Fink, J., Kobsa, A., & Nill, A. (1996, October). *User-oriented adaptivity and adaptability in the AVANTI Project.* Paper presented at the conference "Designing for the web: Empirical studies," Redmond, WA.

Fink, J., Kobsa, A., & Schreck, J. (1997). *Personalized hypermedia information provision through adaptive and adaptable system features: User modeling, privacy and security issues.* Proceeding of the workshop "Adaptive Systems and User Modeling on the World Wide Web," 6th International Conference on User Modeling, 1997. Chia Laguna, Sardinia.

Firdiyiyek, Y. (1999). Web-based courseware tools: Where is the pedagogy? *Educational Technology, 39*(1), 29–34.

Firooznia, F., & Andreadis, D. K. (2006). Information literacy in introductory biology. *Journal of College Science Teaching, 35*(6), 23-27.

Fisher, F. (1995). *Growing healthy technology: a process for developing effective strategies to integrate education and technology.* Yakima, WA: Educational Technology Support Center 105.

Flammia, G. (1997). XML and style sheets promise to make the Web more accessible. *IEEE EXPERT, 12*(3), 98-99.

Formica, S. W., & Harding, W. M. (2001). *Evaluation results for middle school drug prevention and school safety coordinators online continuing education events: Summary report.* Report prepared for Education Development Center, Inc., and the United States Department of Education.

Formica, S. W., & Harding, W. M. (2002). *Evaluation results for middle school drug prevention and school safety coordinators online continuing education events: Six-month follow-up report.* Report prepared for Education Development Center, Inc., and the United States Department of Education.

Formica, S. W., Harding, W. M., & Giguere, P. J. (2002, November). *Evaluation results from distance learning courses for U.S. Department of Education Middle School Coordinators.* Paper presented at the annual conference of the Association for Educational Communications and Technology, Dallas, Texas.

Fredenborg, J. (1995). *Fritz Heider's "The sychology of interpersonal relations": A detailed citation analysis.* Oslo, Norway: University of Oslo Library, Faculty of Social Sciences Library.

Freeman, L. C. (1980). The gatekeeper, pair dependency, and structural centrality. *Quality and Quantity, 14*, 585-592.

Freeman, L. C. (2000). Visualizing Social Networks. *Journal of Social Structure, 1*(1). Retrieved on December 11, 2004 from http://www.cmu.edu/joss/content/articles/volume1/Freeman.html.

Freeman, L. C., Webster, C. M., & Kirke, D. M. (1998). Exploring social structure using dynamic three-dimensional color images. *Social Networks, 20*, 109-118.

Freire, P. (1972). *Pedagogy of the oppressed.* Harmondsworth: Penguin.

Gagne, R. (1985). *The conditions of learning* (4th ed.). New York: Holt, Rinehart, and Winston.

Galbraith, M. W. (Ed.). (1998). *Adult learning methods.* (2nd ed). Malabar, FL: Krieger.

Gallant, J. P., Thyer, B. A., & Bailey, J. S. (1991). Using bug-in-the-ear feedback in clinical supervision: Preliminary evaluations. *Research on Social Work Practice, 1*(2), 175-187.

Gardner, H. (1983). *Frames of mind.* New York: Basic Books.

Garrison, D. R., & Archer, W. (2000). *A transactional perspective on teaching and learning: A framework for adult and higher education.* Oxford, UK: Pergamon.

Garrison, D. R., Anderson, T., & Archer, W. (2000). Critical inquiry in a text-based environment: Computer conferencing in higher education. *The Internet and Higher Education, 2*(2-3), 87-105.

Garrison, D.R. (1992). Critical thinking and self-directed learning in adult education: an analysis of responsibility and control issues. *Adult Education Quarterly, 42*(3), 136-148.

Garrison, D.R., & Anderson, T. (2003). *E-Learning in the 21ˢᵗ century: A framework for research and practice.* London: Routledge.

Garrison, D.R., & Cleveland-Innes, M. (2005). Facilitating cognitive presence in online learning: Interaction is not enough. *American Journal of Distance Education, 19*(3), 133-148.

Garrison, D.R., Anderson, T., & Archer, W. (2000). Critical inquiry in a text-based environment: Computer conferencing in higher education. *The Internet and Higher Education, 2(2-3),* 87-105.

Garrison, D.R., Anderson, T., & Archer, W. (2001). Critical thinking and computer conferencing: A model and tool to assess cognitive presence. *American Journal of Distance Education, 15*(1), 7–23.

Garton, L., Haythornthwaite, C., & Wellman, B. (1997). Studying online social networks. *Journal of Computer Mediated Communication, 3*(1). Retrieved September 23, 2002, from http://www.ascusc.org/jcmc/vol3/issue1/garton.html

Gasparini, S. (2004). Implicit versus explicit learning: Some implications for L2 teaching. *European Journal of Psychology of Education, 19*(2), 203-219.

Gearhart, D. (2001). Ethics in distance education: Developing ethical policies. *Journal of Distance Learning Administration:* State University of West Georgia, Distance Learning Center. Retrieved June 7, 2006, from http://www.westga.edu/~distance/ojdla/spring41/gearhart41.html

George, R., & Luke, R. (1995, November). *The critical place of information literacy in the trends towards flexible delivery in higher education contexts.* Paper delivered at the Learning for Life Conference. Retrieved March 15, 2006, from http://www.city.londonmet.ac.uk/deliberations/flex.learning/rigmor_content.html

Giguere, P. J., Formica, S. W., & Harding, W. M. (2004). Large-scale interaction strategies for Web-based professional development. *American Journal of Distance Education, 18*(4), 207-223.

Gillespie, F. (1998). Instructional design for the new technologies. *New Directions for Teaching and Learning, 76*, 39-52.

Glaser, B., & Strauss, A. (1967) *The discovery of grounded theory: Strategies for qualitative research.* New York: Aldine de Gruyter.

Glass, G., & Smith, M. (1978). *Meta-Analysis of research on the relationship of class-size and achievement.* San Francisco, California: Far West Laboratory for Educational Research and Development.

Glass, G., & Smith, M. (1979). *Relationship of class size to classroom processes, teacher satisfaction and pupil affect: A meta-analysis.* San Francisco, California: Far West Laboratory for Educational Research and Development.

Glisky, E., & Schacter, D. (1988). Long-term retention of computer learning by patients with memory disorders. *Neuropsychologia, 26*(1), 173-178.

Gobet, F., & Simon, H. A. (1996). Templates in chess memory: A mechanism for recalling several boards. *Cognitive Psychology, 31*, 1-40.

Gobet, F., & Simon, H. A. (1998). Pattern recognition makes search possible: Comments on Holding (1992). *Psychological Research, 61*, 204-208.

Golder, S. A., & Donath, J. (2004, September 19-22). Social roles in electronic communities. Presented at Association of Internet Researchers IR 5.0. Brighton, England. Retrieved May 12, 2005, from http://web.media.mit.edu/~golder/projects/roles/golder2004.pdf

Goldman, S. R., Williams, S. M., Sherwood, R. D., Hasselbring, T. S., & Cognition and Technology Group at Vanderbilt. (1999). *Technology for teaching and learning with understanding: A primer.* Nashville, TN:Vanderbilt University.

Gordon, D. T. (2000). *The digital classroom: How technology is changing the way we teach and learn.* Boston: Harvard Education Letter.

Gorham, J. (1988). The relationship between verbal teacher immediacy behaviors and student learning. *Communication Education, 37,* 40-53.

Gorham, J., & Zakahi, W. (1990). A comparison of teacher and student perceptions of immediacy and learning: Monitoring process and product. *Communication Education, 39,* 355-367.

Gorsky, P., & Caspi, A. (2005). Dialogue: A theoretical framework for distance education instructional systems. *British Journal of Educational Technology, 36*(2), 137-144.

Gorsky, P., & Caspi, A. (2005). A critical analysis of transactional distance theory. *Quarterly Review of Distance Education, 6*(1), 1-11.

Gorsky, P., Caspi, A., & Smidt, S. (2007). Use of instructional dialogue by university students in a difficult distance education physics course. *Journal of Distance Education, 22*(1), 1-22.

Gorsky, P., Caspi, A., & Trumper, R. (2004). University students' use of dialogue in a distance education physics course. *Open Learning, 19*(3), 265-277.

Gorsky, P., Caspi, A., & Trumper, R. (2006). Campus-based university students' use of dialogue. *Studies in Higher Education. 31*(1), 71-87.

Gorsky, P., Caspi, A., & Tuvi-Arad, I. (2004). Use of instructional dialogue by university students in a distance education chemistry course. *Journal of Distance Education, 19*(1), 1-19.

Govindasamy, T. (2002). Successful implementation of e-Learning Pedagogical considerations. *Internet and Higher Education, 4,* 287-299.

Grabe, M., & Grabe, C. (1998). *Integrating technology for meaningful learning* (2nd Ed.). Boston: Houghton Mifflin Company.

Grabowski, B. L. (1996). Generative learning: Past, present, future. In Jonassen, D. H. (Ed.), *Handbook for educational communications and technology* (pp. 897-907). New York, NY: Simon and Schuster Macmillan.

Gudykunst, W. B. (1998). *Bridging differences: Effective intergroup communication* (3rd Ed.). Thousand Oaks, CA: Sage.

Gunawardena, C. N, Lowe, C. A., & Anderson, T. (1997). Analysis of a global online debate and the development of an interaction analysis model for examining social construction of knowledge in computer conferencing. *Journal of Educational Computing Research, 17*(4), 397-431.

Gunawardena, C. N. (1995). Social presence theory and implications for interaction and collaborative learning in computer conferences. *International Journal of Educational Telecommunications, 1*(23), 147-166.

Gunawardena, C. N., & Zittle, F. J. (1997). Social presence as a predictor of satisfaction within a computer-mediated conferencing environment. *The American Journal of Distance Education, 11*(3), 8-26.

Guri-Rosenblit, S. (2001). The tower of babel syndrome in the discourse on information technologies in higher education. *Global E-Journal of Open and Flexible Learning, 1*(1), 28-38.

Hannafin, M. (1997). The case for grounded learning systems design: What the literature suggests about effective teaching, learning, and technology. *Educational Technology Research and Development, 45*(3), 101-117.

Harasim, L., Hiltz, S. R., Teles, L., & Turoff, M. (1997). *Learning networks: A field guide to teaching and learning online.* Cambridge, Massachusetts: MIT Press.

Harding, W. M., Formica, S.W., & Scattergood, P. (2001, October). *Evaluation of trainings in substance abuse and violence prevention for middle school coordinators.* Paper presented at the 129th annual meeting of the American Public Health Association, Atlanta, GA.

Harper, S. G. (1999). *Counseling and the internet.* Retrieved November 30, 1999, from http://www.find-articles.com.

Harris-Bowlsbey, J. (2000). The internet: Blessing or bane for the counseling profession? In J. W. Bloom & G. R. Walz (Eds.), *Cybercounseling and cyberlearning: Strategies and resources for the millennium* (pp. 39-50). Alexandria, VA: American Counseling Association and CAPS with ERIC Counseling and Student Services Clearinghouse.

Harvey, J. H. (1989). Fritz Heider, (1896-1988) (Obituary). *American Psychologist, 44,* 570-571.

Haynes, R., Corey, G., & Moulton, P. (2003). *Clinical supervision in the helping professions: A practical guide.* Pacific Grove, CA: Thomson: Brooks/Cole.

Haythornthwaite, C. (1998). *Network structure among computer-supported distance learners: Multiple relations, multiple media, and time.* Retrieved March 11, 2003, from http://alexia.lis.uiuc.edu/ ~haythorn/LEEP3_2.html

Head, J. T., Lockee, B. B., & Oliver, K. M. (2002). Method, media, and mode: Clarifying the discussion of distance education effectiveness. *Quarterly Review of Distance Education, 3*(3), 261-68.

Health Level Seven, Inc: The clinical document architecture. (2002). Retrieved December 11, 2002, from http://www.hl7.org

Hearne, J. D., Poplin, M., Schoneman, C., & O'Shaughnessy, E. (1988). Computer aptitude: An investigation of differences among junior high students with learning disabilities and their non-learning-disabled peers. *Journal of Learning Disabilities, 21,* 489-492.

Heberling, M. (2002, Spring). Maintaining academic integrity in online education. *Journal of Distance Learning Administration, 5*(1). Retrieved December 27, 2006, from http://www.westga.edu/~distance/ojdla/spring51/heberling51.html

Heider, F. (1958). *The psychology of interpersonal relations.* New York: John Wiley & Sons, Inc.

Heim, M. (1992). The erotic ontology of cyberspace. In M. Benedikt (Ed.), *Cyberspace: First steps.* Cambridge: MIT Press.

Help Us Define PC Ease of Use. (2004, June 16). *PC Magazine.* Retrieved October 24, 2006, from http://www.pcmag.com/print_article2/0,1217,a=129735,00.asp

Henderson, C. (1995). *College freshmen with disabilities: A triennial statistical profile.* Washington DC: American Council on Education, HEATH Resource Center. (ERIC Document Reproduction Service No. ED387971)

Henri, F. (1992). Computer conferencing and content analysis. In A. R. Kaye (Ed.), *Collaborative learning through computer conferencing: The Najaden papers* (pp. 115-136). New York: Springer.

Henri, F. (1992). Computer conferencing and content analysis. In A.R. Kaye (Ed.), *Collaborative learning through computer conferencing: The Najaden papers* (pp. 115-136). New York: Springer.

Herman, A., & Swiss, T. (Eds.). (2000). *The world wide web and contemporary culture theory.* New York: Routledge.

Herring, S. C. (2000, Winter). Gender differences in CMC: Findings and implications. *The CPSR Newsletter, 18*(1), 3-11. Retrieved June 6, 2006, from http://www.cpsr.org/prevsite/publications/newsletters/issues/2000/Winter2000/herring.html

Hestenes, D. (1987). Toward a modeling theory of physics instruction. *American Journal of Physics, 55*(5), 440-454.

Hestenes, D. (2006). *Modeling instruction in high school physics, chemistry, and physical science.* Retrieved July 25, 2006, from http://modeling.asu.edu/modeling-HS.html

Hill, J. R., Raven, A., & Han, S. (2002). Connections in web-based learning environments: A research-based model for community building. *Quarterly Review of Distance Education, 3*(4), 383-393.

Hill, J., & Hannafin, M. (1997). Cognitive strategies and learning from the world wide web, *Educational Technology Research and Development, 45,* 37-64.

Hillman, D. C., Willis, D. J., & Gunawardena, C. N. (1994). Learner-interface interaction in distance education: An extension of contemporary models and strategies for practitioners. *The American Journal of Distance Education, 8*(2), 30-42.

Hiltz, S. R., Coppola, N., Rotter, N., Turoff, M., & Benbunan-Fich, R. (2000). Measuring the importance of collaborative learning for the effectiveness of ALN: A multi-measure, multi-method approach. *Journal of Asynchronous Learning Networks, 4*(2). Retrieved December 6, 2006, from http://www.sloan-c.org/publications/JALN/v4n2/v4n2_hiltz.asp

Hmelo-Silver, C. E., & Azevedo, R. (2006). Understanding complex systems: Some core challenges. *The Journal of the Learning Sciences, 15*(1), 53-61.

Hmelo-Silver, C. E., & Pfeffer, M. G. (2004). Comparing expert and novice understanding of a complex system from the perspective of structures, behaviors, and functions. *Cognitive Science, 28*, 127-138.

Ho, S. (2002). Evaluating students' participation in on-line discussions. In *Proceedings of AusWeb 2002, The Eighth Australian World Wide Web Conference,* Queensland, Australia. Retrieved December 5, 2006, from http://ausweb.scu.edu.au/aw02/papers/refereed/ho/paper.html

Hoffman, B. (1995). Integrating technology into schools: Eight ways to promote success. *Technology Connection, 2(6)*,14-15.

Hoffman, R. (2002). Strategic planning lessons learned from a big-business district. *Technology & Learning, 22(10)*,26-38.

Hothi, J. & Hall, W. (1998, June). An evaluation of adapted hypermedia techniques using static user modeling. In *Proceedings of the Second Workshop on Adaptive Hypertext and Hypermedia, (pp. 45-50).* Pittsburgh, USA.

Howell-Richardson, C., & Mellar, H. (1996). A methodology for the analysis of patterns of participation within computer-mediated communication courses. *Instructional Science, 24*, 47-69.

Hron, A., & Friedrich, H. F. (2003). A review of web-based collaborative learning: Factors beyond technology. *Journal of Computer Assisted Learning, 19*, 70-79.

Huffman, S. P., & Rickman, W. A. (Spring, 2003). Keep it SIMPLE: Technology planning strategy. In *Proceedings of Society of Information Technology and Teaching*, Albuquerque, NM: Spring 2003 International Conference.

International Data Group (IDC). (2005, October 5) With nearly 12 billion instant messages each day, IM is growing into a serious business collaboration tool, IDC finds. Retrieved May 25, 2006, from http://www.idc.com/home.jhtml

Jacko, J. A., Rosa, R. H., Scott, I., Pappas, C. J., & Dixon, M. A. (2000). Visual impairment: The use of visual profiles in evaluations of icon use in computer-based tasks. *International Journal of Human-Computer Interaction, 12*(1), 151-164.

Jackson, C. (2005, February). Integrating information literacy into an undergraduate law course. Paper presented at the UKCLE seminar on teaching and learning for legal skills trainers, 16 February 2005. http://www.ukcle.ac.uk/resources/biall/jackson.html

James, V. L. (2006). *The creation of emotionally detached customers.* Retrieved December 22, 2006, from www.crmmarketplace.com/content/news/article.asp?docid=%7B8C7798E0-E36E-433C-BEBE-00085E5E6167%7D

Janusik, L. A., & Wolvin, A. D. (2002). Listening treatment in the basic communication course text. In D. Sellnow, (Ed.), *Basic Communication Course Annual* (Vol. 14, pp. 164 – 210). Boston: American Press.

Jenkins, H., Clinton, K., Purushotma, R., Robinson, A. J., and Weigel, M. (2006). Confronting the challenges of participatory culture: Media education for the 21st Century. Retrieved December 12, 2006, from http://www.digitallearning.macfound.org/atf/cf/%7B7E45C7E0-A3E0-4B89-AC9C-E807E1B0AE4E%7D/JENKINS_WHITE_PAPER.PDF

Jetten, J., Postmes, T., & McAuliffe, B. (2002). We're all individuals: Group norms of individualism and collectivism, levels of identification, and identity threat. *European Journal of Social Psychology, 32,* 189-207.

Johansen, R., Vallee, J., & Spangler, K. (1988). Teleconferencing: Electronic group communication. In R. S. Cathcart and L. A. Samovar (Eds.), *Small group communication: A reader* 5th Ed. (pp. 140-154). Menlo Park, CA: Institute for the Future.

Johnson, J. C., Borgatti, S. P., Luczkovich, J. J., & Everett, M. G. (2001). Network role analysis in the study of food webs: An application of regular role coloration. *The Journal of Social Structure, 2*(3). Retrieved September 2, 2004, from http://www.cmu.edu/joss/content/articles/volume2/JohnsonBorgatti.html

Johnson. J. C., Richardson, D. C., & Richardson, J. S. (2002, September). *Network visualization of social and ecological systems.* Paper presented at the Russian-American Workshop on Studies of Socio-Natural Co-Evolution from Different Parts of the World, Academgorodok, Siberia.

Johnston, W., Dark, V., & Jacoby, L. (1985). Perceptual fluency and recognition judgments. *Journal of Experimental Psychology: Learning, Memory, & Cognition, 11*(1), 3-11.

Jonassen, D. (1999). Designing constructivist learning environments. In C. M. Reigeluth (Ed.), *Instructional-design theories and models: A new paradigm of instructional theory, Vol. II* (pp. 215-239). Mahwah, NJ: Lawrence Erlbaum.

Jonassen, D. H. (1988). *Instructional designs for microcomputer courseware.* Hillsdale, NJ: Lawrence Erlbaum Associates

Jonassen, D. H. (1996). *Computers in the classroom: Mindtools for critical thinking.* Englewood Cliffs, NJ: Prentice-Hall.

Jonassen, D. H. (2000). *Computers as mind tools for schools: Engaging critical thinking* (2nd Ed.). Upper Saddle River, New Jersey: Merrill.

Jonassen, D. H., & Wang, S. (1993). Acquiring structural knowledge from semantically structured hypertext. *Journal of Computer-Based Instruction, 20*(1), 1-8.

Jonassen, D., & Rohrer-Murphy, L. (1999). Activity theory as a framework for designing constructivist learning environments. *Educational Technology, Research & Development, 47*(1), 61-79.

Jones, M. G., Harmon, S. W., & Lowther, D. (2002). Integrating web-based learning in an educational system: A framework for implementation. In R. A. Reiser & J. V. Dempsey (Eds.), *Trends and issues in instructional design and technology* (pp. 295-306). Upper Saddle River, NJ: Merrill/Prentice Hall.

Kanuka, H., Rourke, L., & Laflamme, E. (2006). The influence of instructional methods on the quality of online discussion. *British Journal of Educational Technology.* Retrieved from http://www.blackwell-synergy.com/doi/pdf/10.1111/j.1467-8535.2006.00620.x

Kanz, J. E. (2001). Clinical-supervision.com: Issues in the provision of online supervision. *Professional Psychology: Research and Practice, 32,* 415-420.

Kaplan, D. (2006, October). Ethical use of technology in counseling [CT Online -- Ethics update]. *Counseling Today Online.* Retrieved December 7, 2006.

Karmaker, N. L. (2002). Online privacy, security and ethical dilemma: A recent study. Association for the Advancement of Computing in Education, ERIC IR021765.

Katz, R. N. (2006). *The ECAR study of undergraduate students and information technology, 2006: Key findings.* Retrieved December 22, 2006, from http://www.educause.edu/ers0607/

Kearney, P., Plax, T. G., & Wendt-Wasco, N. J. (1985). Teacher immediacy for affective learning in divergent college courses. *Communication Quarterly, 33,* 61-74.

Kearsley, G. (2004). *Explorations in learning and instruction: The theory into practice database.* Retrieved January 15, 2007, from http://tip.psychology.org/

Kearsley, G., & Shneiderman, B. (1998). Engagement Theory: A Framework for technology-based teaching and learning. *Educational Technology, 38*(5), 20-23.

Kennedy, B. (Ed.). (2000). *The cybercultures reader.* New York: Routledge.

Kerka, S. (1996). Distance learning, the Internet and the World Wide Web. Retrieved May 8, 2006 from http://www.cete.org/acve/docgen. asp?tbl=digests&ID=21

Kerka, S. *Distance learning, the Internet, and the World Wide Web.* (ERIC Document Reproduction Service No. ED 395 214, 1996).

Kerr, E. B. (1986). Electronic leadership: A guide to moderating online conferences. *IEEE Transactions on Professional Communications, 29*(1) 12-18.

Kettler, A., Klensin, J.C., Medin, M., Partridge, C., Schutzer, D., et al. (2001). *The Internet's coming of age, Vol. 2005.* Washington, DC: National Academy Press.

Kiesler, S., Seigel, J., & McGuire, T. W. (1984). Social psychological aspects of computer-mediated communication. *American Psychologist, 39*(11), 1123-1134.

King, J. C., & Doerfert, D. L. (1996). *Interaction in the distance education setting.* Retrieved January, 1996, from http://www.ssu.missouri.edu/ssu/AgEd/NAERM/ s-e-4.htm

Klitzke, M. J., & Lombardo, T. W. (1991). "A bug-in-the-eye" can be better than "bug-in-the-ear": A teleprompter technique for on-line therapy skills training. *Behavior Modification, 15*, 113-117.

Knowles, M. S., Holton, E. F., & Swanson, R. A. (1998). *The adult learner: The definitive classic in adult education and human resource development.* Houston: GULF.

Ko, S., & Rossen, S. (2001). *Teaching online: A practical guide.* New York: Houghton Mifflin Co.

Kolb, D. A. (1984). *Experiential learning: Experience as the source of learning and development.* Englewood Cliffs, NJ: Prentice-Hall, Inc.

Kozma, R. B. (1987). The implications of cognitive psychology for computer-based learning tools. *Educational Technology, 27*(11), 20-25.

Kremers, M. (1993). Student authority and teacher freedom. In B. Bruce, J. Kreeft Peyton, & T. Batson (Eds), *Network-based classroom: Promises and realities* (pp 113-123). New York: Cambridge.

Kuh, G.D., & Hu, S. (2001). Effects of student-faculty interaction in the 1990s. *Review of Higher Education, 24*(2), 309-332.

Kukla, R. (1992). Cognitive models and representation. *The British Journal for the Philosophy of Science, 43*(2), 219-232.

Kules, W. (2000). *User modeling for adaptive and adaptable software systems.* Retrieved December 11, 2002, from University of Maryland, College Park, Department of Computer Science Web site at http://www.otal.umd. edu/uuguide/wmk/

Lance, G.D. (2002). Distance learning and disability: A view from the instructor's side

Landa, L. N. (1987). The creation of expert performers without years of conventional experience: The Landamatic method. *Journal of Management Development, 6*(4), 40-52.

Landa, L. N., & Kopstein, F. F. (Scientific Editor), & Bennett, V., Translator. (1974). *Algorithmicization in learning and instruction.* Englewood Cliffs, NJ: Educational Technology Publications.

Landa, L. N., & Kopstein, F. F. (Scientific Editor), & Desch, S., Translator. (1976). *Instructional regulation and control: Cybernetics, algorithmicization, and heuristics in education.* Englewood Cliffs, NJ: Educational Technology Publications.

LaRose, R., & Whitten, P. (2000). Re-thinking instructional immediacy for web courses: A social cognitive exploration. *Communication Education, 49*, 320-338.

Layne, C. M., & Hohenshil, T. H. (2005). High tech counseling: Revisited. *Journal of Counseling & Development, 83*, 222-226.

Leigh, W. A., Lee, D. H., & Lindquist, M. A. (1999). *Soft skills training: An annotated guide to selected programs*. Washington, DC: Joint Center for Political and Economic Studies.

Lesh, R. (2006). Modeling students modeling abilities: The teaching and learning of complex systems in education. *The Journal of the Learning Sciences, 15*(1), 45-52.

Levenburg, N. M., & Major, H. T. (2000). Motivating the online learner: The effect of frequency of online postings and time spent online on achievement of learning goals and objectives. In *Proceedings of the International Online Conference On Teaching Online in Higher Education*. Indiana University-Purdue University: Fort Wayne.

Lewitt, E., & Baker, L. (1996). Child indicators: Children in special education. *The Future of Children, 6*(1), 139-152.

Liddle, H. A. (1991). Training and supervision in family therapy: A comprehensive and critical analysis. In A. S. Gurman & D. P. Kniskern (Eds.), *Handbook of family therapy* (Vol. 2, pp. 638-697). New York: Brunner/Mazel.

Liese, B. S., & Beck, J. S. (1997). Cognitive therapy supervision. In C. E. Watkins Jr. (Ed.), *Handbook of psychotherapy supervision* (pp. 114-133). New York: John Wiley & Sons.

Lim, B., Plucker, J., & Nowak, J. (2001). We are what we weave? Guidelines for learning by web design. *Educational Technology, 41*(6), 23-27.

Lim, B-R. (2004). Challenges and issues in designing inquiry on the web. *British Journal of Educational Technology, 35*(5), 627-643.

Lin, G. Y. (2004). Social presence questionnaire of online collaborative learning: Development and validity. In *Proceedings of the 27th AECT Annual Convention*, (pp. 588-591). Bloomington, IN: Association for Educational Communications and Technology.

Lindlif, T. R., & Shatzer, M. J. (1998). Media ethnography in virtual space: Strategies, limits, and possibilities.

Journal of Broadcasting and Electronic Media, 42(2), 170-189.

Littleton, K., & Whitelock, D. (2005). The negotiation and co-construction of meaning and understanding within a postgraduate online learning community. *Learning Media and Technology. 30*(2), 147-164.

Löhner, S., Van Joolingen, W. R., Savelsbergh, E. R., & Van Hout-Wolters, B. (2005). Students' reasoning during modeling in an inquiry learning environment. *Computers in Human Behavior, 21*, 441-461.

Ludlow, B. L. (2002). Web-based staff development for early intervention personnel. *Infants and Young Children, 14*(3): 54-64.

Luppicini, R. (2006). Review of computer mediated communication research for education. *Instructional Science*. Retrieved from http://www.springerlink.com. ezaccess.libraries.psu.edu/content/v02314727u816016/fulltext.pdf

MacGeorge, E. L., Homan, S. R., Dunning, J. B., Elmore, D., Bodie, G. D., Evans, E., et al. (in press). Student evaluation of audience response technology: Influences of aptitude, learning, and learning conceptualizations. *Journal of Computing in Higher Education*.

Maier, F., & Größler, A. (2000). What are we talking about? A taxonomy of computer simulations to support learning. *Systems Dynamics Review, 16*(2), 135-148.

Main, J. (1987). The Russian who makes pros out of amateurs. *Fortune, 76*.

Mallen, M. J., Vogel, D. L., & Rochlen, A. B. (2005). The practical aspects of online counseling: Ethics, training, technology, and competency. *The Counseling Psychologist, 33*, 776-818.

Mallen, M. J., Vogel, D. L., Rochlen, A. B., & Day, S. X. (2005). Online counseling: Reviewing the literature from a counseling psychology framework. *The Counseling Psychologist, 33*, 819-871.

Malopinsky, L., Kirkley, J., Stein, R., & Duffy, T. (2000, October 26,). *An instructional design model for online problem based learning (PBL) environments: The learn-*

ing to teach with technology studio. Paper presented at the Association for Educational Communications and Technology Conference (AECT), Denver, Colorado.

Mangurian, L., Feldman, S., Clements, J., & Boucher, L. (2001). Analyzing and communicating scientific information. *Journal of College Science Teaching, 30*(7), 440-445.

Martinez, A., Dimitriadis, Y., Rubia, B., Gomez, E., Garrachon, L., & Marcos J. A. (2002). Studying social aspects of computer-supported collaboration with a mixed evaluation approach. In Stahl, G. (Ed.), *Proceedings of Computer Support for Collaborative Learning (CSCL) 2002 Conference*, Jan. 7-11, Boulder, Colorado, (pp. 631-632).Mahwah, NJ: Lawrence Erlbaum,

Marton, F., & Saljo, R. (1976). On qualitative differences in learning: 1. Outcome and process, *British Journal of Educational Psychology, 46*, 4-11.

Mason, R. (1991). Moderating educational computer conferencing. *DEOSNEWS, 1*(19). Retrieved January 1, 2007, from http://www.ed.psu.edu/acsde/deos/deosnews/deosnews1_19.asp

Mauzey, E., Harris, M. B. C., & Trusty, J. (2000). Comparing the effects of live supervision interventions on novice trainee anxiety and anger. *The Clinical Supervisor, 19*, 109-120.

Mayer, R. E., & Moreno, R. (2003). Nine ways to reduce cognitive load in multimedia learning. *Educational Psychologist, 38*(1), 43-52.

Mayer, R. E., Dow, G. T., & Mayer, S. (2003). Multimedial learning in an interactive self-explaining environment: What works in the design of agent-based microworlds? *Journal of Educational Psychology, 95*(4), 806-813.

McAdams, D. P. (1998). *Power, intimacy, and the life story: Personalogical inquiries into identity.* New York: Guilford.

McAfee, O. & Leong, D. J. (2002). *Assessing and guiding young children's development and learning (3rd Ed.).* Boston, MA: Allyn & Bacon.

McArdle, K., & McGowan, I. (1997). Professional development through reflective inquiry. In R. Hudson, S. Maslin-Prothero, & L. Oates, (Eds.), *Flexible learning in action case studies for higher education.* (pp. 61-66). London: Kogan Page.

McCarthey, S. J., & McMahon, S. (1992). From convention to invention: Three approaches to peer interactions during writing. In R. Hertz-Lazarowitz & N. Miller (Eds.), *Interaction in cooperative groups.* New York: Cambridge University Press.

McCollum, E. E., & Wetchler, J. L. (1995). In defense of case consultation: Maybe "dead" supervision isn't all that dead after all. *Journal of Marital and Family Therapy, 21,* 155-166.

McCroskey, J. C. (1970). Measures of communication-bound anxiety. *Speech Monographs, 37,* 269-277.

McDowell, L. (2002). Electronic information resources in undergraduate education: An exploratory study of opportunities for student learning and independence. *British Journal of Educational Technology, 33*(3), 255-266.

Mead, S., Spaulding, V., Sit, R., Meyer, B., & Walker, N. (1997). Effects of age and training on world wide web navigation strategies. In *Proceedings of the Human Factors and Ergonomics Society 41st Annual Meeting*, (pp. 152-156).

Mehrabian, A. (1969). Some referents and measures of nonverbal behavior. *Behavior Research Methods and Instrumentation, 1*(6), 205-207.

Miller, G. A. (1956). The magical number seven, plus or minus two: Some limits on our capacity for processing information. *The Psychological Review, 63*(2), 81-97.

Miller, K. L., Miller, S. M., & Evans, W. J. (2002). Computer-assisted live supervision in college counseling centers. *Journal of College Counseling, 5*(2), 187-192.

Miller, S. M., & Miller, K. L. (2000). Theoretical and practical considerations in the design of web-based instruction. In B. Abbey (Ed.), *Instructional and cognitive impacts of web-based education.* Hershey, PA: Idea Group Publishing.

Miller, S. M., & Miller, K. L., (1999). Using instructional theory to facilitate communication in web-based courses. *Educational Technology and Society, 2* (3). Retrieved from http://ifets.gmd.de/periodical/vol_3_99/miller. html

Milrad, M. (2002). Using construction kits, modeling tools and system dynamics simulations to support collaborative discovery learning. *Educational Technology & Society, 5*(4), 2002. Retrieved August 16, 2006, from http://ifets.ieee.org/periodical/vol_4_2002/milrad.html

Milrad, M., Spector, J. M., & Davidson, P. (2002). Model facilitated learning. In S. Naidu (Ed.), *eLearning: Technology and the development of learning and teaching*. London: Kogan Page Publishers.

Milsum, J.H. (1966). *Biological control systems analysis*. NY: McGraw-Hill.

Mindes, G. (2007). *Assessing young children (3rd Ed.)*. Upper Saddle River, NJ: Merrill/Prentic Hall.

Moody, J. (2004). Distance education. Why are the attrition rates so high? *The Quarterly Review of Distance Education, 5*(3), 205-210.

Moore, M. (1993). Theory of transactional distance. In D. Keegan (Ed.), *Theoretical principles of distance education* (pp. 23-38). New York: Routledge.

Moore, M. G. (1972). Learner autonomy: The second dimension of independent learning. *Convergence 5*(2). 76-88.

Moore, M. G. (1989). Three types of interaction. *The American Journal of Distance Education, 3*(2), 1-6.

Moore, M. G. (2005). Editorial: Blended learning. *The American Journal of Distance Education, 19*, 129-132.

Moorhouse, A., & Carr, A. (1999). *The correlates of phone-in frequency, duration and the number of suggestions made in live supervision. Journal of Family Therapy, 21*, 241-249. Retrieved November 30, 2006, from Academic Search Premier database.

Moreno, J. L. (1934). *Who shall survive? Foundations of sociometry, group psychotherapy, and sociodrama*.

Washington DC: Nervous and Mental Disease Publishing Co.

Morice, J. (2002). *Lights and wires: Effective e-learning*. Paper to the World Conference on Educational Multimedia, Hypermedia & Telecommunications, Denver, CO.

Morrell R., Mayhorn C., & Bennett J. (2000). A survey of world wide web use in middle-aged and older adults. *Human Factors 42*(2), 175-82.

Myrick, R. D., & Sabella, R. A. (1995). Cyberspace: A new place for counseling. *Elementary School Guidance & Counseling, 30*, 35-44.

National Board for Certified Counselors. (2005 copyright) *Standards for the practice of Internet counseling*. Retrieved November, 30, 2006, from http://www.nbcc. org/webethics2

National Education Association (2000). *A survey of traditional and distance learning higher education*. Washington, DC: Author

National Education Association. (1986). *What research says about class size*. Washington DC: Professional and Organizational Development/Research Division.

Navarro, P., & Shoemaker, J. (2000). Policy issues in the teaching of economics in cyberspace: Research design, course design, and research results. *Contemporary Economic Policy, 18*(3), 359-366.

Neukrug, E. S. (1991). Computer-assisted live supervision in counselor skills training. *Counselor Education & Supervision, 31*, 132-138.

Neuliep, J. W. (2002). Assessing the reliability and validity of the generalized ethnocentrism scale. *Journal of Intercultural Communication Research, 31*, 201-215.

Neuliep, J. W., & McCroskey, J. C. (1997). The development of a U.S. and generalized ethnocentrism scale. *Communication Research Reports, 14*, 385-398.

Neuliep, J. W., & McCroskey, J. C. (1997). The development of intercultural and interethnic communication apprehension scales. *Communication Research Reports, 14*, 385-398.

Nevgi, A., Virtanen, P., & Niemi, H. (2006). Supporting students to develop collaborative learning skills in technology-based environments. *British Journal of Educational Technology*, 37(6), 937-947.

Newman, D. (1990). Opportunities for research on the organizational impact of school computers. *Educational Researcher, 19(3)*, 8-13.

Nissenbaum, H. (1999). The meaning of anonymity in an information age. In A. Spinello & H. T. Tavani (Eds.), *Readings in cyberethics* (2nd ed.), (pp. 450-461). Sudbury, MA: Jones and Bartlett Publishers.

Nitko, A. J. (2001). *Educational assessment of students, 3rd Ed.* Upper Saddle River, NJ: Merrill Prentice-Hall.

Nitko, A. J. (2004) *Educational assessment of students, 4nd Ed.* Upper Saddle River, NJ: Pearson/Merrill Prentice-Hall.

Nunan, T. (1996, July). *Flexible Delivery—What is it and why is it a part of current educational debate?* Paper presented at the Higher Education Research and Development Society of Australasia annual Conference "Different Approaches: Theory and Practice in Higher Education." Perth, Western Australia. Retrieved March 15, 2006 from http://www.city.londonmet.ac.uk/deliberations/flex.learning/nunan_content.html

O'Neil, J. (1995). Teachers and technology: Potential and pitfalls. *Educational Leadership. 53(2),* 10-12.

Office of the Privacy Commissioner. (2006). Federal privacy law. Retrieved September 29, 2006, from http://www.privacy.gov.au/act/

Olt, M. R. (2002) Ethics and distance education: strategies for minimizing academic dishonesty in online assessment. *Journal of Distance Learning Administration.* Retrieved October 16, 2006, from http://www.westga.edu/~distance/ojdla/fall53/olt53.html

OSEP: Office of Special Education Programs. (2001). *Twenty-third Annual Report to Congress on the Implementation of the Individuals with Disabilities Education Act.* Retrieved December, 8, 2003, from http://www.ed.gov/offices/OSERS/OSEP/Products/OSEP2001AnlRpt

Oswald, D. F. (2002). A conversation with Glenn E. Snelbecker. *Educational Technology*, September-October, 59-62.

Palloff, R. M., & Pratt, K. (1999). *Building learning communities in cyberspace: Effective strategies for the online classroom.* San Francisco: Jossey-Bass.

Papert, S. (1993). *The children's machine: Rethinking school in the age of the computer.* New York, NY: Basic Books.

Park, D. C. (1999). The basic mechanisms accounting for age-related decline in cognitive function. In D.C. Park & N. Schwartz (Eds.), *Cognitive aging: A primer* (pp. 3-22). Philadelphia, PA: Psychology Press.

Parrott, L. III. (2003). *Counseling and psychotherapy.* Pacific Grove, CA: Brooks/Cole.

Pask, G. (1975). *Conversation, cognition, and learning.* New York: Elsevier.

Paulsen, M. F. (1995). Moderating Educational Computer Conferences. In Z. L. Berge and M. P. Collins (Eds.), *Computer-mediated communication and the online classroom. Vol. 3: Distance learning* (pp. 81-90). Cresskill, NJ: Hampton Press.

Pea, R. D. (1994). Seeing what we build together: Distributed multimedia learning environments for transformative communications. *Journal of the Learning Sciences, 3*(3), 285-299.

Pellegrino, J., Chudowsky, N., & Glaser, R. (Eds.). (2001). *Knowing what students know: The science and design of educational assessment.* Washington, DC: National Academy Press.

Pelz, B. (2004, June). (My) Three principles of effective online pedagogy. *Journal of Asynchronous Learning Networks*, 8(3), 33-46. Retrieved December 27, 2006, from http://www.sloan-c.org/publications/JALN/v8n3/v8n3_pelz.asp

Perkins, D. (1990). On knowledge and cognitive skills: A conversation with David Perkins. *Educational Leadership, 147*(5), 50-53.

Perkins, D. N., & Unger, C. (1999). Teaching and learning for understanding. In C.M. Reigeluth (Ed.), *Instructional-design theories and models,* Vol. 2, (pp. 91-114). Mahwah, NJ: Lawrence Erlbaum Associates.

Perse, E. I., Burton, P., Kovner, E., Lears, M.E., & Sen, R. J. (1992). Predicting computer-mediated communication in a college class. *Communication Research Reports, 9*(2), 161-170.

Popham, W. J. (1999). *Classroom assessment: What teachers need to know (2ⁿᵈ Ed.).* Boston, MA: Allyn & Bacon.

Poplin, M. (1988). Holistic/constructivist principles of the teaching and learning process: Implications for the field of learning disabilities. *Journal of Learning Disabilities, 21,* 401-416.

Poplin, M. (1988). The reductionistic fallacy in learning disabilities: Replicating the past by reducing the present. *Journal of Learning Disabilities, 21,* 389-400.

Poplin, M., Drew, D., & Gable, R. (1984). *Computer aptitude, literacy, and interest profile.* Austin, TX: PRO-ED.

Porter, C. E. (2004). A typology of virtual communities: A multi-disciplinary foundation for future research. *Journal of Computer-Mediated Communication, 10*(1). Retrieved December 2, 2004, from http:/www.ascusc.org/jcmc/vol10/issue1/porter.html.

Postmes, T., Spears, R., & Lea, M. (1998). Breaching or building social boundaries? SIDE-effects of computer-mediated communication. *Communication Research, 25,* 689-715.

Postmes, T., Spears, R., & Lea, M. (2002). Inter-group differentiation in computer-mediated communication: Effects of depersonalization. *Group Dynamics, 53*(6), 3-16.

Powers, W. G., Bodie, G. D., & Fitch-Hauser, M. (2005). Improving training outcomes: An innovative approach. *International Journal of Applied Training and Development, 1.* Retrieved April 1 from http://www.management-journals.com/journals/training/index.php.

Powers, W. G., Bodie, G. D., & Fitch-Hauser, M. (2006, April). *Initial testing of an online learning system in an extracurricular context.* Paper presented at the annual convention of the Southern States Communication Association, Dallas/Fort-Worth, TX.

Race, P. (1996) Practical pointers to flexible learning. Retrieved March 15, 2006, from http://www.city.londonmet.ac.uk/deliberations/flex.learning/race_content.html

Radcliffe, D. F. (2002). Technological and pedagogical convergence between work-based and campus-based Learning. *Educational Technology & Society, 5*(2). Retrieved March 15, 2006, from http://ifets.ieee.org/periodical/vol_2_2002/radcliffe.html

Rainbow, S. W., & Sadler-Smith, E. (2003). Attitudes to computer-assisted learning amongst business and management students. *British Journal of Educational Technology. 34,* 615-624.

Reber, A. S. (1967). Implicit learning of artificial grammars. *Journal of Verbal Learning and Verbal Behaviour, 5,* 855-863

Reeves, T. C. (2000). Alternative assessment approaches for online learning environments in higher education. *Journal of Educational Computing Research, 23*(1), 101-111.

Reffay, C., & Chanier, T. (2003). How social network analysis can help to measure cohesion in collaborative distance-learning. In B. Wasson, S. Ludvigsen, & U. Hoppe (Eds.), *Computer-supported collaborative learning, designing for change in networked learning environments.* In *Proceedings of the International Conference on Computer Support for Collaborative Learning 2003* Dordretch, *(Vol. 2* pp. 343-352). The Netherlands: Kluwer Academic Publishers.

Reiff, H., & Gerber, P. (1994). Social/emotional and daily living issues for adults with learning disabilities. In P.J. Gerber & H.B. Reiff (Eds.), *Learning disabilities and adulthood,* (pp. 72-81.)

Reigeluth, C. (1998). *Instructional design theories and models: A new paradigm of instructional theory. Volume II.* Mahwah, NJ: Erlbaum.

Reio, T. G., & Crim, S. J. (2006). *The emergence of social presence as an overlooked factor in asynchronous online learning.* Paper presented at the Academy of Human Resource Development International Conference (AHRD). Columbus, OH.

Reisetter, M., & Boris, G. (2004). What works: Student perception of effective elements in online learning. *Quarterly Review of Distance Education, 5*(4), 277-291.

Rennie, F. (2003). The use of flexible learning resources for geographically distributed rural learners. *Distance Education, 4(1)*, 25-39.

Rezmierski, V., & Soules, A. (2000) Security, anonymity: The debate over user authentication and information access. *Educause Review, March-April*, 22-30. Retrieved December 27, 2006, from http://www.educause.edu/ir/library/pdf/ERM0022.pdf

Rheingold, H. (1994). *The virtual community: Finding connection in a computerised world.* London: Secker & Warburg.

Rich, E. (1979). User modeling via stereotypes. *Cognitive Science, 3*, 329-354.

Richardson, D. C., & Richardson, J. S. (1992). The kinemage: A tool for scientific communication. *Protein Science 1*, 3-9.

Richardson, J. C., & Swan, K. S. (2003). Examining social presence in online courses in relation to students' perceived learning and satisfaction. *Journal of Asynchronous Learning Networks, 7*(1), 68-88.

Rickards, L. D. (1984). Verbal interaction and supervisor perception in counseling supervision. *Journal of Counseling Psychology, 31*, 262-265.

Ritchie, D., & Volkl, C. (2000). Effectiveness of two generative learning strategies in the science classroom. *School Science and Mathematics, 100*(2), 83-89.

Roberts, N. G., Andersen, D. F., Deal, R. M., Grant, M. S., & Shaffer, W. A. (1983). *Introduction to computer simulation: The system dynamics modeling approach.* Reading, MA: Addison-Wesley.

Rogers, C. (1965). *Client-centered therapy.* London: Constable.

Rogers, C. (1969). *Freedom to learn.* Columbus, OH: Merrill.

Rogers, C. (1969). *Freedom to learn.* Columbus: Merrill Publishing Co.

Rogers, C. R. (1969). *Freedom to learn.* Columbus, OH: Merrill.

Rosenberg, M. (2001). *E-Learning. Strategies for delivering knowledge in the digital age.* New York: Merrill Lynch.

Roszkowski, M. J., Devlin, S. J., Snelbecker, G. E., Aiken, R. M., & Jacobsohn, H. G. (1988). Validity and temporal stability issues regarding two measures of computer aptitude and attitudes. *Educational and Psychological Measurement, 48*, 1029-1035.

Rourke, L., & Anderson, T. (2002). Exploring social presence in computer conferencing. *Journal of Interactive Learning Research, 13(3)*, 259-275.

Rourke, L., Anderson, T., Garrison, D., & Archer, W. (1999). Assessing social presence in asynchronous text-based computer conferencing. *Journal of Distance Education, 14*(2), 50-71.

Rourke, L., Anderson, T., Garrison, D.R., & Archer, W. (2001). Assessing social presence in asynchronous text-based computer conferencing. *Journal of Distance Education, 14*(2). Retrieved September 1, 2006, from http://cade.athabascau.ca/vol14.2/rourke_et_al.html

Rousseau, G., Jamieson, B., Rogers, W., Mead, S., & Sit, R. (1998). Assessing the usability of online library systems. *Behaviour & Information Technology, 17*, 274-281.

Rovai, A. A. (2002). A preliminary look at the structural differences of higher education classroom communities in traditional an ALN courses. *Journal of Asynchronous Learning Networks, 6*(1), 41-56.

Rovai, A. P. & Baker, J. D. (2005, Spring). Gender differences in online learning. *Quarterly Review of Distance Education, 6*(1), 31-45. Retrieved June 6, 2006, from EBSCO Full text Database.

Rowe, N. (2004). Cheating in online student assessment: Beyond plagiarism. *Journal of Distance Learning Administration*. Retrieved September, 23, 2006, from http://www.westga.edu/%7Edistance/ojdla/summer72/rowe72.html

Rubin, R. B., Plamgreen, P., & Sypher, H. (1994). *Communication research measures*. New York: Guilford.

Rumelhart, D. E. (1980). Schemata: The building blocks of cognition. In R. J. Shapiro, B. C. Bruce and W. F. Brewer (Eds.). *Theoretical issues in reading comprehension*. Hillsdale, NJ: Erlbaum.

Russell, T. (1999). *The no significant difference phenomenon*. Montgomery, AL: International Distance Learning Certification Center.

Ryan, K., & Cooper, J. M. (2004). *Those who can, teach (10ᵗʰ Ed.)*. Boston, MA: Houghton Mifflin Company.

Salmon, G. (2000). *E-moderating: The key to teaching and learning online*. London: Kogan Page.

Salpeter, J. (2003). Web literacy and critical thinking: A teacher's tool kit. *Technology and Learning, 23*(8), 22-34.

Samarawickrema, R. G. (2005). Determinants of learner readiness for flexible learning: Some preliminary findings. *Distance Education, 26(1),* 49-66.

Saskatchewan Education. (1991). *Instructional approaches: A framework for professional practice*. Regina, SK: Saskatchewan Education.

Scherl, C. R., & Haley, J. (2000). Computer monitor supervision: A clinical note. *The American Journal of Family Therapy, 28*, 275-282.

Schunk, D. H. (2000). *Learning theories: An educational perspective*. New Jersey: Prentice-Hall.

Scott, C. R. (1999). Communication technology and group communication. In L.R. Frey, D.S. Gouran, & M.S. Poole (Eds.), *The handbook of group communication theory and research* (pp.432-472). Thousand Oaks, CA: Sage.

Scott, J. (2000). *Social network analysis: A handbook*. Second edition. London: Sage Publications.

Sellnow, D. D., Child, J. T., & Ahlfeldt, S. L. (2005). Textbook technology supplements: What are they good for? *Communication Education, 54*, 243-253.

Selye, H. (1956). *The stress of life*. New York: McGraw-Hill.

Selye, H. (Ed.) (1980). *Selye's guide to stress research*. New York: Reinhold.

Sener, J. (2004). Escaping the comparison trap: Evaluating online learning on its own terms. *Innovate, 1*(2). Retrieved December 7, 2004, from http://innovateonline.info/print.php?id=11.

Shachar, M., & Neumann, Y. (2003). Differences between traditional and distance education academic performances: A meta-analytic approach. *International Review of Research in Open and Distance Learning, 4*(2), Retrieved January 15, 2007, from http://www.irrodl.org/content/v4.2/

Shaw, H. E., & Shaw, S. F. (2006). Critical ethical issues in online counseling: Assessing current practices with an ethical intent checklist. *Journal of Counseling & Development, 84*, 41-53.

Shea, V. (1994). *Netiquette*. Retrieved June 7, 2006, from http://www.albion.com/netiquette/corerules.html

Sherry, L. (1996). Issues in distance learning. *International Journal of Educational Telecommunications, 1*(4), 337-365. Retrieved September 11, 2006, from http://carbon.cudenver.edu/~lsherry/pubs/issues.html

Short, J. A., Williams, E., & Christie, B. (1976). *The social psychology of telecommunications*. New York: John Wiley & Sons.

Short, J. A., Williams, E., & Christie, B. (1976). *The social psychology of telecommunications*. London: John Wiley & Sons.

Shreve, G., & Zeng, M. L. (2003). Integrating resource metadata and domain markup in an nsdl collection. In *DC-2003: Proceedings of the International DCMI Metadata Conference and Workshop* (pp. 223-229). Seattle, Washington.

Silverman, D. (2001). *Interpreting qualitative data: Method for analysing talk, text, and interaction.* London: Sage.

Simon, H. (1969). *The sciences of the artificial*, Cambridge, MA: MIT Press.

Simon, H. A. (1981). Herbert Simon: A software psychologist who isn't. *Psychological Association Monitor,* 15.

Simon, H. A., & Newell, A. (1971). Human problem solving: The state of the theory in 1970. *American Psychologist, 26,* 145-159.

Simonson, M. (2004). Class size: Where is the research? *Distance Learning, 1*(4), 56.

Simora, F. (Ed.). (1991). *The Bowker annual library and book trade almanac* (36 Ed.). New Providence, NJ: R. R. Bowker.

Sims, R. (2000). An interactive conundrum: Constructs of interactivity and learning theory. *Australian Journal of Educational Technology, 16*(1), 45-57. Retrieved May 17, 2006, from http://www.ascilite.org.au/ajet/ajet16/sims.html

Smith, C. (1997). Teaching by e-mail. In R. Hudson, S. Maslin-Prothero, & L. Oates, (Eds.), *Flexible learning in action case studies for higher education.* (pp. 34-38). London: Kogan Page.

Snelbecker, G. E. (1967). Influence of therapeutic techniques on college students' perceptions of therapists. *Journal of Consulting Psychology, 31,* 614-618.

Snelbecker, G. E. (1974). *Learning theory, instructional theory, and psychoeducational design.* New York: McGraw-Hill.

Snelbecker, G. E. (1984). *"Functional Relevance": Key to successful computer applications.* Unpublished manuscript. Wyndmoor, PA: Snelbecker, G.E.

Snelbecker, G. E. (1985). *Learning theory, instructional theory, and psychoeducational design.* Latham, MD: University Press of America. (Reprint of book originally published by McGraw-Hill in 1974).

Snelbecker, G. E. (1986). *Will computers survive in education? Some practical suggestions.* Luncheon Address at the Fifth Annual Microcomputer Conference, Sagninaw, Michigan.

Snelbecker, G. E. (1988). Heider's comprehensive contributions. *Contemporary Psychology, 33,* 925.

Snelbecker, G. E. (1989). *Instructional design, teachers, and functional relevance.* Paper presented in the symposium "Instructional Design and the Public Schools: A Conversation with the Authors of the Journal of Instructional Development. Special Issue." Presented at the Annual Meeting of the Association for Educational Communications and Technology, Dallas, TX.

Snelbecker, G. E. (1991). *Global concepts: An instructional perspective—differentiated instructional systems design.* Presented in Symposium at the National Conference of the American Society for Training and Development, San Francisco, CA.

Snelbecker, G. E. (1993). Practical ways for using theories and innovations to improve training. In G. M. Piskurich (Ed.), *The ASTD handbook of instructional technology* (pp. 19.3-19.26). New York: McGraw-Hill.

Snelbecker, G. E., Bhote, N. P., Wilson, J. D., & Aiken, R. M. (1995). Elementary versus secondary school teachers retaining to teach computer science. *Journal of Research on Computing in Education, 27*(3), 336-347.

Snelbecker, G. E., Bhote-Edjulee, N. P., Aiken, R. M., & Wilson, J. D. (1992). *Demographic variables, experience, aptitudes and attitudes as predictors of teachers' learning about computers.* Paper presented at the Annual Meeting of the American Educational Research Association, San Francisco, CA. (ERIC Document Reproduction Service No. 344 877, SP 033 785).

Snelbecker, G. E., Miller, S. M., & Zheng, R. (2004). Thriving, not merely surviving, with technology in education: Implications for teachers, administrators, policy makers, and other educators. *Journal of Christian Education and Information Technology, 6,* 13-53.

Snelbecker, G. E., Miller, S. M., & Zheng, R. (2006). Learning sciences and instructional design: Observations, reflections, and suggestions for further exploration. *Educational Technology, 46*(4), 22-27.

Snelbecker, G. E., Milier, S. M., & Zheng, R. (2007). Function relevance and online design. In R. Zheng & P. Ferris (Eds.), *Understanding online instructional modeling: Theories and practice.* Hershey, PA: Idea Group.

Snelbecker, G.E. (1999). Some thoughts about theories, perfection, and instruction. In C.M. Reigeluth (Ed.), *Instructional-design theories and models: A new paradigm of instructional theory, bolume II*, (pp. 31-50). Mahwah, NJ: Erlbaum.

Spinello, R. A. (2003). Cyberethics; morality and law in cyberspace (2nd Ed.). Sudbury, MA: Jones and Bartlett Publishers, Inc.

Sproull, L., & Kiesler, S. (1986). Reducing social context cues: Electronic mail in organizational communication. *Management Science, 32*, 1492-1513.

Stacey, E. (2002). Quality online participation: establishing social presence. *Research in Distance Education 5: Revised papers from the 5th Research in Distance Education Conference*, (pp. 138-153). Deakin University, Geelong.

Stahl, G. (2004). Building collaborative knowing. Elements of a social theory of CSCL. In Strijbos, J. W., Kirschner, P. A. & Martens, R. L. (Eds.). *What we know about CSCL: And implementing it in higher education* (pp. 53-86). Amsterdam, Kluwer.

Stoltenberg, D. D., McNeill, B., & Delworth, U. (1998). *IDM supervision: An integrated developmental model for supervising counselors and therapists.* San Francisco: Jossey-Bass.

Stone, S., Poplin, M., Johnson, J., & Simpson, O. (1992). *Non-traditional talents of the learning disabled: Divergent thinking and feeling.* Unpublished manuscript, Claremont Graduate School.

Stothard, S. (1994). The nature and treatment of reading comprehension difficulties in children. *Reading development and dyslexia.* Retrieved September 16, 2006, from PsycINFO database.

Strauss, A., & Corbin, J. (1998) *Basics of qualitative research: Techniques and procedures for developing*

grounded theory. Thousand Oaks, CA: Sage Publications.

Sundland, S. M. (1960). *Psychotherapists' self-perceptions, and patients' perceptions of their therapists.* Unpublished doctoral dissertation, The Ohio State University.

Supreme Court of the United States. (2001, October). *Gonzaga University and Roberta S. League v. John Doe.* Case No. 01-679. Retrieved December 28, 2006, from http://www.aclu.org/FilesPDFs/gonzaga.pdf

Swan, K., & Shih, L. F. (2005). On the nature and development of social presence in online course discussions. *Journal of Asynchronous Learning Networks, 9*(3), 115-136.

Swanson, H. (1993). Working memory in learning disability subgroups. *Journal of Experimental Child Psychology, 56*, 87–114.

Swanson, L. (1999, May). *Intervention research for students with learning disabilities: A meta-analysis of treatment outcomes.* Paper presented at the meeting of Keys to Successful Learning: A National Summit on Research in Learning Disabilities, Washington, D.C.

Swinth, K. R., & Blascovich, J. (2002, October). *Perceiving and responding to others: Human-human and human-computer social interaction in collaborative virtual environments.* Paper presented at the 5th Annual International Workshop PRESENCE 2002, Porto, Portugal. Retrieved January 28, 2007, from http://www.temple.edu/ispr/prev_conferences/proceedings/2002/Final%20papers/Swinth%20&%20Blascovich.pdf

Tammelin, M. (1998). From telepresence to social presence: The role of presence in a network-based learning environment. In Tella, S. (Ed). *Aspects of media education: Strategic imperatives in the information age.* University of Helsinki. Retrieved September 14, 2006, from http://hkkk.fi/%7Etammelin/MEP8.tammelin.html

Tarver, S., Ellsworth, P., & Rounds, D. (1980). Figural and verbal creativity in learning disabled and non-learning-disabled children. *Learning Disability Quarterly, 3*, 11-18.

Tavangarian, D., Leypold, M., Nolting, K., Roser, M., & Voigt, D. (2004). Is e-learning the solution for individual learning? *Electronic Journal of e-Learning, 2*(2), 273-280.

Tehan, R. (2005, December). Personal data security breaches: Context and incident summaries. *CRS Report for Congress.* Retrieved December 28, 2006, from http://digital.library.unt.edu/govdocs/crs//data/2005/upl-meta-crs-8258/RL33199_2005Dec16.pdf

Tennyson, R., & Schott, F. (1997). Instructional design theory, research, and models. In R. Tennyson, F. Schott, N. Seel, & S. Dijkstra (Eds.), *Instructional design: International perspectives. Vol. 1.* Mahwah, NJ: Erlbaum.

Thomas, S., & Busby, S. (2003). Do industry collaborative projects enhance students' learning? *Education & Training, 45,* 226-235.

Tolmie A., & Boyle, J. (2000). Factors influencing the success of computer mediated communication (CMC) environments in university teaching: A review and case study. *Computers and Education, 34,* 119-140.

Trevino, L. K., Daft, R. L., & Lengel, R. H. (1990). Understanding managers' media choices: A symbolic interactionist perspective. In J. Fulk & C. Steinfield (Eds.), *Organizations and communication technology* (pp. 71-94). Newbury Park, CA: Sage.

Trevino, L. K., Lengel, R. H., & Daft, R. L. (1987). Media symbolism, media richness, and media choice in organizations. *Communication Research, 14,* 553-574.

Tu, C., & McIsaac, M. (2002). The relationship of social presence and interaction in online classes. *The American Journal of Distance Education, 16*(3), 131-150.

Turkle, S. (1997). *Life on the screen: Identity in the age of the internet.* New York, NY: Touchstone.

U. S. Census Bureau. (1990). *Statistical abstract of the United States 1990* (110 Ed.). Washington, DC: Bureau of the Census.

U. S. Census Bureau. (1992). *Statistical abstract of the United States 1992* (112 Ed.). Washington, DC: Bureau of the Census.

UCLA Center for Communication Policy. (2003). *Surveying the digital future: the UCLA Internet report, year three, UCLA Center for Communication Policy.* Retrieved May 12, 2003, from UCLA Center for Communication Policy Web site: http://www.ccp.ucla.edu/pdf/UCLA-Internet-Report-Year-Three.pdf

Uebbing, S. J. (1995). *Planning for technology.* The Executive Educator, *17(11),* 21-23.

United States Department of Education. (2006). *Family Educational Rights and Privacy Act (FERPA).* Retrieved December 28, 2006, from http://www.ed.gov/policy/gen/guid/fpco/ferpa/index.html

Van Merrienboer, J.J.G. (1997). *Training complex cognitive skills: A four-component instructional design model for technical training.* Englewood Cliffs, NJ: Educational Technology Publ.

Van Merrienboer, J.J.G., Clark, R. E., & de Croock, M. B. (2002). Blueprints for complex learning: The 4C/ID-model. *Educational Technology Research and Development Journal, 50*(2), 39-64.

Velasco, C., & Mohamad, Y. (2002, May). *Web services and user/device profiling for accessible internet services provision.* Paper presented at CSUN's Seventeenth Annual International Conference: "Technology and Persons with Disabilities." Los Angeles, CA.

Viegas, F. B., Boyd, D., Nguyen, D. H., Potter, J., & Donath, J. (2003). Digital artifacts for remembering and storytelling: *PostHistory* and *social network fragments*. Retrieved March 21, 2004, http://web.media.mit.edu/~fviegas/papers/posthistory_snf.pdf

Vygotsky, L. (1978). *Mind in society.* Cambridge, MA: Harvard University Press.

Wagner, E.D. (1997, Fall). Interactivity: From agents to outcomes. In T.E. Cyrs, (Ed.), *New Directions for Teaching and Learning, 71,* 19-26. Jossey Bass.

Walther, J. B. (1992). Interpersonal effects in computer-mediated interaction: A relational perspective. *Communication Research, 19,* 52-90.

Walther, J. B. (1997). Group and interpersonal effects in international computer-mediated collaboration. *Human Communication Research, 23*, 342-369.

Wantz, R. A., Tromski, D. M., Mortsolf, C. J., Yoxtheimer, G., Brill, S., & Cole, A. (2003). Incorporating distance learning into counselor education program: A research study. In J. W. Bloom & G. R. Walz (Eds.), *Cybercounseling and cyberlearning: An encore.* (ERIC Document Reproduction Service No. ED 481146).

Wasserman, S., & Faust, K. (1994). *Social network analysis: Methods and applications.* New York: Cambridge University Press.

Wegerif, R. (1998). The social dimension of asynchronous learning networks. *Journal of Asynchronous Learning Networks, 2*(1). Retrieved July 23, 2003, from http://www.aln.org/alnweb/journal/vol2_issue1/wegerif.htm

Weigel, V. B. (2002). *Deep learning for a digital age.* San Francisco, CA: Jossey Bass, a Wiley Company.

Westerman, S. J., Davies, D. R., Glendon, A. I., Stammers, R. B., & Matthews, G. (1995).

Wheatley, G. (1991). Constructivist perspectives on science and mathematics learning. *Science Education, 75*, 9-21.

White, N. (2001). *Community member roles and types.* Retrieved August 12, 2006, from http://www.fullcirc.com/community/memberroles.htm

Wikipedia: The Free Encyclopedia. (2007). Retrieved January 15, 2007 from http://en.wikipedia.org/wiki/Rule_of_thumb

Wilensky, U., & Resnick, M. (1999). Thinking in levels: A dynamic systems approach to making sense of the world. *Journal of Science Education and Technology, 8*(1), 3-19.

Willging, P. A. (2004). Using social network analysis to study teamwork dynamics. In T. N. Garavan, E. Collins, M. J. Morley, R. Carbery, C. Gubbins, & L. Prendeville (Eds.), *Proceedings of the Fifth UFHRD/AHRD Conference.* University of Limerick, Ireland.

Williams, B., Blowers, P., & Goldberg, J. (2004). Integrating information literacy skills into engineering courses to produce lifelong learners. Retrieved June 9, 2006, from http://www.asee.org/acPapers/2004-2405_Final.pdf

Wilson, B. (1999). *The dangers of theory-based design.* Retrieved from http://www.cudenver.edu/~brent_wilson/dangers.html

Wilson, B. G, & Jonassen, D. H. (1989). Hypertext and instructional design: Some preliminary guidelines. *Performance Improvement Quarterly, 2*(3), 34-39.

Wilson, B. G., Jonassen, D. H., & Cole, P. (1993). Cognitive approaches to instructional design. In G. M. Piskurich (Ed.), *The ASTD handbook of instructional technology* (pp. 21.1-21.22). New York: McGraw-Hill. Retrieved from http://www.cudenver.edu/~brent_wilson/training.html

Windschitl, M. (1996). Student epistemological beliefs and conceptual change activities: How do pair members affect each other? *Journal of Science Education and Technology, 6*, 24-38.

Winn, W., & Snyder, D. (1996). Cognitive perspectives in psychology. In D. Johassen (Ed.). *Handbook of research for educational communications and technology* (pp. 112-142). New York: Simon and Schuster Macmillan.

Witherby, A. (1997). Peer mentoring through peer-assisted study sessions. In R. Hudson, S. Maslin-Prothero, & L. Oates, (Eds.), *Flexible learning in action case studies for higher education.* (pp. 28-33). London: Kogan Page.

Witt, P. L., & Schrodt, P. (2006). The influence of instructional technology use and teacher immediacy on student affect for teacher and course. *Communication Reports, 19*, 1-15.

Wittrock, M. C. (1992). Generative learning processes of the brain. *Educational Psychologist, 27*(4), 531-41.

Wolstenholme, E. (1990). *System enquiry: A system dynamic approach.* New York: Wiley & Sons.

Woods, R., & Ebersole, S. (2003). Social networking in the online classroom: Foundations of effective online learning. *EJournal, 12-13*(1). Retrieved August 28, 2003, from http://www.acs.ucalgary.ca/ejournal/archive/v12-13/v12-13n1woods_print.html

Woolfolk, A. (2001). *Educational psychology (8ᵗʰ ed.).* Needham Heights, MA: Allyn & Bacon.

Word, E., Johnston, J., Bain, H., Fulton, D., Boyd-Zaharias, J., Lintz, M., et al.(1990). *Student/Teacher Achievement Ratio (STAR): Tennessee's K-3 class-size study.* Nashville: Tennessee State Dept. of Education.

Wu, H., de Kort, E., & De Bra, P. (2001). A reference architecture for adaptive hypermedia systems. In *Proceedings of the 12th ACM Conference on Hypertext and Hypermedia,* (pp.141-150). Århus, Denmark.

Wu, Y. B., & Chen, X. (2005). Assessing student learning with automated text processing techniques. *Journal of Asynchronous Learning Networks, 9*(3). Retrieved November 12, 2006, from http://www.sloanc.org/publications/jaln/v9n3/v9n3_wu.asp

Yang, H. (2001). Mission possible: Project-based learning preparing graduate students for technology. In C. Crawford et al. (Eds.), *Proceedings of Society for Information Technology and Teacher Education International Conference 2001* (pp. 2855-2857). Chesapeake, VA: AACE.

Yang, H. (2006, October). *STEP on social presence for online teaching and learning.* Paper presented at the AECT Annual Convention, Dallas, TX.

Yang, H. (2007). Establishing social presence for online collaborative learning: STEP and practices. In R. Zheng & P. S. Ferris (Eds.), *Understanding online instructional modeling: Theories and practices.* Hershey, PA: Idea Group Publishing.

Yang, H., & Maina, F. (2004). STEP on developing active learning community for an online course. In C. Crawford et al. (Eds.), *Proceedings of Society for Information Technology and Teacher Education International Conference 2004* (pp. 751-760). Chesapeake, VA: AACE.

Yang, S. C. (1996). Designing instructional applications using constructive hypermedia. *Educational Technology,* November-December, 45-50.

Zadeh, L. (1976). A fuzzy-algorithmic approach to the definition of complex or imprecise concepts. *International Journal Man-Machine Studies, 8,* 249-291.

Zadeh, L. (1989). Knowledge representation in fuzzy logic. *IEEE Transactions on Knowledge and Data Engineering, 1,* 89-100.

Zhu, E. (2006). Interaction and cognitive engagement: An analysis of four asynchronous online discussions. *Instructional Science, 34,* 451–480.

About the Contributors

Bobbe Baggio is an author, consultant, and educator with more than 25 years of experience in education and information technologies. Proficient in all areas of instructional design for online learning from needs analysis to application development, she serves clients from the corporate, government, and higher education sectors. She believes in research-based instructional design and her priority is to provide products and services that match the learners' needs. Her prior experience includes being a senior scientist, management consultant, director of IT, VP of software development, sales, and marketing representative, and educator. Her education includes a BA from Waynesburg College, MA from West Virginia University, MS from Lehigh University, and PhD candidate at Capella University.

Yoany Beldarrain is an author and conference presenter on the topic of distance education. She has more than 15 years experience in the K-20 field, covering curriculum, instruction, and supervision. She is an instructional leader at Florida Virtual School, where she is responsible for the direct supervision of online instructors. She believes in empowering instructors and students to become agents of change within the online learning environment. She is a Fulbright-Hays Scholarship recepient and a PhD candidate at Capella University specializing in Instructional Design for Online Learning. She earned her MS in educational leadership from Nova Southeastern University, and her BS in elementary education from Florida International University.

Graham Bodie (MA, Auburn University, 2002) is a third-year doctoral student at Purdue University who has already achieved distinction as a researcher in the areas of listening, information processing, and communication pedagogy. His work on these topics has been presented at regional, national, and international conferences and has been published in several journals. Graham currently serves as the member-at-large, special projects, and chair of the Research Committee with the International Listening Association. Prior to returning to academics, Graham worked as research analyst for Godwin Group Advertising, where he employed quantitative and qualitative methodologies to effectively answer client questions and concerns which ultimately served as part of client marketing strategies and/or branding efforts.

Brian H. Cameron is a professor of Practice in the College of Information Sciences and Technology at The Pennsylvania State University. Prior to joining Penn State, he was director of Information Technology for WorldStor, Inc., a storage service provider (SSP) in Fairfax, VA. He has also held a variety of technical and managerial positions within IBM and Penn State. His primary research and consulting interests include enterprise integration, storage networking, emerging wireless technologies, and the use of simulations and gaming in education. He has designed and taught a variety of courses on topics that include networking, enterprise integration, storage networking, project management, and IT consulting.

Avner Caspi received his doctorate in cognitive psychology at Tel Aviv University. His research interests include instructional theory, the role of dialogue in instructional systems and socio-psychological aspects of Internet use.

Eran Chajut received his doctorate in cognitive psychology at Tel Aviv University. His research agenda includes selective attention, stress, attitude change and decision making. He has co-authored several university texts including *Theories of Learning and Instruction*. In addition, he serves as an advisor for the development of computer games for cognitive training.

Roy B. Clariana is an associate professor in the College of Education at The Pennsylvania State University. In this role, Dr. Clariana pursues his scholarly interests and teaches graduate-level courses on evaluating learning outcomes, integrating technology in schools, instructional design, designing Web-based instruction, and project management. Dr. Clariana is an accomplished writer and researcher. His primary interests lie in the area of modeling technologies, computer-based instruction, the representation of structural knowledge, and feedback. Dr. Clariana has numerous awards, most recent and notable is the Fulbright Teaching and Research Award, Oulu, Finland, January-June, 2005.

Michele R. Cummins is a senior research associate for Social Science Research and Evaluation, Inc. (SSRE). Her research, publication, and presentation experience addresses diverse areas such as youth health behavior, substance use and abuse, domestic violence, foster and adoptive care, peer leadership, and assessing program fidelity. Ms. Cummins leads SSRE's student survey division and has consulted to over 40 communities on the design, implementation, analysis, and reporting of data from student health surveys. She has worked with local agencies, state agencies, foundations, and federal agencies such as the Center for Substance Abuse Prevention, the Center for Mental Health Services, the National Institute of Justice, and the National Highway Traffic Safety Administration. Currently evaluating multiple federal training and technical assistance centers, Ms. Cummins provides training and technical assistance on issues related to prevention, needs assessment, and evaluation, covering topics such as evidence-based prevention, program fidelity and adaptation, logic modeling, evaluation design, data collection methods, and effective data presentation.

Bruce J. Diamond, (PhD) is an associate professor at William Paterson University in the Department of Psychology. Affiliations include Kessler Institute for Rehabilitation, Kessler Medical Rehabilitation Research and Education Corporation and UMDNJ-NJ Medical School. Dr. Diamond (along with Dr. Shreve) was PI on Demonstration Project D2: "Telerehabilitation: Social Support and A Test of Cognitive Rehabilitation on the Internet" (NIDRR). Dr. Diamond has published on the topics of cognition, telerehabilitation, and information technology accessibility. He is a clinical neuropsychologist specializing in brain disorders and rehabilitation with research interests in the cognitive neuroscience of memory, executive function and information processing.

Scott W. Formica is a research associate at Social Science Research & Evaluation, Inc., (SSRE). He has extensive experience in designing, administering, and managing multiple research projects. Mr. Formica has published articles on a variety of public health and prevention issues such as booster seat use in low-income communities and substance abuse prevention programming in middle schools. He has spoken at numerous federal conferences and has facilitated small groups of grantees on evaluation-related topics such as basic research designs, developing logic models, assessing program fidelity, and using evaluation data for sustainability. Current projects include evaluations of two training and technical assistance centers funded by the Substance Abuse and Mental Health Service Administration's Center for Mental Health Services, and the evaluation of the Massachusetts Strategic Prevention Framework State Incentive Grant funded by SAMHSA's Center for Substance Abuse Prevention. Mr. Formica has also consulted to and evaluated grants from the U.S. Department of Education.

Deb Gearhart is the director of e-education services at Dakota State University in Madison, South Dakota. She has over 20 years of experience in distance education. Before joining Dakota State she spent 10 years with the Department of Distance Education at Penn State. Dr. Gearhart manages the e-learning program, with online degree programs and the University's videoconferencing courses. She earned a MEd in adult education with a distance education emphasis and an MPA in public administration, both from Penn State. She completed her PhD program in education from Capella University. She is an assistant professor of educational technology at DSU and teaches distance education courses in the masters in educational technology program.

Paul Giguere (MS, EdD) is director of distance learning in Friedman School of Nutrition, Science and Policy, Tufts University. He was senior scientist for Education Development Center, Inc. (EDC) in Newton, Massachusetts, responsible for investigating and implementing distance learning systems, theories, and practices with regard to the delivery of training and professional development for projects primarily based in the Center for Health and Human Development Programs (HHD) at EDC. Dr. Giguere is also on the faculty of UMass Online where he teaches and lectures on such topics as computer science theories and the ethical issues of technology in society. He also serves as a principal investigator of a National Science Foundation-funded project entitled *"A distributed hybrid approach for creating a community of practice using NSF funded manufacturing engineering technology curriculum modules."*

Paul Gorsky received his doctorate in science education from Technion, Israel Institute of Technology. His R&D interests include instructional theory, instructional technologies, the role of dialogue in instructional systems, and the development of intelligent, flexible and adaptive instructional systems. In addition, Dr. Gorsky founded and chairs a nationwide not-for-profit organization, "Science and Reasoning 2000," which offers extra-curricular, hands-on, inquiry based activities to gifted and "science-oriented youth" throughout Israel.

Wayne Harding (EdM, PhD) is director of projects for Social Science Research & Evaluation, Inc. (SSRE). Dr. Harding has over 30 years of research experience. He has been an investigator on grants and/or contracts from such U.S. agencies as The National Institute on Drug Abuse, The National Institute on Alcoholism and Alcohol Abuse, United States Education Department, the Centers for Disease Control and Prevention, National Highway Traffic Safety Administration, The National Institute on Mental Health, The National Institute of Justice, the Health Resources and Services Administration, the Center for Substance Abuse Prevention, and the Center for Mental Health Services. He has authored over 120 research reports and made over 150 presentations to both professional and general audiences.

Margaret Fitch-Hauser is an associate professor and former chair of the Department of Communication and Journalism at Auburn University. She is a published scholar in the field of listening and information processing and has served as an expert witness in several fraud litigations. Her current research efforts focus on cultural differences in listening related measures and situations. Professor Fitch-Hauser also has 30 years experience as a consultant, trainer, and coach. She has worked with people from a variety of organizations ranging from large multinational firms to small businesses. Margaret specializes in helping clients discover and develop their own communication and relationship styles and strengths. She does this by listening, diagnosing, and working with the client to problem solve and strategically map a path to improvement.

Stephanie Huffman is an assistant professor at the University of Central Arkansas. Her primary areas of scholarship include educational, informational, and instructional technology, library science, and technology leadership.

Sigrid Kelsey is an associate librarian in the Louisiana State University Libraries, where she works as the electronic resources and Web development coordinator. She has authored two articles about the e-struction program, published in *Louisiana Libraries* and *The Reference Librarian*. Over the years, her e-struction programs have reached hundreds of students.

Kenneth L. Miller received a BA in sociology, an MS in education (Counseling) degree, and a PhD (Counselor Education) from Purdue University. He has held assistant professorships at California State University, San Bernardino, The Citadel, and the University of Hawaii at Manoa. He is currently an associate professor in the Department of Counseling and Special Education at Youngstown State University. Dr. Miller has numerous publications and has made over 100 conference presentations. His research interests include technology use in clinical supervision, theoretical considerations in the design of web-based instruction, child abuse prevention, and measurement of cultural bias and discrimination. He is co-author of the *Survey of Cultural Attitudes and Behaviors.*

Susan M. Miller received her BA in psychology from the University of Chicago, MS in instructional design, and PhD in educational psychology from Purdue University. Dr. Miller held assistant professor positions at Temple University and Texas A & M University where she taught courses in cognition, learning, instruction, instructional design and technology, program evaluation, and research methods. Dr. Miller has numerous publications and has made approximately 80 professional presentations. Dr. Miller's current research interests focus on understanding students' problem-solving strategies and designing technology-based learning and virtual environments to enhance reasoning and critical thinking skills. Dr. Miller has conducted a series of studies to assess cultural bias in educational institutions and is co-author of the *Survey of Cultural Attitudes and Behaviors.*

Patricia A. Nordstrom is currently a doctoral candidate in the Instructional Systems at the Pennsylvania State University, and a project manager for the Survey Research Center at Penn State, University Park, PA. Ms. Nordstrom holds a BS in agronomy and a MEd in extension education from Pennsylvania State University. Her scholarly work focuses on online education, adult education and training and development.

William G. Powers is a professor and former chair of the Department of Communication Studies and associate dean in the College of Communication at Texas Christian University. He is well known for integrating communication education theory and research with practical application in modern business and industry contexts. To that end, he remains personally involved in working with business groups and in guiding students through internships in the Dallas/Fort Worth area. His Concept Keys online learning system was originally developed to assist with those efforts. Dr. Powers is an avid researcher with over 150 books, articles, and papers with an intensive interest in areas and applications associated with communication accuracy and communication skills leading to interpersonal and professional success.

Wendy Rickman is a clinical instructor and director of the Technology Learning Center for the College of Education at the University of Central Arkansas. Her primary areas of scholarship include educational technology, library science, and educational leadership.

Michael F. Russo has been the instruction coordinator at the LSU Libraries since July, 2001. Besides being a published novelist, his articles about information literacy include "For Better or Worse: Gauging the Efficacy of Online Information Literacy" (*Professional Studies Review*, Vol. 1 no. 2) and "Information Literacy Training at LSU: First Steps" (*Louisiana Libraries*, Vol. 66, No. 1). He earned his MLIS in 2000 from Louisiana State University and holds a Master's degree in English from the University of Wisconsin in Milwaukee. Until August 29, 2005, he was a resident of the lost city of New Orleans.

Glenda Hostetter Shoop currently serves as the director of Curriculum Development and Evaluation at the Penn State College of Medicine, Hershey, PA. In this role, she provides the leadership in managing all aspects of system operations and responsibilities in the Office of Medical Education, and offers guidance in curriculum design and program evaluation. She also is a doctoral candidate in the instructional systems program at The Pennsylvania State University, and maintains a number of scholarly interests among which are online learning environments, the relationship between meta-cognition and cognition, methods of evaluation, and systems theory.

Gregory M. Shreve, PhD is a professor and chairman of modern and classical languages at Kent State University. He received his doctorate in anthropology from Ohio State University and a Certificate of Advanced Study in information science from the University of Pittsburgh. Research specialties include translation, language informatics, software design and localization, and intercultural issues in information science. Shreve is founder of the Institute for Applied Linguistics at Kent State, the country's foremost university-based translation program. He is the general editor of the monograph series *Translation Studies* and co-author of several influential books on translation including *Cognitive Processes in Translation and Interpreting*.

Glenn Snelbecker (PhD, Cornell University, 1961) is a professor of psychological studies in education at Temple University, Philadelphia, PA. His training and experience as an educational psychologist and clinical psychologist led to American Psychological Association Fellow status in both areas. He was director/co-director of "technology and education" projects for over 20 years, and external evaluator for federally-funded computer projects. His book, book chapters and journal papers on learning theory, instructional theory, instructional technology, and psychoeducational design have been used in many countries. In August, 2004, he served as keynote speaker for two international conferences, in Busan and Seoul, Korea, and as Scientific Committee Member for international "design" conferences.

Maud Walsh is an associate professor in the Louisiana State University School of Plant, Environmental, and Soil Sciences, where her primary responsibilities are teaching and advising undergraduate students in the environmental management and plant and soil science curricula. Walsh's research interests include the geological record of early life on Earth and environmental remediation and restoration. Walsh has been involved for several years in several professional development programs for middle-school science teachers that focused on inquiry-based learning in the sciences, especially earth and environmental sciences.

Haomin Wang is an associate professor and manager of instructional technology at Dakota State University. He received his MA in applied linguistics and PhD in education from Northern Arizona University. He has taught undergraduate courses in multimedia and hypermedia development, and graduate courses in distance learning systems design, Web-based instruction, and instructional programming. His research interests include affordances of media, distributed cognition, instructional hypermedia, and adaptive courseware design. He is author of *Designing and Developing Web-Based Instruction* and producer of various Web applications at Dakota State University.

Pedro A. Willging is currently an adjunct professor at the University of La Pampa, Argentina, where he is the director of a research project related to open source learning management systems. Pedro has a PhD in education from the Department of Human Resource Education at the University of Illinois at Urbana-Champaign. His work experience includes development of e-learning materials and research of virtual environment interfaces. His current research focuses on social network analysis and visualization of online interactions.

Barbara Johnson Wilmes is an associate professor at the University of Central Arkansas. Her primary areas of scholarship include teaching and learning and technological environments to improve student performance, and application of assessment to improve teaching and student performance.

Harrison Hao Yang, EdD, currently is a professor of the Department of Curriculum and Instruction at the State University of New York at Oswego, and holds an adjunct professorship at the Chinese University of Hong Kong. He served as coordinator of educational technology at the Center for Instructional Technology of Florida International University, assistant professor, and associate professor at SUNY Oswego.

Index

288